D0970205

CHINA'S RISE

CHALLENGES AND OPPORTUNITIES

CHINA'S RISE

CHALLENGES AND OPPORTUNITIES

C. FRED BERGSTEN

CHARLES FREEMAN

NICHOLAS R. LARDY

DEREK J. MITCHELL

PETERSON INSTITUTE FOR INTERNATIONAL ECONOMICS

CENTER FOR STRATEGIC AND INTERNATIONAL STUDIES

WASHINGTON, DC

SEPTEMBER 2008

**PETER G. PETERSON INSTITUTE
FOR INTERNATIONAL ECONOMICS**
1750 Massachusetts Avenue, NW
Washington, DC 20036-1903
(202) 328-9000   FAX: (202) 659-3225
www.petersoninstitute.org

C. Fred Bergsten, *Director*
Edward Tureen, *Director of Publications,
  Marketing, and Web Development*

**CENTER FOR STRATEGIC
AND INTERNATIONAL STUDIES**
1800 K Street, NW
Washington, DC 20006
(202) 887-0200 FAX: (202) 775-3199
www.csis.org

John J. Hamre, *President and CEO*
James Dunton, *Director of Publications*

*Typesetting by BMWW
Printing by United Book Press
Cover design by Sese-Paul Design*

Copyright © 2008 by the Peter G. Peterson
Institute for International Economics and
the Center for Strategic and International
Studies. All rights reserved. No part of this
book may be reproduced or utilized in any
form or by any means, electronic or me-
chanical, including photocopying, record-
ing, or by information storage or retrieval
system, without permission from the
Institute.

For reprints/permission to photocopy
please contact the APS customer service
department at Copyright Clearance Center,
Inc., 222 Rosewood Drive, Danvers, MA
01923; or email requests to:
info@copyright.com

Printed in the United States of America
10 09 08   5 4 3 2 1

**Library of Congress Cataloging-in-
Publication Data**

China's rise : challenges and opportunities /
C. Fred Bergsten . . . [et al.].
    p. cm.
    Includes bibliographical references and
index.
    ISBN 978-0-88132-417-4 (alk. paper)
    1. China—Economic conditions—2000–
2. China—Foreign economic relations.
3. Democratization—China.   4. China—
Politics and government—2002–
I. Bergsten, C. Fred, 1941–   II. Peterson
Institute for International Economics.
III. Center for Strategic and International
Studies (Washington, D.C.)

HC427.95.C4566 2008
330.951—dc22
                            2008028925

The views expressed in this publication are those of the authors. This publication is
part of the overall program of the Institute and the Center, as endorsed by their Boards
of Directors, but does not necessarily reflect the views of individual members of the
Boards or the Advisory Committees.

Contents

Preface   vii

Chronology of Main Events   xiii

Introduction   1

1   China's Challenge to the Global Economic Order   9

2   China Debates Its Future   33

3   Democracy with Chinese Characteristics? Political Reform and the Future of the Chinese Communist Party   57

4   Center-Local Relations: Hu's in Charge Here?   75

5   Corruption in China: Crisis or Constant?   91

6   Sustaining Economic Growth in China   105

7   Energy Implications of China's Growth   137

8   Why Does the United States Care about Taiwan?   169

9   China's Military Modernization   191

10   China and the World   209

11   Conclusion   235

Bibliography   241

About the Authors   245

About the Organizations   249

Acknowledgments   253

Advisory Committee   255

Index	259

Tables
Table 6.1	Government expenditure on social programs, 2002–07	122
Table 7.1	Energy demand by sector, 2005	142
Table 7.2	GDP by sector, 2005	142
Table 7.3	Industrial profit margins, on an earnings-before-tax basis	148
Table 7.4	Global steel industry: Production, market share, and industry concentration, 2006	149
Table 7.5	Industry concentration in China	150
Table 9.1	Competing statistics on China's military expenditure, 2006	200
Table 10.1	China's top trading partners, 2007	210
Table 10.2	China's rank among countries' top trading partners	221
Table 10.3	China's top five sources of crude oil imports, 2003–07	222

Figures
Figure 5.1	Perceived level of corruption in China, 1984–2006	93
Figure 6.1	Investment as percent of GDP, 1978–2007	107
Figure 6.2	Household consumption as percent of GDP, 1978–2007	107
Figure 6.3	Government consumption as percent of GDP, 1978–2007	108
Figure 6.4	Net exports of goods and services, 1992–2007	109
Figure 6.5	Manufacturing and services share of urban investment, 1995–2007	111
Figure 6.6	Losses of unprofitable industrial enterprises, 1995–2007(e)	113
Figure 6.7	Industry profits as percent of GDP, 1998–2007(e)	113
Figure 6.8	Current account balance as percent of GDP, 1994–2007	115
Figure 6.9	Household savings and interest income, 1992–2003	119
Figure 7.1	Energy intensity of the Chinese economy, 1953–2007	139
Figure 7.2	Energy demand, historic and recent forecasts, 1974–2030	140
Figure 7.3	China's share of global production, 2006	143
Figure 7.4	Industrial electricity prices, 2006	145

Boxes
Box 1.1	Other economic superpowers?	10
Box 1.2	Will China dump its dollars?	18
Box 2.1	"Emancipation of the mind" campaigns	43
Box 9.1	China's defense budget	192
Box 9.2	Aircraft carriers	198

Preface

China remains a country of complexity and contradiction. It has become an economic powerhouse and an increasingly influential global player, raising the prospect that it will be a future rival to the United States in world affairs. At the same time, China's unbalanced growth fuels unsustainabilities and inequities in its political and social system, raising longer-term questions about its domestic stability. Abroad, China is widely welcomed as an engine of economic growth, even as its military modernizes and its increasing footprint creates palpable discomfort about its impact on global stability and the international system.

For Americans and others in the international community, coping with the rise of China has emerged as the key challenge of the 21st century. Formulating an effective strategy to do so, however, demands a far richer and more nuanced understanding of China's fundamental social, political, and economic context than that shaping the current public debate in the United States and elsewhere.

The China Balance Sheet Project, a joint endeavor by the Center for Strategic and International Studies (CSIS) and the Peterson Institute for International Economics, was established in 2005 with the intention of providing a balanced and objectively reasoned source of information on China for government officials, business and other private-sector leaders, the media, and the interested public alike. Our first book, *China: The Balance Sheet—What the World Needs to Know Now about the Emerging Superpower*, was published in April 2006. Translated into several languages, that book—and the one-page issue summaries derived from it provided on www. chinabalancesheet.org—has become a standard reference for policymakers, journalists, and students around the world, fulfilling an unmistakable need for authoritative and balanced discussion of China's contemporary economic, military, political, social, and international policies and perspectives. It has been widely quoted by top officials of both governments, including US Secretary of the Treasury Henry Paulson, Jr. and former Chinese Vice Premier Wu Yi.

In May 2007, the two institutions held a full-day national conference to continue the discussion of China and US-China relations. At that session, we released *The China Balance Sheet in 2007 and Beyond*, a compilation of papers that delved into topics including Beijing's internet censorship policies, the rule of law in China, and China's relations with India and Russia. Keynote presentations were delivered by Secretary of the Treasury Henry Paulson, Jr.; Robert Zoellick, president of the World Bank and former US deputy secretary of state; and Craig Mundie, chief research and strategy officer for Microsoft.

This book seeks to take the analysis several important steps further by connecting China's development directly to US and global interests, and offering a series of possible policy responses. It begins by looking at the global economic challenge posed by China, a central theme throughout the volume, in a chapter written by Dr. C. Fred Bergsten, director of the Peterson Institute. It then turns to the emerging policy debates on all these issues in China, where an intellectual climate is forming that is more open, diverse, and creative than many outsiders realize.

As in the earlier two publications, the book then assesses the likely development of China itself under three headings: domestic political and social affairs, economic policy, and foreign and security policy. The authors divided lead responsibility for the discussion according to their expertise. Charles Freeman, holder of the Freeman Chair in China Studies at CSIS, took primary responsibility for the chapters devoted to China's domestic policies. Dr. Nicholas Lardy, senior fellow at the Peterson Institute, addressed China's domestic economy. Trevor Houser and Daniel Rosen of the Peterson Institute coauthored chapter 7 on China's energy issues. Derek Mitchell, senior fellow in the International Security Program at CSIS, took on the multifaceted challenges of China's foreign and security policy. All these authors have published extensively on their areas of expertise.

In the process, we would like to thank many people for their contributions. Melissa Murphy was instrumental in writing chapters 2, 3, and 5 and Andrew Wedeman of the University of Nebraska-Lincoln in the writing of chapter 5 on corruption. David Finkelstein of the Center for Naval Analyses provided the first draft of and substantial intellectual input into chapter 9 on China's military modernization.

We have been enormously assisted in the preparation of the book by an Advisory Committee of high-level experts on China and US-China relations. The full committee met with the authors and their team to discuss the book in its early stages and helped shape its ultimate direction through their invaluable comments and suggestions. It should be noted, however, that the findings and opinions in this book rest with the authors. They do not necessarily represent the views of our Advisory Committee members, contributing authors, and others who have provided support.

A full list of Advisory Committee members, contributing authors, and other supporting individuals is provided at the end of this volume.

Our gratitude extends particularly to Bates Gill, director of the Stockholm International Peace Research Institute (SIPRI) and former holder of the Freeman Chair in China Studies, for his immeasurable support of the project and to Ben W. Heineman, Jr., senior fellow at the Belfer Center for Science and International Affairs at Harvard University's John F. Kennedy School of Government, member of the CSIS Board of Trustees, and former senior vice president-general counsel of GE, who conceived of the project and has greatly aided it.

Eve Cary and Carl Rubenstein at CSIS served as project coordinators for the China Balance Sheet Project and provided administrative support to the project leads. Adam Posen, deputy director and senior fellow at the Peterson Institute for International Economics advised the project. Invaluable research assistance was provided by Eve Cary and Alyson Slack at CSIS and Giwon Jeong at the Peterson Institute. Additional research help was provided by Shiuan-ju Chen, Orlando Crosby, Fergus Green, Xuan Gui, Liana Lim Hinch, Arthur Kaneko, Stephen Meyers, Alexis Rado, Shelley Su, Pak To Wong, and Xiao Zhang. Carla Freeman at Johns Hopkins' School for Advanced International Studies provided editorial assistance. Edward A. Tureen of the Peterson Institute provided editorial advice and oversaw the publication process. Madona Devasahayam of the Peterson Institute served as an expert copyeditor and editorial coordinator.

After the publication of *China's Rise: Challenges and Opportunities*, the project will remain active through conferences and briefings, and possible further studies, and will remain an important source for balanced and salient information on China through the project's website (www.china balancesheet.org) and through its publications.

The Center for Strategic and International Studies (CSIS) provides strategic insights and policy solutions to decision makers in government, international institutions, the private sector, and civil society. A bipartisan, nonprofit organization headquartered in Washington, DC, CSIS conducts research and analysis and develops policy initiatives that look into the future and anticipate change. CSIS's work is made possible thanks to the generous support of individuals, private foundations, US and international government agencies, and corporations.

The Peterson Institute for International Economics is a private, nonprofit institution for the study and discussion of international economic policy. Its purpose is to analyze important issues in that area and to develop and communicate practical new approaches for dealing with them. The Institute is completely nonpartisan. It is funded by a highly diversified group of philanthropic foundations, private corporations, and interested individuals.

Financing for the China Balance Sheet Project comes from a combination of general institutional resources and external support. External underwriters include ACE Ltd, American International Group, The Boeing Company, Caterpillar, Citigroup, The Coca-Cola Company, FedEx, General Electric, General Motors, Goldman Sachs, Microsoft, Pfizer, and Procter & Gamble. These institutional supporters and underwriters had no editorial role in, or control over, the content of this book.

China's rise provides the United States and global community with a great number of both challenges and opportunities. As the United States and others prepare to meet those challenges and seize those opportunities, it will be crucial to have a clear and objective understanding of the nature and implications of China's emergence. The China Balance Sheet project will continue its effort to provide such a contribution to the ongoing debate and discussion about China in coming years.

JOHN J. HAMRE
President and CEO
Center for Strategic and
International Studies

C. FRED BERGSTEN
Director
Peterson Institute for
International Economics

July 2008

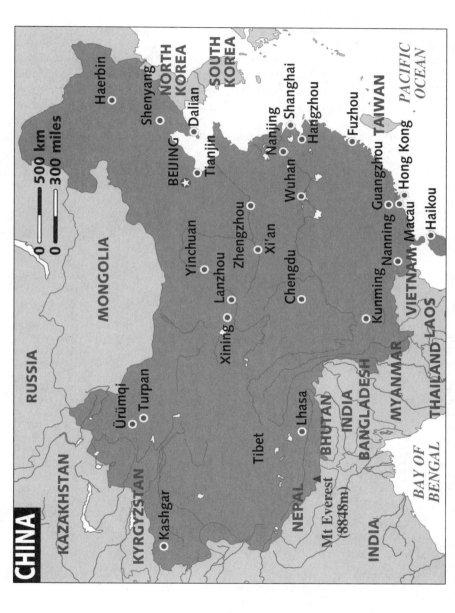

Source: Lonely Planet Images Map/Lonely Planet Images

Chronology of Main Events

Date	Event
October 1, 1949	Mao Zedong and the Communist Party of China announce the founding of the People's Republic of China (PRC); Zhou Enlai becomes first premier.
December 1949	Chiang Kai-shek and the Kuomintang (KMT) flee to Taiwan.
1950s	
October 1950	China enters the Korean War.
December 24, 1952	China undertakes its first Five-Year Plan (1953–57) focused on economic development.
January 1958	Mao Zedong launches the Great Leap Forward, which is abandoned in 1961.
March 15, 1959	China suppresses a massive uprising in Tibet.
1960s	
June 1960	Sino-Soviet split.
October 11, 1962	China attacks India over border dispute.
October 1964	China successfully tests its first nuclear bomb.
August 13, 1966	Mao Zedong launches the Cultural Revolution, which lasts until 1976.
1970s	
April 1970	China puts its first satellite into orbit.

(chronology continues next page)

Date	Event
July 1971	Henry Kissinger secretly visits China.
October 1971	The Republic of China (ROC) is expelled from the United Nations and the Chinese seat in the General Assembly and Security Council is given to the PRC.
February 21, 1972	President Richard Nixon visits China and signs the Shanghai Communiqué, normalizing relations with the PRC.
April 5, 1975	Chiang Kai-shek dies and is replaced by Chiang Ching-kuo as president of Taiwan.
January 8, 1976	Premier Zhou Enlai dies.
September 9, 1976	Mao Zedong dies and is succeeded initially by Hua Guofeng, who subsequently is outmaneuvered by Deng Xiaoping.
1978	Deng Xiaoping becomes de facto ruler; officially launches the Four Modernizations (agriculture, industry, science and technology, and national defense), formally marking the beginning of the reform era.
	China introduces one-child family policy.
March 1979	Deng Xiaoping sets forth the Four Cardinal Principles—to keep to the socialist road, to uphold the people's democratic dictatorship, leadership by the Communist Party, and Marxism-Leninism-Mao Zedong Thought. These four principles define the parameters of permissible dissent in the PRC. Opposition to any one of these principles meets with swift and strong suppression.
January 1979	Deng Xiaoping visits the United States and the Jimmy Carter administration officially recognizes the PRC.
April 1979	The US Congress passes the Taiwan Relations Act.
July 1979	Law of the People's Republic of China on Chinese-Foreign Joint Ventures comes into force.

Date	Event
1980s	
April 1980	PRC becomes a member of the International Monetary Fund.
May 1980	PRC becomes a member of the World Bank.
August 1980	China's National People's Congress creates four special economic zones in Zhuhai, Xiamen, Shenzhen, and Shantou.
September 1980	Zhao Ziyang is appointed premier.
November 1987	Li Peng becomes premier.
January 13, 1988	Chiang Ching-kuo dies. Lee Teng-hui becomes Taiwan's first native-born president.
March 1989	Protest breaks out in Tibet.
April 15, 1989	Reformist leader Hu Yaobang dies, sparking protests in Tiananmen Square in his memory.
May 15, 1989	Soviet leader Mikhail Gorbachev visits China.
June 4, 1989	The People's Liberation Army (PLA) opens fire on protestors in Tiananmen Square. The West imposes an arms embargo on China.
1990s	
December 1990	Stock markets open in Shanghai and Shenzhen.
July–October 1991	US Congress links most favored nation (MFN) status to human rights conditions.
1992	China reestablishes friendly relations with Russia.
March 1993	Jiang Zemin becomes president.
May 1993	President Bill Clinton renews MFN but issues executive order requiring China to improve human rights record.
September 1993	President Clinton introduces "constructive engagement" policy for dealing with China.
January 1, 1994	The official renminbi exchange rate and the foreign exchange swap market rate are unified at the latter rate, starting a market-based, managed floating rate system.

(chronology continues next page)

Date	Event
May 1994	President Clinton delinks human rights and MFN.
June–August 1995	Lee Teng-hui visits the United States, prompting Chinese military exercises.
March 1996	China conducts missile tests off the coast of Taiwan and two US aircraft carriers are dispatched. Lee wins Taiwan's first direct presidential election.
February 19, 1997	Deng Xiaoping dies.
July 1, 1997	Hong Kong is returned to Chinese sovereignty.
September 1997	Deng Xiaoping's Theory is established as the Party's guiding ideology alongside Marxism-Leninism-Mao Zedong Thought.
October 1997	President Jiang Zemin visits the United States.
March 1998	Zhu Rongji succeeds Li Peng as premier and announces reforms in the wake of the Asian financial crisis.
July 22, 1998	Jiang Zemin calls on the Chinese military to withdraw from business.
May 8, 1999	Chinese embassy in Belgrade, Yugoslavia accidentally bombed by NATO forces.
November 15, 1999	China and the United States reach a bilateral agreement on China's accession to the World Trade Organization (WTO).
2000s	
March 18, 2000	DPP candidate Chen Shui-bian is elected president in Taiwan's first change of power between political parties.
October 10, 2000	The United States grants China permanent normal trade relations (PNTR) status, paving the way for WTO accession.
April 1, 2001	2001 collision between a US EP-3 surveillance aircraft and a PLA fighter sours US-China relations.

Date	Event
April 24, 2001	President George W. Bush approves the largest package of arms sales to Taiwan in nearly a decade.
June 15, 2001	Shanghai Cooperation Organization is created from original Shanghai Five members (China, Russia, Kazakhstan, Kyrgyzstan, and Tajikistan) plus Uzbekistan.
July 13, 2001	Beijing is awarded the 2008 Summer Olympics.
August 13, 2001	Japanese Prime Minister Junichiro Koizumi makes first of several visits to Yasukuni Shrine.
December 11, 2001	PRC joins the WTO.
January 1, 2002	Taiwan joins the WTO.
February 21, 2002	President Bush visits China on the 30th anniversary of President Nixon's visit to China.
September 2002	Chinese officials and representatives of the Dalai Lama meet for the first time since 1991.
November 2002	The Three Represents Theory credited to Jiang Zemin becomes the Party's guiding ideology.
March 2003	Fourth generation of leadership installed: Hu Jintao is president and Wen Jiabao is premier.
March–April 2003	China and Hong Kong are hit by the severe acute respiratory syndrome (SARS) virus. Strict quarantine measures are enforced to stop the disease from spreading.
August 27–29, 2003	Beijing hosts first round of Six Party Talks between China, the United States, North Korea, South Korea, Japan, and Russia.
October 15, 2003	China launches first manned spacecraft.
November 2003	Zheng Bijian, head of the Central Party School and senior adviser to President Hu Jintao, coins the term "peaceful rise" at the Boao Forum for Asia.
December 2003	Premier Wen Jiabao visits the United States.
March 20, 2004	Taiwan President Chen Shui-bian is reelected.

(chronology continues next page)

Date	Event
November 2004	China reaches open-market agreement with 10 southeast Asian nations that covers 25 percent of the world's population.
March 14, 2005	China's National People's Congress passes an Anti-Secession Law.
April 2005	Widespread anti-Japanese riots throughout China over a Japanese textbook's description of World War II.
July 21, 2005	China's central bank announces that the renminbi will appreciate against the dollar by 2 percent and says that it will peg the renminbi to a basket of currencies and allow it to fluctuate within a narrow 0.3 percent range.
August 1–2, 2005	Deputy Secretary of State Robert Zoellick visits Beijing for the first round of senior dialogues.
August 2, 2005	China National Offshore Oil Corporation (CNOOC) withdraws its $18.5 billion bid to buy Unocal Corp., citing "unprecedented political opposition" in the United States.
September 21, 2005	Zoellick delivers a speech that calls for China to be a "responsible stakeholder."
November 13, 2005	Explosion at a chemical plant poisons the Songhua River, cutting off water supplies to millions of people.
November 19, 2005	President Bush visits China.
December 7–8, 2005	The United States and China conduct the second round of senior dialogues.
December 14–15, 2005	First US-China Strategic Economic Dialogue (SED) in Beijing. Presidents Bush and Hu establish this Cabinet-level forum to develop strategies to reach shared long-term objectives while managing short-term challenges in the US-China economic relationship.
April 18–21, 2006	Hu Jintao visits the United States, his first state visit.
May 2006	China completes work on the Three Gorges Dam.

Date	Event
July 2006	The China-Tibet railway, the world's highest train route, begins operation.
January 2007	The Chinese military successfully conducts a missile test in space, shooting down an old satellite.
April 2007	Wen Jiabao becomes the first Chinese premier to address Japan's parliament.
May 22–23, 2007	Second US-China Strategic Economic Dialogue in Washington. Leaders from both countries agree to increase market access, open the financial sector, foster energy security, protect the environment, and strengthen the rule of law.
October 2007	The Scientific Development Concept credited to Hu Jintao becomes the Party's guiding socioeconomic ideology.
December 12–13, 2007	Third US-China Strategic Economic Dialogue in Beijing. Both countries agree to conduct extensive cooperation over a 10-year period to address environmental sustainability, climate change and energy security.
January 2008	Snowstorms affect 100 million Chinese and cause severe economic disruption.
March 2008	Anti-China protests erupt in Tibet.
	KMT candidate Ma Ying-jeou is elected president of Taiwan.
May 2008	A severe earthquake in Sichuan kills an estimated 70,000 people.
June 17–18, 2008	Fourth US-China Strategic Economic Dialogue in Annapolis, Maryland. Both countries sign a Ten-Year Energy and Environment Cooperation Framework that sets goals and lays out concrete next steps to address environmental sustainability, climate change, and energy security.

Introduction

China is not a superpower, nor will it ever seek to be one. If one day China should change its color and turn into a superpower, if it too should play the tyrant in the world, and everywhere subject others to its bullying, aggression and exploitation, the people of the world should . . . expose it, oppose it and work together with the Chinese people to overthrow it.

—Deng Xiaoping, speech at the UN General Assembly, April 1974

Twenty-five years ago, in the early years of China's opening, the cultural, economic, and political gulf between China and the United States was vast. If you were one of the foreigners living in Beijing at the time—one of the lucky 1,200—that gulf could produce its share of quirks. A night out could mean a trip to the "Disco" at Ethnicities Hotel on the western side of Tiananmen Square, where one drank warm beer and watched a handful of local Chinese—typically children of high-ranking officials from the leadership compound at Zhongnanhai—shimmy across the dance floor to "Rudolph the Red-Nosed Reindeer," "Jingle Bells," and (endlessly) "Fernando" by the Swedish group ABBA. Any effort at communication between foreigners and Chinese was quickly rebuffed by conspicuous, leisure-suited representatives of the Public Security Bureau. The city's streets were deserted after 7 p.m. or so, and one could zoom across town at the end of an evening in a matter of minutes to one's heavily guarded foreigners-only compound to call it a day.

That Beijing is long gone now. The city's art and music scenes are vibrant and sophisticated, although one still encounters quirks now and again. Foreigners and Chinese congregate and connect without fear of official molestation. That same trip across town at any time of day or night will take nearly an hour given the traffic in Beijing (1,100 new cars are introduced into the city every day).

China has changed much in the last 25 to 30 years, and not just for foreigners living there (now numbering 150,000 in Beijing alone). Chinese citizens increasingly work where they want, live where they want, travel where they want, and interact *how* they want in ways unimaginable

30 years ago. Their lives are also more complicated than they were back then, changed by an economy that has grown 13 times since it began to open up in 1978 and a government that has scrambled to keep political pace with the dramatic social changes that have accompanied the economic development.

American China watchers have the somewhat annoying competitive habit of comparing their first China experiences. Those who lay claim to the early 1970s have special bragging rights. The more recent one's first trip to China, the less intimate is one's relationship with China. This is a somewhat foolish hierarchy. But in many ways, like carbon dating, the date one first experienced China says a lot about one's perceptions not only of China's rise as a global power but also about the appropriate American response to that rise. The earlier the experience, the more likely one is to focus not on shortcomings in China's development but on how far China has come. The more recent one's China experience, the more likely one is focused on where China needs yet to go or, more pointedly, the more one takes for granted China's status as competitor to US interests. Ultimately, any American who has sought to understand China has encountered a country of serious contradictions. A precise definition of China's challenges and opportunities (despite the promise of this book) is impossible because China is so dynamic. This inability to define the challenges and opportunities is unfortunate, because China is front and center of any US administration's leading foreign policy considerations.

China presents difficult strategic questions for the United States and its global leadership. Will China fit into the current and long-standing international architecture designed in the postwar era by the United States? Is a new global system needed that will incorporate China more fully? Must China itself be a key architect of such a system? How should we define the nature of the "China challenge," and how does it balance against the opportunities presented by the nation's rise? These questions define the key challenges that increasingly characterize US-China relations.

As the 21st century unfolds, the stakes have never been higher nor the need greater for getting US policy toward China right. Yet there is often more heat than light in the US debate about China. To address this pivotal issue, the Center for Strategic and International Studies (CSIS) and the Peterson Institute for International Economics launched a joint multiyear project, the China Balance Sheet Project, that brings together leading experts to examine the key questions, uncover the pertinent facts, and analyze the dynamics underpinning China's domestic transformation and emergence as an international power—as well as its implications for the United States and the world.

China: The Balance Sheet—What the World Needs to Know Now about the Emerging Superpower, the project's initial publication, addressed the critical questions of whether China is facing continued growth or economic downturn, political democratization or disorder or continued authoritarian rule, and whether the emerging superpower presents an economic opportunity or threat, a security partner or rival. In so doing, the book provides policymakers, students, and the interested public alike with comprehensive, authoritative, and accessible analysis in order to begin an informed debate about the challenge of a rising China.

In *China: The Balance Sheet* the authors and their institutions sought to lay out a number of issues presented by China's rise. Part of the motivation of that book was to counter fears about China with facts about China. Too little is known about China's impact on US global interests, and that book attempted to provide context for the debate about China—to both allay fears and dispel sanguinity about the China phenomenon.

This book attempts to take the concept of *China: The Balance Sheet* a step further, to more pointedly focus on the implications of China's rise and dig deeper into the impact of that rise on US interests and policy assumptions. Our motivations here are to sharpen understanding of China's domestic and international considerations as a means of directing a response to that rise.

US policy toward China, after all, has been fundamentally consistent for the last 30 years or so (and is one of the few US policies for which this is true). This has not been a foolish consistency by any means, but the China of today is not the China of 30 years ago. At a minimum, a reexamination of US approaches to China given the dramatic change in circumstances is warranted. Part of this need is driven because China's rise has had a transformative impact not just on its own people but also on the entire global context. In 1978 Deng Xiaoping exhorted China to throw off the chains of its planned economy and become a modern, developed country. The United States and other Western powers made the bold decision to welcome China to develop within the US-led global economic and security architecture. It worked. In 1978, with a quarter of the world's population, China represented less than 0.5 percent of total global economic output. Thirty years later, China accounts for between 7 and 10 percent, depending on the methodology one uses. In the process, it has gained economic, political, and military clout that stands in sometimes sharp contrast to that of the United States and the architecture that provided the incubator to China's rise. The Washington Consensus, the ten-point strategy for economic and political development that has formed the cornerstone of US-led multilateral institutions since the end the World War II, is now confronted by a striking alternative model in China.

In the authors' view, a static response to such a dynamic change in circumstances would be unwise. In accounting terms, a balance sheet is a snapshot of assets and liabilities at any given time, a somewhat static view. In *China: The Balance Sheet*, we attempted to provide such a snapshot of China's rise. In this book, we attempt to capture the dynamism of China in something more akin, in accounting terms, to an income statement. One goal of this book is primarily to articulate a need to rethink the tools we use to deal with the challenges and opportunities of China's rise. We offer some alternative policy formulations herein to stimulate debate.

China and the United States have bridged significant differences in the last 30 years. The two countries have built a record of cooperation and engagement of which both governments can be proud. There is no reason why the United States cannot continue to work with China and welcome it into the global community in which the United States has been the dominant player. Understanding the challenges and weighing the opportunities to best manage that process would be a wise exercise. We hope that this book will help in that exercise.

Reader's Guide to the Book

Chapter 1, "China's Challenge to the Global Economic Order," discusses China's rise to the status of a global economic superpower and its impact on the institutions and norms of the global economic system. The chapter concludes that China's rise could pose a threat to the United States and world stability simply by virtue of its economic weight but also because it is challenging some of the key rules and conventions on which the postwar regime has been based. However, there is opportunity for a constructive realignment of global economic leadership that incorporates China in the top tier of that reordered regime. In response to China's rise, the United States should develop a much closer "G-2" relationship with China, through which the two coordinate their approaches and attempt to steer the global governance process on a number of key issues, perhaps starting with global warming and sovereign wealth funds but extending to more traditional trade, monetary, energy, and foreign assistance issues as well. The United States and China should start holding annual, or even semiannual, summit meetings to both implement and symbolize this new relationship.

Chapter 2, "China Debates Its Future," examines the dynamic intellectual debate in China that now swirls around the most fundamental political, economic, and foreign policy questions confronting the country. The answers and policies that flow from this debate will help shape China's future, impact US-China relations, and influence the world at large. While the unprecedented level of more open and public debate is an encouraging sign, calls for a return to traditional Communist Party tenets on the political front and more forceful assertion of narrowly defined Chinese national interests are worrisome. The chapter suggests that the United States make a concerted effort to monitor these debates in order to formulate informed and effective policy responses.

Chapter 3, "Democracy with Chinese Characteristics? Political Reform and the Future of the Chinese Communist Party," examines the Party's plan to implement "democracy with Chinese characteristics." The chapter concludes that China's political reform is likely to traverse the same gradual development path as economic reform and can be characterized as "instrumental, incremental, and idiosyncratic." Despite challenges, not least of which is bridging the gap between the rhetoric and reality of promised political reform, the Party is far from being on the brink of collapse and more likely to remain in power for the foreseeable future. While attempts to export "Western" democracy to China are likely to fall on deaf ears, the chapter suggests that the United States can apply selective pressure on China when the Party fails to live up to its own promises and violates the political and legal reforms it has put in place. A "track two" dialogue among Chinese and American academic and nongovernmental institutions to discuss the merits and demerits of liberal, East Asian, and even Chinese-style democracy should be encouraged.

Chapter 4, "Center-Local Relations: Hu's in Charge Here?" discusses how central policies are often not implemented properly or at all by local governments and the implications of this for social stability, environmental and health issues, US-China relations, and the Chinese public's perceptions of the central government's legitimacy. The chapter concludes that although Chinese leaders have taken steps to correct the problem, the implementation of central laws at the local level may continue to be a significant challenge for Chinese leaders in the future. The chapter recommends that the United States work to build interest coalitions in China that include officials at the local level, as well as encourage visiting US officials, politicians, and business groups to visit provincial capitals and establish working relationships with local-level officials.

Chapter 5, "Corruption in China: Crisis or Constant?" evaluates the current level of corruption in China, investigates the causes, types, and perpetrators of corruption—including incidents that involve government officials such as the buying and selling of offices and the "criminalization" of the state—and looks at the resulting impact on the stability of the Chinese Communist Party. The chapter's main conclusion is that corruption has remained at approximately the same level since 2000 and that as yet it has neither undercut growth nor significantly undermined the Party, though the Party's response to corruption will be crucial to its future. The chapter suggests that the United States should continue aiding China with the construction of its legal system and implementation of the rule of law.

Chapter 6, "Sustaining Economic Growth in China," discusses how China has been making efforts to shift its source of economic growth from investment and export-led development to domestic consumption, the benefits of which would include more rapid job creation, reduction in the increase of energy consumption and environmental degradation, more equal distribution of income, and a reduction in the country's excessive trade surpluses, as well as continuation of strong economic growth. However, the chapter concludes that the rebalancing process has been more difficult than expected and that China's current economic growth may be more unbalanced than it was in 2004, due to a number of factors. The chapter suggests that the Chinese government step up policy action in the fiscal, financial, pricing, and exchange rate domains, all of which are characterized by mispricing of key elements of the economy (energy, interest rates, and the exchange rate). Failure to do so may lead to more moderate growth rates than in previous years, continued upward pressure on global oil and commodity prices, continued trade tensions with other countries, and further increases in China's energy use and carbon emissions.

Chapter 7, "Energy Implications of China's Growth," explores the ties between macroeconomic trends and energy outcomes. It describes how aspects of China's current development model—most notably its energy-intensive heavy industry and investment-led growth—have contributed to serious energy and environmental problems, as well as less optimal growth and employment outcomes, for both China and the international community. The chapter notes that while Chinese leaders are becoming more aware of the problem and what is needed to fix it, notably a broad rebalancing program with structural and institutional reforms, they have been slow to make the necessary policy changes. The United States can leverage change in China by improving the sustainability of its own energy profile and should work with China on climate change through a multilateral climate framework.

Chapter 8, "Why Does the United States Care about Taiwan?" addresses the relationship between Taiwan and the United States—noted as the most sensitive issue in US-China relations—and focuses on a number of reasons for US interest in Taiwan, including maintaining credibility with allies, a desire to protect a democratic system, and strong trade ties with the island. The chapter also notes the limits on US support of Taiwan. Though US political and military support for Taiwan has grown increasingly complicated, the original reasons for supporting Taiwan remain valid and important to US interests. To maintain peace across the Taiwan Strait and honor the commitment to Taiwan, the chapter suggests that the United States take a number of steps, including insisting that Taiwan coordinate any moves toward sovereignty with Washington, engaging more directly with Taiwanese officials, supporting Taiwan's membership in appropriate international organizations that do not require statehood, and being prepared militarily to defend Taiwan in a crisis.

Chapter 9, "China's Military Modernization," discusses China's recent military modernization, noting that the People's Liberation Army (PLA) has made substantial strides in improving its operational and institutional capacities through the development, acquisition, and fielding of new weapons systems; institutional and systemic reforms; and development of new war-fighting doctrines. The chapter concludes that even if the modernization of the PLA is for strictly peaceful purposes, a more capable PLA has the potential to significantly alter the strategic balance in Asia and will have a noteworthy impact on Asian countries as well as the United States. The chapter recommends that the United States should respond in several ways: The United States should (1) modernize its own forces; (2) reach out to the PLA; (3) continue to maintain a presence in Asia; and (4) make an effort to conduct military diplomacy and operational cooperation in Asia.

Chapter 10, "China and the World," discusses China's emerging role in the global system, its relationships with a number of important countries, the role of soft power in its foreign policy, and the goals and principles underlying its foreign policy. The chapter concludes that China's increasing engagement with the world is not a disturbing development, but rather an expected and welcome one, as China will be an invaluable help in addressing a wide range of global problems. The chapter recommends that in response to China's rise, the United States should take several steps, including refraining from exaggerating the threat from China, maintaining its alliance system in East Asia, and renewing its attention to the developing world.

1

China's Challenge to the Global Economic Order

We know we have to play the game your way now but in ten years we will set the rules!

— Chinese ambassador to the World Trade Organization
during China's negotiations to enter the institution

China has become a global economic superpower. It has the second largest national economy[1] and is the second largest exporter.[2] It has by far the world's largest current account surplus and foreign exchange reserves. Growth has averaged 10 percent for the past 30 years, the most stunning record in history. Real GDP in 2006 was about 13 times the level of 1978, when Deng Xiaoping initiated economic reforms.

A country must meet three criteria to be a global economic superpower. It must be large enough to significantly affect the world economy. It must be dynamic enough to contribute importantly to global growth. It must be sufficiently open to trade and capital flows to have a major impact on other countries.

Three economies now meet these criteria. The United States remains the largest national economy, the issuer of the world's key currency, and in most years the leading host (and home) country for foreign investment. The European Union is now the largest economic entity and the largest trader, even excluding commerce within its membership, and its euro increasingly competes with the dollar as a global currency.

China, however, is far more deeply integrated into the world economy than either of the other economic superpowers. Despite being a continental economy like both of them, and despite three decades of autarky prior to the 1978 reforms, trade accounts for more than twice as much of China's economy as it does for the United States or the European Union as a group. Hence China's dramatic expansion has a powerful effect on the rest of the world. It shared global growth leadership with the much larger United States during the record world expansion of 2004–07 and, with

---

Box 1.1 Other economic superpowers?

China is often paired with India in discussions of global economic superpowers, but there is no comparison between them at this time. India's GDP is less than half that of China's, and trade accounts for less than half as much of its overall economy. The annual growth in China's trade exceeds the total level of India's trade. China attracts more foreign direct investment each year than India has received in the 60 years since its independence. India is now developing dramatically and could start growing faster than China and is the most likely candidate to become the fourth global economic superpower in a decade or so, but China will totally dominate its Asian neighbor on all three of the key criteria for the foreseeable future.

Japan is the only other possible contender for global economic superpower status. There were indeed periods, in the 1980s and even into the early 1990s, when Japan appeared to be playing such a role. When the yen reached its peak in 1995, at about 80:1 against the dollar, Japan's total GDP was fully 80 percent that of the United States (despite a population that was less than half as large). The country's competitive prowess led to widespread perceptions of "Japan as Number One." But its trade and other economic transactions with the rest of the world remained relatively limited as a share of its economy, its financial markets never liberalized sufficiently to enable the yen to play an important international role, its economy collapsed for the entire decade of the 1990s, and its population is now declining. Japan has already lost to China its regional dominance and with it any pretensions to global leadership. Japan missed its moment.

---

the current US slowdown, has become the undisputed chief driver of world growth.[3] (See box 1.1 on other contenders for economic superpower status.)

China poses a major challenge to the United States and the rest of the world simply by virtue of its status as a new global economic superpower. Such rising powers can disturb the existing international order and trigger security as well as economic conflicts. The most notorious cases are Germany in the late 19th century and Japan and Germany again in the early 20th century. There are, of course, more benign cases as well, notably the United States in the late 19th century and the European Union and Japan in the second half of the 20th century.

The challenge is vastly complicated in the case of contemporary China because it is a historically unique global economic superpower in three very important senses. It is still a poor country with per capita income of around $3,000, less than 10 percent that of the European Union and United States. It is still a nonmarket economy—one in which the government makes major decisions on prices and allocating goods and resources—to an important extent despite the dramatic marketization of the past three decades. In political terms, it is, of course, not yet a democracy—and perhaps its greatest challenge to the overall global system is its determination to become a successful high-income country without thorough reform of its authoritarian political system. All three elements reduce the likelihood that China will easily accept the systemic responsibilities that traditionally accompany superpower status, and they in fact lead some to conclude that acceptance of such responsibilities by China would not even be in the interest of the United States. The integration of China into the existing global economic order would in any event be a far more daunting effort than the integration of Japan from the early 1970s, difficult and still incomplete as that task has proved to be.

The challenge posed by China in security terms is less dramatic but still of great significance, as described in chapters 8 to 10. China has been expanding and modernizing its military capacity rapidly and, though it cannot yet match the United States on a global basis, its forces have become capable of much wider projection and will soon enable it to operate outside its region. The country's economic success is expanding its ability to support and deploy military assets with sufficient speed to alarm many of its neighbors and pose potential threats in ever-wider theaters. China, of course, remains a nuclear power with delivery systems that could reach at least some parts of the United States.

A third cluster of political issues is also part of the "China challenge" to existing international norms: nonproliferation, self-determination, human rights, labor standards, and others. International standards, with greater or lesser precision, exist in all these areas. As in the economic domain, China adheres to most of them in principle but often deviates in practice. China's challenge on these topics most frequently arises through its cooperation with countries that are violating the agreed international norms, such as Iran on nuclear proliferation or Burma on human rights, and thus undercuts the ability of the global order to address those problems effectively. Most fundamentally, "there is the strong possibility that China is trying to develop a new model of politics that it will call democratic but that will not include the elements of pluralism, contestation and direct elections that the U.S. regards as essential parts of democracy."[4] Hence, "the China challenge" ranges well beyond the economic dimension, which is the focus of this chapter.

The Systemic Challenge

The revealed preference of the incumbent powers, in this case primarily the United States and the European Union in terms of the international economic order, is to seek to coopt the powerful newcomer into the global regime that they have built and defended for a prolonged period. There are increasing signs, however, that China is not comfortable with the current international economic system. As described in chapter 2, both Chinese officials and scholars are actively discussing alternative structures in which China can be present at the creation and thus serve as a coequal partner in constructing the regime. As noted in chapter 3, China "not only wants to sit at the table but also be given a seat at the top." Mark Leonard concludes that "The first thirty years of the People's Republic reform program have been mainly about China joining the world . . . [while] the story of the next thirty years will be about how . . . China reaches out and shapes the world."[5] By early 2008, China was bold enough to publicly and harshly criticize the United States for its own shortcomings in managing the world economy, especially the failure of its regulatory regime to prevent the global financial crisis; the steady fall of the dollar, which was pushing up oil and other commodity prices; and its allegedly discriminatory rules against incoming foreign investments.[6]

In numerous areas of its economic interaction with other countries, China is now pursuing strategies that conflict with the norms, rules, and institutional arrangements that attempt to structure the global order. This can be viewed simply as the usual free-riding and skirting of responsibility by a powerful player, cleverly exploiting the gaping loopholes in and weak enforcement of existing international rules to pursue its perceived national interests. Moreover, China is hardly alone in deviating from the existing rules of the game. The United States and European Union themselves, the key architects of the current system and its putative defenders, clearly flout those norms on occasion even if they are usually careful to adhere to the letter of the law, as when the United States implements its antidumping rules in ways that violate the spirit (and even perhaps the letter) of the World Trade Organization (WTO) rules. Other major emerging-market economies, such as India and Brazil, also deviate from systemic purity from time to time.

As the powerful newcomer that jars existing economic and political relationships at a systemic level, however, China has a profound interest in the effectiveness of international rules and institutions. It should be seeking to fortify the robustness of the system, whether the present version or an alternative more to its liking, to prevent widespread economic conflict. This chapter attempts to develop a strategy for pursuing that objective that will be attractive to both China itself and the United States and that could therefore play a central role in both future US-China relations and global adjustment to "the China challenge."

There is no evidence that China's challenges to the current economic order derive from any cohesive, let alone comprehensive, strategy concocted by the political or even intellectual leadership of the country. It is certainly not based on any desire to restore Marxist or Communist economic principles. Despite periodic calls for "a new international economic order," each component seems to have emerged pragmatically within the individual issue-areas. To date, China's alternative approaches have emerged de facto and piecemeal rather than across-the-board or even with explicit articulation. China's recent behavior, however, compounds its size as a challenge to the existing world economic regime.

Like the United States and many other countries, China is experiencing considerable negative domestic reaction to its cooperation with other countries and international institutions on economic issues. The nearly universal backlash against globalization, responding mainly to the uneven distributional effects of that phenomenon, is clearly present in China and explains at least part of its current attitude toward the world economy. "New Left" intellectuals are vocal in their criticism of Western models of development and global cooperation as described in chapter 2. Their questioning of China's present economic strategy pointedly includes its international dimension. A new round of internal debate on all these issues is planned for the post-Olympics period starting in late 2008.

The Chinese version of the backlash, as in most countries, has a unique national flavor. In China's case, the Communist Party's claim to continuing authoritarian power now rests primarily on its ability to maintain rapid economic growth. That growth, however, has spawned distributional and environmental consequences that have provoked widespread domestic protests against the Party's leadership. Hence the government's response addresses key elements of the present development model, including some of its international aspects, as well as political processes within the country. Economic nationalism is clearly on the rise in China, as manifest in portions of the new Anti-Monopoly Law and the government's new supervisory role over mergers and acquisitions vis-à-vis foreign firms. China's challenge to the world economy links directly to its core internal agenda and the debates over how it should proceed on a series of vital domestic issues.

Such a systemic challenge represents a worrisome evolution in China's behavior over time. At the very outset of its reform process, in the late 1970s, China was eager to join (and to displace Taiwan in) the International Monetary Fund (IMF) and World Bank. These institutional ties subsequently played important, and apparently highly welcome, roles in China's early development success. Subsequently, China not only endured a lengthy negotiation and ever-escalating set of requirements to join the WTO but proactively used the promarket rules of that institution to overcome domestic resistance to internal reform. It seemed quite willing to operate within the existing system until relatively recently. But the attitudes of countries can change dramatically with changes in their objective circumstances, and China appears to be undergoing a significant evolution in its attitude toward the global economic order as it recognizes its vastly increased capability to influence global events.

Trade

On trade, China has been playing at best a passive and at worst a disruptive role with respect to the global system. Its current account surplus in 2007 approximated 11 percent of its GDP. Its annual global surplus came in at $372 billion and, even if it declines a bit in 2008, will still be by far the largest in the world. Its hoard of foreign currency exceeded $1.8 trillion by mid-2008 and is by far the world's largest despite the continued low incomes of the Chinese population. These results are unprecedented for a major trading country and place substantial pressures on the global economy.

Moreover, these surpluses are generated to a large extent by China's massive intervention in the foreign exchange markets to prevent the needed appreciation of its currency, the renminbi. China has the right to peg its currency under IMF rules, but it does not have the right to intervene massively in the foreign exchange market, as it has for the past five years, to maintain a substantially undervalued price for its national currency and thus enormously boost its international competitive position. This behavior violates the most basic norms of the IMF Articles of Agreement, which require members to "avoid manipulating exchange rates . . . to avoid effective balance of payments adjustment or to gain unfair competitive advantage" and whose implementing guidelines explicitly proscribe the use of "prolonged, large-scale, one-way" intervention to maintain competitive undervaluation.[7] The US current account deficit is, of course, at the heart of the global imbalances and stems largely from internal US economic problems and policy errors. China's large trade surpluses compound the problem substantially, however, and to an important extent result from policies that are widely regarded around the world as unfair and indeed inconsistent with the global rules.

Large and persistent trade and currency imbalances have traditionally been major sources of protectionist pressures in deficit countries. This is particularly true in the United States, where the surges of import relief actions in the early 1970s and mid-1980s were predicated on sizable currency misalignments that ultimately required substantial depreciations of the dollar. Present restrictive attitudes are indicated by the numerous bills proposed in the US Congress to address the China currency issue with trade sanctions if other remedies fail. Similar attitudes can be increasingly observed in Europe as well, especially now that it has replaced the United States as China's largest export market.

On trade policy itself, China makes no effort to hide its preference for low-quality, politically motivated bilateral and regional arrangements over more economically meaningful (and demanding) multilateral liberalization through the WTO or even high-quality agreements with individual trading partners. Since China is the world's largest surplus country and second largest exporter, and thus has enormous impact on world trading patterns and policies, this poses two important challenges to the existing global regime.

First, China's rejection of the compromise proposed for the Doha Round in July 2008 was a key reason for the historic failure of that multilateral initiative. China in fact declared throughout most of the negotiations that it should have no liberalization obligations whatsoever in the Round and even invented a new category ("recently acceded members") to justify its recalcitrance. Such a stance by a major trading power is akin to rejection or abstention by the United States or the European Union, either of which would have torpedoed the Doha Round or even precluded it from ever getting off the ground.

We know from history that the global trading system is dynamically unstable: It either moves forward toward steady liberalization or falls backward under the constant pressure of protectionism and mercantilism. The demise of the Doha Round represents the first failure of a major multilateral negotiation in the postwar period and places the entire WTO system in jeopardy. Whatever one thinks of the virtues of the Doha initiative, or indeed of the current global rules that proscribe preferential agreements unless they meet fairly rigorous economic criteria, these are central norms of the existing system, the violation of which will, over time, severely undermine the entire regime.

China is, of course, not the only culprit in the Doha drama. The United States and European Union were unwilling to enact the needed reductions in their agricultural support programs, though to their credit they placed extensive offers on the negotiating table and kept the round alive. Other emerging-market economies, especially India, were also unwilling to open their markets meaningfully. But China, with its major stake in open trade because of its heavy dependence on global markets and its huge surpluses, exhibited the sharpest contrast between its objective interests and its revealed policy.

Second, China's pursuit of bilateral and regional trade agreements with neighboring countries is almost wholly political. Its "free trade agreement" with the Association of Southeast Asian Nations (ASEAN) accepts those countries' own penchant for weak accords, covering only a small share of its commerce with them in an effort mainly to assuage their fears of being swamped (especially in terms of attracting foreign investment) by their huge neighbor. When China has agreed to consider liberalization pacts with countries that seek economically meaningful agreements, such as Australia, progress has been limited.[8]

The United States and other major trading powers, of course, factor foreign policy considerations into their selection of partners for regional and especially bilateral trade agreements. But they also insist on reasonably high economic standards that conform to the (admittedly loose and poorly enforced) rules of the WTO, especially coverage of "substantially all" trade. China is able to escape legal application of those rules by continuing to declare itself a "developing country" and invoking the systemic norm of "special and differential treatment." But for China, as a major global trading power, to hide behind such loopholes provokes substantial international strains and represents a second fundamental challenge to the global trading system.

In addition to jeopardizing the WTO system directly by undermining both the Doha Round and the norms for multilateralism, China's trade policy strategy will do so indirectly, and probably even more importantly, by leading to the creation of a loose but potent Asian trading bloc. The network of bilateral and plurilateral agreements in the region, which started with China-ASEAN, is now steadily expanding to include virtually all other possible permutations: parallel Japan-ASEAN and Korea-ASEAN deals; many other bilateral agreements including perhaps China-India; a "10+3" arrangement, which brings together the 10 ASEAN countries and all three northeast Asian countries (China, Korea, and Japan); and maybe even a "10+6," which broadens the group to include Australia, India, and New Zealand. Especially with the failure of the Doha Round, this evolution is likely to produce an East Asia Free Trade Area led by China within the next decade as part of its broader strategy of promoting regional identity and solidarity.

Such a regional grouping centered on China will, as noted earlier, be full of exceptions and deviations from WTO norms that limit its economic impact. But it is still virtually certain to trigger a sharp backlash from the United States and European Union, and probably numerous developing countries, because of its new discrimination against them (despite their own adoption in the past of similarly discriminatory agreements such as the North American Free Trade Agreement [NAFTA] and the European Union itself). Even more important systemically, it will create a tripolar global regime with a new Asian pole to counterpoise the existing power centers in Europe and North America. Such a configuration is not inherently antithetical to multilateral cooperation, and could even abet it if managed to that end, but would pose a serious threat to the present institutional construct and could accelerate the deterioration of today's global system. It comports nicely, however, with China's foreign policy goal of promoting a multipolar world that constrains the global power of the United States.

China's challenges to the global trading system fuse in its opposition to the US proposal in the Asia Pacific Economic Cooperation (APEC) forum in 2006 for a Free Trade Area of the Asia Pacific. This APEC initiative was immediately endorsed by a number of smaller member economies that fervently want to prevent trade conflict between the group's two superpowers. It seeks to head off the potential confrontation between an Asia-only trading bloc and the United States, which could "draw a line down the middle of the Pacific," curb and eventually consolidate the proliferating "noodle bowl" of preferential pacts in the Asia-Pacific region, and offer an economically meaningful "Plan B" for widespread trade liberalization in the event of a definitive failure of the Doha Round.[9] China has clearly opposed the idea, however, revealing its preference for bilateral deals without much economic content and its disinterest in pursuing strategies to defend the broader trading order.

International Monetary System

China's challenge to the international monetary order is at least as serious. Alone among the world's major economies, China has rejected the adoption of a flexible exchange rate policy, which would promote adjustment of its balance-of-payments position and help avoid a buildup of large imbalances. As noted earlier, it has in fact intervened massively in the currency markets to maintain a substantially undervalued exchange rate, which has produced huge trade and current account surpluses that are by far the largest counterparty to the US trade and current account deficits. These imbalances and the unprecedented flow of international funds that they require could trigger at almost any time a crash of the dollar and "hard landing" of the global economy, severely compounding the current financial crisis (box 1.2). China's challenge to the international monetary order also adds considerably to the risks it is posing for the global trading system, as noted above.

To date, however, China has resisted the pleas of the United States and others to conform to the international monetary norms. Its announced move to "a managed floating exchange rate based on market supply and demand" in July 2005 has still produced only a modest rise in the trade-weighted rate of its currency, despite the recent acceleration of its bilateral appreciation against the dollar, and a small moderation at best in the continued huge surpluses in its external accounts. Its intervention in the currency markets to block faster appreciation has in fact at least doubled since that time, implying a policy that is less rather than more market-oriented.

Hence China's behavior poses a fundamental challenge to the operation of the global monetary regime and to the effectiveness of its institutional guardian, the International Monetary Fund. China has in fact questioned the basic concept of international cooperation in dealing with these problems, claiming that the exchange rate is "an issue of national sovereignty" when it is of course a quintessential international question in which foreign counterparties have an equivalent interest. Far from accepting IMF advice, it has strenuously objected even to the principle of Fund involvement in the issue. Underlying this debate is the implicit threat that China might promote creation of an Asian Monetary Fund—based on the Chiang Mai Initiative, which provides the fulcrum for Asian

Box 1.2   Will China dump its dollars?

China's foreign exchange reserves had risen to about $1.8 trillion, by far the largest national hoard in the world, by May 2008. They were rising by about $50 billion every month as the authorities intervened in the currency markets to limit the appreciation of the renminbi, and so could easily climb to $2 trillion or more by the end of the year. China does not publish the composition of its holdings, but most estimates suggest that 60 to 75 percent, or more than $1 trillion, are invested in dollar assets (with most of the rest in euros and perhaps a smattering in yen and other currencies).

Some observers worry that these holdings represent a major Chinese threat to the United States. They fear that China could "dump" some or all of its dollars, driving down the exchange rate of the US currency in a rapid and disorderly manner. This could trigger a sharp rise in US inflation and interest rates, especially since any such action by the Chinese, or even serious rumors thereof,[1] would presumably lead to panicky dollar sales by other holders around the world. Such a sequence would have particularly costly effects during a period when the US economy is simultaneously hovering near recession and experiencing uncomfortably high inflation, as in 2008.

Such a step by the Chinese is highly unlikely, however, for three reasons: First, any partial sale of their current dollar holdings (or rumors thereof) would drive down the value of their remaining dollar holdings, probably sharply. The Chinese authorities are already under considerable domestic criticism for the sizable losses they have incurred as the dollar has dropped over the past six years, by a cumulative average of 25 to 30 percent against other currencies, by more than 50 percent against the euro and some other plausible alternatives, and by even more against "real" assets such as oil and many other commodities. Since it would be technically impossible for the Chinese to sell anything close to their dollar total of $1 trillion or so instantaneously, they would be shooting themselves in the financial foot in a major way through such action.

Second, Chinese sales of dollars would drive up the price of whatever currencies they converted into. The authorities would sharply raise the price of their own renminbi if they sold dollars to other Chinese entities, such as banks or companies, for local currency. The resulting appreciation of the renminbi would adversely affect China's trade competitiveness and represent a total reversal of the country's currency policy of the past five years, under which they have bought large amounts of dollars to maintain an undervalued exchange rate. It would thus be more plausible for China to sell dollars for euros and other foreign currencies. Such a move would be highly unwelcome to the Europeans and other recipients of the shifts,

(box continues next page)

Box 1.2   Will China dump its dollars? *(continued)*

however, because their currencies would then become overvalued, with negative effects on their international competitiveness, and could trigger additional protectionist reactions against China as a result.

Third, unlike the sizable but gradual appreciation of the renminbi that China should permit to help correct the global imbalances, China would be branded an international pariah if it were to "dump" its dollars in a precipitous manner that generated global financial and economic instability. This would be opposite the international praise they rightly garnered during the Asian financial crisis in 1997–98 when they helped counter further contagion and possible worldwide panic by avoiding sympathetic depreciation of their own currency. Dollar "dumping" would rightly attract far more international opprobrium than China has already endured in recent years for keeping its currency so undervalued through overt manipulation.

The only plausible circumstance under which China might "dump" its dollars is if it thought the United States might be about to freeze those holdings itself, as it did with Iran's dollar assets in 1979 after the revolution in that country and its takeover of the US embassy. China has already protected itself against this risk to a considerable extent by holding many of its dollars outside the United States, however, and such a sequence could only occur in the extremely unlikely event of very sharp confrontation between the two countries over Taiwan or some other political "hot spot." The much more likely scenario is that China will gradually diversify its reserve composition away from the dollar over time, primarily at the margin by converting a modest portion of its additional dollar acquisitions into euros and perhaps other currencies.

---

1. Rumors that Kuwait planned to sell $100 million in dollar assets, which were never confirmed, were a major factor in triggering the free fall of the US currency in late 1978, which remains the most serious dollar crisis to this time.

---

monetary cooperation, in addition to the regional trade plans described earlier—and further erode the global role of the IMF.

Energy

On energy, China's challenge is less frontal because no body of agreed global doctrine, rules, and institutions exists. Moreover, China's search for "assured sources of supply" can lead to increased global production of oil and gas and thus help alleviate upward pressure on prices and any possible shortages. The challenge in this area is no less important, however, because China will become the world's largest consumer of energy over the next few years and has been a major contributor to the dramatic rise in world oil prices over the past five years (chapter 7).

There are at least two conflicting regimes in this issue-area: the (periodically effective) producer cartel embodied in the Organization of Petroleum Exporting Countries (OPEC) and the (very loose and incomplete) consumer anticartel in the International Energy Agency (IEA). China has essentially challenged both with its drive to line up "secure sources of supply" by providing support to Chinese oil companies in their pursuit of overseas oil investment through tied aid and other types of assistance that member countries of the Organization for Economic Cooperation and Development (OECD) have sought to discipline. Beijing's efforts in Sudan and Iran have been of particular concern as they have led China to constrain the efforts of the UN Security Council to impose sanctions on those countries. As with the other issue-areas, China is hardly alone in its search for "equity oil" and allegedly preferred access. But as a major driving force of the single most important commodity market in the world, the country has a particular interest in, and responsibility for, forging systemic responses rather than trying to carve out exceptions and special privileges for itself.

The other consuming countries have not sought to engage China in their cooperative arrangements, however, at least until very recently. It has been denied membership in the IEA because it is not a member of the OECD, which requires its members to be committed to an open market economy and democratic pluralism. The United States, for its part, rejected the proposed takeover of Unocal by the China National Offshore Oil Corporation (CNOOC) in 2005 and thus indicated an unwillingness to permit perfectly normal and reasonable Chinese investment in additional energy resources.[10] As indicated in chapter 7, China will become an active and constructive partner in ensuring the security of international energy markets only if it is allowed to help shape energy policy at the multilateral level and if Chinese oil companies are allowed to compete freely for investment opportunities in the United States and other Western countries.

Foreign Aid

On foreign aid, China has already become a major donor (depending on how aid is defined) and poses a direct challenge to prevailing norms by ostentatiously ignoring the types of conditionality that have evolved throughout the donor community over the past quarter century. It rejects not only the social conditions (human rights, labor standards, and environmental norms) that have become prevalent but also the basic economic criteria (starting with poverty alleviation and good governance) that virtually all bilateral and multilateral aid agencies now require as a matter of course.

As with its trade and commodity pacts, China's "conditionality" is almost wholly political: insistence that the recipient countries support China's positions on global issues, in the United Nations and elsewhere, and funnel their primary products to it as reliable suppliers. As with trade, China has now become such a sizable player that its deviation from global norms matters a great deal. It provides its recipients with an escape from despised "Western conditionality" or the Washington Consensus that is both financially profitable and politically satisfying to them but that may vitiate any lasting value they can obtain from Chinese assistance itself and, even more so, from the non-Chinese assistance that it may supplant.

Global Implications

All these policies, and the national mindset they represent, reveal that China's attitude toward its global economic responsibilities has not kept pace with the breathtaking ascent of its security and (especially) economic impact on the rest of the world. China continues to behave primarily like a small country with little systemic effect and therefore systemic responsibility. In economic terms, it acts like a price-taker rather than the price-maker with enormous, sometimes decisive, influence on critical global economic outcomes it has so clearly become.

Such a lag in perceptions is not difficult to understand, particularly for a very conservative leadership that is still guided to an important extent by Deng Xiaoping's directive to maintain a low international profile. Indeed, the central thrust of contemporary Chinese foreign policy is to avoid international developments that could disrupt the country's ability to focus on its huge domestic challenges. Moreover, the speed at which China has assumed international prominence, and its systemic consequences, is difficult for even the most experienced observers to assimilate.

Even the strongest defenders of the current global system would also concede that at least some of China's criticisms are valid. Neither the United Nations, the WTO, the IMF, the World Bank nor their putative steering committees like the Group of Seven (G-7) have been models of effectiveness in recent years or even decades. The Doha Round would have achieved very little liberalization of world trade after almost a decade of effort. The IMF has failed to enforce its own rules and is being forced to downsize. The G-7 has adopted a mutual nonaggression pact among its members, under which they basically agree not to criticize each other very loudly, and their criticisms of outsiders (like China) ring hollow as a result. Global policy cooperation, let alone coordination, has largely gone out of style.

The significance of China's challenge will depend importantly on who else will join its effort. China is, of course, a significant challenger solely on its own because of its massive, and rapidly growing, economic weight and its formidable, though lesser, security counterpart. It will probably be unable to win widespread acceptance for alternative approaches, however, without a considerable array of important allies—who can be attracted either by persuasion or by coercion. Most of its Asian neighbors can already be counted on to support its initiatives or at least not oppose them, due to its preponderant impact on the region, as already observed in APEC, and an Asian economic bloc is in the making as noted earlier. Its increasing number of close economic partners, especially in Africa, are in a similar position and will tend at least to be neutral to avoid antagonizing a China that has demonstrated its willingness to retaliate against noncooperation. Its alliance with India in blocking the Doha Round bears close watching.

Challenges to the international order are not a new phenomenon, at least at the rhetorical level. "North-South conflict" has ebbed and flowed in intensity for over three decades. OPEC was initially perceived as a champion of the "South" for systemic reform after the first oil shock in the early 1970s (before it became clear that developing countries would suffer even more than rich nations from its manipulation of world energy markets. Abetted by a bevy of nongovernmental organizations (NGOs), some poor countries have continued to press for systemic modifications even as a growing number of emerging-market economies sought to enter the "rich men's club" and some of its formal institutions (with Korea and Mexico entering the OECD, and those two along with Brazil, China, and India becoming more-or-less regular invitees to side meetings of the G-7/G-8).

The challenge from China is fundamentally new and vastly more important than any of these earlier phases. It is different because it is based on pragmatic pursuit of very specific national interests rather than any ideological attack. It is much more salient because of the massive, and rapidly growing and multifaceted, economic weight of the challenger. OPEC and Japan, the only serious previous challengers to the postwar global order, in fact sought to join rather than alter the system. The challenge from China, though still in its early days, is potentially far more serious.

A New Approach

The United States should, therefore, implement a subtle but sharp change in its basic economic strategy toward China. Instead of focusing on bilateral problems and complaints, and seeking to coopt China into a global economic system that it would try to continue leading by itself, the United States should seek to develop a true partnership with China to provide joint leadership of that system, even if the system requires substantial modifications to persuade China to play that role. The two economic superpowers should begin to pursue together the development of coordinated, or at least cooperative, approaches to global issues that can be resolved effectively only through their active co-management. Such a "G-2" approach would accurately recognize, and be perceived by the Chinese as accurately recognizing, the new role of China as a legitimate architect and steward of the international economic order.

The proposed strategy is importantly different from current US policy. The present approach seeks to wean or coopt, whether one wants to use polite or blunt terminology, China into the global economic order that the United States has helped construct and sought to lead for over 60 years. Such a fondness for the status quo is understandable, given both the fundamental success of that regime throughout most of its existence and the prominent role it provides for the United States.

But China is quietly uncomfortable with the very notion of its integration into the current international system, which it had no role in developing. Moreover, the current system has become increasingly ineffective over the past decade or so, as outlined earlier. This is due importantly to its growing political illegitimacy as its decision-making machinery fails to evolve sufficiently to provide adequate voice for the emerging powers, of which China is by far the most important. Systemic reform is needed in any event, and the Chinese catalyst for it could turn out to be quite fortuitous and extremely healthy.

The ineffectiveness of the current system also derives from its failure to address the interrelationships among key issues. Currency imbalances foster trade protectionism. Capital-intensive development strategies accelerate environmental degradation. Energy imbalances lead to financial distortions and even crises. All these economic issues must be seen in the context, and addressed with full recognition, of the broad political and security settings within which they take place. It will be essential to address these seemingly separate topics much more holistically if management of the global economic system is to improve significantly.

Present US policy purports to include tough enforcement measures when China fails to cooperate on specific issues, and Congress frequently calls for much more of that medicine. The United States has in fact taken China to the dispute settlement mechanism at the WTO in a number of cases and has won virtually all of them, mainly through settlements out of court, but with very modest results. There have been a few instances of unilateral US "safeguard actions," but their economic impact has been minuscule. On the much bigger exchange rate issue, the administration has been unable to mobilize the IMF or the G-7 and has itself been unwilling to label China a "currency manipulator" even when its massive intervention has been obvious.[11] The Congress has not followed through on any of its own trade or currency threats. The United States has done very little to counter China's moves on energy and aid.

China contends that external pressure, especially when applied publicly, is counterproductive and virtually forces it to reject the proposed courses of action.[12] But the revealed impotence of hard-line US bilateral efforts derives primarily from three basic domestic factors: the clear benefits to many Americans of attractive Chinese products and financial support, its need for Chinese cooperation on noneconomic issues ranging from North Korea to Iran, and the keen interest of many US-based companies in avoiding confrontations with Beijing for fear of retaliation. There is simply too much US opposition to "tough" policies for them to be sustained, even if adopted on occasion. Foreign allies for a confrontational approach are even harder to find, for similar reasons. The likely continuation of this futility suggests that there is no real alternative to a cooperative approach. It indeed implies that the main, or perhaps only, hope for persuading China to start providing constructive systemic leadership lies in convincing it of the critical importance to itself of doing so and then actively partnering with it to that end.

The proposed strategy would treat old issues in new ways. The United States and China could agree to construct their proposed bilateral and regional trade agreements, including megadeals like the Free Trade Area of the Americas and an East Asia Free Trade Area, in ways that would support subsequent multilateral liberalization and even permit eventual linkage between the regional bodies. There would be recognition that dollar overvaluation has reflected errant US fiscal policy and inadequate US private saving just as renminbi undervaluation has reflected inadequate Chinese internal demand and excessive intervention. Competitive currency misalignments would be treated as deviations from the agreed norms of the IMF and as beggar-thy-neighbor policies that hurt all trading partners, especially including other poor countries (as India and others are now vocally emphasizing). The United States could escort China, figuratively if not literally, into the IEA so that the two together could help organize the response of consuming countries to high global oil prices and longer-run security of supply.

The proposed strategy could apply even more forcefully to the creation of new international norms and institutional arrangements to govern economic issues where no such arrangements have previously existed. The two most important candidates at present are global warming and sovereign wealth funds. China is a central player on both. On the former, it likely has passed the United States as the world's largest emitter of greenhouse gases. On the latter, its recently created sovereign wealth fund—the China Investment Corporation—could quickly become one of the world's largest as China is by far the world's largest holder of foreign exchange reserves, the source of financing for most such funds. There will be no possibility of constructing effective global regimes on these issues without full and active participation by China and indeed close cooperation between China and the United States.

China's challenge to the current global economic order could in fact come to a head on these two topics. To date, China has steadfastly refused to contemplate binding constraints on its aggregate emissions of greenhouse gases (and other developing countries, including India, are hiding behind its resistance). So has the United States, but that stance fortunately seems likely to change dramatically with a new US administration in 2009, and the United States may even seek to take an aggressive lead in forging a new international compact on the issue. Moreover, as noted in chapter 7, China now seems willing to commit to "nationally appropriate mitigation actions" under a post-Kyoto framework. Hence there may well be a fruitful opportunity for new US-China collaboration on the issue.

Such a regime, however, could also lead to the installation of trade or other barriers in participating countries against carbon-intensive products from countries with less exacting (or no) standards. A US-China trade war with retaliation and counterretaliation could result unless the two countries cooperate intensively in constructing a new global regime on the issue. Such a regime would, of course, be implemented through a much broader grouping of nations, in which China could maintain its role as a leader of the developing countries, but can be forged in the first instance only through intimate if informal "G-2" collaboration.

China has already indicated some skepticism about the emerging consensus on the adoption of new international guidelines, even if voluntary and nonbinding, on the structure and investment activities of sovereign wealth funds. The United States is championing such codes, primarily to head off the risk of protectionist domestic reactions to specific investments, because it so desperately needs the foreign money to fund its huge external and internal deficits. It is especially dependent on China, with its massive currency reserves and large annual additions to them from its ongoing surpluses. A frontal clash could develop over this issue as well, triggered either by Chinese rejection of proposed new guidelines or US rejection of particularly sensitive Chinese investments (as in the CNOOC case).

Hence the United States should reach out to Beijing on both global warming and sovereign wealth funds, as well as modify its approach in a number of ongoing negotiations, to start implementing the new strategy. The basic idea is to develop a very informal but increasingly effective "G-2" between the United States and China to help guide the global governance process on an increasing number of economic topics. The concept would not apply in the security area, where the issues and relationships are very different, but could have a major impact on both the functioning of the world economy and on the China-US economic relationship.

Such a new steering committee would not seek to displace any of the existing international economic institutions. Other major countries, notably the European Union and on some issues Japan and the large oil exporters, would, of course, need to remain deeply involved as well. The new rules, codes, or norms would frequently be implemented through existing multilateral institutions, like the IMF, WTO, and IEA. Some of them might work through new worldwide organizations created to deal with truly new issues, such as a Global Environmental Organization to manage climate change policy.[13] But effective systemic defenses in today's world must start with active cooperation between its two dominant economies, the United States and China.

It would be impolitic for the two governments to use the term "G-2" publicly, and they should not do so. For the strategy to work, however, the United States will have to accord true priority to China as its main partner in managing the world economy. This will be true even vis-à-vis the European Union, the other global economic superpower and traditional partner in any de facto "G-2" that may have existed in the past, in important part because the European Union still has neither a cohesive policy nor an effective spokesman except in a very few issue-areas (like international trade, where it *has* spoken with a single voice from its creation and has thus played a central global role). The European Union, Japan, and perhaps some other traditional US allies might be unhappy with the relative downgrading of their own relationship with the United States. But their pique should be assuaged by the enhanced effectiveness of the global economy, which is the objective of the exercise, and would be minimized if the "G-2" structure were pursued diplomatically without fanfare. In any event, nothing short of the intimate relationship implied by the "G-2" concept is likely to attract China, and engage the United States sufficiently, to create the effective leadership core that the two countries and the world as a whole need so desperately.

Initial steps are already being taken toward implementing this concept. After the initial proposal for a US-China "G-2,"[14] Robert Zoellick as deputy secretary of state in the second George W. Bush administration launched a Senior Dialogue with Chinese counterparts, and Secretary of the Treasury Henry Paulson, Jr. escalated the engagement in 2007 to a Strategic Economic Dialogue (SED) among the leaders of 10 or so cabinet agencies in each country. On the military side, Secretary of Defense Robert Gates recently inaugurated a direct hotline with his Chinese counterparts to respond to any crisis risks. The beginnings of an institutional framework for a working G-2 have thus been put in place, and patterns of cooperation are already developing on some topics, including the environment and international finance. Energy and the environment were in fact central topics of discussion at the third and fourth meetings of the SED in December 2007 and June 2008. These recent innovations have produced useful, if not dramatic, results and should certainly be continued.

But it is not nearly enough to seek to induce China to become a "responsible stakeholder" in the global system, as the US government has sought to do since Zoellick initiated that concept in 2005, though that would be an important step forward. It must be seen, and accorded full rights, as a true leadership partner in the evolving global economy of the 21st century. As Harry Harding has recently testified to the Congress,[15] China "should be invited to participate in the norm drafting process . . . [and] should be treated as a rule-maker and not simply as a rule-taker."[16]

It may in fact prove impossible to persuade China to behave like a "responsible stakeholder" without according it full leadership status.

The logical next step is for China and the United States to initiate annual, or even semiannual,[17] summit meetings to both symbolize and implement such a new relationship. Only the heads of government can integrate the wide range of economic and foreign policy/national security issues that must be included in the partnership. Only they can make decisions on the essential trade-offs within and among the key areas, even within the economic domain. Only the regular convocation of summits can galvanize officials of the two countries to develop the intensive procedures for consultation and cooperation that are essential underpinnings for an effective "G-2." The SED or some equivalent cabinet-level body should prepare for, and carry out the decisions of, the heads of government on an increasingly routinized basis.

A partnership for global economic leadership between a rich developed country and a poor developing country would be unprecedented in human history, as befits the uniqueness of China's becoming the first poor economic superpower. Examples of such cooperation, however, suggest that converting bilateral disputes into systemic management initiatives can be extremely effective. In the late 1970s, for example, the United States was applying countervailing duties to scores of Brazilian products because Brazil's export subsidies accounted for almost half the value of all its foreign sales. A frontal assault on the subsidies was politically unacceptable in Brazil, but the two countries agreed to cooperate closely, and in fact took the lead, in negotiating a new Subsidy Code in the General Agreement on Tariffs and Trade (GATT). That code simultaneously became the linchpin of a successful Tokyo Round, a basis for adding an injury clause to the US countervailing duty law, and a foundation for phasing out the Brazilian rebate policy. That US-Brazil trade issue greatly resembles, both bilaterally and systemically, the China currency issue of today.

Are the United States and China ready to substantially reorient their policies toward each other and, indeed, their entire foreign economic policies? At least three shifts in mindset will be needed in the United States: acceptance of a true partner in managing global economic affairs, working intimately with an Asian country rather than the traditional European allies, and collaborating with an authoritarian political regime instead of the usual democracy. All three will pose substantial challenges for any American policymaker seeking to carry out such a new approach, not least because of the domestic political resistance that will be encountered on each of them.

Is China ready for such cooperation with the United States or indeed to play a responsible leadership role in the world economy under any institutional setting?[18] The historical answer is that no country, even the British and American hegemons during their eras of dominance, has been "ready" for such a role until it was forced upon the country by its own national interests and the realities of the global economic situation. As a country that is still quite poor in the aggregate, and whose currency remains inconvertible and protected by extensive capital controls, China will be sorely tempted to resist and instead maintain its demeanor as a small country or, at most, as a leader of the developing nations. As noted earlier (and in chapter 2), an internal backlash against globalization (as in the United States) is challenging some of the basic tenets of the country's international economic engagement. The revealed preference for systemic challenges outlined earlier indicates a willingness to jeopardize global stability.

It would seem that China is rapidly approaching a position, however, where the consequences of its chosen strategy of integration with the world economy will push it to assume ever-increasing responsibility for the successful functioning of that economy. Its trade exceeds 60 percent of GDP, twice the share in the United States or the European Union as a group, and that ratio continues to rise rapidly. Its foreign financial assets are approaching half the size of its economy and are a major component of its national wealth, and they too will steadily become much larger. China has almost surely passed the point where its leadership can responsibly, or even in its own narrow political interests, pursue a policy of benign neglect.

China's own central interest in an effectively functioning world economy is the cardinal reason why it might be willing to participate in a new joint leadership arrangement with the United States. Its broad foreign policy interests in projecting "soft power" worldwide and avoiding confrontation with the United States reinforce such a stance. So does the Party's desire to solidify central control over the provinces, as discussed in chapter 4, because deeper global engagement (such as participation in the WTO's dispute settlement mechanism and strengthening the independence of monetary policy by adopting a more flexible exchange rate system) will almost always tend to add to the decision-making power of the national authorities. Intellectuals in China are hotly debating whether China should work within the system or proceed unilaterally, perhaps including with harsh criticism of the United States over alternative models of financial regulation and currency management (as has already begun to surface in the wake of the US housing and financial crises of 2007–08). US willingness to pursue genuine partnership in shaping the future international economic order could tilt the outcome in a constructive direction. From China's standpoint, the historic challenge is to alter the global system in its direction without precipitating widespread conflict as other emerging powers have done in the past.

If China proves to be leery of getting too close to the United States and would be more inclined to accept the needed global leadership responsibilities in a different institutional setting, perhaps because the United States maintains a cautious stance toward Beijing on security issues, alternatives are available. The European Union could be a member from the outset of a "G-3" of the current global economic superpowers, especially now that it has become China's largest trading partner, source of new technologies, and host to Chinese students. The "new G-5" recently created by the IMF to conduct its intensified multilateral consultative process, which adds Japan and Saudi Arabia (to represent the oil producers) to these three, is another if less promising possibility. China could simply be invited to join the existing G-7 and/or G-8.[19] The central need is to embrace China in an effective leadership compact in light of its critical role in the world economy and its legitimate desire to be engaged in systemic management at all relevant stages of the process, including the creation of any new rules and (formal or informal) institutions. China itself will have to judge which of these institutional approaches would be most attractive and convey that preference to the rest of the world.

But there remains the question whether China would prefer to continue going it largely alone, challenging the existing global system rather than joining with the United States or anyone else in an effort to modify that system in a gradual and orderly manner. Even the closest observers outside China, and maybe even the Chinese themselves, cannot know the answer to that question any more than they can foresee the orientation of overall Chinese foreign policy in the years and decades ahead.

The only way to test these ideas is to try the proposed approach in specific cases. The upcoming negotiations to create a global architecture to counter global warming, with their critically important trade policy dimension and huge implications for energy policy along with the emissions controls themselves, offer a compelling opportunity. As indicated in chapter 7, the United States and China could fruitfully cooperate on a number of climate change issues in addition to working out the needed overarching regime: carbon capture and sequestration, industrial energy efficiency, biofuels, green buildings, and nuclear power. Full Chinese cooperation is essential, and the United States has no chance of succeeding on the issue unilaterally or even in effective partnership with only the Europeans and other rich countries.

The new US administration that will take office in early 2009 is committed to launching a major global initiative on the issue. The two countries have already pledged, at the SED meeting in June 2008, to work closely on energy and the environment for the next 10 years. Hence climate change is a tailor-made test case for a new "G-2," coupling informal China-US collaboration at the core of the process with the conduct of formal negotiations and implementation in broader groupings that imbed China with other developing as well as industrialized countries.

Under seven successive presidents, the United States has chosen to engage rather than confront China on the eminently sensible view that confrontation could only provoke the evolution of a hostile China, which would be profoundly contrary to US interests. China's impressive economic advance is likely to continue, perhaps leading it to become the world's largest economy as well as the world's largest trading nation, and the United States should thus on similar logic make every effort to engage it as a true partner in steering global economic affairs. The initiative could fail, but its success would bring huge benefits, and the effort itself would pay important dividends for the United States in terms of both relations with China itself and the broader US image in Asia and around the world.

Bilateral issues will, of course, remain between the United States and China, in both the economic and security spheres, as between any pair of countries with high levels of trade and investment. But even those issues could be more easily resolved in a relationship that emphasizes the global coleadership responsibilities of the partners by providing a much broader context, and a much wider basis for trust and cooperation, within which to address them than can possibly exist today.

Conclusion

China's challenge to the existing norms, rules, and institutions of a growing number of components of the global economic order could be enormously disruptive both to the United States and to world stability. That challenge could escalate further as China's economic power, military capabilities, and self-confidence continue to grow rapidly and as the effectiveness of the existing regime and the scope for US leadership of it continue to erode. Peaceful transfer of international power has been elusive over the centuries of human history, and the numerous failures thereof have proven to be extremely dangerous.

On the other hand, the opportunity for an orderly realignment of global economic leadership has seldom been so promising. There is very little threat of conflict between China and the United States, nor indeed between any of the other great powers, into which they might be drawn. Overall relations between the two, while wary on both sides, have improved substantially in recent years. Economic, and especially financial, interdependence between them has deepened substantially. Institutional linkages, as noted above, are at an early stage but are clearly being constructed at the direction of the top leadership in both countries. As Henry Kissinger has recently reminded us, US foreign policy must evolve steadily from its transatlantic focus of the past to an inevitable transpacific focus for the future.[20]

There is considerable risk in continuing to respond to each issue that arises in a primarily bilateral and ad hoc manner. There is very little shared basis, as yet, for seeing such issues in a common framework that can produce routine rather than confrontational solutions. The proposed initiative to create a US-China "G-2" should, at a minimum, limit the risk that individual disputes will escalate and disrupt both the relationship and broader economic activities. At best, it could create a process that will, over time, generate sufficient trust and mutual understanding to produce active cooperation on at least those occasions when the national interests of the two countries come close to intersection.

It may be difficult for some to foresee such active cooperation between countries that possess such starkly different characteristics. At the same time, those same two countries possess noteworthy similarities, from their entrepreneurial cultures to their global foreign policy perspectives. Their international positions, as the incumbent power retaining great capabilities and the rising power with far-reaching aspirations, are converging on paths that make the proposed cooperation not only possible but also seemingly inevitable at least to an important degree. It will clearly take time to develop the proposed "G-2" and even the essential cooperation on global warming through which it might be launched. But the next administration in the United States should make a major effort to pursue that prospect as a, if not the, central purpose of its overall foreign policy.

Notes

1. With exchange rates calculated at purchasing power parity per the standard practice of the International Monetary Fund and World Bank. Using market exchange rates, China's economy is now the fourth largest in the world but will shortly pass Germany to move into third place behind only the United States and Japan.

2. China is the third largest trading nation but it is running a huge trade surplus so its exports far exceed its imports, and it is the second largest exporter, trailing only Germany and ahead of both Japan and the United States.

3. China accounts for about 10 percent of global output (with exchange rates at purchasing power parity) and is growing at about 10 percent annually. Hence, it alone accounts for about one percentage point of total world growth, or about one-quarter of the current global expansion rate of a bit less than 4 percent.

4. Harry Harding, testimony before the Senate Foreign Relations Committee, Washington, May 15, 2008.

5. Mark Leonard, *What Does China Think?* (New York: PublicAffairs, 2008).

6. Edward Wong, "Booming, China Faults US Policy on the Economy," *New York Times*, June 17, 2008.

7. Morris Goldstein and Nicholas R. Lardy, eds., *Debating China's Exchange Rate Policy* (Washington: Peterson Institute for International Economics, 2008).

8. Its bilateral free trade agreement with New Zealand, signed in early 2008, is an anomalous exception with a very small country (China's 50th largest trading partner) that appears to be largely motivated by gratitude for New Zealand's being the first country to approve China's WTO accession and the first to grant it "market economy" status.

9. C. Fred Bergsten, "A Free Trade Area of the Asia-Pacific in the Wake of the Faltering Doha Round: Trade Policy Alternatives for APEC," in *The APEC Trade Agenda? The Political Economy of a Free Trade Area of the Asia-Pacific*, eds. Charles E.

Morrison and Eduardo Pedrosa (Singapore: Pacific Economic Cooperation Council and APEC Business Advisory Council, 2007).

10. The US "rejection" resulted from an emotional and highly political outburst from Congress when the takeover was proposed rather than from the standard policy procedures of the US government, which were never involved in the case because CNOOC withdrew its bid in the face of the congressional onslaught.

11. C. Randall Henning, *Accountability and Oversight of US Exchange Rate Policy* (Washington: Peterson Institute for International Economic, 2008).

12. Chapter 3 similarly notes that efforts to force liberal democracy on China "remain ineffective and ultimately counterproductive."

13. Daniel C. Esty, *Greening the GATT: Trade, Environment, and the Future* (Washington: Institute for International Economics, 1994).

14. C. Fred Bergsten and the Institute for International Economics, *The United States and the World Economy: Foreign Economic Policy for the Next Decade* (Washington: Institute for International Economics, 2005).

15. Harding, testimony before the Senate Foreign Relations Committee.

16. In the same vein, but with slightly less ambition, Richard Haass has proposed a "selective partnership" through which China and the United States look for opportunities to work together at high levels on specific issues where their interests intersect, including to "provide a setting to establish rules that would shape international relations and to design institutions for buttressing those rules." Richard N. Haass, testimony before the Senate Foreign Relations Committee, Washington, May 15, 2008.

17. The other two economic superpowers, the United States and the European Union, have held "home and home" annual summits in each partner area for a number of years. Both their substantive and symbolic value is severely limited, however, by the absence of a single recognizable leader for the European Union as a counterpart to the president of the United States and the limited scope of EU competence on many issues, and their operational results have been minimal. China-US summits, even if they became routinized, would probably command much more attention and have greater policy potential.

18. Robert Kagan asks whether "a determinedly autocratic government can really join a liberal international order?" and argues that "Chinese rulers . . . like all autocrats are most pragmatic about keeping themselves in power (and that) we may want to keep that in mind as we try to bring them into our liberal international order." Robert Kagan, "Behind the 'Modern' China," *Washington Post,* March 23, 2008.

19. Russia has participated in the annual summit meetings of the traditional G-7 (Canada, France, Germany, Italy, Japan, United Kingdom, and United States) since the early 1990s, so they have become a G-8. The finance ministers of the traditional group, however, continue to function as a G-7. I have earlier suggested including China in the "Finance G-7" but not in the more political G-8 if concerns about its lack of democracy are viewed as barring it from the latter.

20. Henry A. Kissinger, "The Three Revolutions," *Washington Post,* April 7, 2008.

2

China Debates Its Future

Many countries in the world have paid a very high price and learned a very painful lesson in transforming their economic systems. . . . We have to learn from these mistakes and keep them in mind at all times. To carry on walking the path leading to socialism with Chinese characteristics, we have to find a Chinese way to carry on economic reform, political reform, cultural reform and social reform.

—*China Reform Times*, May 21, 2008[1]

To understand the challenges facing China and US-China relations and consider potential US policy responses to them require insight into the context in which they will evolve, resolve, or dissolve. One critically important—but underappreciated—way to grasp this context is to observe the dynamic intellectual debate in China that now swirls around the most fundamental political, economic, and foreign policy questions confronting the country's future. China's intellectual atmosphere—reflecting the country as a whole—is far more open, diverse, and in flux than most outsiders appreciate. The answers and policies that flow from this diverse intellectual debate will shape China's future and, for better or for worse, influence the world as well.

Scrutinizing this debate in China is important because China's top leaders are increasingly paying attention to the intellectuals and their divergent views in setting policy. Absent formal, and politically institutionalized, channels for the expression of public opinion, Chinese intellectuals continue in their traditional behind-the-scenes role of articulating diverse social interests. Historically, these debates have also served as a window into the opaque world of China's elite politics. Individual intellectuals and the arguments they champion have often served as proxies for the differences over ideology, policies, and plans among China's top leaders, official airing of which has been proscribed by the Chinese Communist Party (CCP).[2]

President Hu Jintao's work report to China's 17th CCP Congress in October 2007, emerged in part from the intellectual and ideological ferment of the past several years. The report charts a pragmatic but cautious middle course that has some comparatively progressive elements but for the most part stays true to the status quo while accommodating some "new leftist" and nationalist sentiments. On the economic front, Deng Xiaoping's "basic line" of prioritizing economic development set more than 15 years ago at the 13th CCP Congress has been strongly reendorsed and features prominently throughout Hu's work report. It is significant that the CCP's most authoritative ideological document, the Party charter, was amended at the 17th Party Congress to formally enshrine Hu's Scientific Development Concept—an overarching strategy that endorses continued development, but development that acknowledges and addresses the downsides of overly rapid growth, is "people centered," and is sustainable—as part of the Party canon.

At the same time, on the political front, Hu even put forward certain modest political reforms, acknowledging the "growing enthusiasm of the people to participate in political affairs." However, the Four Cardinal Principles (upholding the socialist path, people's democratic dictatorship, CCP leadership, and Marxism-Leninism-Mao Zedong Thought[3]), traditional ideological tenets not used widely for many years, also reappear in the work report. As to foreign policy, the guidance of opening to the outside world and pursuing "peaceful development" is clearly articulated, even as a more assertive approach to economic and security matters is more evident.

In straddling this middle ground, Hu Jintao apparently attempted to quell and settle much of the ongoing intellectual debates by killing three birds with one stone. The "Right" was firmly reminded that economic reform would precede political reform and that any political reform would proceed incrementally and absolutely under the leadership of the CCP. The "New Left" was put on notice that market-oriented reforms, opening up, and economic development remained the Party's central task and that there was no going back. And, by reclaiming ownership of the Four Cardinal Principles and enshrining the Scientific Development Concept, Hu also managed to outmaneuver those on the "Old Left" who had begun to accuse the leadership of abandoning the Party's core principles.

With these critical recent developments in mind, the following sections describe the economic, political, and foreign policy debates in China—and the leadership's responses to them—during the past several years, especially before, during, and after the 17th CCP Congress. These debates are shaping and will continue to shape Beijing's responses to the many fundamental and vexing challenges it faces at home and abroad. Americans and their leaders need to understand and follow these debates to be able to cooperate with China in constructing new, forward-looking, and sustainable institutions and rules to effectively meet the challenges facing these two countries and the world—from energy security, corruption, and human rights to sustainable development and regional stability.

Role of Policy Intellectuals

The contribution of intellectual debate to policy decisions is a venerated and often high-stakes tradition in Chinese political culture dating back to ancient times. While intellectual activism was tightly and at times ruthlessly manipulated and controlled during most of the Maoist era, a far livelier environment has steadily emerged to accompany the course of China's reforms since 1978. Such debates typically intensify in the run-up to the Party Congress, held every five years. The eventual "winners" and "losers" in these debates become apparent when the policies adopted at the Party Congress—which guide China's development for the ensuing five years—are made public. For example, following economic and political retrenchment in the wake of the 1989 Tiananmen Square crackdown, the 14th Party Congress in 1992 signaled that the reformers led by Deng Xiaoping had prevailed over the conservatives led by Chen Yun. After a bitter proxy debate among intellectuals over "what is socialist and what is capitalist?" the Congress endorsed the creation of a "socialist market economic system," heralding a new era of rapid market reform. Once the Party sets the political and economic "line" at the Congress, however, it traditionally signals an end to the debate; those who continue to overstep this line face rebuke from the Party, or worse. Following the 14th Party Congress, conservative leaders including Yao Yilin and Song Ping lost their positions on the all-powerful Political Bureau Standing Committee, and the director of the Party's mouthpiece *Renmin Ribao* (*People's Daily*), Gao Di, was removed.[4]

In short, debates among intellectuals in China are not simply "academic," but often prove to be important early indicators of divergent interests and, ultimately, policy outcomes. A number of intellectuals and Chinese "think tanks" are assuming increasingly important roles in policymaking: Many leading intellectuals serve as advisers to China's leaders, and their ideas are often clearly discernible in government policies.[5] Despite facing sensitive political limitations and being vulnerable to manipulation by the Party, intellectuals are increasingly mediating between state and society as a subtle dance plays out among political thinkers, policymakers, and the public. Wang Shaoguang, a Yale-educated, leading Chinese intellectual based in Hong Kong, commented that "the breadth and depth with which intellectuals today participate in politics is unprecedented . . . . In setting the orientation of their policies, the leaders listen to the intellectuals directly or indirectly."[6] The United States must carefully observe these debates to improve its understanding of both how and why the Chinese leadership will choose to address the many economic, political, and diplomatic challenges it faces.[7] In addition, as China's global influence grows, understanding the country's intellectual debate and how it influences policy will be critical to informing effective policy responses in capitals around the world.

Current Dynamics

In the run-up to the 17th CCP Congress in October 2007, a confluence of social, political, economic, and cultural developments produced one of the most open and wide-ranging intellectual debates on the country's economic and political future yet in post-1949 China. The debate was remarkable in several respects. First, in what the CCP acknowledges is a "new historical starting point" in the "new period" of 29 years of reform,[8] the increasingly apparent downsides of rapid economic development—including corruption, income inequality, regional economic disparities, environmental degradation, increased demand for public goods and decreased ability of the state to supply them, and the social unrest all these problems have spawned—have prompted an unprecedented reevaluation of Deng Xiaoping's legacy and pose fundamental questions about China's current growth path and the nature of reform going forward. At the same time, the CCP leadership is well aware that to stay in power it has to formulate the correct policy responses to these pressing issues as it continues to lead China's development. Given the stakes, it is not surprising that China's top intellectuals were engaged in an often rancorous debate aimed at influencing the leadership prior to the 17th Party Congress. Many critical and strategic questions—settling on a proper model for sustainable growth, opening up the governance system to accept greater transparency and accountability, and determining China's role in regional and global affairs—were vigorously deliberated but not fully resolved, assuring that policy debate will continue.

Second, apart from the intensity of the current debate, what also marks this latest "Beijing Spring"[9] is that not all of the intellectuals engaged in it work within the system of official and semiofficial "think tanks" and Party-state organizations.[10] China's expanded education system and the commercialization of culture have opened up opportunities for "non-establishment" intellectuals working outside this system to take part in the discussion.[11] The ongoing marketization of Chinese media and explosion of the internet in the country have dramatically opened avenues through which a wide range of views are communicated, including in newspapers, journals, and online sources, often well before the CCP Propaganda Department can clamp down on or prevent such public airing of controversial debates and opinions. The current debate on China's future goes well beyond a simplistic dichotomy between "reformers" and "conservatives," reflecting the growing pluralization of opinion and interests that has taken place in China in the last decade.

Third, the lively intellectual discourse in the country underscores that China cannot be perceived as a rigid, monochromatic state. Such a perception fails to account for the divergence of views and pressures on China's leadership, and how these forces increasingly affect an already complex decision making process. As Wang Shaoguang writes:

> Intellectuals play a large role in influencing public opinion and thus influencing public policy. All public policy changes in recent years were basically preceded by shifts in public opinion. Take the migrant worker issue, the 'three rural issues' [*san nong*—agriculture, peasants and rural areas], and health care reform. In all cases, the issues first took off on the internet before being picked up by the print media and even television. From there it made its way onto the public agenda and became a policy issue and ultimately public policy.[12]

Finally, and perhaps most remarkably, the scope of the current debate has expanded to encompass discussion of political reform and steps toward "democratization." While this discussion can proceed only within certain limits, these topics are no longer taboo. China's top leaders now routinely express their interest in seeing China move toward greater openness and democracy—though definitely not in the Western sense and definitely with the leadership of the CCP intact.

Reevaluation of Reform

One of the most important economic turning points for China emerged amid lively intellectual debate in the run-up to the 14th CCP Congress in 1992, as Deng Xiaoping sought to reassert his control over policymaking, which he had lost to his conservative rival Chen Yun after the Tiananmen Square crisis. The Congress' historic decision to back Deng's economic policy line set China on the path of rapid market reform and delivered a virtually irreversible setback for Party conservatives, who had argued in favor of a "planned economy with market regulation." Although heated discussions about the economy continued among intellectuals throughout the 1990s, these discussions concerned the scope and speed of reform and not a fundamental reevaluation of Deng's reform project itself.

Today, however, a more fundamental reevaluation is beginning to take place within intellectual circles. This reevaluation has been prompted by the realization that, unlike in the 1980s and 1990s, when reform benefited nearly all Chinese, today the gap between "winners" and "losers" in China is widening. Increasing resentment among marginalized groups toward those whose political and economic connections ensure that they profit from reform is spilling over into the streets: China has seen an unprecedented increase in the number and size of protests, demonstrations, and incidents of social unrest.[13] Concerns over the impact of China's entry into the World Trade Organization (WTO) and the negative impact of globalization, and the return to China of many Western-educated intellectuals infused with postmodernist ideas, have led to a critique of the neoclassical, neoliberal economics that had provided the ideological underpinning for reform policies promoting China's rapid economic development.[14] Amid increasing concerns about widening income gaps, regional disparities, pervasive corruption, environmental degradation, and deteriorating social services, as well as the debates over private property protections and the admission of entrepreneurs into the CCP, intellectuals have raised fundamental questions about China's current development path, asking whether it is negating Chinese socialism and whether it is time to consider alternatives.

Debating Development

The intellectuals who provoked the latest major debate over China's economic line have became known as the "New Left"[15]—a pejorative term in China because "Leftists" have long been associated with the radicals of the Cultural Revolution[16] or more recently with the "Old Left" conservatives, who opposed market reform and opening in the 1980s.[17] Many on the "New Left" are critical of neoclassical, neoliberal economics identified with the so-called Washington Consensus[18] and blame China's social ills on the rapid reform policies of Deng Xiaoping and former president Jiang Zemin. However, "New Left" intellectuals do not advocate a return to orthodox Marxism, as some of their "Old Left" predecessors did. Rather, they have more in common with international critiques of globalization and neocolonialism.[19]

A number of "New Left" thinkers are concerned with social justice issues, particularly the so-called *san nong* or "three rural" issues pertaining to hardships faced by peasants (*nongmin*), the agricultural sector (*nongye*), and rural communities (*nongcun*). Others promote the rights of migrant workers, and still others are involved in China's nascent environmental movement. In challenging Western models of development, some "New Left" and other intellectuals are actively exploring a "third way" for China, akin to what has been called the Beijing Consensus.[20]

The issue that brought the "New Left" into the limelight was their critique of state-owned enterprise (SOE) reform in China, particularly the perceived injustice of the privatization process and corruption it engendered. The most famous proponent of this view is a Hong Kong–based economist, Larry Lang, a vehement opponent of SOE reform and, according to public polls, the most popular economist in China. The "New Left" intellectuals have also criticized financial liberalization—particularly the sale of banks to foreigners—warning of "economic colonization" and loss of economic sovereignty, which dovetails with the rise in popular economic nationalism—or "economic patriotism," as the *China Daily* termed it. This discourse has not been confined to the pages of economic journals but has had a real impact: Government technocrats faced increased questioning and opposition in discussions not only of SOE reform and foreign participation in China's financial system but also in preventing passage of a law to formalize private property ownership.[21]

Moreover, foreign companies have also felt the heat of the "economic security" debate, with the Carlyle Group and Goldman Sachs, among others, mired in protracted negotiations over the purchase of Chinese companies. In a sign that the leadership was clearly listening to the debate and anxious to deflect criticism, in September 2006, regulations were issued that strengthened the government's supervisory role over mergers and acquisitions and added two more state agencies—and considerably more red tape—to the approval process. The international business community was further alarmed when China's Anti-Monopoly Law, 13 years in the making, was finally adopted in August 2007—with stipulations that require foreign purchasers of Chinese companies to go through special checks in order to ensure that the deal will have no adverse impact on China's "national security."

But the "reformist" or "liberal" camp has not sat silently in the face of these critiques. In February 2006—just prior to the 4th Plenary Session of the 10th National People's Congress (NPC) in March and approval of the 11th Five-Year Program to set the broad economic development strategy for 2006–10—commentator "Huangfu Ping," a pseudonym for Zhou Ruijin, who provided the intellectual foundation for Deng's political comeback in 1992, published his first article in 15 years. He argued that it is wrong to blame market reforms for current social problems and wrongheaded to rehash the old ideological debates over whether the Chinese system should be called "capitalist" or "socialist." Instead, he blamed societal problems on the lack of progress in administrative and management reform. Given that the "Huangfu Ping" commentaries of the early 1990s were reportedly commissioned by Deng's daughter, Deng Nan, and tacitly approved by then-mayor of Shanghai, Zhu Rongji,[22] there was considerable speculation that retired and current leaders were involved in the publication of these most recent commentaries.

While the Hu Jintao–Wen Jiabao vision for the future direction of China's economic development initially appeared to encourage the "New Left"—by acknowledging concerns about equity, corruption, and a fraying social safety net and by casting their policies in terms of building a "new socialist countryside" and realizing a "harmonious society"[23]—the Party's overarching Scientific Development Concept, which guides these policies, pays at least equal attention to continuing market economic reforms. The 11th Five-Year Program laid out at the NPC, while signaling a shift in emphasis from GDP-oriented growth to social welfare, was, therefore, aimed at balancing different interests and consolidating a consensus on China's future direction at a time of unprecedented social transformation and intellectual debate. Wen Jiabao displayed the delicate balancing act at his news conference during the March 2006 NPC. He frankly admitted that reform was going through a "very difficult period," but, in a clear swipe at "New Left" critics, stated that "backpedaling offers no way out" in solving China's problems and that reform would "unswervingly push forward."[24] Earlier, President Hu Jintao made similar remarks at a meeting of deputies from Shanghai, a city that has been at the forefront of China's modernization. Hu's remarks made headlines in all major Chinese newspapers, with some analysts concluding that this put an official end to the ideological debate.[25]

However, such optimism proved premature. On March 20, conservative economist Liu Guoguang reignited the discussion, publishing an article in *Zhongguo Qingnian Bao* (*China Youth Times*) on the need for more central planning.[26] Party authorities took other steps apparently to moderate the "Old" and "New Left": An outspoken left-of-center publication, *Bingdian* (*Freezing Point*) was closed in January 2006, Larry Lang's popular Shanghai TV show was canceled in March 2006, and the editors of the left-leaning *Dushu* (*Reading*), including Wang Hui, were removed in July 2007. In the midst of these intellectual battles, in April 2006, the minutes of an internal meeting among policy analysts and government officials held by the China Society for Economic Reform, a think tank affiliated with the State Council, were leaked onto the internet, revealing "unprecedented controversy and dissent" among China's leading policy intellectuals.[27] Even on the eve of the 17th CCP Congress in late 2007, some 170 left-wing Party members published an open letter to Hu Jintao calling on the Party to defend its traditional ideals in the face of the new "capitalist class."[28]

Policy Response

The importance of these intellectual policy debates is reflected in the effort by Hu and Wen to steer a consensus course. It is difficult to judge whether Hu and Wen genuinely share "New Left" convictions or whether it was politically expedient to do so. It appears that they at times supported the "New Left" position in part because it played into their effort to reduce the continuing influence of former President Jiang Zemin and his so-called Shanghai clique of close political and intellectual associates. By coopting "New Left" tenets and allowing public criticism of Jiang's reform legacy, Hu and Wen articulated an alternative policy prescription to address China's pressing issues—an approach popular among the Chinese masses if not among some of their Political Bureau colleagues. Building particularly on public anger over corruption, Hu and Wen moved against "Shanghai clique" stalwart and Jiang protégé Chen Liangyu, the mayor of Shanghai, who had openly opposed their policies, firing him for corruption in September 2006. Ironically, Hu and Wen were following a Party tradition: Jiang Zemin had used the same gambit to remove his rival, Beijing Mayor Chen Xitong in 1995. Indeed, during their tenures both Deng Xiaoping and Jiang Zemin tacked to the "Left" when necessary, before pulling back to a middle course—which is apparently what Hu and Wen were attempting to do before the 17th CCP Congress in October 2007.

In a highly unusual move, on the eve of the 5th Plenary Session of the 10th NPC in March 2007, Premier Wen Jiabao published an article in the *People's Daily*, in which he countered Leftist charges that China's reform had strayed too far from socialist ideals and was the cause of the nation's socioeconomic problems. On the contrary, Wen held that social injustice and corruption are part and parcel of China's "immature" socialist system, reviving Deng Xiaoping's dictum that China will be at the "primary stage of socialism" for 100 years.[29] The premier reminded critics that, at this stage, economic development is the Party's "central task" and warned that "big policy mistakes," particularly the "disastrous ten-year long Cultural Revolution," led to major missed opportunities in China's development. Pushing the point further, two highly contested pieces of legislation, the Property Law and Corporate Income Tax Law, were passed during the NPC session in March 2007.

On June 25, 2007, during a speech to Central Party School (CPS) cadres,[30] President Hu Jintao effectively laid out the leadership's policy platform before the 17th Party Congress and put intellectuals of all persuasions on notice about where the economic line would fall. Hu said that pursuing the "socialist road with Chinese characteristics" was "correct" and that, while "changing the mode of economic development" and "putting people first," the "central task" remained seizing "economic construction"—Deng Xiaoping's "basic line" adopted at the 13th CCP Congress in 1987 and reasserted and accelerated in 1992.[31] In August 2007, Xing Bensi, an adviser to Jiang Zemin and former vice president of the CPS, argued that solving China's problems "can only be alleviated and resolved through sustained economic development and continued deepening of reform, and we should never go back to the old path before reform and opening up."[32]

Hu Jintao's work report at the 17th CCP Congress in October 2007 further reaffirmed the mainstream view that Deng Xiaoping's vision of reform and opening up, "being a new great revolution," is the "only way to realize the great rejuvenation of the Chinese nation."[33] While acknowledging the difficulties of implementing these reforms, Hu responded to Leftist critics by stating bluntly that "standing still or turning back would lead us nowhere." Reaffirming that the CCP's "central task" remains economic construction, while striving for more equitable and sustainable development, the Party will clearly continue market reforms, strengthen protections for property rights, and pursue further SOE reform, with greater regulatory oversight.[34]

Of particular interest to the international community is the emphasis in the work report on the importance of enhancing "independent innovation" and supporting indigenous research and development. The Political Bureau study meeting held on the eve of the 17th CCP Congress was also significant. At the session, Professor Wang Xinkui of the Shanghai Institute of Foreign Trade and Research Fellow Long Guoqiang of the State Council Development Research Center discussed the hotly debated topics of opening up wider to the outside world and assuring China's economic security. Hu Jintao gave a speech at the session, which served as a preview to his work report, in which he strongly endorsed opening up and further integration into the global economy while at the same time emphasizing the need to "improve laws and regulations for safeguarding national economic security."[35]

Following the Party Congress, Vice Premier Zeng Peiyan was reported to have called for the restriction of foreign capital in key areas and "sensitive industries" in order to defend China's economic security, suggesting that multinational companies could face further roadblocks in their attempts to invest in China's domestic companies and industrial sectors.[36] The intellectual debate is likely to focus on this issue going forward. In September 2007, the influential business magazine *Caijing* (*Finance and Economics*) carried an article by Qinghua University law professor Wang Baoshu critical of the Anti-Monopoly Law, particularly the inclusion of a "national security review" for foreign investors.[37] At the same time, the book *Currency Wars*, which takes a negative look at the global investment industry and warns against the opening up of China's financial sector, was a publishing success in China at the end of 2007.[38] In spite of some of the conclusions drawn at the 17th CCP Congress, the debates over China's economic future will continue, especially as the downsides of economic growth persist.

Indeed, as China prepares to celebrate the 30th anniversary of reform in 2008, a new round of debate has been launched not only evaluating the past three decades but also looking ahead to decide the future path China should traverse. At the 17th CCP Congress, Hu Jintao laid out both the opportunities and challenges facing China at this new stage of development and called for an "emancipation of the mind" in order to correctly handle the focal issue confronting the CCP of coordinating economic growth and social development moving forward. While a seemingly esoteric concept to a foreign audience, these "emancipation" campaigns cannot be underestimated, and they have been launched at critical junctures in the course of China's modernization (see box 2.1).[39] This "third emancipation of the mind" campaign calls on cadres to "break the old rules" and "practices and systems that are out of keeping with the scientific development concept," in particular, admonishing them to not neglect education, public health, the environment, and other social development indicators of "most concern to the people" in pursuit of rapid GDP growth.[40]

This debate in turn will affect—and has already affected—how Beijing chooses to respond to outside pressures on such economic issues as renminbi revaluation, promoting domestic consumption, energy policy, and

---

Box 2.1   "Emancipation of the mind" campaigns

The Chinese Communist Party's "emancipation of the mind" (*sixiang jiefang*) campaigns are aimed at forging ideological consensus and support for the central leadership's overarching policies. They have historically been launched by the Party leadership at critical junctures in the course of China's modernization: in 1978, as former paramount leader Deng Xiaoping battled Maoist opponents of the initial reform and opening up policy, and in 1992, as Deng once again battled opposition from Party conservatives trying to roll back market economic reforms.

The third emancipation of the mind campaign, which is being launched in 2008, the 30th anniversary of China's reform and opening up, was first mentioned in President Hu Jintao's work report to the 17th National Party Congress in October 2007 and again in Premier Wen Jiabao's report to the National People's Congress in March 2008. It appears aimed not only at containing and steering the ongoing intellectual debate about the next phase of China's economic and political reform but also at breaking through ongoing entrenched bureaucratic and local-government resistance to implementing the central leadership's Scientific Development Concept, in particular, to addressing the continued neglect of education, public health, the environment, and other social development indicators in pursuit of rapid GDP growth.

The campaigns involve intensive study sessions and meetings for officials as well as local-level investigations into the implementation of central directives. In addition to getting cadres to toe the official line, however, the campaigns also provide officials and intellectuals with the space to experiment with economic and now political reform—although within parameters still set by the Party.

Experiments with political-administrative reform under the rubric of the emancipation of the mind campaign are being spearheaded by a close associate of Hu Jintao, Wang Yang, who is the party secretary of Guangdong Province, which has been the location of many of China's pioneering economic reforms and where the second emancipation of the mind campaign was launched. Given the historical precedent, much hinges on the success of the third campaign not only for the Hu-Wen administration's policy platform but also for China's future development trajectory.

---

further opening of the domestic market to foreign investment and influence. These and other key challenges to the Chinese development agenda and their implications for US-China relations are discussed in this book.

Democracy Debated

In recent years, the intellectual discourse in China has also significantly expanded beyond economics to include discussion of political reform and foreign policy, with nationalism a common underlying theme linking the cross-cutting debates. Given the enduring images and perceptions of the 1989 Tiananmen Square protests, it might come as a surprise that many proponents of political change in China today eschew the "May Fourth Movement"[41] ethos, which first looked to Western science and democracy to "save China" at the beginning of the 20th century and which was revived by liberals in the 1980s. At the same time, many of today's intellectuals are not adherents of orthodox Marxism-Leninism either. Rather, some of the most vigorous debates among Chinese policy intellectuals concern the notion of a "democratic deficit," pointing to the political and economic difficulties that followed from the rapid introduction of Western-style democracy in places such as Russia and other former Soviet republics, as well as Iraq, Indonesia, and Taiwan. "New Left" critics also charge that only China's nouveau riche will benefit from Western "capitalist-style" democracy. Debate now often centers on whether Western-style democracy is right for China or whether a "third way" for political reform can be found.

The democracy debate has coincided with—and indeed allowed to proceed because of—a growing recognition by the Party that in order to stay in power it needs to implement more serious political reform to accompany economic reform, a strategic calculation first proposed by Deng Xiaoping in 1980 but then postponed because of the divisions within the leadership that were laid bare in the post-Tiananmen Square crackdown in 1989.[42] For the Party, political reform traditionally focused on administrative improvement, Party- and institution-building, and limited grass-roots democracy—all aimed at keeping the Party in control.[43] That intellectuals have been allowed to widely discuss "democratization" for the first time since 1989 is significant. Du Daozheng, editor of the liberal journal *Yanhuang Chunqiu* (*Chinese Spring and Autumn*), told reporters that for the first time "such a complicated and important theoretical issue was discussed fairly . . . there was no abuse, name-calling, threats, punishment, bans or dismissals."[44]

As the 17th CCP Congress approached, the democracy debate intensified, filling online chat rooms and animating discussions in China's official and nonofficial media outlets. In December 2006, Yu Keping, deputy director of the Party's Central Translation Bureau and reportedly a close advisor to Hu Jintao, published an article in *Xueshi Shibao* (*Study Times*) entitled "Democracy is a Good Thing," offering a vision of gradual, incremental democratization with Chinese characteristics. In the article he highlighted the words of Hu Jintao, who said at Yale University in April 2006, "without democracy, there will be no modernization." Emboldened by the debate, the 86-year-old former vice president of Renmin University, Xie Tao, published an article in the liberal journal *Yanhuang Chunqiu*, urging China to follow the road of social democracy socialism found in Northern Europe. The article set off a firestorm of controversy, with supporters and opponents holding a series of competing symposiums to discuss Xie's article. The debate also reanimated the Old Leftists, who, having found limited outlet for their articles in the mainstream media, posted them on Maoflag.net and other sympathetic websites. In July 2006, after 17 former top officials and Marxist scholars posted a letter accusing China's leaders of betraying the revolution and steering the country in the wrong direction, Maoflag.net was shut down temporarily.

Official Line Weighs In

Beginning in the early part of 2007 and extending through the summer, the Party stepped up its efforts to rein in and forge consensus on the political reform debate. The first official reaction to the democracy debate came in the form of Premier Wen Jiabao's aforementioned *People's Daily* article published in February 2007. To contain the discussion, Wen revived Deng Xiaoping's dictum that China is at the "primary stage of socialism" during which economic development must precede political reform. Implicitly rejecting Western models, Wen stated that China should "take its own path in enhancing democracy."[45] Perhaps most authoritatively, a *People's Daily* commentator's article, which has the imprimatur of the Political Bureau, declared that President Hu Jintao's June 25, 2007 CPS speech had established the "political, ideological, and theoretical foundation" for the upcoming 17th CCP Congress.[46] Indicating caution on political reform, Hu reiterated the Party's basic line set at the 13th Party Congress of "one central task" (economic construction) and "two basic points" (upholding reform and opening up and upholding the Four Cardinal Principles of the socialist path, people's democratic dictatorship, CCP leadership, and Marxism-Leninism-Mao Zedong Thought). But Hu's additional comments on the need to move forward "commensurate with the continuous rise of our people's enthusiasm for political participation," to "enrich the form of democracy" and "broaden the democratic channel," reflected comparatively progressive notions that policy intellectuals had voiced over the previous one to two years.[47] The CCP's vision for China's political reform is discussed in detail in chapter 3.

These debates and their outcomes will affect developments in 2008 and beyond on some of the most fundamental questions and challenges confronting China's domestic political future, including such problems as leadership accountability, improved governance, endemic official corruption, center-local relations, and the future role of the Party. The outcomes of these debates will likewise affect the tenor and tone of US-China relations and China's relations with the West more broadly, especially on issues of human rights, civil liberties, media censorship, rule of law, and development of a more responsive, just, and democratic political system in China.

Foreign Policy: Rise of Nationalism or Peaceful Rise?

As with economic and domestic political questions, foreign policy issues, no longer considered within the sole purview of state and Party organs, are increasingly the subject of intensifying debate in China. The debate on foreign policy evolves from many of the same sources and echoes many of the same themes as the debates on economic and political development. In examining China's growing role in the world, intellectuals question whether modernization necessarily involves emulating the West or following Western-built norms and institutions within the international system. Others have been influenced by international critiques of neoliberalism and postcolonialism—the Washington Consensus versus Beijing Consensus debate, which played out as differences among the leadership over China's entry into the WTO and the impact of globalization became apparent.[48] Coming out of this discourse are the hotly debated issues now finding concrete expression in official government policy—including laws and regulations aimed at ensuring economic security and building indigenous innovation capacity, which have a direct impact on international business interests. Still other intellectuals have been preoccupied with traditional "hard power" issues such as China's military modernization and how to respond to the superpower status and "hegemony" of the United States in the post–Cold War period.

Nationalism Debated

The sides in the current Chinese foreign policy debate can be roughly divided into those who argue the need for China to pursue its interests more assertively and unilaterally and those who argue a rising China's interests are best served through further steady and peaceful integration within the international system. Those who advocate a more assertive, "nationalist" approach believe China must more consciously marshal its growing resources to realize the country's interests, which for too long have been suppressed by foreign forces intent on keeping China down. This viewpoint has a deep history in Chinese thinking—drawing strength from the view that from the mid-19th to mid-20th century, China was devastatingly humiliated at the hands of foreign powers—but in recent years has seen resurgence as China's development and popular confidence levels have steeply risen. While openly displayed in reaction to specific international events—such as visits by the Japanese prime minister to the Yasukuni Shrine, the accidental bombing of the Chinese Embassy in Belgrade by US warplanes in May 1999, or more recently the Beijing Olympics torch relay—nationalist sentiments at both elite and popular levels are frequently expressed on issues ranging from economic security, to indigenous innovation capacity, to traditional foreign policy issues such as relations with the United States, Japan, Russia, and Taiwan.[49]

Today, a good portion of nationalist concern is pointed at the US government, which, in contrast to the past, is increasingly seen as unfriendly toward China. Changes in Chinese popular thinking toward the United States are starkly illustrated: Tiananmen protestors erected the "Goddess of Democracy" statue in homage to the United States in 1989, but 10 years later, following the accidental bombing by US warplanes of the Chinese embassy in Belgrade, furious protestors pelted the US embassy in Beijing with eggs and bricks and set some US consulate buildings in Chengdu on fire. Such attitudes slowly built up over the course of the 1990s: 87.1 percent of Chinese in a 1995 poll identified the United States as the country "least friendly" toward China.[50] More recently, according to a BBC poll conducted in 2006, 62 percent of Chinese polled had a negative view of the United States, up from 42 percent in 2005 (these trends reflect a broader deterioration in positive views of the United States across much of the globe in recent years).

It is all too tempting—but ultimately misleading—to dismiss these developments as merely the cynical manipulation of public opinion by government and Party organs to stoke nationalist sentiments, distract attention away from China's pressing socioeconomic problems, and position the CCP as the one and only legitimate defender of the country's interests. There is some evidence the leadership has turned to this ploy (and not always successfully), but looking to this explanation alone obscures serious discussions, debates, and changes within the collective Chinese consciousness regarding the outside world, and particularly the United States. Suisheng Zhao has termed this process the "demythification" of the West in China. This trend can be clearly traced in intellectual debates, which have at various times intersected with leadership politics, both influencing and being influenced by the formulation of Chinese foreign policy.

Intellectuals disagree over the particular causes of nationalism in the current period and hence the ability and the interest of Chinese authorities to control its expression. But most believe rising nationalism is inevitable, and debate whether the government should seek to guide it in constructive ways. Most mainstream scholars agree that Chinese nationalism is largely reactive—it emerges most openly and vociferously in response to specific international events deemed insulting to the Chinese people, such as the US bombing of the Chinese embassy in Belgrade in 1999, the Japanese prime minister's visits to the Yasukuni shrine, and the former Taiwan leader Lee Teng-hui's visit to the United States in 1995. However, unhappy with this "reactionary" aspect of nationalist sentiment, Wang Xiaodong, whose views are representative of the "New Left," argues that expressions of nationalist sentiment should be more systematic, confident, and militant in order to provide stronger ideological support for strengthening the Chinese nation.[51] On the other hand, critics of nationalism, including Xu Jilin, Ren Bingqiang, and Wang Dingding believe its reactionary nature indicates that Chinese nationalism is empty, offensive, and unconstructive.[52]

Still other intellectuals believe that the current nationalism is rational and essentially a form of patriotism, while others are less optimistic.[53] In practice, Chinese authorities appear to tread a thin line, which restrains extreme nationalism but encourages patriotic displays. For example, official media such as *Zhongguo Qingnian Bao* (*China Youth Times*), *Huanqiu Shibao* (*Global Times*), and *Xuexi Shibao* (*Study Times*) have highlighted Japan-bashing campaigns on the internet while also running editorials denouncing narrow-minded nationalism.[54]

The publication of the 1996 best-seller *China Can Say No* and journals such as *Zhanlue yu Guanli* (*Strategy and Management*) provided a platform for the articulation of ideas with a nationalist slant from many of the "New Left" intellectuals already writing on economic and political issues. Intellectuals such as Wang Xiaodong, He Xin, Gan Yang, and Fang Ning grabbed the headlines with their polemics, often highly critical of the United States. In response, "mainstream" intellectuals such as Xiao Gongqin and Shen Jinru—who wrote the rejoinder, "China Will Not Be 'Mr. No' "—mobilized in order to counter the "New Left" and to support rapprochement with the United States and China's integration within the international community. At the time, the Chinese leadership was deeply divided over the specific question of entry into the WTO as well as the larger question of relations with the United States, and they tolerated the intellectual debate as far as it supported their respective positions.[55]

Integrating China

For the most part, however, the Chinese leadership has remained wary of "New Left" ideas in the foreign policy arena because their brand of "populist nationalism" also has an antigovernment slant to it, which can quickly get out of hand—as it did during anti-Japanese demonstrations in the spring of 2005. As a result, the leadership has to increasingly take into account emergent and popular intellectual ideas that resonate widely with the public, particularly those related to historically sensitive topics such as relations with Japan, the Taiwan issue, and "economic security." Nonetheless, establishment intellectuals and foreign ministry professionals have largely managed to maintain control over the foreign policymaking process and put forward a goal of steadily and peacefully integrating a more powerful China with the international system.

In their 2007 *China Quarterly* article, Bonnie Glaser and Evan Medeiros trace the evolution of China's foreign policy and the influence of establishment intellectuals who work outside the formal government bureaucracy in formulating it, as China grappled with establishing a theoretical foundation for its "new diplomacy" and global activism in the 21st century.[56] In particular, they examine how the concept of "peaceful rise"—first articulated by Zheng Bijian, former chairman of the China Reform

Forum and reportedly a Hu Jintao confidant—became one of the new concepts the Hu administration introduced into China's foreign policy.[57]

By 2004, however, the term began to be dropped from the official lexicon as debate arose within the leadership and among intellectuals and the general public about its usage. These debates critically evaluated many aspects of the term, including that it would constrain China's policy options in dealing with Taiwan, that the goal of a "peaceful rise" is unattainable, that the term "rise" would actually engender more concern, that the term contradicts Deng Xiaoping's basic guidance on foreign affairs, that it could set back much needed military modernization, and that it could incite populist nationalism. Most interesting was the fact that the debate took place at all and in such a public way, calling into question a senior-level policy pronouncement. As a result of the debates and criticism, the more acceptable term "peaceful development" found its way into official usage.

The formulation of China's foreign policy and its theoretical foundation further crystallized in April 2005, as President Hu Jintao introduced the concept of building a "harmonious world" at the Asia-Africa summit in Jakarta and expounded on it at the United Nations summit in September. The concept, which complemented Hu's domestic policy of establishing a "harmonious society," represents an effort to respond to the challenges of globalization and calls for the establishment of a new international political and economic order based on "multilateralism, mutually beneficial co-operation and the spirit of inclusiveness."[58] While a new term, "harmonious world" in practice differs very little from mainstream concepts espoused by Chinese leaders since the beginning of the reform era: that China's interests are best served through a foreign policy that seeks a peaceful external environment so that the country can devote its energies principally to domestic economic development, reassure neighbors and key partners about China's benign intentions, and avoid confrontation with other major powers, especially the United States.

In another reflection of ongoing debate about China's foreign policy and the need for the Party and government to put its authoritative stamp on such discussions, a rare and critically important work conference on foreign affairs was held in August 2006, bringing together all leading foreign ministry officials and diplomats from overseas. According to Chinese press accounts, the meeting set out the "important principles that must be followed in order to build a harmonious world." The "central authorities" reportedly "expounded in all-round and systematic fashion on the idea of building a harmonious world, and established this as a guideline and policy principle for Chinese diplomacy."[59] The need for the leadership to clarify its foreign policy direction and the debate that surrounded it suggests differences of opinion not only among intellectuals but within the officialdom as well.

Since the foreign affairs work conference, much of the open debate on Chinese foreign policy has subsided and cohered around the general concept of seeking a "harmonious world." Discussion within mainstream think tanks and other intellectual circles have for the time being concluded that the "framework" of a harmonious world was in place, that it now needs to be "put it into concrete practice," and that this approach "projected a new image for China as a responsible power."[60] At the 17th CCP Congress in October 2007, Hu Jintao in his formal work report made frequent reference to following the path of "peaceful development" and the need to build a "harmonious world," thereby further solidifying these ideas in the lexicon of official Chinese foreign policy.[61]

Nevertheless, while this broad framework appears solidly in place, it remains open to critiques and adaptation on a number of specific issues. Chinese leaders will not pursue a "harmonious world" at all costs and will remain highly sensitive to slights to the country's growing national pride. Over the past year, China's tougher stance on foreign economic policy and on Taiwan and the Chinese antisatellite test, for example, are just a few indicators of the greater assertiveness that lies not far beneath the surface within circles of government, military, and intellectual elites. While Chinese leaders will want to lead with a more constructive and "harmonious" approach to their dealings with the outside world, they will need to remain ever mindful of and at times accommodate the growing sense of confident nationalism that has come with China's growth and success of recent years.

Looking Ahead

While the past several years have seen an unprecedented degree of open and at times highly public debate in China over critical economic, political, and foreign policy issues, the run-up to the 17th CCP Congress and the Congress itself served in part to forge agreement and assert leadership consensus to guide both ideological and policy thinking over the next five years. Nevertheless, in following what was arguably the liveliest and most open intellectual debate China has witnessed since reform and opening up began in 1978, it is important to ask whether the confluence of social, political, economic, and cultural developments that helped nurture the discourse were a temporary phenomenon or a sign of deeper and more meaningful change.

For the near term, these developments will have pluses and minuses for the United States and US-China relations, with both encouraging signs and continuing and new difficulties on issues that matter to Americans and American interests. At a broad level, it is encouraging to see an unprecedented level of more open and public debate in Chinese intellectual circles, traditional media, the internet, and amongst government analysts. At the same time, however, calls for a return to traditional Communist Party tenets and for more forceful assertion of narrowly defined Chinese national interests are more worrisome. More specifically, regarding economic questions, current results of these policy debates mean continued opportunity for the United States and others to benefit from increased trade and investment with China, but growing protectionist impulses in the country, especially concerning foreign investment, will need to be watched. On the political front, Americans can be encouraged by the leadership's incremental and potential steps toward a more open and just society in China but dismayed by the overarching atmosphere of CCP power and the lack of accountability and abuses that go with it. As for foreign relations, China is expected to continue to make some encouraging and constructive contributions consistent with global norms, regional expectations, and US interests, but these will remain tempered by growing New Left and nationalist sentiments within the broader population.

Notes

1. *Zhongguo Gaige Bao* (*China Reform Times*), "Pro-Reform Paper Considers Emancipation of Mind," May 21, 2008, in Open Source Center (OSC): CPP2008053061 5001.

2. The following information on China's intellectual debates draws from a more detailed discussion in Melissa Murphy, *Decoding Chinese Politics: Intellectual Debates and Why They Matter* (Washington: Center for Strategic and International Studies, January 2008).

3. "Marxism-Leninism reveals the universal laws governing the development of the history of human society. It analyzes the contradictions inherent in the capitalist system that it is incapable of resolving internally and shows that socialist society will inevitably replace capitalist society and ultimately develop into communist society. The Chinese Communists have untiringly striven to integrate Marxism with the concrete practice in China and adapted it to Chinese conditions. Combining Marxism-Leninism with the concrete practice of the Chinese revolution, the first generation of the CCP's central collective leadership, with Mao Zedong as its core, settled such basic questions as the nature, motive, and object of the new democratic revolution and the road to socialism in China. And Mao Zedong Thought was thus established, which is Marxism-Leninism applied and developed in China" ("Ideological and Theoretical Basis of the Communist Party of China," *China Daily*, July 10, 2007, www.chinadaily.com).

4. For further discussion of this period, see Joseph Fewsmith, *China Since Tiananmen: The Politics of Transition* (New York: Cambridge University Press, 2001).

5. A number of intellectual advisers have subsequently moved into powerful Party and government positions, including Wang Huning, former professor at Fudan University and adviser to Jiang Zemin, appointed to the Secretariat of the 17th CCP Central Committee in October 2007. Also, in the 1980s, China Investment Corporation (CIC) Chairman and former Vice Finance Minister Lou Jiwei worked at the Research Center of Economic Development, a State Council think tank, before coming to the attention of former Premier Zhu Rongji.

6. *Nanfeng Chuang* [*Southern Wind Window*], "Wang Shaoguang: Lishi de luoji yu zhishifenzi mingyun de bianqian" ["Wang Shaoguang: The Logic of History and the Changing Fate of Intellectuals"], January 24, 2007, www.tecn.cn. Wang Shaoguang along with Hu Angang pioneered work on the problems of decentralization, tax reform, and China's regional disparities in the 1980s, issues that subsequently became front and center for the CCP. See Fewsmith, *China Since Tiananmen*, 132.

7. Under Hu Jintao, a regular mechanism for discussion between Party leaders and intellectuals has been established, reviving a practice first begun by former CCP General Secretary Hu Yaobang in 1985. Since 2002, the Political Bureau has held more than 40 "study sessions"—currently about once a month—during which leading intellectuals from think tanks and universities are invited to discuss topics of concern with the leadership, ranging from rule of law to rural issues to financial and political reform.

8. Xinhua News Agency, "Hu Jintao zai zhongyang dangxiao fabiao zhongyao jianghua" ["Hu Jintao Makes an Important Speech at the Central Party School"], June 25, 2007, http://news.xinhuanet.com.

9. "Beijing Spring" refers to brief periods of political liberalization beginning in 1978, which have usually been followed by clampdowns. The name is derived from "Prague Spring," an analogous event that occurred in Czechoslovakia in 1968.

10. Former General Secretary Zhao Ziyang employed think tankers to help formulate his economic policies in the 1980s, in part to circumvent the official bureaucracy, then a conservative bastion. See Barry Naughton "China's Economic Think Tanks: Their Changing Role in the 1990s," *China Quarterly*, no. 171 (September 2002): 625.

11. One example is the best-seller by Wang Shan, *Luo Yi Ning Ge'er, Disanzhi Yanjing Kan Zhongguo* [*Looking at China Through a Third Eye*] (Taiyuan: Shanxi People's Publishing House, 1994), a highly critical look at China's reform with a nationalistic slant, by a then-young writer.

12. *Nanfeng Chuang*, January 24, 2007.

13. Official Chinese statistics put the number of "public order disturbances" at 87,000 in 2005, up from 8,700 in 1993 and 74,000 in 2004. According to official Chinese sources, the number of more narrowly defined "mass incidents" fell by 22 percent in the first 10 months of 2006 to 17,900. In 2008, it was reported that "figures of mass incidents and participants decreased by 2.7 percent and 17.1 percent, respectively" in 2007, without further elaboration. See Xinhua News Agency, "China's Public Security Organs Promote Safety," April 20, 2008, www.chinapeace.org.cn.

14. The "reformers" or "liberals" comprised a group of Party elders and intellectuals including Wan Li, Liu Ji, Li Shenzhi, Shen Jiru, Ma Licheng, Liu Junning, Xu Youyu, and Zhou Ruijin aka Huangfu Ping. Today, some of the mainstream intellectuals are Gao Shangquan, Shen Baoxiang, Lu Zhongyuan, Zhou Qiren, Lin Yifu, Mao Yushi, Jiang Ping, Xu Xiaonian, Wu Jinglian, Xing Bensi, Fan Gang, Li Yining, Zhang Weiying, Sheng Hong, and Zhang Shugang.

15. The "New Left" is a loose and heterogenous group that would not necessarily identify itself as such and includes intellectuals operating outside the establish-

ment, including Wang Hui, Chen Xin, Larry Lang, Zhang Qingde, Yang Fan, Cui Zhiyuan, Han Shaogong, Li Tuo, Zhang Chengzhi, Li Shaojun, Yang Bin, Zuo Dapei, Zhang Xudong, Han Deqiang, Gan Yang, Zhang Kuan, Gong Xiantian, Wang Xiaodong, Wang Shaoguang, and Hu Angang.

16. A slogan introduced by Mao Zedong in 1940, noted again by Liu Shaoqi in 1958, and used more frequently in connection with leftist attacks on the "cultural front" in late 1965 and early 1966. The expression was used to denote the Great Proletarian Cultural Revolution, a political campaign officially inaugurated in August 1966 to rekindle revolutionary fervor of the masses outside formal party organizations. The Cultural Revolution decade (1966–76) can be divided into three periods: 1966–69, from the militant Red Guard (the young "soldiers" of the Cultural Revolution) phase to the 9th National Party Congress; 1969–71, the period of the zenith and demise of Lin Biao; and 1971–76, the period of Mao's declining health and the ascendancy of the Gang of Four (term used by the post-Mao leadership to denote the four leading radical figures—Jiang Qing [Mao's fourth wife], Zhang Chunqiao, Yao Wenyuan, and Wang Hongwen—who played a dominant political role during the Cultural Revolution). At the August 1977 11th National Party Congress, the Cultural Revolution was declared officially to have ended with the arrest in October 1976 of the Gang of Four (Library of Congress, Federal Research Division, Country Studies/Area Handbook Series—China, www.loc.gov/rr/frd [accessed June 20, 2008]).

17. The "Old Left" or "conservatives" are typically associated with Party elders and intellectuals such as Chen Yun, Wang Zhen, Hu Qiaomu, Li Peng, Deng Liqun, Yu Quanyu, Gao Di, and Liu Guogang. Some members of the Chinese Academy of Social Sciences (CASS), particularly its Marxism Institute established in 2005, are also considered "conservative/leftist," including Chen Kuiyan, Li Shenming, Liu Fengyan, Zhang Shuhua, and Zhang Quanjing. They were recently involved in the compilation of a DVD that blamed the fall of the Communist Party of the Soviet Union on the "ideological errors" of Nikita Khrushchev and Mikhail Gorbachev, seen as a veiled criticism of both Jiang Zemin and Hu Jintao. See "OSC Analysis—China: Lessons From CPSU Demise Reflect CPC Policy Debate," June 15, 2007, in OSC: CPF20070615534001.

18. The Washington Consensus is a 10-point strategy for economic and political development that has formed the cornerstone of US-led multilateral institutions since the end of World War II.

19. For a discussion of the influence of works by Edward Said, Michel Foucault, Fredrick Jameson, et al., see Fewsmith, *China Since Tiananmen*, 114. A number of Western academics have begun to look to China for lively discussions in "critical theory"; see Steven Venturino, "Inquiring After Theory in China," *Boundary*, no. 33 (February 2006): 91–113.

20. See Joshua Cooper Ramo, *The Beijing Consensus* (London: Foreign Policy Centre, May 2004). Ramo notes that whether China's reform project ends in success or failure, "the Beijing Consensus is already drawing a wake of new ideas that are very different from those coming from Washington," and are "marking a path for other nations around the world" to follow. It should be noted that much controversy surrounds the validity of the "Beijing model," though the discussion is beyond the scope of this chapter.

21. An interesting anecdote underscores the link between intellectuals, the Party, and policymaking in China: Gong Xiantian is an outspoken "New Left" critic of the property law, who charged that private property rights were unconstitutional. In 2005, he received a call from NPC Chairman Wu Bangguo to discuss his views. In the final version of the law, among other amendments, a clause was inserted that the law must not contradict the Constitution. See Lesley Hook, "The Rise of China's New Left," *Far Eastern Economic Review*, April, 2007.

22. Fewsmith, *China Since Tiananmen*, 45.

23. Creating a "harmonious society" (*héxié shèhuì*) is the end goal of the Scientific Development Concept, a policy program that seeks to balance China's pursuit of economic growth with paying equal attention to solving social welfare issues and putting the "people first." The concept, which aims to ultimately create overall societal balance and harmony, is identified with the Hu-Wen administration and was first proposed during the 4th Plenum of the 16th Central Committee of the Communist Party of China (CPC) in 2004.

24. CCTV, "Wen Jiabao Zongli jizhe zhaodaihui" ["Premier Wen Jiabao News Conference"], March 14, 2006, www.cctv.com.

25. Xinhua News Agency, "Top Leaders Join Lawmakers, Advisors in Group Discussions," March 7, 2006, www.npc.gov.cn. See also Su Xin, "Deepen Reform at a New Starting Point in History," People's Forum column, *People's Daily*, March 9, 2006, translated by National Technical Information Service, US Department of Commerce; and Joseph Kahn, "A Sharp Debate Erupts in China Over Ideologies," *New York Times*, March 12, 2006, www.nytimes.com.

26. Liu Guoguang, "Shehui Zhuyi Shichang Jingji ye Xuyao Jihua" ["The Socialist Market Economy Also Needs Planning"], *Zhongguo Qingnian Bao* [*China Youth Times*], March 20, 2006.

27. Joseph Kahn, "At a Secret Meeting, Chinese Analysts Clashed Over Reforms," *New York Times*, April 7, 2006.

28. *Boxun News*, "Excerpts from PRC Leftists' 17 September Open Letter to Hu Jintao," September 21, 2007.

29. Xinhua News Agency, "Wen Jiabao: Guanyu shehuizhuyi chuji jieduan de lishi renwu he wo guo dui wai zhengce de ji ge wenti" ["Wen Jiabao: Several Questions Concerning the Historical Duty of the Primary Stages of Socialism and Our Nation's Foreign Policy"], February 26, 2007, http://news.xinhuanet.com. The "primary stage" idea was first developed by Zhao Ziyang and incorporated into the 13th CCP Congress as ideological justification for further liberalization and reform. The term fell out of use after 1989.

30. Cadres are persons who hold responsible administrative positions in either the Party or the governmental apparatus throughout China.

31. Xinhua News Agency, "Hu Jintao zai zhongyang dangxiao fabiao zhongyao jianghua" ["Hu Jintao Makes an Important Speech at the Central Party School"], June 25, 2007, http://news.xinhuanet.com.

32. *Beijing Ribao*, "CPC Theorist Says Development Key to Solving Contradictions Among People," August 6, 2007.

33. CCTV, "Dang de shiqi da kaimu: Hu Jintao zuo baogao" ["The Opening Ceremony of the 17th Party Congress: The Report of Hu Jintao"], October 15, 2007, http://news.cctv.com.

34. Ibid.

35. Xinhua News Agency, "Hu Jintao Speaks at CPC Political Bureau Study on Opening Up, Economic Security," September 29, 2007.

36. *South China Morning Post*, "Restrictions Urged on Foreign Capital in 'Key Areas,'" October 31, 2007.

37. *Caijing*, "Qinghua Law Professor Wang Baoshu Criticizes Anti-Monopoly Law," September 2, 2007.

38. *South China Morning Post*, "Book About 'Dark Side' of Global Bankers Top Draw for Mainland Chinese," November 5, 2007.

39. *Nanfang Dushi Bao*, "Xin yi lun sixiang jiefang cong nail qibu?" ["What Should Be the Starting Point for a New Round of Discussion of Mind Emancipation?"], March 3, 2008, www.eeo.com.cn.

40. Zhonggong Shandong Shengwei Dangxiao [Chinese Communist Party School of Shandong Province], "Wo xiao juxing di san ci jiefang sixiang da taolun zhuanti yantaohui" ["Convening of the Third Specialized Symposium on 'Emancipation of the Mind'"], May 12, 2008, www.sddx.gov.cn.

41. The May Fourth Movement was a Chinese intellectual movement (1917–21) that advocated strengthening and reforming China through the application of Western science and democracy. Following the end of World War 1, on May 4, 1919, pressure for reform culminated in a protest by Beijing university students against the Versailles Peace Conference's decision to transfer former German concessions in China to Japan. The movement inspired future generations of student activists and intellectuals, especially after the launch of reform and opening up in 1978.

42. Deng Xiaoping, "On the Reform of the System of Party and State Leadership," August 18, 1980, in *Selected Works of Deng Xiaoping 1975–1982* (Beijing: Foreign Languages Press, 1983).

43. A summary and analysis of these measures in recent years is provided in C. Fred Bergsten, Bates Gill, Nicholas Lardy, and Derek Mitchell, *China: The Balance Sheet: What the World Needs to Know Now about the Emerging Superpower* (New York: PublicAffairs Books, 2006), chapter 3.

44. Richard McGregor, "China Struggles to Define Democracy," *Financial Times*, June 12, 2007.

45. Xinhua News Agency, February 26, 2007.

46. "OSC Analysis: Hu Speech Sets Agenda for 17th Party Congress," July 1, 2007, in OSC: CPF2007072539001.

47. Xinhua News Agency, "Hu Jintao zai zhongyang dangxiao fabiao zhongyao jianghua" ["Hu Jintao Makes an Important Speech at the Central Party School"], June 25, 2007, http://news.xinhuanet.com.

48. Cooper Ramo, *The Beijing Consensus*, 33.

49. For a good summary of Chinese scholars' debate over the origins of nationalism in Chinese thinking, see Chen Xueming, "Dangdai Zhongguo Minzu Zhuyi Sichao Yanjiu Zongshu" ["Summary of Trends and Research in Contemporary Chinese Nationalism"], *Guangdong Sheng Shehui Zhuyi Xueyuan Xuebao* [*Journal of the Guangdong Institute of Socialism*], no. 22.1 (January 2006): 104–108.

50. Xinhua News Agency, "Jiang Zemin zhuan: Jiang Zemin de jingli" ["Biography of Jiang Zemin: Jiang Zemin's Experience"], March 23, 2005, http://news.xinhuanet.com.

51. Wang Xiaodong, *Zhongguo de Minzu Zhuyi Bixu Xiang Xifang Xuexi* [*Chinese Nationalism Should Learn from the West*] (Chinese Democracy and Justice Party, February 5, 2003), www.cdjp.org.

52. Ren Bingqiang, "Zhongguo Minzu Zhuyi de Chongxin Xingqi: Yuanyin, Tezheng ji Yingxiang" ["The Reemergence of Chinese Nationalism: Reasons, Characteristics, and Influence"], *Xuehai* [*Sea of Learning*] (January 2004): 78–82.

53. Zhang Yonghong, "Dangdai Zhongguo Minzu Zhuyi Toushi" ["Perspectives on Contemporary Chinese Democracy"], *Xinjiang Daxue Xuebao* [*Xinjiang University Journal*], no. 32.1 (March 2004): 39; Lin Zhibo, "Dangdai Zhongguo Shifou Xuyao Minzu Zhuyi?" ["Does Today's China Need Democracy?"], *Shidai Chao* [*Trends of the Era*], no. 24 (December 2004): 46–47.

54. See "Xuni Shijie de 'Kangri'" ["Japanese Resistance in a Hypothetical World"], *Zhongguo Qingnian Bao* [*China Youth Times*], April 13, 2005; and Ma Licheng, "Weihe Buyao Xiaai de Minzu Zhuyi" ["Reasons For Not Wanting A Narrow Democracy"], *Xuexi Shibao* [*Study Times*], November 18, 2002. See also Zhang Wenmu, "Yong Guojia Zhuyi Daiti Minzu Zhuyi" ["Replacing 'Nationalism' With 'Statism'"], November 12, 2003, www.cngdsz.net; Wang Yiwei, "Yong Aiguo Zhuyi Chaoyue Minzu Zhuyi" ["Patriotism Trumps Nationalism"], *Huanqiu Shibao* [*Global Times*], January 31, 2005.

55. The magazine *Zhuanlue yu Guanli* [*Strategy and Management*] was reportedly closed down in September 2004 after publishing an article critical of China's policy toward North Korea.

56. Bonnie S. Glaser and Evan S. Medeiros, "The Changing Ecology of Foreign Policymaking in China: The Ascension and Demise of the Theory of 'Peaceful Rise,'" *China Quarterly*, no. 190 (2007): 291–310.

57. See Zheng Bijian, "China's 'Peaceful Rise' to Great-Power Status," *Foreign Affairs* 84, no. 5 (September/October 2005): 18–24. See also "Full Text: China's Peaceful Development Road," White Paper, State Council Information Office, December 22, 2005, http://english.people.com.cn.

58. *China Daily*, "Hu Calls for a Harmonious World at Summit," September 16, 2005.

59. *Guoji Wenti Yanjiu*, "China Reform Forum Member Yue Xiaoyong Discusses Harmonious World Theory," July 13, 2007, translated in OSC: CPP20070724455003.

60. *Shijie Jingji Yu Zhengzhi*, "PRC Scholar Summarizes Academic Conference on PRC Foreign Strategy," May 14, 2007, translated in OSC: CPP20070525455002.

61. CCTV, "The Report of Hu Jintao."

3

Democracy with Chinese Characteristics? Political Reform and the Future of the Chinese Communist Party

China should take its own path in enhancing democracy. We never view socialism and democracy as something that is mutually exclusive. . . . We should focus on efforts to promote economic development, protect lawful rights and interests of the people, fight corruption, increase public trust in government, strengthen government functions and enhance social harmony. And we should continue the reform in the political system by expanding democracy and improving the legal system. This will enable other members of the international community to better appreciate and accept the path of development taken by the Chinese people.

— Wen Jiabao, February 26, 2007[1]

That the ruling Chinese Communist Party (CCP) has apparently recognized the need for political reform to accompany economic reform is much welcomed. Less certain, however, is the likely trajectory of this reform path over the coming decades and its implications not only for the CCP and the Chinese people but also for the United States.

Buoyed by the success of adhering to Deng Xiaoping's wily advice to "cross the river by feeling the stones" in the economic realm, the Party clearly intends to pursue its own distinct path in the political realm. In China's gradual transition to "democracy," the Party is once again eschewing the "shock therapy" of radical reform closely associated with the Washington Consensus[2] and intends to borrow selectively from various democratic systems to build a so-called deliberative democracy (*xieshang minzhu*),[3] which combines authoritarian Party leadership, expansion of popular participation in the political process, and governance through the rule of law, while rejecting universal suffrage, true parliamentary bodies, and contested multiparty elections.

Deng Xiaoping outlined the initial plans for China's political reform in a famous speech to the Party leadership in August 1980;[4] however, the process was stymied in the wake of the 1989 Tiananmen Square crisis and collapse of the Soviet Union. The lessons learned from that period and the recognition that lack of political reform is impeding further socioeconomic development has put the issue back on the Party's agenda. The current "fourth generation" leadership—the Hu Jintao–Wen Jiabao administration—articulated its own vision of China's political future in a white paper on building "socialist democracy with Chinese characteristics," first unveiled in 2005.[5]

While there is much to dispute about Chinese-style democracy and it is difficult to predict whether it will succeed over the long term, it is clear that, for the foreseeable future, the CCP will lead China's political reform, which will remain largely instrumental, incremental, and idiosyncratic. *If* all goes according to the Party's plan, in the coming decades the United States is likely to encounter a "democratic" China that resembles its East Asian neighbor Singapore more closely than any Western liberal democracy.

Evolution of China's Political Reform: Instrumental, Incremental, and Idiosyncratic

While the CCP apparently now accepts the need for more serious political reform, it is important to understand that, for the Party, political reform remains a means to an end—an instrument to help ensure continued "socialist modernization." The Party is pursuing "democracy with Chinese characteristics" primarily to address the socioeconomic and political challenges that have emerged in the course of China's modernization, including a widening income gap, increasing regional disparities, corruption, environmental degradation, and rising demand for public goods amid the state's decreased ability to supply them, as well as the social unrest these problems have helped spark. These challenges threaten the realization of China's development goals upon which the CCP's legitimacy now largely rests, and as such, political reforms are ultimately aimed at retaining the Party's ruling status.

The Tiananmen Square crisis in 1989 and demise of the Soviet Union soon thereafter served as a warning for the CCP: Rather than burying its head in the sand, the Party investigated the rise and fall of not only the Communist Party of the Soviet Union (CPSU) but also other ruling parties around the world. In 2004 the leadership soberly admitted that the organization was in disarray and that its ruling status "will not remain forever if the Party does nothing to safeguard it."[6] The Party, therefore, adopted a decision to absorb the "negative" lessons from the collapse of the Soviet bloc as well as the "positive" lessons of ruling parties, not only in East Asian countries such as Singapore and Japan but also as far afield as Cuba and Mexico.

Subsequently, the Party began to implement incremental reforms aimed at strengthening party building and ruling capacity, including gradually increasing "inner-party democracy" and cautiously expanding grass-roots political participation through village-level elections, as well as establishing the rule of law and adjusting center-local, party-state relations.[7]

While some Chinese academics joined the international discourse over the notion of "democratic deficit," which points to the political and/or economic difficulties that have followed rapid introduction of Western-style liberal democracy in developing nations,[8] others examined China's historical tendency toward political radicalization—associated with tragedies such as the Cultural Revolution—calling henceforth for evolutionary rather than revolutionary responses to the nation's problems.[9] The discourse has supported the Party's contention that the decision to pursue China's own development path of economic before political reform and incremental rather than rapid democratization is the correct one. The Party's future leaders—the so-called fifth generation now rising to power—all of whom experienced the Cultural Revolution firsthand, are unlikely to diverge from this path.

In addition to being incremental, China's political reform remains highly idiosyncratic. The Party rejects the "one size fits all" notion of democratization, choosing instead to draw on an eclectic mix of Marxism with both Western and traditional Chinese schools of thought adapted to suit China's particular sociopolitical circumstances and stage of economic development. An example is instituting what the CCP calls a system of multiparty cooperation rather than multiparty competition. According to the white paper on democracy:

> In building socialist political democracy, China has always adhered to the basic principle that the Marxist theory of democracy be combined with the reality of China, borrowed from the useful achievements of the political civilization of mankind, including Western democracy, and assimilated with the democratic elements of China's traditional culture and institutional civilization. Therefore, China's socialist political democracy shows distinctive Chinese characteristics.[10]

Although the basic guideline for building "democracy with Chinese characteristics" was outlined in the white paper, it remains very much a work in progress and the subject of fierce debate both inside and outside the CCP.[11] As with China's economic reform, in the coming years we can expect periods of policymaking characterized by *fang/shou* (loosening, then tightening), steps forward and backward, especially if the Party fears control of the process is slipping through its hands. The CCP will experiment with political reform—keeping what works and discarding what does not—adopting Deng Xiaoping's other famous aphorism, "It doesn't matter whether the cat is black or yellow as long as it catches mice."

China's political reform project is also more inclusive than is at first apparent. Characterizations of China as having a monolithic, top-down policymaking process fail to account for the diverse debate taking place in the country and pressures on China's leadership. As discussed in chapter 2, decision making is becoming increasingly complex and is beginning to reflect disparate social interests. Absent official channels for the expression of public opinion, Chinese intellectuals continue behind the scenes to articulate these diverse interests and mediate between state and society.

Rather than advocating liberal democracy as a response to China's challenges, many new generation intellectuals reject Western "capitalist-style" democracy, charging that it will benefit only the newly rich members of Chinese society, but they do not advocate a return to orthodox Marxism. These "New Left" intellectuals are instead exploring a third way for China's development, akin to the so-called Beijing Consensus.[12] To quote Joshua Cooper Ramo, who first popularized the term:

> The idea that Chinese are all striving for 'the American Way of Life,' as Richard Madsen has observed, is a dangerous misconception. They are striving to make 'The Chinese Way of Life.' As a result, Chinese development has a certain kind of prideful, internal energy that helps the nation's confidence.[13]

In the opaque world of Chinese politics, it is difficult to judge how closely the ideological cleavage among intellectuals in recent years mirrors splits among China's top leadership and the real extent to which the discourse has affected policymaking. However, one indication that the consensus forged by Deng Xiaoping on China's modernization was in serious need of reaffirmation by 2007 was the extent to which Hu Jintao strongly reinforced Deng's "basic line for the primary stage of socialism" at the 17th Party Congress. Moreover, Hu Jintao and Wen Jiabao have found it necessary to launch a third "emancipation of the mind" campaign to garner support for the latest phase of reform (see box 2.1 in chapter 2). As Gao Shangquan, a leading light of China's modernization, commented:

> A large scale debate occurred in 2005 and the issues of the controversy were very focused . . . . Is the reform itself wrong, or has it run into problems? Should we rethink the reform or deny the reform? . . . . This is still a major political issue concerning the party's and country's future and destiny. The debates have been very vigorous, drawing attention from all sectors of society, and the central government is extremely concerned, too."[14]

Putting Theory into Practice

As the debate over reform continues and the CCP traverses its path toward "democracy with Chinese characteristics," the Party has so far proven remarkably responsive, pragmatic, and willing to adapt to China's changing circumstances, which partly explains its resilience in the face of emerging challenges. This approach has enabled the CCP to put in place mechanisms by which the system can be opened enough to retain legitimacy and support, while also maintaining the Party's power. A prime example of the Party's pragmatism is the doctrinal elasticity of former President Jiang Zemin's "Three Represents" theory,[15] which removed the remaining ideological roadblocks preventing once reviled private entrepreneurs from joining the Communist Party. The CCP has thus been largely successful in coopting China's emerging middle class of entrepreneurs and intellectuals—thereby at least slowing the emergence of a critical elite and viable political opposition. The mechanisms the Party has put in place bear more than a passing resemblance to the "soft authoritarianism" of its East Asian neighbors.

The Rule of Law: A Means to Strengthen the Party's Ruling Capacity

In 2004, the leadership openly recognized the need to improve Party governance and frankly acknowledged that the ruling status of the CCP "is by no means a natural result of the Party's founding, and will not remain forever if the Party does nothing to safeguard it."[16] A number of measures to enhance the CCP's ruling capacity, particularly governing the country according to the rule of law, have subsequently been taken.[17]

To stem the "moral degeneration" of Party cadres, in particular corruption among local officials—a source of widespread discontent across the country—the Party launched an old-style rectification campaign for members in January 2005, focusing on intensive education sessions in Party ideology and good governance for cadres at all levels. A cadre responsibility system and improved supervision and oversight mechanisms have also been announced. Hu Jintao's report to the 17th Party Congress emphasized expanding the "democratic rights" of people to supervise local cadres.

The approval of "freedom of information" regulations in April 2007 was a major step toward improving government transparency. These regulations ostensibly give citizens the right to access "nonexempt" government information and compel officials to disclose it—though what information is subject to "exemption" remains at the government's discretion.

Even the National People's Congress (NPC), traditionally considered a "rubber-stamp" body, has shown some signs of independent thinking since the early 1990s: It no longer unquestionably approves all legislation put before it by the State Council, as the protracted drafting process for controversial bills such as the Property Law and Anti-Monopoly Law attests. In 2003, one-tenth of NPC delegates voted against Jiang Zemin staying on as the chairman of the Central Military Commission. The Administrative Supervision Law has enhanced the supervisory role of party congresses at the local level, and practically all draft legislation is now made available for public comment. Elections for people's congress deputies are also becoming more competitive, with some even electing independent candidates.[18]

In February 2008, China issued its first white paper on promoting the rule of law. Emphasizing the progress made in establishing a "modern Chinese legal system" since reform and opening up, the paper includes an appendix of 229 laws now in force. However, the paper points out that China would not "copy indiscriminately" from foreign legal systems but rather proceed from its "actual conditions." The paper reasserts the ultimate authority of the Party over the legal system, noting that "the CPC [Communist Party of China] always plays the role as the core of leadership in directing the overall situation and coordinating the efforts of all quarters in legal construction."[19]

While still far from being a rule-of-law country, China has made progress. Citizens are more conscious of their rights—adding to the danger that rising expectations could spark popular discontent if they go unmet. Significantly, the new politburo's first study session in November 2007 focused on improving and expanding public participation in China's legal system.[20]

Promoting Inner-Party Democracy

The lessons learned from the demise of the CPSU partly prompted the leadership's latest push to promote "inner-party democracy" (*dangnei minzhu*), which has been debated at various junctures in the Party's history. Polls taken of the attitudes of Party members, which revealed widespread apathy and "wavering ideals and beliefs, a weak sense of purpose, and lax organization and discipline,"[21] also reportedly alarmed the leadership. Significantly, inner-party democracy serves as a bellwether for China's incremental democracy project, the aim of which is to establish democracy first within the party, then expand it to society at large—first at the grass-roots level and then at higher levels.[22] As Yu Keping, a leading Party theoretician and adviser to Hu Jintao, has stated: "Without inner-party democracy, China's democracy today is nothing but empty talk."

Efforts are under way to institutionalize CCP procedures and also make them more transparent, in place of the Byzantine "informal politics" that have historically dominated inner-party life. At each level of the Party, members must now vote on major decisions including in the critical area of personnel appointments, and party standing committees at all levels must deliver annual work reports. A proposal that local party congresses be in session more regularly, instead of meeting only once every five years, has been implemented on an experimental basis and was endorsed at the 17th Party Congress. Regulations governing the convening of party congresses, selection for and retirement from official posts, fixed-term limits, and other measures have helped to institutionalize Party processes, diminish the formerly dominant role of paramount leaders and retired elders, and improve the "democratic" character of inner-party deliberations and decision making. To make Party procedures more transparent, the Chinese media now report on politburo meetings as well as discuss the division of responsibilities among its members.

The official media lauded the "democratic processes" applied in the election of the Party's new leaders at the 17th CCP Congress, at which there were 8 percent more candidates than slots available. The Congress decided to expand the scope of multicandidate elections, and Party leaders praised experiments with direct election of party secretaries and members of township party committees in Jiangsu and Sichuan, suggesting these elections may also be expanded.[23]

The institutionalization of Party procedures would also remove one of the most persistent stumbling blocks for Communist parties: leadership succession. The transfer of power to Hu Jintao, Wen Jiabao, and the "fourth generation" of Chinese leadership in 2002–03 was the smoothest and most bloodless in over 80 years of Chinese Communist history. Unlike his predecessors, Hu Jintao has not assumed the mantle of the "core" of his generation, instead preferring to promote the norms of collective leadership. The much-remarked upon failure of Hu Jintao to designate a successor at the 17th Congress could be interpreted more positively as an important step in the evolution from informal, personality-driven politics to a formal, institutionalized, and ultimately more stable leadership system.[24]

Pursuing "Multiparty Cooperation"

Following the 17th Party Congress, China issued its first-ever white paper on the political party system, which, according to a spokesperson, is aimed at clearing up "misunderstandings" commonly held overseas about the political system and emphasizing that China has "established its own unique political party system and its own way to fulfill democracy, which is unique in the world."[25]

China's eight "democratic parties" enjoyed a brief power-sharing relationship with the CCP immediately after the People's Republic was established in 1949. But they were persecuted during the antirightist campaign and Cultural Revolution and subsequently fell into political obscurity. While their rehabilitation could be viewed merely as a means to stave off international criticism, the concept of multiparty cooperation and consultation has actually been the subject of much discussion in China. Central Party School Vice President Li Junru, among others, has expounded on the idea of "deliberative democracy," calling for an expansion of the supervisory role of the NPC and the Chinese People's Political Consultative Conference (CPPCC) as well as consultation with China's eight democratic parties and other nonparty figures.

In March 2005, the NPC adopted "Suggestions on Further Strengthening Multiparty Cooperation and Political Consultation under the Leadership of the CPC," and, in 2007, Wan Gang, a member of the Zhi Gong (Public Interest) Party, was appointed minister of science and technology, and Chen Zhu was named minister of health—the first non-CCP member appointed as minister since reform began.

While an expanded role for consultation and inclusion of non-CCP organizations in China's governance is encouraging, the Party has left no room for doubt about the limits to multiparty cooperation, pointedly recommitting to its Four Cardinal Principles at the 17th Party Congress: upholding the socialist path, people's democratic dictatorship, leadership of the CCP, and Marxism-Leninism-Mao Zedong Thought.

Greater Openness and Democracy at the Grass-Roots Level

Experiments with political reform at the grass-roots level have been under way since the 1980s. In 1987 the government enacted an experimental law on direct village committee elections, which was revised in 1998 to make village elections mandatory and included such requirements as secret ballots and open vote counting. Currently, elections occur in almost 1 million villages across China, affecting about 80 percent of the population in the countryside. Direct elections are also being held at urban residential and township committee levels in some parts of China.

International organizations, including both Republican and Democratic institutions operating under the National Endowment for Democracy as well as the Carter Center, have provided technical assistance for these elections. According to the vice president of the International Republican Institute, Elizabeth Dugan, although the elections were largely devised to "create a release valve to prevent political pressures from exploding" and are controlled by the Party, they have "introduced the element of free choice into the political process."[26] The report card, however, remains mixed. While in some parts of China, the elections "approach free and fair," in other parts "they are weak."[27] To control what the Party would view as too much democratization, especially the loss of Party influence at the local level, nominees for village chief in some areas must now be drawn from Party branch members. A classified party document reportedly found that up to 75 percent of rural party branches are in a "state of collapse" and that other organizations, including "reactionary forces, both traditional clans and triads and also newly established Christian churches," are stepping into the political vacuum.[28]

Some observers note that secret balloting, as well as the more recent empowering of villagers to report on election irregularities and unseat unpopular leaders, has improved the quality and competitiveness of village elections.[29] In some areas, however, elections have exacerbated social and political tensions: Corrupt local leaders who have no intention of adhering to Beijing's rule of law have responded violently to "rights conscious" villagers.[30]

Other experiments with grass-roots political reform are under way across the country, notably the Wenling, Zhejiang Province experiment with "democratic consultation" (*minzhu kentan*), in which ordinary citizens are free to raise questions or give opinions on important issues such as budgets during open meetings with local officials, as well as the permanent party congress representation system.[31] In Sichuan Province, experiments allowing some non-Party members to participate in the nomination of candidates for township elections are also under way.

Amid criticism that the glacial pace of grass-roots political reform has done little to alleviate social tensions—not to mention expand democracy—at the local level, Hu Jintao has called for the deepening of village- and township-level government reform to "safeguard the people's rights to be informed, to participate, to express and to oversee," suggesting some forward momentum is on the horizon.[32] While it remains to be seen how his call will be put in practice, it is the first time the Party has promoted grass-roots democracy, specifically self-government, as a key issue.[33]

Shenzhen: A "Special Political Zone"?

Guangdong Province has been a pioneer in China's modernization and played a unique experiential role in reform and opening up, notably establishing China's first special economic zone in Shenzhen in 1980. Not surprisingly, it is here that the inadequacies of China's current political-administrative system to deal with the social, economic, and political challenges that have emerged during the course of modernization are most visible. Guangdong party secretary and close associate of Hu Jintao, Wang Yang, has been at the forefront of the aforementioned "emancipation of the mind" campaign, calling on the province to set an example for the rest of the nation in implementing the political-administrative reforms that the Party has launched in response to these challenges.[34]

It is speculated that Guangdong will follow the model of China's gradual economic reform and be the first province to establish "special political zones"—speculation heightened recently by publication on the Shenzhen municipal government's website of a draft proposal entitled "Shenzhen's Future Reform."[35] The draft proposal, which has been published to solicit opinions from the public, outlines plans for experiments with both inner-party and grass-roots democracy, including direct election of deputies to the district people's congresses, a permanent representative system for district Party congresses, and mayoral elections. The draft lists key tasks that must be accomplished and envisages that it will take Shenzhen around three years to establish the zone's socialist democracy and legal system; a clean, efficient, and service-oriented government; and a people-centered harmonious society.[36]

Rhetoric Versus Reality

The mechanisms discussed above have helped the Party retain its ruling status, and China's ongoing experiments with political reform are certainly encouraging. But closing the gap between rhetoric and reality—between the policies articulated by the central leadership and their implementation, especially at the local level—is where the rubber hits the road for the CCP going forward (see chapter 4).

There is growing dissatisfaction with local-level government and increasing pressure from "rights conscious" citizens for the Party to not only live up to its own promises but also provide public goods, including better education, healthcare, environmental protection, and clean government. Again, the Party—at least at the level of the central government—has adapted remarkably to China's changing circumstances. For example, the Scientific Development Concept, adopted at the 17th Party Congress, seeks to balance rapid GDP growth while addressing the pressing socio-economic and political issues that have emerged in the course of reform and been the subject of such intense debate.

At the 1st Plenary Session of the 11th NPC in March 2008, Premier Wen Jiabao unveiled an overhauled administrative system, aimed at both streamlining and increasing government transparency, and called on officials to "accept the oversight of the news media and the general public."[37] Wen said the overhaul was designed to:

> . . .build a service-oriented, responsible and honest government ruled by law to carry out the people-centered concept of governance more effectively, earnestly solve problems of the interests of the masses that are most real, most direct, and the cause of the most concern . . . .[38]

Much, therefore, hinges on the success of the third "emancipation of the mind" campaign in fighting entrenched bureaucratic and local government opposition to the economic and political-administrative reforms launched under the Scientific Development Concept.[39] Guangdong Party Secretary Wang Yang warned Party members:

> Cadres with party membership in the province should unite their minds with the requirements of the central authorities . . . . If we do not think of making greater progress and innovation, are unable to work for and lead scientific development, or even become impediments to scientific development, we will be eliminated by the society . . . .[40]

Ongoing Support for the Party

China's political future, as mapped out by the CCP, has been hotly debated not only among theorists who continue to argue over definitions of democracy as well as the sequencing of political reform in post-Communist and developing countries but also among observers both inside and outside China, many of whom dismiss CCP-led democratization altogether.[41]

Within China, some intellectuals, Party advisers, and retired officials are calling for wider political reform.[42] However, while many intellectuals are willing to push the envelope, with some even advocating Northern European-style democratic socialism in China,[43] most support incremental reform under the leadership of the CCP and are engaged in a sincere, in-depth research effort that will likely provide the theoretical underpinning for the Party's political reform policies.[44]

Several possible scenarios for China's political future have been posited:

- A China led by the CCP will remain "authoritarian" for the foreseeable future;[45] absent democracy—measured by liberal democratic standards including multiparty elections and a range of political and civil liberties—the country will likely become "trapped in transition" and be marked by crony capitalism, which has afflicted many developing nations.[46]

- Economic development will, eventually, lead to political freedom and China will traverse the same path as other modernizing countries. Rising income and education levels will produce a middle class, which, when it reaches critical mass, will push for more political rights, in support of either reform within the CCP (possibly renamed) or a change of regime by around 2025.[47]

- China will follow its own path to democracy—actually a variant of the East Asian development model—and pass through a lengthy period of "soft authoritarianism" to what the Party calls "democracy with Chinese characteristics." The CCP will then resemble Singapore's People's Action Party (PAP) or even Japan's Liberal Democratic Party (LDP). The timing is unclear. By comparison, under the leadership of the Leninist Kuomintang (KMT), it took Taiwan nearly 50 years to go from grass-roots elections in the 1950s to its first democratic presidential election in 2000.[48]

While the glacial pace of China's political reform and ongoing egregious human rights violations, religious persecution, and lack of civil and political liberties—illustrated most recently in Tibet—keep it at the bottom of international rankings of "democratic" countries, it is the Chinese people who will ultimately decide the CCP's fate and the kind of China that the United States will face in the coming decades.[49]

Perhaps the most enduring image of China in the popular American imagination is the Tiananmen Square crackdown on June 4, 1989. Those who assume that the only thing standing in the way of liberal democracy in China is the People's Liberation Army (PLA) may be surprised that research suggests not only China's elite but also a majority of the population support CCP-led political as well as economic reform—some 95 percent, according to one poll.[50] While caution is advised when interpreting such polls, survey evidence continues to find that while the Chinese people do demand democracy, they also believe the Party is actually supplying it.[51]

When asked to compare present conditions with those prior to opening up in 1978, not surprisingly, 97 percent said the government's economic performance was much or somewhat better. However, government performance in expanding civil liberties and political rights also received high approval ratings, ranging from 60 to 80 percent.[52]

The impact of China's tragic history of political upheaval, which many in the "fifth generation" now in their late 40s and early 50s experienced firsthand, should not be underestimated; polls find overwhelming support for the Party's prioritization of social stability.[53] Time may actually be on the Party's side. People have only to turn on their television sets to compare the results of "shock therapy" in countries such as Russia, Indonesia, Iraq, and Afghanistan with the relative success of the Party's incremental approach to reform. Until recently, even Taiwan, which many hoped would be the catalyst for wider political reform on the mainland, has had a largely negative impact—the official Chinese media often play up the partisan politics and resulting economic difficulties the island has experienced. There is growing support not only among intellectuals but society at large for a uniquely "Chinese model" of development, which rejects much of the Western liberal democratic blueprint for political reform.[54]

Finally, as long as the majority of Chinese people continue to *perceive* that the Party is providing them with the economic and political goods they demand, the Party will retain "the mantle of heaven." In a 2005 international survey of public attitudes in 17 countries China ranked the highest, with 50 percent of Chinese people feeling they had made personal progress in the last five years and over 70 percent expressing satisfaction with national conditions.[55]

To be sure, the Party faces numerous challenges in the coming years, not the least of which is bridging the gap between the rhetoric and reality of promised political reform and meeting the rising expectations of the Chinese people. However, research suggests that in the absence of any unforeseen external shocks—and continued absence of any viable political opposition—the CCP, far from being on the brink of collapse, is likely to remain in power for the foreseeable future.

Conclusion and Recommendations

It remains to be seen whether the CCP will succeed in the political realm as it has in the economic realm and establish "democracy with Chinese characteristics," in which the system can be opened enough to retain legitimacy and support, while also maintaining the Party's power over the long term. Whether it succeeds or fails will have serious implications for the United States.

There are those who argue that the United States should not engage with a "nondemocratic" China. The idea of regime change or collapse is also actively encouraged in some quarters, though it would result in an economic, political, and humanitarian crisis, which, in an era of globalization, would be devastating not only for China but also the United States and the wider international community. It is in all our long-term interests to see China modernize successfully.

Those who support the promotion of liberal democracy should also be careful not to view it as a panacea for the difficulties in US-China relations. Even a liberal democratic China would continue to pose both an economic challenge and opportunity for the United States. As the history of US-European relations suggests, contentious trade disputes arise even between states with close political values as well as economic interests. While the "peaceful democracy" theory holds that there would be less to fear from China's military modernization and international intentions, given rising nationalism in China and identity politics on Taiwan, there is no guarantee that it will help end the impasse. Furthermore, as elections in other places have shown, one cannot predict whether a democratically elected leader of China would be pro- or anti-American. Certainly, a successful transition, especially one led by the CCP, is likely to lead to a more confident China and one that not only wants to sit at the table but also wants to be given a seat at the top.

The foregoing discussion of the evolution of political reform in China, apparent ongoing domestic support for the CCP, and the international discourse on the "democratic deficit" in developing countries underscores why attempts to force liberal democracy on China are likely to remain ineffective and ultimately counterproductive. Alternatives include:

- Rather than debating whether or not China's reforms are evidence of real democratization and arguing over the yardsticks by which to measure it—which the CCP can brush off as evidence of American "cultural hegemony" and find a receptive audience that supports it— the United States should apply selective pressure on China when the Party fails to live up to its own promises and violates the political and legal reforms it has put in place.

- US policymakers need to accept that in the absence of organized opposition, the CCP will continue to control the pace and scope of political reform in China. However, the United States can still exert a positive influence and the necessary pressure to keep the process moving forward by actively participating in international institutions and multilateral forums and by supporting nongovernmental organizations (NGOs) in their efforts to expand grass-roots democracy, establish rule of law, and improve corporate governance in China.

- In addition to "track one" government-to-government engagement, "track two" dialogue among US and Chinese intellectuals and officials working on political reform issues should be established to seriously discuss the merits and demerits of liberal, East Asian, and even Chinese-style democracy. Further, regular contacts and formal partnerships between US and Chinese think tanks and other NGOs should be encouraged.

- Finally, a "Beijing model" of not only economic but also political development, whether valid or not, is already gaining influence among developing nations. A successful transition to "democracy with Chinese characteristics" led by the CCP would present a de facto alternative to the long-established "Washington model" of development and require a ready response from the United States.[56] A plethora of polls in recent years has shown the steady decline in US "soft power" and moral authority, and policymakers need to take immediate steps to reverse this decline.

Notes

1. Xinhua News Agency, "Wen Jiabao: Guanyu shehuizhuyi chuji jieduan de lishi renwu he wo guo dui wai zhengce de ji ge wenti" ["Wen Jiabao: Several Questions Concerning the Historical Duty of the Primary Stages of Socialism and Our Nation's Foreign Policy"], February 26, 2007, http://news.xinhuanet.com.

2. For a discussion of the Washington Consensus versus Beijing Consensus, see Joshua Cooper Ramo, *The Beijing Consensus* (London: Foreign Policy Centre, May 2004). Ramo notes that whether China's reform project ends in success or failure, "the Beijing Consensus is already drawing a wake of new ideas that are very different from those coming from Washington" and "marking a path for other nations around the world" to follow.

3. Also referred to as "participatory" democracy and "consultative" democracy.

4. Deng Xiaoping, "On the Reform of the System of Party and State Leadership," August 18, 1980, in *Selected Works of Deng Xiaoping 1975–1982* (Beijing: Foreign Languages Press, 1983).

5. Xinhua News Agency, "Zhongguo de minzhu zhengzhi jianshe" ["The Building of China's Democratic Polity"], October 19, 2005, http://politics.people.com.cn.

6. Xinhua News Agency, "Zhonggong zhongyang guanyu jiaqiang dang zhizheng nengli jianshe de jueding" ["CCP Decision on Strengthening the Governance Capacity of the Party"], September 26, 2004, www.people.com.cn. For an excellent discussion of this period, see David Shambaugh, *China's Communist Party: Atrophy and Adaptation* (Washington: Woodrow Wilson Center Press, 2008).

7. Author's interview with Chinese party scholar in Beijing, March 2008. See also Xinhua News Agency, "Zhonggong zhongyang guanyu jiaqiang dang zhizheng nengli jianshe de jueding" ["CCP Decision on Strengthening the Governance Capacity of the Party"], September 26, 2004, www.people.com.cn.

8. Ding Gang, "The Failure of the US Model is Not the Failure of Democracy" ["Meiguo de Shibai Bushi Minzhu de Shibai"], *Huanqiu Shibao*, February 13, 2008,

www.chinaelections.org; and Ding Gang, "Is US Democracy 'Transplantable?'" ["Meiguo Minzhu Nengzai Shijie Puji Ma?"], *China Daily*, February 5, 2008, www.chinaelections.org. Michael McFaul notes that of the 28 former Soviet republics, 22 are now dictatorships or rocky transitional regimes; see McFaul, "The Fourth Wave of Democracy and Dictatorship: Non-cooperative Transitions in the Post-Communist World," *World Politics* 54, no. 2 (January 2002).

9. For example, see Li Zehou and Liu Zaifu, *Farewell to Revolution* [*Gaobie Geming*] (Hong Kong: Cosmos Books, 1996).

10. Xinhua News Agency, October 19, 2005.

11. For a discussion of these debates, see Melissa Murphy, *Decoding Chinese Politics: Intellectual Debates and Why They Matter* (Washington: Center for Strategic and International Studies, 2007).

12. Cooper Ramo, *The Beijing Consensus*.

13. Ibid.

14. *Nanfang Dushi Bao* [*Southern Urban News*], "Xin yi lun sixiang jiefang cong nali qibu?" ["What Should Be the Starting Point for a New Round of Discussion of 'Mind Emancipation'?"], March 3, 2008, www.eeo.com.cn.

15. Jiang Zemin's "Three Represents" theory—that the party must always represent the development trend of China's advanced productive forces, the orientation of China's advanced culture, and the fundamental interests of the overwhelming majority of people—cleared the way for the admission of private entrepreneurs into the Communist Party and a constitutional amendment to include the protection of private property. See Bruce Dickson, *Red Capitalists in China* (Cambridge: Cambridge University Press, 2003); and Bruce Dickson, "Cooptation and Corporatism in China: The Logic of Party Adaptation," in *China's Deep Reform: Domestic Politics in Transition*, eds. Lowell Dittmer and Guoli Liu (Lanham, MD: Rowman & Littlefield, 2006).

16. Xinhua News Agency, "Zhonggong zhongyang guanyu jiaqiang dang zhizheng nengli jianshe de jueding" ["CCP Decision on Strengthening the Governance Capacity of the Party"], September 26, 2004, www.people.com.cn.

17. For a discussion on China's rule of law, see Jamie P. Horsley, "The Rule of Law in China: Incremental Progress," in *The China Balance Sheet in 2007 and Beyond (Phase II Papers)* (Washington: Peterson Institute for International Economics and Center for Strategic and International Studies, 2007).

18. *China Daily*, "Independent Candidate Elected," December 17, 2003.

19. Xinhua News Agency, "Zhongguo fazhi jianshe" ["Establishing the Rule of Law in China"], February 28, 2008, http://news.xinhuanet.com.

20. Xinhua News Agency, "Hu Jintao zhuchi di shiqi jie zhonggong zhongyang zhengzhiju di yi ci jiti xuexi" ["Hu Jintao Presides over the First Group Study Session of the 17th Politburo"], November 28, 2007, http://news.xinhuanet.com.

21. *Ching Chi Jih Pao*, "HK Daily: CPC To Launch Education Campaign To Reinforce Faith in Communism," November 24, 2004, in Open Source Center (OSC): CPP2004112400042.

22. *Nanfang Dushi Bao* [*Southern Urban News*], "Yu Keping: jiefang sixiang yao gei ren yi jihui, zhe jiu shi minzhu" ["Yu Keping: Emancipation of the Mind Is About Providing Opportunity: This Is the Essence of Democracy"], February 21, 2008, www.beelink.com.

23. *People's Daily*, "Li Yuanchao: Tuijin dang nei minzhu jianshe, zengqiang dang de tuanjie tongyi" ["Li Yuanchao: Promotion of Intra-Party Democracy's Construction, Strengthening Party Unity"], November 1, 2007, http://news.xinhuanet.com.

24. For Cheng Li, this might even presage the emergence of a collective leadership with competing factions, a "one party, two factions," formula that would presumably see the party evolve to resemble Japan's ruling Liberal Democratic Party (LDP). However, this evolution would require the CCP elite to mature beyond viewing politics as a zero-sum game in which such factionalism could actually split the party—which is why it is currently proscribed. See Cheng Li, "China in the Year 2020: Three Political Scenarios," *Asia Policy*, no. 4 (July 2007), 17–29.

25. Xinhua News Agency, "Zhongguo de zhengdang zhidu" ["China's Political Party System"], November 15, 2007, http://news.xinhuanet.com.

26. Elizabeth Dugan, "Is Democracy Stirring in China?" (speech to the United Nations Association–National Capital Area Young Professionals for International Cooperation, June 29, 2005).

27. Ibid.

28. Dickson, *Red Capitalists in China*, 48.

29. Kevin O'Brien, "Villagers, Elections, and Citizenship in Contemporary China," in *China's Deep Reform: Domestic Politics in Transition*, eds. Lowell Dittmer and Guoli Liu (Lanham, MD: Rowman & Littlefield, 2006).

30. Agence France Presse, "Murder, Corruption Part of Chinese 'Democracy,'" October 17, 2007.

31. *Nanfeng Chuang* [*Southern Wind Window*], "Wenling minzhu, ouran he biran zhijian" ["Wenling's Democracy: Between Chance Occurrence and Inevitability"], February 5, 2008, http://news.xinhuanet.com.

32. CCTV, "Dang de shiqi da kaimu: Hu Jintao zuo baogao" ["The Opening Ceremony of the 17th Party Congress: The Report of Hu Jintao"], October 15, 2007, http://news.cctv.com.

33. *Caijing*, "Expert Comments on 17th Party Congress Report, Breakthroughs in Political Reform," October 27, 2007 in OSC: CPP20071030456001.

34. *Nanfang Ribao* [*Southern Daily*], "Wang Yang: Ba jiefang sixiang xuexi taolun huodong yinxiang shenru" ["Wang Yang: Deepening the Discussion & Activity Related to 'Emancipation of the Mind'"], March 3, 2008, http://news.southcn.com.

35. Author's interview with Chinese party scholar in Beijing, March 2008. See *Nanfang Ribao*, "Attempting a Major Breakthrough in Political Reform, Democracy and Legal System Again Establishing Special Zones," May 23, 2008, www.nanfangdaily.com.cn.

36. Ibid.

37. Xinhua News Agency, "Government Officials Told to Facilitate Supervision from Public Members," March 5, 2008, http://en.chinaelections.org.

38. Xinhua News Agency, "Shenhua xingzheng guanli tizhi gaige, jianshe renmin manyi de zhengfu" ["Deepening Reform of the Administrative Apparatus, Building a Government that Satisfies the People"], March 4, 2008, http://news.xinhua net.com.

39. Entrenched bureaucratic and business interests are thought to have watered down Beijing's plan to establish "super ministries" in March 2008 as part of the administrative overhaul, seen particularly in the failure to create an energy ministry.

40. *Nanfang Ribao*, March 3, 2008.

41. For further discussion, see Randall Peerenboom, *China Modernizes: Threat to the West or Model for the Rest?* (Oxford: Oxford University Press, 2007). See also James Mann, *The China Fantasy: Why Capitalism Will Not Bring Democracy to China* (New York: Penguin, 2007).

42. Zhu House, former minister of propaganda who was purged in the wake of the Tiananmen Square crackdown, has criticized Chinese-style democracy as "fake democracy" so long as it remains controlled by the CCP, in Wu Yong "Commentary: Can China's Communist Party Implement Democracy?" *UPI Asia Online*, July 20, 2007, www.upiasiaonline.com. See also Liu Junning, "China's Reform: Approaching a Dead End," *China Security* 3, no. 4 (Autumn 2007), 90–102.

43. Murphy, *Decoding Chinese Politics.*

44. Author's interview with Chinese party scholar in Beijing, March 2008. The latest 300-page research report from China's influential Central Party School—reportedly commissioned by the central leadership—charges that the "backwardness of the political system is affecting economic development" and warns of serious social instability unless democratic reforms are implemented that strengthen supervision over the CCP. The report provides a detailed guideline for the gradual implementation of political reform. See Zhou Tianyong, Wang Changjiang, and Wang Anling, *A Hard Task: After the 17th Party Congress: China's Political System Reform Research Report* [*Gongjian: Shi Qi Da Hou: Zhongguo Zhengzhi Tizhi Gaige Yanjiu Baogao*] (Xinjiang: Xinjiang Production and Construction Corps Publishing, October 2007).

45. Andrew Nathan, "Authoritarian Resilience," *Journal of Democracy* 9 (January 2003), 6–17.

46. Minxin Pei, *China's Trapped Transition: The Limits of Developmental Autocracy* (Cambridge: Cambridge University Press, 2006).

47. Bruce Gilley, *China's Democratic Future* (New York: Columbia University Press, 2004). See also Henry Rowen, "When Will the Chinese People Be Free?" *Journal of Democracy* 18 (July 2007), 38–52.

48. Peerenboom, *China Modernizes.* See also Dali Yang, "China's Long March to Freedom," *Journal of Democracy* 18 (July 2007), 58–64.

49. Freedom House, *Freedom in the World 2007: Annual Survey of Political Rights and Civil Liberties*, eds. Arch Puddington, Aili Piano, et al. (New York: Rowman & Littlefield, 2007).

50. Zhengxu Wang, "Public Support for Democracy in China," *Journal of Contemporary China*, no. 16 (November 2007), 561–79.

51. It is difficult to dismiss these findings as the result of political indoctrination or fear of reprisal because the same surveys found people willing to be highly critical of rising inequality, corruption, and other issues. See Tianjin Shi, "How Do Asian People Understand Democracy" (presentation at the Carnegie Endowment for International Peace, November 28, 2007), www.carnegieendowment.org.

52. Zhengxu Wang, *Journal of Contemporary China*, no. 16, 561–79.

53. Liberal reformer Ding Xueliang has warned, "If an anarchic situation appears in China, the violence the Chinese will inflict on each other will far exceed the barbarism inflicted by the Japanese when it invaded in the 1930's." See Fewsmith, *China Since Tiananmen*.

54. See Tang Wenfang, *Public Opinion and Political Change in China* (Stanford: Stanford University Press, 2005). See also Ding Gang, "Emancipate the Mind: Break the Western Discourse Cage" ["Jiefang Sixiang: Tupo Xifang Huayu Laolong"], *Huanqiu Shibao*, February 19, 2008, www.chinaelections.org.

55. Peerenboom, *China Modernizes*.

56. Ian Buruma, "The Year of the 'China Model'," *The Nation*, January 9, 2008.

4

Center-Local Relations: Hu's in Charge Here?

The mountains are high, the Emperor is far away.

— Chinese proverb

Many in the United States believe that China's one-party system gives Beijing total power and control over all levels of government. The image, perhaps left over from the Maoist cult of personality era, of a single leader or core group of leaders responsible for and in command of all aspects of Chinese society still pervades the American imagination. This perception of absolute authority has led US policymakers and industry groups to focus on securing top-down commitments from Chinese leaders to resolve bilateral economic and other issues. That the leaders sometimes do not fulfill these commitments endlessly frustrates the Americans who have sought them, who view this as negligence on the part of Chinese leaders, lack of political will, or even outright malfeasance.

Beijing's ability to unilaterally impose its will throughout China is, however, highly limited. For a variety of reasons discussed in this chapter, China's authoritarian regime lacks the capacity to implement many of its decisions throughout the polity, a limitation that has important implications for policymaking in Beijing. The leadership has to gauge carefully what it can and cannot get away with vis-à-vis local authorities; how much political capital will be required to enact controversial policies at local levels; and how much discretion to allow local authorities in policies set at the national level—recognizing that the center has no capacity to enforce absolute obedience to its edicts. The policy process can frequently result in vague national policy pronouncements that look less like hard and fast rules than abstract guiding principles—exhortations to local authorities to "do the right thing" that leave considerable latitude for local recalcitrance. Even when Beijing issues more categorical commands, local compliance is far from certain.

The central government's ability to make good on its policies and assurances is of great importance to the United States, particularly when key US trade, consumer safety, and environmental interests are involved. It may seem counterintuitive for the United States to be concerned about a *lack of control* by an authoritarian regime such as China's, but it has some fairly fundamental reasons to be concerned about the Chinese central government's capability to implement policies.

If Beijing cannot effectively implement its policies at home, its international agreements on trade and environment issues are of little use. A commitment from Beijing to abide by global intellectual property norms, no matter how well-intentioned, is of scant value if Beijing has only modest authority to actually enforce it within China. Thus, weighing the fairness of China's trade practices can be difficult: One can envision a scenario in which Beijing is penalized by the international community for unfair trade practices but is unable to make significant changes because those practices are beyond its effective control.

America's legal tradition has conditioned Americans to view the passage of a law or rule by the main government authority as binding. In managing trade disputes with China, much of US economic diplomacy is directed toward pressing Beijing to change its laws or regulations that otherwise appear to tolerate disputed behavior. It may be premature for American trade negotiators to declare victory at the passage of a new law without accounting for the center-local disconnect. A more successful US strategy may require Americans to build longer-term benchmarks and a process to verify implementation at all layers of government. That, in turn, may require the US government to deepen its reach into Chinese provinces and spend time cultivating political relationships outside China's bigger cities.

From Decentralization to Recentralization

Decentralization in the 1980s

In 1978 a radical program of decentralization was introduced in China to jumpstart economic development. The program introduced the "fiscal contracting system" (the so-called *fen zao chi fan* or "eating in separate kitchens" policy), which gave each level of government a separate revenue base and required them to balance their own expenditures.[1] In practice, this meant that tax collection became a provincial, rather than central, task, with the center and local governments negotiating the division of tax revenues.[2] Local governments developed their own sources of income, making them less dependent on the central purse.[3] With the central government no longer directly overseeing services provided in local areas, local officials gained significant autonomy from Beijing.[4]

Though decentralization successfully kickstarted China's economy, it also engendered institutional conflict between the central and local governments. Local governments face the dilemma of choosing between following the orders of the central government, which may harm local interests, and focusing on local interests, which may deviate from central plans and objectives.[5]

Decentralization has also fostered endemic corruption in China. Given the broad discretionary power officials have over regulatory issues with little effective oversight, opportunities for self-dealing are great, with potential rewards dramatically outweighing the risks of punishment.[6]

Decentralization has also limited the central government's capacity to use fiscal policy to manage the economy as a whole.[7] Recalcitrant local officials routinely ignore central policies intended to manage boom-bust cycles or otherwise direct economic growth. Beijing's efforts to balance regional growth have been particularly challenging, and its efforts to reduce the widening income disparities between regions and provinces have thus far proven ineffective.[8]

Effort to Recentralize in the Early to Mid-1990s

To address the ill effects of decentralization, the Chinese government began a program of recentralization in the early to mid-1990s.[9] The most significant dimension of recentralization was the creation of the tax division system in 1994, which transferred the role of tax collection back to the central government.[10] The tax division system dramatically increased central government revenue and reduced provincial economic autonomy. The center's share of total government revenue went from only 22 percent in 1993 to nearly 50 percent just three years later.[11]

At the same time that recentralization and the tax division system allowed the center to largely achieve its goal of increased fiscal power,[12] they created unique incentives for local governments to disregard central policies. Before the reforms, local governments' share of total revenue stood at 78 percent.[13] By 2004, however, local governments garnered just 45 percent of total government revenue yet were responsible for 72 percent of total government spending.[14] Beijing continues to devolve responsibility for social welfare programs to local governments but has not transferred significant new funding to them to compensate for the revenue lost from the tax division system.[15] In the face of revenue pressures, many local officials have little recourse but to ignore central directives on such issues as growth planning and resource management.[16] The financial pressure on local governments, coupled with a "growth at any cost" mandate, is responsible for many of China's policy implementation shortcomings.

Current Factors Causing Center-Local Friction

Growth at Any Cost

Local officials are unwilling to follow central government laws primarily because of the intense focus on "growth at any cost" since the early 1990s.[17] Promotion of local officials is largely based on their economic growth record, and the surest way up the ladder is to focus on "growth at any cost."[18] Beijing has instituted metrics for promoting officials based on the attention they pay to environmental health and even intellectual property rights (IPR) protection, but local officials would rather focus on promoting growth.[19] This focus on growth is reinforced by the autonomy—strengthened by the devolution of responsibility to localities during China's post-Mao reforms—that local officials have enjoyed for most of China's history.

Even though the central government is increasingly aware of China's environmental problems, "growth at any cost" has left environmental laws particularly vulnerable. Local officials often see environmental policies and continued growth as opposing choices and almost always opt for economic growth.[20] They gain more from promoting rapid industrialization than from promoting steady, sustainable development, an approach that generally carries considerable environmental costs.[21]

At the root of many local officials' desire to maintain growth in their provinces and localities is a desire to maintain stability and prevent social unrest, particularly since promotions can also depend on an official's ability to suppress social unrest.[22] Factories engaging in counterfeiting or violating product safety rules are often the cornerstones of local economies, providing jobs and revenue. Thus, when local officials uncover environmental, IPR, or consumer safety violations, they often turn a blind eye to avoid facing the dangers from job losses and decreased revenue, including social unrest, destabilization, and possible demotion.

Institutional Weaknesses

China's bureaucratic structure and institutional weaknesses contribute significantly to the gap between central policy and local implementation.

For example, consumer and product safety suffers as a result of nearly a dozen government organizations dealing with various aspects of food safety, including the Ministries of Health and Commerce, and a hodgepodge of laws that cover various aspects of food safety. Local governments often find it difficult to follow ministerial orders and implement laws, even if they are inclined to do so.[23]

The center's structural weaknesses have also led to poor implementation of IPR policies. For example, local governments are responsible for appointing local officials and judges and for their salaries, benefits, and housing.[24] The significant control that the local government exerts over these officials and judges means that they are more loyal to the local than to the central government. This translates into much less severe penalties for counterfeiters.[25]

To enforce its policies at the local level, the central government relies on its local bureaus, which are often ineffective because of their excessive dependence on local governments. In the case of environmental protection, for instance, the center relies on local environmental protection bureaus (EPBs) to implement environmental policies at the provincial and municipal levels down to the district/county level. For their funding, EPBs depend on local governments, which also approve promotions and allocate resources and personnel.[26] This dependence leaves EPBs financially vulnerable and under intense pressure from growth-driven local officials.[27] These EPBs are, therefore, often cash-strapped and understaffed (or with staff that lacks adequate training).[28]

Local and Personal Income Gains

As discussed earlier, the fiscal revenue share of local governments has plummeted since the tax reform of 1994, while their share of spending on social programs has increased.[29] This shortfall in revenue has led to widespread corruption at the local level. In the case of the environment, local governments ignore polluting companies and pressure local EPBs to do the same in order to maintain the local government's tax revenue stream and prevent social unrest[30] and at the same time be able to continue to collect pollution-related fines.[31]

Growth and land policies are also vulnerable to corruption because of the profits local officials can make, as they control both land and building projects. Local officials often seize collectively owned farmland, providing little or no compensation to the displaced, and sell the land at a significant profit. This system gives local officials a powerful incentive to ignore central land management directives.[32]

In addition, local officials often have a personal stake in a province's major enterprises, and when these enterprises are the target of a suit or mediation regarding pollution or labor violations, local officials are quick to become involved and able to sway the court to rule in the favor of the enterprises.[33]

All these weaknesses plague nearly all policy areas of interest to the United States. The next section shows how local governments blatantly ignore central rules and regulations in key areas and why the United States should care. The last sections discuss the steps the center is taking to improve local implementation of its policies in key areas and recommend that the United States, in addition to seeking top-down commitments, should build interest coalitions at the local level.

How Center-Local Relations Affect Key Policies (and Why the United States Should Care)

Environmental Policies

China is on the cusp of environmental catastrophe. According to the World Bank, just 1 percent of China's urban population of 560 million people breathes safe air;[34] 300 million people in China have no access to clean water. Pollution is said to be responsible for 710,000 to 760,000 deaths a year,[35] and official Chinese estimates peg the economic cost of pollution at 8 to 12 percent of China's annual GDP. Environment- and pollution-related protests have increased nearly 30 percent per year since 2000.[36] China's nascent environmental movement has the potential to galvanize nationwide support, cutting across regional and socioeconomic boundaries, and presenting the organized opposition the Chinese Communist Party so fears.[37] Clearly, environmental degradation is upping the ante on China's economic development and social stability considerations (see chapters 6 and 7).

Beijing has attempted to rally support for environmental awareness. The Beijing Olympics in 2008 is being marketed as the "Green Olympics," and stringent environmental standards for a range of new investment projects have been passed.

Despite the tough talk, however, local authorities have thwarted the center's environmental policy at every turn. Local government corruption, cover-ups, misreporting, and lax enforcement have been the rule, rather than the exception, with respect to environmental regulation. Central-government inspections in October 2006 revealed that local governments had checked just 30 percent of projects for compliance before approval, and nearly half of the projects checked did not implement the required pollution controls.[38] In December 2006, the State Environmental Protection Agency (SEPA) noted that national targets to reduce particular pollutants (such as sulfur dioxide) had not been met and that levels had actually risen despite the fact that local governments had broadly reported having hit their targets.[39]

Intellectual Property Policies

The US economy increasingly relies on intellectual property as a fundamental value, and in the fight for global IPR protection today, China is a key battleground.

Despite the central government's efforts to reduce the level of counterfeiting and trademark infringement, IPRs remain fluid throughout much of China. US industry groups variously estimate the problem in the tens of billions of dollars, but any estimate is impracticable. Although IPR protection and enforcement is improving, the problem is outstripping the ability of Chinese authorities to manage or contain it. It is no longer simply a problem for the domestic Chinese market: Chinese products made up 79 percent of the counterfeit goods seized by the European Union in 2006[40] and 81 percent of the total domestic value of US mid-year FY2007 seizures.[41]

Although Beijing has stepped up efforts to combat IPR violations through campaigns and legislation,[42] local officials, with much at stake in preserving IPR-infringing enterprises, have proved a significant obstacle (see earlier section). Raids and seizures take place occasionally, but for the pirates, the profits they can earn far outweigh the risk of punishment. In 2000, average fines in administrative IPR cases were $792, average compensation in those cases for brand owners was $19, and criminal prosecution proceedings were carried out in just 1 in 500 cases[43]—with this record, legal action is hardly a deterrent.

Consumer/Product Safety Policies

Be it adulterated cooking oil, toxic toothpaste, counterfeit medicines, poisonous dog food, or lead-tainted toys, China's record on product safety is a matter of grave concern to consumers in China and throughout the world. With some 80 percent of toys sold in the United States made in China, import safety issues have become a hot topic. In March 2006, Mega Brands, Inc. recalled 3.8 million magnetic building sets made in China, and in August 2007, Mattel recalled 10.5 million Chinese-made toys.[44]

Farm-raised seafood imports from China have also caused a great deal of concern. Chinese exports of agricultural and seafood products to the United States quadrupled from 1996 to 2006, making China the second leading exporter of seafood to the United States. However, between October 2006 and May 2007, the US Food and Drug Administration (FDA) found Chinese seafood contaminated with banned antimicrobial agents such as carcinogens malachite green, nitrofuran, and gentian violet.[45]

Consumer/product safety is of significant concern in Beijing, not only because it threatens China's export juggernaut but also because China's domestic consumers are themselves increasingly restive about the issue. While the central government has acknowledged the problem and taken steps to correct it, local governments continue to ignore it.

Labor and Trade Laws

China's success in implementing labor laws is also of critical interest to the United States, both for humanitarian and economic competitiveness reasons. Chinese workers operate in unsafe conditions and earn very low wages. Despite central regulations to protect them, local government officials, in collusion with factory owners, continue to abuse the workers.[46]

The brick kiln scandal is an extreme example of the gap between central labor laws and local implementation. In August 2007, authorities were alerted to a massive forced labor operation in brick kilns, mines, and workshops.[47] A subsequent investigation discovered 67,000 kilns, mines, and workshops without licenses,[48] and 1,340 people were rescued from forced labor.[49] Reports have surfaced that local government officials, including the police force, were aware of the violations but did little to protect the workers.[50]

In addition to labor laws, local governments routinely violate trade laws. They are often guilty of unfair subsidies and industrial dumping, two particularly significant US concerns. Free or considerably underpriced land is a common subsidy local authorities offer investors in favored projects. Under-cost products factories make at the behest of local governments seeking simply to keep those businesses up and running—against the wishes of Beijing—is one cause of dumping.

Corrupt land transactions are another major problem, as mentioned earlier, particularly with regard to compensation. According to official central audits, local governments often pay little or no compensation to displaced people, misappropriating funds designated for land compensation to give staff bonuses or make up budget shortfalls.[51]

Local governments are responsible for nearly 20 percent of China's investment,[52] much of which is misdirected into sectors with excess capacity, such as steel,[53] while ignoring sectors with more long-term promise, such as labor-intensive agriculture.[54] In addition, to attract both foreign and domestic businesses, local governments turn a blind eye to a wide range of central government laws, allowing companies to ignore minimum wage laws,[55] suppressing union organizations,[56] and granting asylum to environmentally noncompliant businesses.[57]

What It Means for Hu and Wen

President Hu's ambitious Scientific Development Concept, enshrined into Party doctrine at the 17th Party Congress, as well as the goal of a "harmonious society," effectively challenges the status quo by asserting the importance of balance and stability ahead of growth at all cost. As such, the center is on a collision course with existing tensions in center-local relations. To implement its "rebalancing" campaign, Beijing will have to exert its will on local authorities in ways that have been particularly challenging for the past few years.[58]

Hu has taken steps over the past few years to gain better local control, for himself and his political allies in Beijing. He devoted much of his initial five years in office to ensuring that a cadre of like-minded, trusted associates stocked key provincial positions throughout China. Now that he has made considerable headway toward this goal, he arguably has more direct provincial reach than any of his predecessors in memory. Whether the existence of these leaders and Hu's personal authority over them will be adequate to overcome the challenges to local adherence to central policy is an open question.

Steps the Center Is Taking

The central government has taken significant steps to strengthen the effectiveness of its policies and improve its capacity to implement them.

Environmental Policy. In a major move to streamline environmental policy, for example, the March 2008 National People's Congress upgraded environmental issues to the ministry level, replacing SEPA with a Ministry of Environmental Protection. The new ministry will have more staff, a larger budget, and a wider range of responsibilities, including pollution prevention and clean-up and biodiversity management.[59] It is as yet unknown how locally managed EPBs will be reformed, if at all. Additionally, the State Council approved the appointment of six interregional environmental inspectors to increase central government control.[60] One of the most promising efforts of the central government to incentivize environmental policy is its Green GDP Program, which uses "green GDP," determined by subtracting the cost of environmental damage from net GDP, to evaluate the performance of local officials.[61] Though the initiative remains alive, it hit a snag when green GDP was found to be almost zero in some provinces due to the severity of pollution[62] and local officials opposed it.[63] The central government has also developed a "green credit" policy, which suspends lending to polluting companies, and a "green trade" policy, which suspends a polluting company's ability to export.[64]

Consumer/Product Safety. The central government launched a four-month campaign in August 2007 to improve product quality, specifically targeting items such as farm produce, pork, drugs, and exported products linked to human health, and including such measures as a nationwide quality monitoring system.[65] The monitoring system is also part of a larger five-year plan announced in May 2007 and is scheduled to cover 90 percent of the country by 2010.[66] In August 2007, the government also announced an RMB8.8 billion pledge to improve the food and drug safety infrastructure, which will include the renovation of drug testing.[67] Also included in the increased efforts is a new accountability system that makes local governments responsible for the quality of food and drugs manufactured in their jurisdictions and punishes officials for substandard food and drug quality.[68] The government is taking the problem seriously: In July 2007, China executed Zheng Xiaoyu, head of China's State Food and Drug Administration, for taking bribes to approve a substandard antibiotic that led to the deaths of at least 10 people.[69]

Land Policies. The central government issued land policies in September 2006 to combat implementation problems associated with progrowth policies, including a supervisory system to oversee urban land transactions,[70] a National Land Superintendency, and increased inspections.[71] The policies indicate that compliance with land use policy will be used as a performance indicator for leaders at all government levels.[72] Furthermore, local governments will be required to list the revenues they receive from land sales, which will help reduce corruption.[73] Additionally, new laws that came into effect in January 2007 put restrictions on land sales and raised compensation and land use taxes.[74] The central government has also stepped up punishments of local officials, punishing three local officials in August 2006 for permitting construction of an unauthorized power station[75] and a land official in December 2006 for approving shady land deals.[76]

Labor Laws. New labor laws that came into effect in January 2008 require written contracts for employees, limit the use of temporary laborers, make firing employees more difficult, and give unions the power to bargain with employers.[77] In response to the kiln scandal mentioned above, a clause was added to the law stipulating punishment of local officials who "overlook or tolerate labor rights violations."[78]

Intellectual Property Rights. On the IPR front, China's action plans every year are intended as multidisciplinary educational, administrative, and punitive exercises to improve IPR protection. Recent efforts to expand education to the provinces are more ambitious than in years past. In 2006, China raised the number of IPR service centers to 50 nationwide and established a national "12312" helpline. The service centers are responsible for receiving and handling complaints about IPR infringements and offering consulting services.[79] Most importantly for center-local considerations, the various agencies with IPR responsibility have focused on streamlining cooperation, particularly between central ministries and relevant administrative entities and law enforcement and judicial departments.

Implications for the United States and Policy Recommendations

For the United States, managing national concerns on trade and economic issues with a national government as difficult to penetrate as China's is a tall prospect as it is. When that government also has very limited power to control the behavior of its own citizens because local officials protect them, the difficulties become more complex. As noted earlier, local governments have traditionally maintained a strong degree of autonomy from the center. But that does not mean that they have always subverted, or will always subvert, the center's interests. Nor should Beijing accept the center-local disconnect as an excuse for shortcomings in China's governance.

To ensure local government compliance with central-government laws, China will have to stop venerating "growth at any cost" and increase funding of local social programs. As Richard Baum, political science professor at the University of California Los Angeles observes, in discussing how to improve enforcement of food safety regulations, for example, "until the central government fixes the fiscal starvation of local governments, who are funded by a combination of local taxes, kickbacks, and bribes, the problem . . . will remain unsolved."[80]

The United States, for its part, will have to build interest coalitions in China that are not just top down but also offer a broader national consensus, including at the local level, in favor of US positions. Such interest coalition building may require more nuance, patience, and effort than most Americans are used to exercising. The current US temptation to pound away at the top, to browbeat Beijing into agreeing to "do something" about US concerns, may satisfy American lawyerly urges, but it does not take the reality of the governance dynamic in China into account. It will certainly not be effective in the long term at delivering meaningful results for US interests.

At a minimum, visiting US officials, politicians, and business groups should venture beyond Beijing and Shanghai to explore China's lesser-known provincial capitals, establish working relationships with local-level officials, and become familiar with their respective provincial policy priorities. In this regard, expansion of US consulate presence in China's provinces, including the posting of commercial and economic officers, should be encouraged.

Notes

1. Gong Ting, "Corruption and Local Governance: The Double Identity of Chinese Local Governments in Market Reform," *Pacific Review* 19, no. 1 (March 2006): 85–102.

2. Zheng Yongnian, *De Facto Federalism in China: Reforms and Dynamics of Central-Local Relations* (Singapore: World Scientific Publishing Co., 2007).

3. Gong Ting, "Corruption and Local Governance," 85–102.

4. Joseph Kahn and Jim Yardley, "As China Roars, Pollution Reaches Deadly Extremes," *New York Times*, August 26, 2007, www.nytimes.com (accessed October 9, 2007).

5. Gong Ting, "Corruption and Local Governance," 85–102.

6. Ibid.

7. Hehui Jin, Yingyi Qian, and Barry Weingast, "Regional Decentralization and Fiscal Incentives: Federalism, Chinese Style" (working paper 99013, Stanford University, Department of Economics, March 1999).

8. Zheng Yongnian, *De Facto Federalism in China.*

9. Andrew C. Mertha, "China's 'Soft' Centralization: Shifting Tiao/Kuai Authority Relations," *China Quarterly* 184 (December 2005): 791–810.

10. Zheng Yongnian, *De Facto Federalism in China*.

11. Yasheng Huang, "Political Institutions and Fiscal Reforms in China," *Problems of Post-Communism* 48, no. 1 (January/February 2001).

12. Guoli Liu and Lowell Dittmer, "Introduction: The Dynamics of Deep Reform," in *China's Deep Reform: Domestic Politics in Transition*, eds. Lowell Dittmer and Guoli Liu (Lanham, MD: Rowman & Littlefield, 2006).

13. *China Energy Weekly*, "Special Report: Blaming Local Governments," September 8, 2006, www.lexis-nexis.com.

14. Ibid.

15. Ibid.

16. Ibid.

17. Chen Gang, "Lessons for the Taihu Algae Crisis," *Straits Times*, September 1, 2007, www.lexis-nexis.com.

18. Elizabeth Economy and Kenneth Lieberthal, "Scorched Earth: Will Environmental Risks in China Overwhelm Its Opportunities?" *Harvard Business Review* (June 2007).

19. Elizabeth Economy, "China vs. Earth: Searching for a Green Path to Growth," *Nation*, May 7, 2007, 29.

20. Carlos Wing-hung Lo and Gerald Erick Fryxell, "Government and Societal Support of Environmental Enforcement in China: An Empirical Study in Guangzhou," *Journal of Development Studies* 41, no. 4 (May 2005): 558–88.

21. Tracy Quek, "The Man Who Wants to Save a Lake: Beijing's Efforts to Protect the Environment Thwarted by Local Officials' Subterfuge in their Drive for Growth," *Straits Times*, January 21, 2007, www.lexis-nexis.com.

22. Daniel Chow, "Intellectual Property Protection as Economic Policy: Will China Ever Enforce its IP Laws?" (statement at conference on Counterfeiting in China, sponsored by the Congressional-Executive Commission on China, Washington, May 16, 2005), www.cecc.gov.

23. Wang Shanshan, "Cooking Up a Proper Recipe for Safe Food," *China Daily*, May 29, 2007, www.chinadaily.com.cn (accessed October 29, 2007).

24. Eric Priest, "The Future of Music and Film Piracy in China," *Berkeley Technology Law Journal* 21, no. 795 (2006): 820–27.

25. Kan Zu and Bradley Yu, "Getting to the Heart of the Counterfeiting Problem," *Managing International Property* (February 2005).

26. Chen Gang, *Straits Times*, September 1, 2007

27. Koon-Kwai Wong, "Greening of the Chinese Mind: Environmentalism with Chinese Characteristics," *Asia-Pacific Review* 12, no. 2 (November 2005): 39–54.

28. Li Xiaofan, "Environmental Concerns in China: Problems, Policies, and Global Implications," *International Social Science Review* 81, no. 1/2 (2005): 43–57.

29. *China Energy Weekly*, "Special Report: Blaming Local Governments."

30. Benjamin van Rooij, "Implementation of Chinese Environmental Law: Regular Enforcement and Political Campaigns," *Development and Change* 37, no. 1 (2006): 57–74.

31. Congressional-Executive Commission on China, *Annual Report* (Beijing, 2006), www.cecc.gov (accessed on October 24, 2007).

32. Verna Yu, "Former Zhao Ziyang Aide Says PRC Government Unable To Protect Farmer Rights," Agence France Presse, February 28, 2006.

33. Adam Briggs, "China's Pollution Victims: Still Seeking a Dependable Remedy," *Georgetown International Environment Law Review* 18, no. 2 (Winter 2006): 305.

34. Kahn and Yardley, *New York Times.*

35. Ibid.

36. Congressional-Executive Commission on China, *Annual Report.*

37. From March to June 2007, using "new media" tools including chat rooms, cell phones, and websites such as Flickr.com, residents in Xiamen, Fujian Province campaigned against construction of a petrochemical plant, sending over one million emails and letters of complaint to the local government. The issue had been raised at the National People's Congress in March. On June 1, around 10,000 residents took part in street protests. Faced with the first, large-scale protest by urban residents to gain nationwide attention since the Tiananmen Square crackdown, the nervous Xiamen City government announced that the project was being put on hold pending an investigation by central government authorities. See BBC, "'Text Protest' Blocks China Plant," May 30, 2007, http://news.bbc.co.uk.

38. Xinhua News Agency, "A Clean Environment Stems from a Clean Government," November 4, 2006, http://news.xinhuanet.com (accessed October 1, 2007).

39. Quek, *Straits Times.*

40. European Commission, Taxation and Customs Union, "Summary of Community Customs Activities on Counterfeit and Piracy," (Brussels, 2006), http://ec.europa.eu (accessed October 30, 2007).

41. US Customs and Border Protection, "Intellectual Property Rights: Seizure Statistics, Mid-Year FY2007," www.stopfakes.gov (accessed October 30, 2007).

42. In April 2006, the central government launched the Action Program on IPR Protection for 2006–07, which stipulates a stronger legal framework for IPR protection, including closer cooperation between law enforcement and courts, a supervising administration, and strengthened management of trademark and copyright departments at the grass-roots level. The plan also urges local government cooperation and calls for punishments for local officials who fail to protect IPRs or cover up IPR infringements. Xinhua News Agency, "Officials to Be Punished for Lax IPR Enforcement," April 27, 2006, www.china.org.cn (accessed October 29, 2007) and "Government Warns Officials Against IPR Violations," April 28, 2006, http://english.peopledaily.com.cn (accessed October 29, 2007).

43. Chow, "Intellectual Property Protection as Economic Policy."

44. Associated Press, "Mattel Issues New Massive China Toy Recall," August 14, 2007, www.msnbc.msn.com (accessed November 16, 2007).

45. Geoffrey S. Becker, *Food and Agricultural Imports from China*, Congressional Research Service Reports and Issue Briefs, July 1, 2007, www.lexis-nexis.com.

46. Joseph Kahn and David Barboza, "China Passes a Sweeping Labor Law," *New York Times*, June 30, 2007, www.nytimes.com (accessed October 9, 2007).

47. Xinhua News Agency, "1,340 Rescued from Forced Labor," August 13, 2007, www.chinadaily.com.cn (accessed October 1, 2007).

48. Ibid.

49. Ibid.

50. Howard W. French, "Beijing's Lack of Penalties in Labor Cases Stirs Outrage," *New York Times*, July 17, 2007, www.lexis-nexis.com.

51. Xinhua News Agency, "Central Government Seeks Strengthened Authority to Improve Efficiency," March 15, 2007, http://english.peopledaily.com.cn (accessed October 2, 2007).

52. David Lague, "China Punishes 3 for Flouting Growth Curbs," *International Herald Tribune*, August 17, 2008, www.iht.com.

53. Barry Naughton, "The Assertive Center: Beijing Moves Against Local Government Control of Land," *China Leadership Monitor*, no. 20 (Winter 2007), www.hoover.org.

54. Wu Zhong, "GDP Isn't Everything," *The Standard*, March 21, 2005, www.thestandard.com.hk (accessed October 1, 2007).

55. Congressional-Executive Committee on China, *Annual Report*.

56. Unisumoon, "China Maps Out Rules to Protect Workers' Rights," China Internet Information Center, www.china.org.cn (accessed October 31, 2007).

57. *China Law and Practice*, "China Tightens Its Environmental Law Control over New Investment Projects," April 2007, www.lexis-nexis.com.

58. The central government has made implementation of labor laws a priority due to the impact of local-government malfeasance on social stability. In 2005, 300,000 labor-related lawsuits were filed, and in 2003 over 515,000 workers were involved in nearly 11,000 strikes, demonstrations, marches, and collective petitions, a significant increase over the 1,500 in 1994 (Congressional-Executive Commission on China, *Annual Report*, 2006).

59. Wu Jiao and Fu Jing, "Ministry Will Give More Weight to Green Issues," *China Daily*, March 13, 2008, www.chinadaily.com.cn.

60. Chinaorg.cn, "Li Shishi Summarizes in 6 Characters Super-Department Reform" ["Lishi shi liuzi gaikuo dabuzhi gaige"], March 13, 2008, www.chinaorg.cn.

61. Economy and Lieberthal, "Scorched Earth."

62. Kahn and Yardley, *New York Times*.

63. Economy and Lieberthal, "Scorched Earth."

64. *Economist*, "Don't Drink the Water and Don't Breathe the Air," January 24, 2008.

65. Xinhua News Agency, "China Takes Measures to Enhance Product Quality, Food Safety," August 27, 2007, http://news.xinhuanet.com (accessed October 29, 2007).

66. Xinhua News Agency, "China Unveils Food, Drug Safety Plan from 2006 to 2010," May 12, 2007, www.chinadaily.com.cn (accessed October 29, 2007).

67. Xinhua News Agency, "China to Invest $1.2b to Improve Food, Drug Supervision," August 8, 2007, http://news.xinhuanet.com (accessed October 29, 2007).

68. Kristine Kwok, "Local Authorities to be Held Accountable for Product Quality," *South China Morning Post*, July 14, 2007.

69. Alexa Olesen, "China Ex-Food and Drug Chief Executed," *Washington Post*, July 10, 2007, www.washingtonpost.com (accessed October 29, 2007).

70. Naughton, "The Assertive Center."

71. Ibid.

72. Ibid.

73. Ibid.

74. Xinhua News Agency, "China Sends Out Inspectors to Monitor Local Gov't Land Use," December 17, 2006, http://news.xinhuanet.com (accessed October 1, 2007).

75. Lague, *International Herald Tribune*.

76. Xinhua News Agency, "China Sends Out Inspectors."

77. Joseph Kahn and David Barboza, "China Passes a Sweeping Labor Law," *New York Times*, June 30, 2007, www.nytimes.com (accessed October 9, 2007).

78. Jamil Anderlini, "Wary Welcome for China's Labour Reform," *Financial Times*, July 2, 2007, 6.

79. Embassy of the People's Republic of China in the United States of America, "China Sets Up National IPR Protection System," August 28, 2006, www.chinaembassy.org.

80. Quoted in Winghei Kwok, "China: Government Grants Foreign and Domestic Journalists Access to Factories," AsiaMedia, www.asiamedia.ucla.edu (accessed October 29, 2007).

5

Corruption in China: Crisis or Constant?

Resolutely punishing and effectively preventing corruption bears on the popular support for the Party and on its very survival, and is therefore a major political task the Party must attend to at all times.

—Hu Jintao, October 15, 2007[1]

Since the spring of 1989, when anger over high inflation and "official profiteering" brought people out on the streets in support of student-led antigovernment demonstrations, the ruling party in China has recognized that the fight against corruption is a matter of life and death. Yet, two decades later, central authorities continue to face the intractable problem of corruption, especially at the local level. Deficient center-local relations is a major reason why central authorities have been unable to effectively check rising local-level corruption. Some observers suggest that the Chinese state is degenerating into a maze of local "mafia states," as corrupt officials form alliances with criminal networks and use public authority for private plunder.[2] There is no shortage of highly publicized cases of high crimes and misdemeanors—the latest being the corruption scandal that brought down former politburo member, Shanghai Party Secretary Chen Liangyu.

Although some have concluded that either the Party is losing the war on corruption or its attack against it is a sham, evidence suggests that after worsening significantly during the 1980s and 1990s, corruption has remained at roughly the same level since about 2000.[3] As such, corruption appears to have transitioned from being a mounting crisis to becoming a constant threat, suggesting that, despite worrying losses, on the whole China's economy will continue to pay little price: The problem has yet to undercut growth rates or deter foreign direct investment. While corruption does not appear an imminent threat to the Party's ruling status, the political costs in terms of damage to the Party's reputation and legitimacy over the long term do, however, bear watching.

The Party faces tough policy choices in the next phase of China's modernization. The question is whether the leadership has the sufficient will and wherewithal to fully implement its current political-administrative reform policies and reconfigure center-local relations; make the system more responsive, accountable, and transparent; and allow for greater public participation and supervision in government on its path to "democracy with Chinese characteristics." The leadership's response will have an impact not only on curbing corruption but also on the future of the Party and the nation.

Corruption Rising to a Plateau

There is no question that corruption is a serious problem in China. In the past two years, Chen Liangyu and two dozen other Shanghai officials have been charged with "lending" RMB4.3 billion from the municipal social security fund to real estate speculators. Officials linked to one deceased politburo member (Huang Ju) and one sitting member (Jia Qinglin) were detained on bribery charges. The former head of China's State Food and Drug Administration, Zheng Xiaoyu, was executed for accepting bribes to approve a substandard antibiotic that killed at least 10 people. Minister of Finance Jin Renqing lost his job after he was implicated in a sex-for-promotions scandal. And, Beijing Vice-Mayor Liu Zhihua was charged with corruption relating to the vast 2008 Olympics redevelopment project.

On the surface, it would seem that China is on the verge of a crisis.[4] Measuring corruption is, however, notoriously difficult. Neither "systematic" aggregate data nor anecdotal evidence drawn from high-profile cases is necessarily reliable or conclusive; moreover, many of the available indicators can be interpreted in different ways. Rather than showing corruption spiraling out of control, such "hard" indicators as the number of officials indicted and convicted of corruption suggest a distinct leveling off in the incidence of corruption in the past decade.

Experts' evaluations of corruption in China have also not changed dramatically in almost a decade (figure 5.1). Although the trend in the PRS Group data is sharply upward between 1995 and 1996, it flattens out in the later 1990s. Transparency International and World Bank indices also plateau during the same period. In addition, even though China's scores worsened during the 1990s, the perceived level of corruption in China was not extreme by global standards. Both Transparency International and the World Bank rank China in the middle two quartiles of score distribution, worse than average but not among the most corrupt states. Transparency International, in fact, shows it regressing toward the mean. Indeed, China dropped from being the fifth most corrupt out of 54 countries in Transparency International's 1995 Corruption Perceptions Index to 78 out of 158

Figure 5.1   Perceived level of corruption in China, 1984–2006

worst possible score in percent

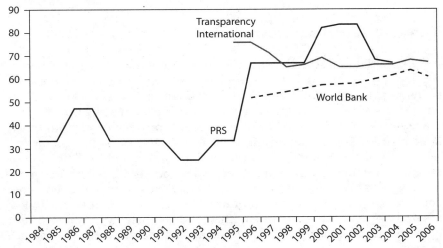

Notes: All indices are recalculated so that high scores correspond to high levels of corruption. PRS data measure the "risk" from corruption and not necessarily its level. For purposes of visual clarity, World Bank governance scores for 1997, 1999, and 2001, which are not estimated in the original dataset, were estimated based on the average of the previous and following years.

Sources: PRS Group, *International Country Risk Guide*; Transparency International, Corruption Perceptions Index, www.transparency.org; World Bank Institute, *Worldwide Governance Indicators*, www.worldbank.org/wbi/governance.

in 2005, 70 out of 163 in 2006, and 72 out of 179 in the 2007 index. These estimates put China on a par with countries including Brazil, India, and Mexico and above Russia and many of the newly democratized former Soviet republics.

High levels of corruption are not unique to the post-1978 reform period. Corruption was widespread during China's imperial period and exploded during the later nationalist period. The Party launched anticorruption drives in 1951–52 and again in 1963–65, although in the turmoil of the Cultural Revolution it is difficult to estimate how prevalent corruption was. In this light, reforms in the 1980s did not necessarily produce a surge in corruption but rather allowed for it to return to earlier levels. The observed leveling off since the mid-1990s might thus be viewed as a return to an "equilibrium level" of corruption.

Although the incidence and extent of corruption may have leveled off, corruption can become more "intense" in the sense that the stakes involved rise or the extent of high-level corruption worsens, precisely what evidence suggests happened in China during the first two decades of reform.[5] Since roughly 2000, however, such steep increases in corruption intensity appear to have given way to what might be interpreted as either a leveling off in intensity or a shift to more moderate increases.[6]

Threat of "Local Kleptocracies"

Aggregate data presented in the previous section may suggest that corruption is not spiraling out of control, but are some segments of the state becoming "local kleptocracies"? Several recent cases display key characteristics associated with kleptocracy, chief among them being that of Chen Liangyu.[7] In September 2006, Chen was abruptly removed from office amid charges that he had arranged illicit loans to real estate developers, with RMB3.45 billion going to the Fuxi Corporation and RMB1 billion to Huawen Holdings. Both Fuxi and Huawen had strong political connections: Chen's son Chen Weili managed Huawen's Shanghai operations, and billionaire Zhang Rongkun controlled Fuxi, which in turn controlled a variety of real estate ventures. Zhang was accused of bribing Chen, other members of the Shanghai political apparatus, and various corporate managers.

Chen certainly was a "chief and a thief," but it is not clear that he had converted the Shanghai apparatus into a graft machine. On the contrary, it appears that he and a relatively small circle of close associates were involved. Most of the senior leadership in Shanghai escaped Chen's fall unscathed. More critically, the Shanghai scandal was part of a much wider phenomenon involving the misappropriation of public funds and corruption across China.

Real estate markets in Shanghai and other urban areas have been red hot for years, fueling high demand for land and investment capital while generating windfall profits for real estate speculators and developers. Under these conditions, it is hardly surprising that officials with access to large blocks of public funds might be tempted to misuse them. According to the State Auditing Administration, RMB4.8 billion in pension and social insurance funds was misappropriated between 2000 and 2006, including RMB1.02 billion in Guangzhou and large sums in Henan, Heilongjiang, Hunan, Zhejiang, and Sichuan.[8] The recent surge in big-money corruption cases can thus be seen as a "feeding frenzy" borne not out of kleptocracy but rather a flood of investment and speculation.

More worrying, however, is new evidence of two forms of corruption that could corrode the state's viability as a governing institution and threaten the legitimacy of the Chinese Communist Party: rising venality of office and alliances between corrupt officials and organized crime, as well as indications that younger officials are increasingly involved.

In the past several years, buying and selling of offices has emerged as a major problem. Perhaps the best known case is the 2003 scandal in Heilongjiang, which revealed a network of bribes-for-jobs involving not only local officials but also senior provincial officials, including the former provincial governor and later minister of land resources, Tian Fengshan. Ultimately, Tian received a life sentence for accepting RMB4 million in bribes from his subordinates.

Another area of concern is evidence of the criminalization of the state. Scholar Minxin Pei argues that the problem has become widespread and offers as evidence 50 cases of what he terms "local mafia states."[9] Perhaps the most serious of these cases occurred in Xiamen, where a ring controlled by well-connected entrepreneur Lai Changxing smuggled RMB53 billion worth of petroleum, cars, cigarettes, and other goods into the country between 1996 and 1999 by buying off most of the municipal apparatus, several provincial officials, and even a vice minister of public security and the general in charge of the People's Liberation Army General Staff's military intelligence bureau. In all, over 600 people, including 360 officials and cadres, were said to be involved. Ultimately, 10 were executed and six received suspended death sentences.[10]

For a Party concerned about preventing rot within its own ranks and avoiding the fate of the former Soviet Union, another worrying phenomenon is that younger cadres are increasingly becoming involved in such crimes. In 2007, it was reported that more than 40 percent of those accused of graft and corruption in Guangzhou were well-educated, high-ranking officials under the age of 45.[11]

In sum, while there is evidence of collusion between officials, police, and organized crime, as well as police corruption, it is hard to determine the severity of the "local mafia state" problem. The roughly 50 cases reported in secondary literature, for example, are spread across some 15 years going back to the early 1990s. Even assuming that the small number of reported cases represents a fraction of the total, available data simply do not appear sufficient to signal that the "local mafia" problem is a serious threat to state integrity. Similarly, the number of officials reportedly punished is so small that it appears that the mafia state exists only in isolated localities and has not become a widespread problem.[12]

Nearly three decades of sustained rapid growth have transformed the Chinese economy and created vast wealth. Speculators and investors are making (and in some cases losing) fortunes. And China's cadres are cashing in on the boom as well. They are skimming off a percentage of the government's investment in new infrastructure, taking a cut from windfall profits from land transfers to private developers, and illegally lending public funds to cash-hungry investors.[13] There is little question that all this comes at a considerable monetary cost; it is estimated that corruption costs could be as high as 3 to 4 percent of China's annual GDP, with corruption-related capital flight costing an additional 2 percent of GDP.[14] But the costs are borne in the context of a rapidly growing economy, which can, arguably, absorb the negative consequences of corruption better than an economy that is either stagnant or growing at a marginal rate.

In a perverse way, the lure of corrupt income is an incentive for cadres to keep the economic boom going. As such, corruption in China today is at least partially a byproduct of growth, not a barrier to it, as is so often the case. China also continues to attract more foreign investment than any other developing country: Total foreign direct investment, including capital flows to the financial sector, hit US$82.7 billion in 2007, up 13.8 percent from 2006.[15]

Over the long term, however, as China's economic growth slows and it endeavors to move up the value chain, the economic costs of corruption could pose a more significant challenge. Moreover, the impact of corruption in the sociopolitical realm has not been benign. Public anger over official corruption has been the catalyst for much of the social unrest that has rocked China in recent years and the reason why the Party leadership acknowledges that it is a "life and death" issue.

Is the Party Over?

Since the late 1990s, the number of officially reported "public order disturbances" has increased dramatically, from around 32,000 in 1990 to 87,000 in 2005.[16] In many cases, anger over local-government corruption has triggered protests, too often erupting into violent clashes between tens of thousands of protestors and police.[17] Most recently, "netizens" blamed the widespread power shortages and transportation problems during China's worst snowstorm in decades on local-level corruption. Public outcry over the collapse of school buildings due to shoddy construction during the Sichuan earthquake likewise prompted nervous officials to promise a thorough investigation and punish those responsible.[18]

Perhaps the most prevalent cause of widespread social unrest is anger over the expropriation of farmland by local officials with little or no compensation to the displaced, often in collusion with developers. In January 2008, it was reported that 2,700 officials had been referred for prosecution on land use violation charges and that over 31,000 cases were under investigation.[19] The May 2007 incident in which police were called in to remove villagers who had laid siege to and then looted the homes of officials in 13 villages in Guangdong Province they suspected of engaging in corrupt land deals[20] is an example of the stories that appear almost daily in the local Chinese press. More worrisome for the authorities—given China's historical link between peasant-led rebellion and regime change—in an apparent organized challenge to official policy: Farmers from Heilongjiang, Shaanxi, Jiangsu, and Tianjin published declarations on the internet in December 2007 claiming ownership of all land in their villages, including land requisitioned by the local government. In response, the State Council issued a notice reiterating opposition to any form of privatization or illegal seizure of farmland and rounded up those responsible for the internet postings.[21]

Thus far, most of the incidents of social unrest remain localized and have been quickly suppressed. Corruption has produced hot spots of unrest, but these flare-ups have failed to set off major wildfires. Most important, there is little evidence that anger over corruption has reached critical levels in cities. So far, the central leadership has been able to cast itself as an opponent of corruption and defender of the "little guy" who bears the brunt of local-level malfeasance.

Nevertheless, in the event of a serious economic downturn or a surge in inflation as happened in 1989, corruption could become a more volatile political factor. More insidious is its long-term potential to undermine the Party's reputation and legitimacy if the public perceives Beijing as being incapable of enforcing its own policies and providing basic public goods, including clean government. In the *2007 Blue Book on China's Society*, published by the Chinese Academy of Social Sciences, cadres surveyed continued to list corruption among their top three concerns.[22] Aware of the high stakes, the central leadership continues to prioritize anticorruption efforts, though to what effect will be discussed in more detail below.

Causes of Corruption Debated

Not surprisingly, corruption has featured prominently in the debate among Chinese intellectuals, with various sides proffering their views on the causes and solutions. It is generally agreed that China's economic reforms, particularly market liberalization in the post-1992 period, opened up more opportunities and provided more incentives for corruption. Traditional reliance on *guanxi* or social connections that blur the line between legal and illegal behavior spread unchecked, filling the vacuum that emerged as norms and values that had previously guided economic and social behavior evaporated during the early stages of reform. At the same time, decentralization in the 1980s and early 1990s amid lagging political system reform, particularly legal reform, expanded local officials' power over funds and resources, giving them more opportunity to engage in corruption, and seriously weakened the central government's ability to combat corruption. Perhaps nowhere are the deficiencies in center-local relations more evident than in the difficulties Beijing has encountered in fighting corruption at the local level, where officials continue to skirt rules and conceal wrongdoing. Given the risk-reward ratio, lack of moral restraints, and official emphasis on rapid growth and wealth accumulation, it is little wonder that corruption has flourished.

Intellectuals, however, widely disagree on the solution to China's corruption; their disagreements center on the role of the Party/state in the economy as well as the pace and scope of political reform. In brief, those on the "Right" argue that Party/state interference distorts the market, breeds official corruption and rent-seeking behavior, and obstructs further reform. In calling for more rapid economic privatization, marketization, and a reduction in the role of the Party/state, many also call for wider and more rapid political reform, citing China's lack of democracy as the root cause of corruption. In contrast, "New Left" intellectuals see neither the free market nor democracy as a panacea, calling instead for a reassertion of the state's role in correcting market failures and better addressing the sociopolitical problems that have emerged in the course of modernization. While calling for political reform, they eschew Western liberal democratic mechanisms—pointing to corruption in countries that have experienced rapid political transitions such as Russia and the former Soviet republics, as well as established democracies such as India and the Philippines. As Yan Sun notes, while the Party's anticorruption policy has proceeded "economically in the direction desired by the new right, it proceeds politically in the direction urged by the new left . . . though in neither case as much as each group would like to see."[23]

Combating Corruption—Is China Campaigned Out?

By the mid-1990s there was widespread concern that decentralization was adversely affecting China's socioeconomic and political development. Granting more autonomy to local officials expanded their monopolistic and discretionary powers over budgets, resources, and investment decisions—increasing the opportunities and incentives to engage in corruption while simultaneously weakening the central government's ability to combat these abuses. The subsequent effort to recentralize, especially the tax reforms adopted in 1994, administrative restructurings, downsizing of China's vast bureaucracy, and attempts to create a professional civil service system, has helped the Party reassert control. However, as discussed in chapter 4, problems in implementing central policies at the local level persist; local officials continue to face the challenge of balancing what are often competing demands from Beijing with those of their local constituents and seek to circumvent central commands or ignore "unfunded mandates."

It would be a mistake, however, to conclude that China has devolved into a "decentralized predatory state," in which a self-interested political-economic elite is perpetuating the existing order and obstructing further reform.[24] The central leadership is fully aware of the challenges facing China and has proven remarkably flexible and willing to experiment with solutions, although with varying degrees of success.

Since 1989, the Party has launched a series of high-profile anticorruption campaigns. In 2005, it launched an old-style rectification campaign partly to address corruption but also the "moral degeneration" of its members. While there are indications that such campaigns bolster the image of Beijing as an anticorruption crusader, there is little evidence that they actually help stem the problem. Such campaigns are primarily aimed at abuses that undermine the economy—such as the illegal privatization of state property—and less frequently address crimes that provoke public resentment such as "official profiteering" and extraction of illegal fees from residents. Moreover, these campaigns actually undercut the institutionalization of the legal system in China, as Party censure and disciplinary measures often replace criminal prosecution.[25] The overlapping functions of the Party's Central Commission for Discipline Inspection (CCDI) and people's state procuratorates (state organs of legal supervision), not to mention oversight from local governments, which continue to appoint cadres to these procuratorates—a system in which the offenders are de facto policing themselves—further undermine attempts to curb corruption.

Nevertheless, in April 2008 the Party announced that it would launch another five-year anticorruption campaign in 2008,[26] and in May, it initiated another education campaign exhorting cadres to "be the Party's loyal guards and the masses' close friends."[27] Closer inspection reveals that the Party recognizes that, alongside traditional campaigns, more fundamental if risky political-administrative reforms are necessary to root out corruption. Veteran leader Chen Yu summed up the dilemma facing the Party: "Fight corruption too little and destroy the country; fight it too much and destroy the Party."

In 2007, China established a National Bureau of Corruption Prevention (NBCP), which circumvents local governments and reports directly to the State Council. Focusing on prevention rather than punishment, the NBCP inspects anticorruption work at various levels, closing loopholes in the current system and standardizing policies for anticorruption work. While it has taken a step in the right direction, China still has much to learn from the examples of Singapore and Hong Kong in firmly establishing the rule of law, a truly independent anticorruption agency, and what the Organization for Economic Cooperation and Development (OECD) has termed an "ethics infrastructure," including effective accountability mechanisms, in order to win the war on corruption. Likewise, China should allow the media to play its role as watchdog. Too often the Party has allowed reporting on local-level malfeasance only to clamp down when reporters begin to uncover cases it does not want reported.

Enhancing the investigative authority of the State Auditing Administration, new regulations reducing officials' discretionary power, and controls on cash transfers as well as improvements in the transparency and accountability of state-owned enterprises are also encouraging moves. In addition, the Party announced a major reshuffle of provincial-level judicial officials in January 2008 after it admitted that "China's judicial and procuratorial system has been successively plagued with major graft incidents involving several provinces."[28] However, as long as local Party officials retain authority over the judicial system through the political-legal committees and the selection of personnel through the nomenklatura[29] system, the problem of undue influence will remain.

To address public anger over official corruption, the Supreme People's Procuratorate announced in May 2008 that rural officials would come under greater scrutiny to protect farmers' interests from corrupt bureaucrats.[30] This move follows central government land policies launched in 2006—notably the establishment of a National Land Superintendency—aimed at addressing expropriation of farmland and corruption at local levels by altering the way land markets operate, reducing local-government discretionary power, and reasserting central authorities' oversight.[31]

The central leadership also recognizes the role of the public and even the media in supervising cadres, especially at the local level; a Central Party School publication recently stated that "public administrators must face it and adapt to it."[32] In a speech on anticorruption, Premier Wen Jiabao called for "soliciting public opinions or holding hearings so as to enhance public participation and receive public supervision" and said that "governance transparency should be further improved to safeguard the public rights to knowledge, participation, expression and supervision."[33]

Experiments with public participation and "democratic consultation" are under way, most notably in Wenling City, Zhejiang Province and Wuxi, Jiangsu Province.[34] When the NBCP launched its website soliciting input from the public in December 2007, it crashed due to the overwhelming response from the public. The Party certainly needs to respond to an increasingly "rights conscious" public frustrated with official corruption if it is to maintain the perception that it is capable of providing basic public goods including clean government.

Conclusion and Recommendations

The central leadership faces tough policy choices: Reforms necessary to curb corruption—and maintain Party legitimacy and ruling status over the long term—could prove a slippery slope. As long as the Party remains above the law and free to police itself, particularly at the local level, corruption will remain rampant. An independent judiciary—or at a minimum an independent anticorruption agency reporting directly to the central leadership—needs to be instituted. While the experiences of countries that have undergone rapid transition to liberal democracy suggest that it is not a panacea, there is certainly room for enhanced accountability and transparency and an increased role for the media and public in supervising government—reforms the Party has in fact promised to implement.

As discussed in chapter 3, Shenzhen—China's first special economic zone, where economic reforms were first implemented—could once again be the first to experiment with what, if implemented, could be far-reaching political reforms.[35] To fight corruption, the municipal government's reform plan published online in May 2007 calls for following the example of Hong Kong's Independent Commission Against Corruption (ICAC): passing special legislation in the zone to carry out anticorruption work, expanding the role of public supervision, and guaranteeing the autonomy of the media in reporting on corruption cases. Officials from Shenzhen have reportedly spent time with the ICAC in Hong Kong, and an independent anticorruption agency could be established in the zone as an experiment.

The United States can certainly play a constructive role in China's anticorruption battle. Indeed, the US government and US nongovernmental agencies have been instrumental in the construction of China's legal system and the ongoing implementation of the rule of law. A number of Chinese intellectuals compare present-day China with 19th century America—with its robber barons and Tammany Hall politics—and acknowledge that China can learn a lot from the American experience in combating corruption and establishing clean government.[36]

Notes

1. Xinhua News Agency, "Hu Jintao zai Zhongguo gongchandang di shiqi ci quanguo daibiao dahui shang de baogao" ["Hu Jintao's Report to the 17th Party Congress"], October 15, 2007, http://news.xinhuanet.com.

2. Minxin Pei, *China's Trapped Transition: The Limits of Developmental Autocracy* (Cambridge, MA: Harvard University Press, 2006).

3. Andrew Wedeman, "Corruption: Crisis or Constant?" (background paper for China Balance Sheet project, Peterson Institute for International Economics and Center for Strategic and International Studies, January 28, 2008), www.china balancesheet.org.

4. The CCDI reported that as of June 2007, it had investigated 24,879 cases involving bribes totaling over RMB6 billion. Xinhua News Agency, "Quanguo chachu shangye huilu an 24,879 jian" ["Across the Country 24,879 Cases of Commercial Bribery Have Been Investigated and Prosecuted"], August 19, 2007. In March 2008, it was reported that the procuratorate investigated more than 209,000 officials from 2002 to 2007, down 13.2 percent from the previous five years, in almost 180,000 cases of embezzlement, bribery, dereliction of duty, and rights violation, down 9.9 percent during the same period; the number of convictions rose 30.7 percent to almost 117,000. See Xinhua News Agency, "Zui gao renmin jianchayuan gongzuo baogao" ["Supreme People's Procuratorate Work Report"], March 22, 2008, http://news.xinhuanet.com.

5. Gong Ting, "New Trends in China's Corruption: Change Amid Continuity," in *China's Deep Reform: Domestic Politics in Transition*, eds. Lowell Dittmer and Guoli Liu (Lanham, MD: Rowan & Littlefield, 2006); Andrew Wedeman, "The Intensification of Corruption in China," *China Quarterly*, no. 180 (December 2004): 895–921.

6. For detailed discussion and data, see Wedeman, "Corruption: Crisis or Constant?"

7. Wang Hongyi, "Six More Jailed in Shanghai Fund Scandal," *China Daily*, September 27, 2007; Bill Savadove, "City Assets Boss in Shanghai Scandal," *South*

China Morning Post, October 24, 2006; Bill Savadove, "How Shanghai Fell Down the Vice Pit," *South China Morning Post,* October 20, 2006; Albert Cheng, "Fighting the Wrong Fights," *South China Morning Post,* December 9, 2006; Lilian Yang, "Cadres Tied to Almost Half of City's Graft Cases," *South China Morning Post,* January 24, 2007; Xinhua News Agency, "Investigation of Shanghai's Billionaire Confirmed Underway," June 4, 2003; Xinhua News Agency, "Senior Chinese Leader Calls for Effective Discipline Inspection System," July 2, 2003; Xinhua News Agency, "Mayor Says Shanghai Has Retrieved All Embezzled Pension Funds," January 28, 2007; Xinhua News Agency, "Commentary: CPC Discipline Watchdog Cracks Down on Officials' Collusion with Businesspeople," January 21, 2007; *Caijing,* "Shanghai Pension Scandal: A Web of Business and Bribes," September 25, 2007; James Kynge and Richard McGregor, "Chinese Scandal of Missing Fund Deepens," *Financial Times (London),* June 9, 2003; Geoff Dyer, "Shanghai 'Scandal' Exposes Darker Side of the Economy," *Financial Times (London),* September 14, 2006.

8. Tschang Chi-Chu, "$1.4b Taken from State Social Funds, Say Auditors," *Straits Times,* November 25, 2006; Xinhua News Agency, "Chinese Audit Report Reveals Theft of 7.1 Bln Social Security Funds," November 23, 2006; Minnie Chan, "Millions Missing from Hunan Pension Fund," *South China Morning Post,* April 8, 2007. Pension funds in China total roughly RMB330 billion, of which RMB230 billion are in the national social security system and RMB100 billion are in various local pension funds including corporate pension funds; Agence France Presse, "China to Centralize Pension Funds after Shanghai Scandal Report," September 26, 2006; and Joseph Kahn, "China Graft Case Snares a Party Boss," *International Herald Tribune,* September 26, 2006.

9. Pei, however, defines this term loosely, and in reality only 32 cases involved officials colluding with organized crime. The other cases involved offenses such as "collective bribery" (7 cases), venality of office (6 cases), bribery and embezzlement (4 cases), and counterfeiting (1 case).

10. *People's Daily,* "Details of Xiamen Smuggling Case Exposed," July 26, 2001.

11. *China Daily,* "Graft, Corruption Cases Have Younger Profile," December 5, 2007.

12. In 2006, a total of 178 police officers were convicted on criminal charges and 273 members of the procuratorate were disciplined for corruption and misconduct. Of these, however, 47 officials were prosecuted for involvement with organized crime; see Xinhua News Agency, "Chinese Courts Convict 178 Police on Criminal Charges," February 8, 2007.

13. Ironically, it is likely that these funds would have been lent to developers anyway, but rather than being lent directly by the fund managers, they would have been improperly lent by the banks in which pension funds are supposed to be deposited: In 2006 auditors uncovered RMB767 billion in irregular lending by banks and other financial institutions. See Rob Delany, "China Tells Banks: Get Tough on Bribery," *International Herald Tribune,* July 17, 2006.

14. Yan Sun, "Corruption, Growth, and Reform: The Chinese Enigma," *Current History* 104, no. 683 (September 2005), 257; see also *South China Morning Post,* "Graft Costs 3pc of GDP: Study," April 12, 2008.

15. *China Daily,* "Nation Top Draw for FDI in 2007," January 22, 2008.

16. According to official Chinese sources, the number of more narrowly defined "mass incidents" fell by 22 percent in the first 10 months of 2006 to 17,900. In 2008, it was reported that "figures of mass incidents and participants decreased by 2.7 percent and 17.1 percent, respectively" in 2007, without further elaboration. See Xinhua News Agency, "China's Public Security Organs Promote Safety," April 20, 2008, www.chinapeace.org.cn.

17. In March 2007, one person was reportedly killed when over 20,000 people clashed with police during a protest over public transportation fee hikes in Yongzhou, Hunan. See *South China Morning Post*, "Over 20,000 Villagers Clash with Police in Protest," March 12, 2007.

18. Xinhua News Agency, "China Vows Firm Hand on Graft, Malfeasance in Quake Relief," May 20, 2008, http://news.xinhuanet.com.

19. Xinhua News Agency, "2,700 Officials Referred for Prosecution on Land Use Violations," January 22, 2008.

20. Lu Geng Song, "Zhongguo weiquan da shiji 2007 nian 4 yue 20 ri zhi 5 yue 20 ri" ["Achievements in Protection of Human Rights in China: 4/20/07–5/20/07"], Human Rights in China, www.renyurenquan.org.

21. *Financial Times*, "December Chinese Peasant Protest New, Serious Challenge to the Party," February 19, 2008.

22. Chinese Academy of Social Sciences, *2007 Zhongguo Shehui Xingshi Fenxi Yu Yuce (Shehui Lanpishu)* [*2007 Analysis and Forecast on China's Social Development (Blue Book of China's Society)*] (Beijing: Social Sciences Academic Press, 2008), 143–54.

23. Yan Sun, "Corruption, Growth, and Reform."

24. Dali Yang, "China: Suffering From Growth Pains or Doomed to Stagnation," in *Is China Trapped in Transition? Implications for Future Reforms* (The Foundation for Law, Justice and Society, 2008), www.fljs.org.

25. For an excellent discussion of these issues, see Melanie Manion, *Corruption by Design: Building Clean Government in Mainland China and Hong Kong* (Cambridge, MA: Harvard University Press, 2004).

26. *Dongfang Zaobao* [*Eastern Morning Edition*], "Zhongguo zhengzhiju tongguo fanfu wu nian guihua" ["The Politburo Approves an Anti-Corruption Five-Year Plan"], April 28, 2008, http://news.hexun.com.

27. Xinhua News Agency, "Zhongjiwei Jianchabu jiu kaizhan'zuo dang de chengken weishi, dang qunzhong de tiexin ren' huodong dawen" ["The Central Commission for Discipline Inspection and the Ministry of Supervision Launch the 'Be a Loyal Protector of the Party and a Confidant of the People' Campaign"], May 5, 2008, http://news.xinhuanet.com.

28. *Nanfang Chuang*, "Behind the Reshuffling of Provincial-Level Judicial Officials," January 16, 2008 in Open Source Center (OSC): CPP20080128530003.

29. A select list or class of people from which appointees for top-level government positions are drawn, especially from a Communist Party.

30. Xinhua News Agency, "Zuigaojian: shenru chaban 8 da lingyu she nong zhiwu fanzui" ["The Supreme People's Procuratorate Investigate and Deal with 8

Types of Agriculture-Related Criminal Activity"], May 8, 2008, www.yn.xinhua net.com.

31. For further discussion of the policy, see Barry Naughton, "The Assertive Center: Beijing Moves Against Local Government Control of Land," *China Leadership Monitor*, no. 20 (Winter 2007), www.hoover.org. See also Xinhua News Agency, "Unified Land Trading Market Launches in Shanghai," March 3, 2008, http://news.xinhuanet.com.

32. *Xuexi Shibao* [*Study Times*], "Cong gonggong shijiao kan gonggong canyu" ["Looking at Public Participation from a Public Point of View"], April 7, 2008, http://bozhiya.kmip.net/studytimes.

33. Xinhua News Agency, "Premier Outlines Anti-Corruption Work, Vows to Build Clean Gov't," April 30, 2008, http://news.xinhuanet.com.

34. He Baogang, "Xieshang minzhu canyuzhe de queding ji qi fangfa" ["Determining Who Will Participate and the Method of Consultative Democracy"], *Xuexi Shibao* [*Study Times*], January 1, 2008, www.china.com.cn.

35. Author's interview with leading Party scholar in Beijing, March 2008. See also *Nanfang Ribao*, "Political Reform Attempting a Major Breakthrough in Democracy and the Legal System Again Establishing a Special Zone Model," May 23, 2008, www.nanfangdaily.com.cn.

36. *Changzhou Shenji Xinxi* [*Changzhou Audit News*], "Zhou Ruijin zai lun jiefang sixiang, cong dujin shidai dao huangjin shidai" ["Zhou Rujin Again Discusses 'Freeing the Mind': From the Gold-Plated Era to the Golden Era"], January 30, 2008, www.czsj.gov.cn.

6

Sustaining Economic Growth in China

China's economic growth is unsteady, unbalanced, uncoordinated, and unsustainable.

—Wen Jiabao, March 2007

Premier Wen Jiabao's statement at his press conference following the close of the annual meeting of China's legislature in March 2007 was remarkable for two reasons. First, China's growth record is the envy of the world, with expansion averaging 10 percent for three decades. Second, since the assessment came from the man who had been in charge of the economy for the previous five years, it was an unusual self-criticism. What thinking underlies Premier Wen's assessment, and what policies is he promoting to make China's growth more sustainable?

Premier Wen and the rest of China's top political leadership seek to rebalance the sources of economic growth. In place of investment and export-led development, they have endorsed transitioning to a growth path that relies more on expanding domestic consumption. The Chinese Communist Party formally embraced this goal as early as December 2004 at the annual Central Economic Work Conference.[1] Since then, Premier Wen has reiterated the goal of making domestic consumption a much more important source of China's economic growth.[2]

China's goal of rebalancing the sources of economic growth is laudable. It increases the likelihood of China's sustaining its strong growth, creating jobs more rapidly, improving the distribution of income or at least slowing the pace of rising income inequality, and reducing China's outsized increases in energy consumption and carbon emissions. It also would help reduce global economic imbalances and thus lessen the risks to the global economy and reduce the possibility that China would be subject to protectionist pressure, especially in Europe and the United States. For these reasons, US Treasury Secretary Henry Paulson, Jr. has repeatedly urged Chinese leaders to rebalance the sources of growth, and Federal Reserve

Chairman Ben Bernanke, in his only speech on the Chinese economy, focused his remarks almost entirely on the case for rebalancing.[3]

But rebalancing the sources of economic growth has proven to be a much greater challenge than initially expected, and in certain respects China's economic growth has become even more imbalanced since 2004. Although the growth of investment expenditures moderated slightly after 2004, net exports of goods and services soared. China's external surplus ballooned to a global record in 2006 and continued to expand at a breakneck pace in 2007. Most importantly, private consumption expenditure as a share of GDP continued to fall through 2007.

Sources of China's Economic Growth

China has been the fastest growing economy in the world for over three decades, expanding at 10 percent a year in real terms. As a result, real GDP in 2006 was about 13 times the level of 1978, when Deng Xiaoping launched China on the path of economic reform.[4] China is now the world's third largest trader and, measured at market exchange rates, its fourth largest economy. It is highly likely to move up a notch in each category in 2009. Given this stunning long-term success, why would China's leadership seek to shift to a new growth paradigm? In global perspective, how imbalanced is China's recent economic growth?

In all economies, the expansion of output is the sum of the change in three components: consumption (both private and government), investment, and net exports of goods and services. Expanding investment has been a major and increasingly important driver of China's growth. As shown in figure 6.1, investment averaged 36 percent of GDP in the first decade or so of economic reform, relatively high by the standard of developing countries generally but not in comparison with China's East Asian neighbors when their investment shares were at their highest.[5] But since the beginning of the 1990s, China's average investment rate has been higher and in 1993 and again in 2004–07 exceeded 40 percent of GDP, a level above the experience of China's East Asian neighbors in their high growth periods.[6] Rising investment has been fueled by a rise in the national saving rate, which reached an unprecedented level of more than half of GDP in 2006.[7] Rising investment was particularly important in 2001–05, when on average it contributed just over half of China's economic growth, an unusually high share by international standards.[8]

The growth of both household and government consumption has been rapid in absolute terms throughout the reform period. But in most years, growth of consumption has lagged the underlying growth of the economy, a lag that has become particularly noticeable since 2000. As shown in figure 6.2, in the 1980s household consumption averaged slightly more than half of GDP. This share fell to an average of 46 percent in the 1990s. But

Figure 6.1   Investment as percent of GDP, 1978–2007

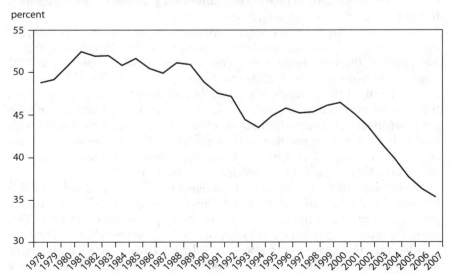

percent

Sources: National Bureau of Statistics of China, *China Statistical Yearbook 2007*; ISI Emerging
Markets, CEIC Database.

Figure 6.2   Household consumption as percent of GDP, 1978–2007

percent

Sources: National Bureau of Statistics of China, *China Statistical Yearbook 2007*; ISI Emerging
Markets, CEIC Database.

Figure 6.3   Government consumption as percent of GDP, 1978–2007

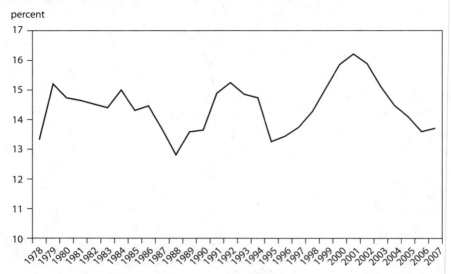

Sources: National Bureau of Statistics of China, *China Statistical Yearbook 2007*; ISI Emerging Markets, CEIC Database.

after 2000, household consumption as a share of GDP fell sharply—and by 2007 accounted for only 35 percent of GDP, the lowest share of any major economy in the world.[9] In the United States, household consumption accounted for 70 percent of GDP in the same year.[10] In the United Kingdom, it was 63 percent, and in India, 56 percent.[11]

As shown in figure 6.3, government consumption as a share of GDP has been relatively stable, averaging around 14 percent throughout the reform period. But it declined from a peak of over 16 percent of GDP in 2001 to under 14 percent in both 2006 and 2007.

As a result of these trends in household and government consumption, the relative importance of consumption as a source of growth during the past two decades diminished substantially, particularly compared with that of investment. In the first half of the 1980s, consumption growth accounted for almost four-fifths of China's economic expansion, whereas since 2003, this share has fallen to less than two-fifths.[12]

Beginning in 2005 the growth of net exports of goods and services also became, for the first time in almost a decade, a major source of economic growth. As shown in figure 6.4, net exports of goods and services in 2005 more than doubled to reach $125 billion, or 5.4 percent of GDP. They expanded rapidly in the ensuing two years, by 2007 reaching $305 billion, or 8.9 percent of GDP. On average, in 2005–07 the expansion of net exports accounted for over a fifth of China's growth.[13]

Figure 6.4   Net exports of goods and services, 1992–2007

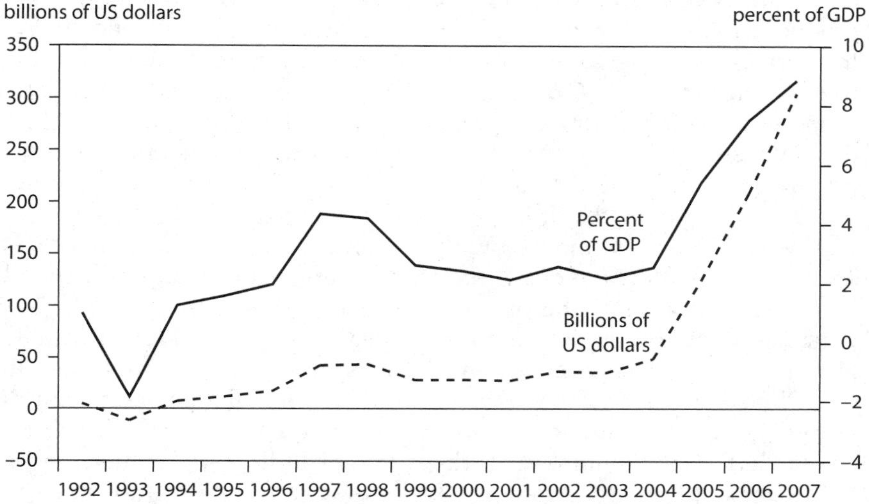

billions of US dollars   percent of GDP

Sources: National Bureau of Statistics of China, *China Statistical Yearbook 2007*; ISI Emerging Markets, CEIC Database.

In sum, despite the decision of the Party in 2004 to increase the role of domestic consumption demand in sustaining economic growth, consumption as a share of GDP has continued to fall and its contribution to China's economic growth has been modest. The government has been successful in slightly moderating the growth of investment. By 2007 the investment share of GDP had fallen by one percentage point and the contribution of investment to GDP expansion had fallen to about two-fifths, substantially less than the extraordinarily high average of 60 percent in 2003–04. On the other hand, net exports of goods and services have soared both absolutely and as a share of GDP, and thus their contribution to economic growth is currently unusually large, leading Premier Wen to opine at the National People's Congress in the spring of 2006 that "we must strive to reduce our excessively large trade surplus."

Rethinking China's Growth Strategy

Several considerations informed the formal decision of China's leadership in 2004 to rebalance the sources of growth. First, investment-driven growth, or what the Chinese sometimes call extensive growth, appeared to be leading to less efficient use of resources. By some metrics, as investment growth accelerated, the efficiency of resource use declined. Multifactor productivity growth, a critical contributor to economic expansion in all economies, averaged almost 4 percent per annum in the first 15 years of economic reform (1978–93) but has slowed to only 3 percent since 1993.[14] In short, as the investment share of GDP rose, the contribution of productivity improvements to GDP growth fell. In the words of Martin Wolf, chief economics commentator for the *Financial Times*, the surprising thing about the Chinese economy in recent years is not, as is so frequently asserted, how fast it is growing but rather, given the outsized share of output devoted to investment, that it is not growing even faster.[15]

The second reason underlying the leadership decision to rebalance the sources of growth is the desire to increase personal consumption and alleviate or at least slow the pace of increasing income inequality. In 2005 personal consumption in China was 30 percent less in real terms than the level that would have been achieved if the household consumption share of GDP had remained at the 1990 level rather than falling by more than 10 percentage points. India offers a useful comparison. In 2004 China's per capita GDP was two-and-a-half times that of India. But, because household consumption as a share of GDP was so much lower in China, per capita consumption exceeded that in India by only two-thirds.[16] The ultimate purpose of economic growth everywhere is to improve human welfare. By this standard, China is falling far below potential.

Similarly, a portion of the increase in income inequality in recent years can be attributed to the highly imbalanced regional pattern of growth. The positive differential in the pace of growth in coastal provinces compared with the national average has increased along with the sharply higher pace of growth of foreign trade (particularly exports) that has occurred since 2000.[17] Moving away from heavy reliance on export-led growth thus is consistent with President Hu Jintao's emphasis on creating a more "harmonious society," which requires, among other things, more balanced development between coastal and inland areas.

Third, China's extensive development has generated very modest gains in employment. Between 1978 and 1993, employment expanded by 2.5 percent per annum, but between 1993 and 2004, when the investment share of GDP was much higher than in the 1980s, employment growth slowed to only slightly over 1 percent.[18] The recent more capital-intensive pattern of growth contributed to a slower pace of job creation for the simple reason that the steel, aluminum, cement, and other investment goods industries employ far fewer workers per unit of capital than do consumer goods industries, not to mention the even less favorable comparison with services. But, as shown in figure 6.5, as investment boomed and the renminbi became increasingly undervalued, the share of investment in urban areas going to the services sector declined from 63 percent in 1999 and 2000 to 55 percent by 2007. Over the same period, the share of investment going to manufacturing doubled from 15 to 30 percent.[19] This clearly slowed the

Figure 6.5   Manufacturing and services share of urban investment, 1995–2007

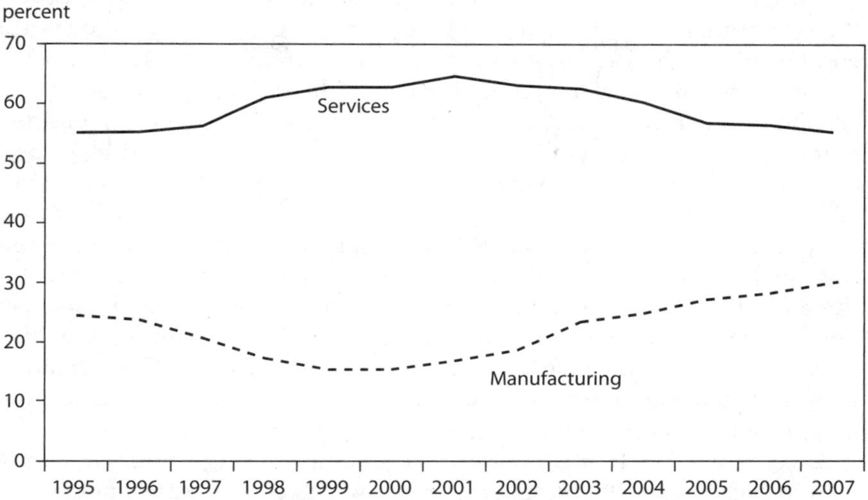

percent

Note: Investment in services includes property development.

Sources: National Bureau of Statistics of China, *China Statistical Yearbook 2007*; ISI Emerging Markets, CEIC Database.

rate of growth of job creation compared with what would have occurred with more balanced growth.

The fourth reason China's leadership wishes to transition to a more consumption-driven growth path is burgeoning energy consumption and its detrimental effects on the environment. Investment-driven growth has required the output of machinery and equipment, and the inputs to produce them, to grow much more rapidly than the output of consumer goods. Rapid growth of output of investment goods, in turn, disproportionately increases the demand for energy.[20] China's energy elasticity of GDP growth (the number of units of energy required to produce an additional unit of output) averaged a modest 0.4 in the 1980s and 1990s, leading over time to a substantial reduction in the amount of energy required to produce each unit of GDP. But this ratio almost tripled to an average of 1.1 in 2001–06.[21] Although China continued to achieve energy efficiency gains in the production of virtually all products, from 2001 through 2006 these gains were no longer sufficient to offset the effect of the rapid expansion of the most energy-intensive sectors of manufacturing, especially steel, chemicals, and cement.[22]

Since two-thirds of China's energy comes from coal, the burgeoning demand for energy generated by capital-intensive growth boosted coal consumption by two-thirds between 2000 and 2005. Coal consumption reached more than 2 billion tons in 2005, almost twice the level of coal consumption in the United States, even though China's economy is only one-sixth the size of that of the United States. As a result, China is now the largest emitter of greenhouse gases. China is home to 16 of the 20 cities with the worst air pollution on the globe. Because of the massive increase in coal consumption, the State Environmental Protection Agency (SEPA) reported that rather than sulfur dioxide emissions declining in 2000–2005 by 10 percent to 18 million tons as planned, they rose to 25.5 million tons by 2005, 42 percent above the goal.[23]

A fifth factor motivating China's leadership is less obvious but still important. Excessive reliance on investment and net exports to drive growth threatens to undo some of the progress China has made in recent years in developing a commercial banking system. A critical component of this process has been the injection of almost RMB4 trillion ($500 billion), mostly from the government, to cover past loan losses and to raise capital adequacy to meet prudential standards.[24]

Excess investment in some sectors of manufacturing could eventually lead to excess capacity and falling prices, which could create a new wave of nonperforming loans. These loans would erode the substantial improvements that state-owned banks have made in their balance sheets over the past few years and could push some city commercial banks, which on average are far weaker, into insolvency. An undervalued currency naturally raises profitability in the export sector—i.e., manufacturing—and thus tends to tilt investment in that direction. This has certainly been the case in China in recent years, where, as already noted, the share of investment going into manufacturing has doubled. Part of this shift of investment toward manufacturing reflects the increased demand for capital goods associated with the rapidly rising rate of investment in the first half of this decade (figure 6.1). But this shift has almost certainly been reinforced by the fillip to manufacturing profitability provided by an increasingly undervalued currency.

The National Development and Reform Commission (NDRC) has acknowledged that excess investment will have adverse financial consequences.[25] In its report to the National People's Congress in 2006, it pointed out that "adverse effects of surplus production capacity in some industries have begun to emerge. Prices for the products of these industries dropped and inventories grew, corporate profits shrank and losses mounted, and potential financial risk has increased."

The rapid increase in the magnitude of financial losses of unprofitable industrial enterprises supports this analysis. As shown in figure 6.6, after several years of stability, losses more than doubled in 2003–06 and then fell slightly in 2007. Since net profits of all enterprises rose sharply in this period (see figure 6.7), the dispersion of the profitability of China's industrial firms has apparently sharply increased over the past three years.

Figure 6.6   Losses of unprofitable industrial enterprises, 1995–2007(e)

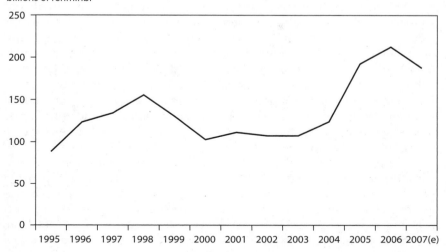

billions of renminbi

(e) = estimate

Sources: National Bureau of Statistics of China, *China Statistical Yearbook 2007*; ISI Emerging Markets, CEIC Database; author's calculations.

Figure 6.7   Industry profits as percent of GDP, 1998–2007(e)

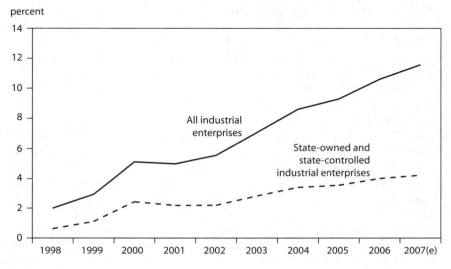

percent

(e) = estimate

Sources: National Bureau of Statistics of China, *China Statistical Yearbook 2007*.

The continued decline in the share of nonperforming loans in the banking system in the past few years is not necessarily a sign that all is well. By 2007, on the back of five consecutive years of double-digit growth and an increasingly undervalued currency, profitability in the tradable goods sector—i.e., manufacturing—had surged to unprecedented levels (see figure 6.7). Thus most corporates have been in a strong position to service their bank debt. Distress in the banking system could emerge, however, either from a slowdown in economic growth over the next few years or from a significant appreciation of the currency. The former would reduce profitability throughout the economy while the latter would concentrate the reduction in profits to firms producing tradable goods. In either case the ability of firms to service their bank debt could be impaired.[26]

A final factor underlining the leadership's desire to transition to a more consumption-oriented growth path is that excessive reliance on expansion of net exports—i.e., a growing trade surplus—raises the prospect of a protectionist backlash in the United States, Europe, and other important markets for Chinese exports. China's central bank, the People's Bank of China, was perhaps the first to explicitly acknowledge this factor in its *Report on the Implementation of Monetary Policy 2005Q2*, in which it candidly stated that China's excessive trade surplus "will escalate trade frictions."[27]

In sum, for a variety of reasons China's top political leadership and its leading economic advisory institutions came to the view by late 2004 that sustaining long-term rapid growth required a significant modification of the underlying growth strategy.

Implications for the Global Economy

If realized, China's new growth strategy would have positive implications not only for China but also for the global economy. As shown in figure 6.8, China's current account surplus has soared in recent years. In 2006 it reached $249 billion, making China, for the first time, the world's largest global current account surplus country. The surplus expanded further to $372 billion, or 11 percent of GDP in 2007, both unprecedented for a large country that is not a large exporter of resources such as oil.[28] In 2007 China's current account surplus as a share of GDP was almost three times that of Japan in the mid-1980s when its current account surplus as a share of GDP peaked. China now is the second largest contributor to global economic imbalances, after only the United States, which has the world's largest current account deficit. China's successful transition to a pattern of growth driven more by domestic consumption demand necessarily entails a reduction in China's national saving rate relative to its investment rate. That, in turn, would reduce China's current account surplus. Thus rebalancing of China's economic growth would contribute to a reduction of global economic imbalances as well.

Figure 6.8 Current account balance as percent of GDP, 1994–2007

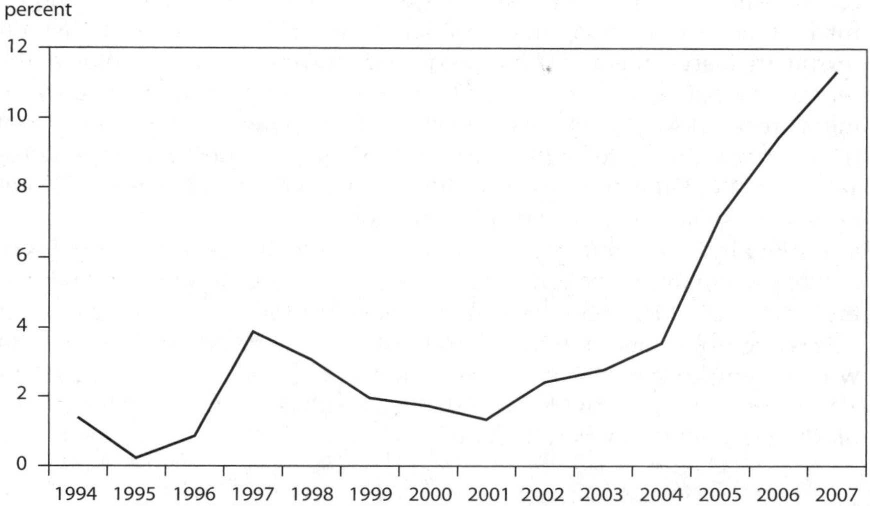

percent

Sources: National Bureau of Statistics of China, *China Statistical Yearbook 2007*; State Administration of Foreign Exchange of China, www.safe.gov.cn.

Similarly, rebalancing economic growth would reduce upward pressure on global oil prices. Although China accounts for less than 10 percent of global oil demand, its increasingly energy-intensive growth path between 2000 and 2006 meant that China alone accounted for more than 30 percent of the increase in global oil demand and global oil imports, far more than any other country. On current trends China alone will continue to account for 30 percent of the increase in global oil demand to 2030.[29] Rebalancing growth would reduce (1) the pace of growth of China's domestic energy consumption, (2) upward pressure on global oil prices, and (3) the pace of growth of China's carbon emissions.[30]

Promoting Consumption-Driven Growth

Promoting domestic consumption demand as a more important source of economic expansion requires that the growth of household and/or government consumption increase faster than the combined growth of investment and net exports. The government can promote consumption via fiscal, financial, exchange rate, and price policy. Fiscal policy options include cutting personal taxes, increasing government consumption expenditures (i.e., government noninvestment outlays), or introducing a dividend tax on state-owned companies. Financial reform could increase interest income received by households, thus raising household disposable income and potentially consumption. The government's policy of maintaining caps on interest rates on bank deposits has reduced substantially the return on savings, reducing household incomes below the level that would prevail in a more liberalized interest rate environment. Appreciation of the renminbi would simultaneously reduce net exports and allow the government greater flexibility in the use of interest rate policy.[31] As will be argued later, higher real interest rates on bank lending are almost certainly necessary to reduce China's excessive rate of investment, which in turn is a prerequisite to a successful transition to a more consumption-driven growth path. Finally, price reforms could contribute to the rebalancing of economic growth. In recent years the Chinese authorities have tightly limited the extent to which rising global oil prices are reflected in the domestic prices of gasoline and diesel fuel. Similarly, they have limited the extent to which rising coal prices are reflected in the domestic price of electricity. These policies have provided a growing subsidy to manufacturing, particularly energy-intensive production.

Fiscal Policy

One obvious policy to stimulate private consumption is to cut personal taxes, thus raising disposable income and personal consumption expenditures. In addition, governments can increase their own budgetary expenditures, notably those on health, education, welfare, and pensions, to add to domestic consumption demand. The low level of social expenditures on the eve of the Party's decision to rebalance the sources of economic growth was reflected in the very limited share of the population covered by health, unemployment, and workers' compensation insurance. In 2003 only about half the urban population was covered by basic health insurance and less than a fifth of the rural population was covered by a cooperative health insurance program initiated on a trial basis in 2002.[32] In the same year, only 14 percent of China's workforce was covered by unemployment insurance, and only 6 percent was covered by workers' compensation. In 2003 the pension scheme covered 116 million workers, only 16 percent of those employed, plus 39 million retirees.[33]

The government has considerable potential to increase its social expenditures without raising taxes on households. Raising taxes likely would depress household consumption, offsetting to some degree the increase in government consumption. The government could simply reduce its own investment expenditures and reallocate the funds to consumption.[34] The government itself directly undertakes about 5 percent of all investment, an amount equivalent to a little over 2 percent of GDP.[35] In addition, the government budget provides "capital transfers," which are used to finance additional investment expenditures.[36] For 2004 these capital transfers were RMB380 billion, the equivalent of 6 percent of all fixed investment.[37] Thus the government's direct and indirect investment outlays combined amount to about 5 percent of GDP. Reducing the government's direct investment and cutting capital transfers would free up resources to increase government consumption—i.e., outlays for health, education, welfare, and pensions. This would contribute significantly to a rebalancing of the structure of demand away from investment and toward consumption.

Increased government consumption expenditures also would contribute indirectly to increasing household consumption as a share of GDP by reducing the household saving rate, which rose significantly in the 1990s and has been running at about 25 percent of disposable income since 2000.[38] One reason for the rise in the saving rate was the reduction in the social services provided by the government and state-owned enterprises. For example, the share of total health outlays borne by individuals on an out-of-pocket basis increased from around 20 percent in 1978 to a peak of 60 percent in 2001.[39]

Increased provision of health care and unemployment compensation through the government budget can reduce household precautionary saving. As families gain confidence that the government will provide more of these services, they voluntarily will reduce their own saving—i.e., increase consumption as a share of their own disposable income. Similarly, greater government provision of educational services and old age support could lead to a reduction in saving associated with lifecycle events, such as children's education and retirement.

In other countries, increased government provision of health services has stimulated increased household consumption.[40] For example, the introduction of National Health Insurance in Taiwan, which raised the fraction of the insured population from 57 percent in 1994 to 97 percent in 1998, substantially reduced household uncertainty about future health expenditures and thus stimulated increased consumption. Households that previously enjoyed no health insurance coverage increased their consumption expenditures by an average of over 4 percent.[41] Thus, China's transition to a more consumption-driven growth path needs to start with increased government consumption expenditures but with time is likely to be reinforced by changes in household consumption and saving decisions.

Finally, corporate tax policy should contribute importantly to the rebalancing of China's sources of economic growth. As shown in figure 6.7, from 1999 through 2007, profits of industrial enterprises in China soared from 3 percent to almost 12 percent of GDP.[42] Although these profits are subject to China's corporate income tax, estimated retained after-tax earnings of industrial firms in 2006 amounted to 8 percent of GDP, compared with an estimated 1.5 percent in 1998.[43] In addition, industrial firms retain depreciation funds that amount to another 6 to 7 percent of GDP.[44]

Unfortunately, in state-owned firms these funds are not subject to a significant rate of return test prior to being reinvested. The reason is that the only available legal alternative to reinvestment is low-yielding bank deposits. Taking into account the relevant measure of inflation, the real after-tax rate of return on corporate deposits is typically negative.[45] Given a negative real rate of return on deposits, it is rational for enterprise managers to reinvest all retained profits and depreciation funds—even when the investment projects have slightly negative anticipated rates of return.

Given the strong upward trend in profits as a share of GDP since 1999 and an apparent upward trend in depreciation funds as a share of GDP as well, retained earnings have become an increasingly important source of investment financing in China's corporate sector and have contributed to the rising investment share of GDP in recent years.

For a number of years, the authorities have discussed requiring state-owned enterprises to pay dividends to their owner—the government.[46] A dividend tax would directly reduce business saving and investment as well as provide the government with additional resources that could be used to enhance government-provided social services.

Financial Reform

The decline in household consumption as a share of GDP (figure 6.2) reflects not only an increase in savings as a share of household disposable income in the 1990s but also a decline in the share of disposable income in GDP. Between 1992 and 2003 household disposable income as a share of GDP fell by 4.8 percentage points.[47]

Part of the explanation of this decline is increasing financial repression. China's financial sector has been undergoing far-reaching reform for more than a decade, suggesting that the degree of repression has eased. However, from the point of view of households this is not the case. As shown in figure 6.9, although household deposits in the banking system as a share of GDP increased by about two-thirds between the early 1990s and 2003, the stream of pre-tax interest earnings generated by these savings declined from an average of about 5 percent in 1992–95 to only 2.5 percent of GDP in 2003. The contribution of interest earnings to disposable income has declined even further since the government introduced a 20 percent tax on interest income in 1999.

The reason for this decline was government interest rate policy on savings deposits. As inflation rose to record highs in 1993, the flow of savings deposits into the banking system plummeted. To avert a crisis the government in July introduced so-called value-guarantee deposits designed to insulate longer-term deposits from inflation. These accounts paid a base interest rate plus a subsidy interest rate. The subsidy rate, calculated when the deposit matured, was set so that the total nominal interest rate offset the inflation that occurred while the funds were on deposit. Thus savers willing to shift their funds into longer-term time deposits received a real rate of return that was at least zero. These value-guarantee deposits

Figure 6.9 Household savings and interest income, 1992–2003
(percent of GDP)

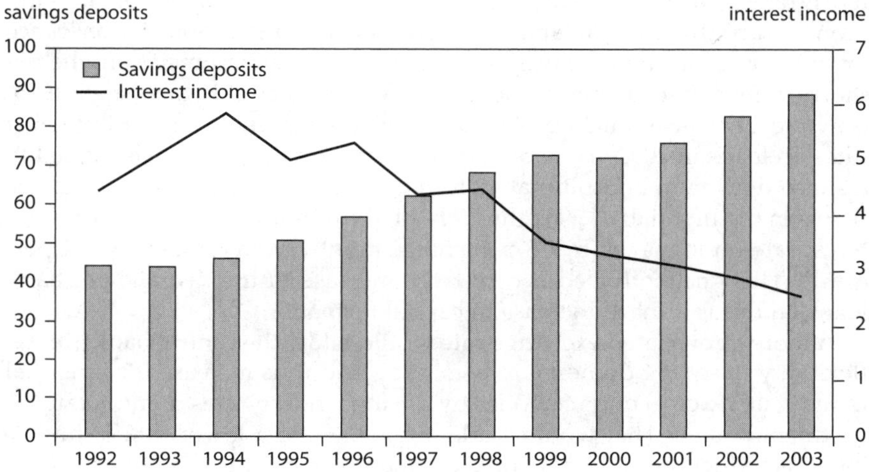

savings deposits   interest income

Sources: National Bureau of Statistics of China, *China Statistical Yearbook 2006*; ISI Emerging Markets, CEIC Database.

were offered to new depositors from July 1993 through April 1996.[48] Subsequently, however, the government fixed interest rates on household savings deposits that were much lower in real terms, leading to the decline in interest income reflected in figure 6.9.

The shrinking contribution of after-tax interest income to household disposable income accounts for almost two-thirds of the decline in household disposable income as a share of GDP between 1992 and 2003. More importantly, if interest earnings after the early 1990s had grown in line with the stock of household bank deposits and the tax on interest income had not been introduced, by 2003 the contribution of interest income to household disposable income would have been 8.9 percent of GDP, 6.4 percentage points greater than the actual contribution.

Exchange Rate Policy

Exchange rate policy should be a third element supporting China's transition to a more consumption-driven growth path for two reasons. First, through its effect on relative prices, appreciation of the renminbi will reduce the growth of exports and increase the growth of imports, reducing China's external imbalance. Second, China's highly undervalued exchange rate constrains the independence of monetary policy.[49] China's central bank has had some success in sterilizing large foreign capital inflows, a key element in its program of controlling the growth of monetary aggregates and bank credit. But it has generally been reluctant to raise domestic interest rates, since that would reduce the carry costs of foreigners moving money into China in anticipation of further renminbi appreciation. Since lower carry costs increase profits from any renminbi appreciation, the authorities fear that raising domestic interest rates could cause capital inflows to become unmanageably large. Fixed nominal domestic interest rates on loans in 2002–03, when domestic price inflation was rising, led to a sharp decline in and ultimately to negative real interest rates on loans. Between the first half of 2002 through the third quarter of 2004, the real interest rate on loans fell by 13 percentage points, from almost 9 to –4 percent.[50] This decline fueled a very large increase in the demand for bank loans and thus a sharp increase in capital formation.

A more appreciated exchange rate would allow the central bank greater flexibility in setting domestic interest rates and thus increase the potential to mitigate macroeconomic cycles by raising lending rates to moderate investment booms. That would lead, on average, to a lower rate of investment. A reduction in the rate of investment is a critical component of the policies to transition to a more consumption-driven growth path. In the absence of a reduction in investment, increased consumption demand would lead to inflation.

Price Reform

A final policy domain is pricing. Among the most important prices that are currently not in accordance with relative scarcities and social preferences are those for land, energy, water, utilities, and the environment.[51] All of these are important manufacturing inputs, so more appropriate pricing, including enforcement of existing environmental standards, would tend to reduce investment in manufacturing, particularly the most energy-intensive industries, and increase investment in services. Appropriate pricing at a minimum means full cost recovery and more ambitiously would mean marginal opportunity cost pricing—i.e., include the cost of environmental damage in both production and consumption as well as the opportunity cost of resource depletion.[52]

China's Pursuit of Consumption-Driven Growth

Fiscal Policy

Even before the December 2004 Central Economic Work Conference, which formally endorsed the transition to a more domestic consumption-driven growth path, in mid-2004 the government initiated a program to raise farm incomes by reducing the agricultural tax levied on farm income.[53] The government reduced the tax in stages, with the largest reductions in 2004 and 2005, and eliminated it entirely by 2007.

The early initiative to eliminate the agricultural tax was followed in 2006 with a doubling, from RMB800 to RMB1,600, in the monthly income exempt from the personal income tax levied on wage earners. The government raised the exemption amount to RMB2,000 per month in 2008.

Another policy that raised disposable income above the levels it would otherwise have achieved was the reduction in the tax on interest income to 5 percent effective August 15, 2007.

The central government also has encouraged local governments to raise the minimum wage in urban areas, potentially increasing the incomes and thus consumption of low-income workers.

Taken together, the first three of these initiatives are raising household incomes above the levels they would otherwise attain. Cumulatively, in the four years ending in 2007 the agricultural tax burden was reduced by an average of RMB133.5 billion per year,[54] an amount equal to an average of 0.7 percent of GDP in those years. Similarly, the State Tax Bureau estimated that raising the personal income tax exemption in 2006 would reduce the personal income tax take by RMB28 billion in 2006, or 0.13 percent of GDP.[55] A further reduction of RMB30 billion was anticipated as a result of the further increase in the exemption in 2008. The cut in the tax on interest income similarly will increase household disposable income by at least RMB30 billion in 2008.

The fourth initiative, minimum wage policy, appears to have had at most only a modest effect on household income for two reasons. First, the Regulations on the Minimum Wage of the Chinese Ministry of Labor and Social Security give local governments considerable leeway in setting the minimum wage.[56] These governments have raised minimum wage rates at a pace substantially below the growth of average wages in their locality. In Beijing, for example, in recent years the minimum wage has been increased at an annual rate of less than 8 percent, far below the 16 percent pace of increase in the average wage of workers and staff in the city.[57] As a result, the minimum wage in Beijing fell from a third of the average wage of workers and staff in the city in 1999 to only a fifth in 2007.[58] Second, the share of the workforce earning the minimum wage appears to be quite small. In Beijing, for example, minimum wage workers accounted for only 2.4 percent of the workforce in 2002.[59] Given the low ratio of the minimum wage to the average wage and the small share of the workforce earning the minimum wage, recent annual increases in the capital's minimum wage had only a minuscule effect on the total wage bill.

In summary, the cuts in taxes on rural and urban incomes instituted in 2004 raised household disposable income by about 1 percent of GDP per year above the level it would otherwise have attained, contributing mod-

Table 6.1   Government expenditure on social programs, 2002–07
(billions of renminbi)

Year	Education	Health	Social security and employment	Total	Percent of GDP
2002	300.61	66.33	268.91	635.85	5.28
2003	335.21	83.08	271.22	689.52	5.08
2004	385.43	93.59	318.56	797.58	4.99
2005	452.78	113.26	378.71	944.75	5.14
2006	546.43	142.12	439.41	1,127.96	5.32
2007	706.54	197.38	539.60	1,443.51	5.78

Source: Xinhua News Agency, "The Course of Improvements in the People's Livelihood from the Perspective of Public Finance Expenditure over the (Past) Five Years," March 7, 2008, http://news.xinhuanet.com.

estly to higher levels of household consumption expenditures than would otherwise have been achieved.[60]

Government expenditures on health, education, and pensions and unemployment programs have increased significantly since 2004, with a record increase in 2007. As shown in table 6.1, by 2007 budgetary expenditures on education, health, social security, and employment combined were RMB1,444 billion, an increase of four-fifths compared with 2004. Of course this was a period of exceptionally rapid growth of the economy and of government budget revenues, so the increase is less impressive relative to those metrics.

One rationale for increased social outlays is Premier Wen's program to create a "new socialist countryside." The program entails increasing subsidies for grain producers, designed to raise the incomes of some of China's poorest farmers; expanding the coverage of the rural cooperative medical system, which was first rolled out on a trial basis in 2002; and eliminating educational fees for rural primary education.

The increase in expenditures on programs tied to the new socialist countryside initiative is impressive.[61] Central government outlays on the rural cooperative medical system rose to RMB11.4 billion in 2007, a twenty-fold increase compared with 2005, raising the number of rural residents covered by the program to more than 730 million, quadruple the number covered in 2005. This program is now available in 86 percent of China's county-level administrative units, an increase of more than seven-fold compared with 2004. The central government has budgeted RMB25.3 billion for this program in 2008, allowing both a broadening of the program to all administrative regions and an increase in the subsidy provided to each participant.

The government budgeted RMB220 billion ($27.5 billion) over five years (2006–10) to provide free rural primary school education, a significant commitment. Expenditures on this initiative in 2006 were RMB36.6 billion, allowing the government to eliminate tuition and miscellaneous school fees for 52 million students in 12 western provinces. Outlays jumped to RMB69 billion in 2007 as the program was extended to central and eastern provinces, reaching a total of 150 million students.

The government also greatly expanded some programs that reach primarily urban residents. Compared with 2004, by 2007 the number of workers covered by basic retirement, health, unemployment, and workers' compensation insurance expanded by 23, 80, 10, and 78 percent, respectively.[62]

Despite the initiatives summarized earlier, combined government expenditures at the national and subnational levels on education, health, and pensions and employment programs rose by less than one percentage point of GDP between 2004 and 2007, and a chunk of that increase simply offset the decline that occurred in 2003 and 2004—i.e., the share of GDP devoted to these programs in 2007 was only 0.5 percentage points higher than in 2002. Similarly, expenditures on these programs as a share of total government fiscal outlays increased by just over one percentage point between 2004 and 2007. But because of the decline in 2003, social expenditures as a share of the consolidated government budget in 2007 were only slightly more than in 2002.

The apparent contradiction between the large percentage increases in central government expenditures on selective social programs, notably the new rural cooperative medical system, and the somewhat more modest increase in total social outlays, is explained in part by the overwhelmingly dominant role of provincial and local governments in financing social programs. In 2005, for example, subnational governments financed 94 percent of all government spending on education and 98 percent of all government spending on public health. Thus until subnational governments increase the priority they assign to funding education and health programs, total expenditures on these programs will rise much more slowly than central government outlays.

Corporate tax policy initiatives are not facilitating a rebalancing of the sources of economic growth. On September 8, 2007 the State Council announced that the government would begin collecting dividends from state-owned industrial companies in 2007.[63] Dividends are being levied at 10, 5, and 0 percent of after-tax profits earned in 2006, depending on the sector in which the firm operates. For example, highly profitable firms in the petroleum, electric power, and telecommunications sectors are to pay at the rate of 10 percent of their after-tax profits, and firms in less profitable sectors such as steel, transportation, electronics, trade, and construction industries will pay at the rate of 5 percent, while a few firms, such as those in the military industry, are exempt from paying dividends at least for an initial three-year period. In 2007, as part of the phase-in process, dividends were to be paid at half of these statutory rates.

Three factors have undermined the potential of the dividend tax to contribute to economic rebalancing. First, the dividend tax rates are too low.
The magnitude of dividend payments to be collected from central state-
owned firms under the administrative guidance of China's State-Owned
Asset Supervision and Administration Commission (SASAC) in 2007 was
set at only RMB17 billion. That amount is vanishingly small, only 4 percent of the 2006 after-tax profits of the firms controlled by SASAC. Even if
the half-rate phase-in had not been used and dividend payments had to-
taled RMB34 billion, that amount was only one-tenth of 1 percent of 2007
GDP. A more robust effort, for example, might have required all state-
owned and state-controlled industrial companies, including those under
the administrative guidance of local SASAC bureaus, to pay half their
after-tax income as dividends. This would have amounted to RMB325 billion or 1.3 percent of 2007 GDP.[64] Additional dividends could also be collected from state-owned firms in the service sector, raising the potential of
a dividend tax to reduce corporate savings and investment and thus contribute to rebalancing.

Second, and perhaps more importantly, it is not clear what portion of
these dividend payments will be available to finance social programs and
other forms of government consumption and what portion will be used to
finance investment. Li Rongrong, the chairman of SASAC, initially argued
that dividend payments should not be made to the Ministry of Finance,
where they might be subject to budgetary allocation and thus could potentially fund additional social services. Rather, he asserted that dividend
payments should be made directly to SASAC, which he said SASAC
would use to finance additional investment outlays. If this approach had
been adopted, a dividend policy would not have reduced the corporate
saving and investment rate and would not have contributed to a rebalancing of the sources of economic growth.[65]

While the debate on the disposition of dividend payments is probably
far from over, a compromise seems to be emerging in which dividend
payments are to be partially allocated to a capital management budget
managed separately from the fiscal budget by the Ministry of Finance
and partially allocated to support social programs. Proposals for the use
of dividends paid by central state-owned enterprises are to come from
SASAC, with the Ministry of Finance determining the final capital management budget and distributing the funds directly to units that will
spend it. The amounts to be used for noninvestment expenditures appear
to be under debate. When the dividend tax and the capital management
budget were first announced in mid-September, it was said that "when
necessary some" of the dividend tax payments could be used to fund social security expenditures.[66] A few months later in December 2007, when
more details were announced, it was said that a majority of the dividend
payments could be used to support social and pension programs.

A third reason corporate tax policy is not contributing to rebalancing is that the introduction of the dividend tax in 2007 coincided with a reduction in the corporate income tax rate. Domestic firms had long complained that their statutory tax rate of 33 percent was well above the 15 percent rate paid by foreign-invested firms. After years of debate the government decided to unify the rate paid by indigenous and foreign firms at 25 percent beginning in 2007. This reform reduced the corporate income tax payments of indigenous firms by an estimated RMB134 billion, offsetting by a factor of almost eight the additional dividend tax collection.[67] The result is that retained earnings of the corporate sector as a share of GDP continued to expand in 2007.

Financial Reform

Reforms of the banking system in recent years have not reduced the degree of repression of the banking system from the perspective of Chinese households. Central bank policy continues to place caps on the interest rates that banks can pay on deposits and floors on the interest rates that they can charge on loans, presumably to prop up bank profitability. This, in turn, makes it more likely that banks will be able to write off future nonperforming loans from their own earnings, thus minimizing the potential fiscal burden of additional bank recapitalization programs.

One measure of growing financial repression is the expanding differential between the interest rate households receive on savings deposits compared with consumer price inflation. In the first quarter of 2008 the central bank fixed the maximum interest rate banks could pay on household demand deposits at 0.72 percent, unchanged from February 2002.[68] But inflation, as measured by the consumer price index, had ticked up by almost 9 percentage points—from –0.8 percent in 2002 to 8 percent in the first quarter of 2008.[69] Thus the real rate of return on demand deposits went from 1.52 to –7.28 percent. The central bank has increased rates paid by banks on term deposits but by far less than the increase in inflation. For example, the one-year term deposit rate in the first quarter of 2008 was 4.14 percent, an increase of only 2.06 percentage points since February 2002. That increase is less than a fourth of the increase in the pace of inflation and has converted a real return of 3 percent in 2002 into a real return of –3.86 percent. If households in the first quarter of 2008 had received the same real rate of interest on their demand and time deposits as in 2002, the additional interest income they would have received would have been the equivalent of about 6 percent of GDP. Thus declining real returns to savings have significantly depressed household disposable income as a percentage of GDP.

Jonathan Anderson, a keen observer of China's financial and banking system, believes that "if the government were to completely liberalize interest rates tomorrow we believe average deposit rates would rise sharply."[70] But interest rate liberalization seems to have fallen off the reform agenda in Beijing. The last step of interest rate liberalization was in October 2004 when the central bank gave commercial banks the authority to raise lending rates without limit from the benchmark rates set by the central bank. However, benchmark interest rates set by the central bank on deposits remain rigid caps.

The implicit taxes imposed on households by the distorted interest rate structure fixed by the central bank resulted in a massive subsidy for corporate borrowers, further increasing profits in the corporate sector. In the first quarter of 2008 the benchmark interest rate paid by corporate customers for a one-year loan was 7.47 percent. But in March, prices for the machinery and equipment and other capital goods that firms would purchase to expand their businesses rose 7.95 percent, making the real rate of interest for corporate borrowers –0.5 percent, an extraordinarily low rate in an economy expanding at 10.6 percent.

Exchange Rate Policy

In July 2005 the Chinese authorities revalued the renminbi by 2.1 percent vis-à-vis the US dollar and announced that the currency could fluctuate by up to 0.3 percent per day and that the renminbi would be managed with reference to a basket of currencies, rather than simply being pegged to the US dollar. These reforms could have contributed to a slowing of the growth of China's external surplus and given the People's Bank of China greater flexibility in adjusting interest rates.

Cumulatively, by the end of the first quarter of 2008, the renminbi had appreciated by 18 percent vis-à-vis the dollar. But, as calculated by the International Monetary Fund, JPMorgan, and other investment banks, on a real effective basis the currency had appreciated by only 11 percent.[71]

Why have China's net exports as a share of GDP continued to rise rapidly while its exchange rate, on a real trade-weighted basis, has been appreciating by more than 3 percent per year since mid-2005? Normally, with a lag of a few quarters, an appreciating currency leads to a slowing expansion and then an absolute reduction in a country's trade surplus. One hypothesis is that the conventionally calculated real effective exchange rate of the renminbi understates China's growing competitiveness in international markets. JPMorgan and other institutions calculate the real exchange rate by comparing the rate of movement of prices in China and in its trading partners. For example, if while the nominal effective exchange rate of the renminbi was unchanged China experienced one percentage point more price inflation than the average of its trading partners, the real exchange rate of the renminbi would appreciate 1 percent. The problem is that the inflation measures used by investment banks and international financial organizations appear to be a poor measure of the prices of China's exports. For example, despite an 18 percent nominal appreciation of the renminbi vis-à-vis the US dollar, from June 2005 through March 2008 the price of Chinese goods imported into the United States had increased by only 2.5 percent.[72] Available data do not suggest that Chinese exporters cut their profit margins in order to avoid passing through the renminbi appreciation to US consumers. The most likely explanation is that productivity growth in China's export sector was sufficiently high that firms producing exports could absorb the effect of the rising value of the renminbi on their export earnings. In short, productivity growth in the export sector over the period must have been about 15 percent. Over that period, prices in China's major trading partners rose on average by about 8 percent. Thus the Chinese currency would have needed to appreciate in nominal terms by almost a quarter to maintain the initial level of competitiveness of Chinese exports. But nominal appreciation of the renminbi against its trading partners was only 7 percent, so Chinese goods grew in competitive terms. This calculation suggests that taking into account the rapid productivity growth in export manufacturing, China's real effective exchange rate depreciated by about 15 percent. In contrast, the standard calculation, which does not take into account the concentrated nature of productivity growth in China, shows appreciation of 11 percent between June 2005 and the end of March 2008.

Price Policy

In the 1980s, when China was still self sufficient in crude oil and not so deeply integrated into the global economy, the domestic price of crude was a small fraction of the international level. But in the 1990s the Chinese government gradually raised crude oil prices to international levels and by 1998, when convergence was completed, adopted a formal plan to adjust domestic crude oil prices monthly to keep them in line with international prices. Similarly, the government raised the retail prices of refined petroleum products toward international levels and in mid-2000 adopted a program to adjust these prices on a monthly basis so that refined product prices reflected crude prices.[73] However, as the global price of crude oil began to rise rapidly in 2004, Chinese pricing policy changed. The domestic price of crude continued to be adjusted in line with the international price, but only a part of the rising price was passed through to retail prices. As a result, in 2005 China's major oil companies lost money on their refining operations, part of which was offset with government subsidies.

By early 2008 retail prices in China for gasoline and diesel fuel were the lowest of any oil-importing country in the world. Sinopec, China's largest oil refiner, reported in April that it lost RMB25 billion on its refining operations in the first quarter of 2008. The government provided

RMB7.4 billion to offset a portion of its losses, but the firm's net profit plunged by two-thirds. In June 2008 the NDRC raised the retail prices for diesel and gasoline by 18 and 17 percent, respectively. These increases will still leave Chinese refiners with significant operating losses and no return on the capital employed in refining. Thus unless the authorities raise the retail prices of diesel and gasoline further or the global price of crude falls and retail prices are not adjusted downward, shortages of refined products subject to price control are likely to persist.

A similar development has emerged in electric power. Until recently thermal power generators have been profitable—i.e., full-cost pricing has been in effect. This was insured in part by a 2005 policy that called for an adjustment in electric power rates if the price of coal rose by more than 5 percent in a half-year. Like the policy for pass-through of rising crude prices to prices of gasoline and diesel fuel, it was abandoned as coal prices rose sharply. Long-term contract coal prices paid by China's five main power-generating companies rose 9 percent in 2007 and an additional 10 percent beginning in January 2008. Moreover, the market price of coal rose much more rapidly, meaning that coal companies frequently defaulted on their contracts, forcing generators to buy a larger share of their coal needs at the market price. At the same time, however, the price the generators received for the power they deliver to the grid companies had remained unchanged since the summer of 2006. With coal accounting for 60 to 70 percent of the total cost of electricity, by the first quarter of 2008, the five largest generators all lost money on their thermal power business.

The NDRC also in June raised the average price paid by industrial users of electric power by RMB0.025 per kilowatt hour or about 5 percent. Barring an unexpected decline in the price of coal, this increase, like the one for fuels, is unlikely to restore profitability to the generating business. The price increase is too small and households are exempt. Abandoning full-cost prices is likely to lead to shortages of electric power as generators pare production.

Glass Half Full or Half Empty?

The government has taken some steps to initiate the transition to a more consumption-driven growth path. For example, outlays on social programs increased more rapidly, particularly in 2005–07, which should contribute over time to a reduction in precautionary savings by households. Cuts in taxes on agricultural, wage, and interest income added modestly to the growth of household income.

But some policies are undermining the goal of rebalancing. For example, recent corporate tax reform has had the perverse effect of raising after-tax retained earnings of Chinese firms, contributing to the ongoing high rate of investment; interest rate caps on savings deposits in the face of rising inflation mean that the real returns to savers are increasingly penurious while the subsidy to corporate borrowers is soaring. Adjusting for productivity gains in the production of export goods, an alternative measure of the real effective exchange rate suggests that the Chinese currency has depreciated rather than appreciated over the past three years, adding to China's external imbalance. And increased government intervention has resulted in a growing subsidy of energy use, likely undermining the goal of reducing the energy intensity of economic growth.

The adverse effect of these policies is reflected in some measures that show economic growth actually has become even more unbalanced since 2004. In 2005–07, the pace of investment demand moderated slightly, as reflected in a cumulative one percentage point reduction in investment as a share of GDP compared with 2004. But China became increasingly dependent on a growing trade surplus to sustain high growth. Net exports jumped from 2.5 percent of GDP in 2004 to 8.9 percent of GDP in 2007 and accounted for one-fifth of China's economic growth in 2005–07. Over the same period household and government consumption as a share of GDP declined by 5.3 percentage points of GDP.[74]

Energy consumption per unit of GDP fell by 1.2 percentage points in 2006 and an additional 3.3 percent in 2007. However, this falls short of the government's goal of reducing the consumption of energy per unit of output by 4 percent annually in the five years through 2010. And even after these improvements, energy intensity per unit of GDP remains well above the average of the first two decades of economic reform.

Other macro measures also suggest the limited effect of rebalancing policies. The share of investment in urban areas allocated to manufacturing continues to rise, reaching 30 percent by 2007, while the share devoted to investment in the services sector continues to fall. This is not surprising. China is a market economy in which firms respond to price signals. China's undervalued exchange rate boosts profitability in manufacturing, a trend that is reinforced by low or even negative real interest rates on loans and the more recent underpricing of energy.

The same trend is reflected in the share of services in GDP. In the first 25 years of economic reform, the share of services in GDP roughly doubled, reaching 41 percent in 2002–03. This is a typical pattern of development for a rapidly growing low-income country. But since then the services share has actually declined slightly, a very peculiar if not wholly unprecedented development for a country with a per capita income of about $2,000 to $3,000.

This evidence suggests that a transition toward more consumption-driven growth in China will require more vigorous government policy action than we have seen to date in all four domains—fiscal, financial, exchange rate, and pricing. The implications for the global economy of slow policy adjustment in China are adverse. China's external surplus will grow much more moderately in 2008 and could even shrink in absolute terms, but this would reflect as much the slowdown of growth in the United States and elsewhere as the modest currency appreciation seen to date. Absent more appreciation of the currency, China's external surplus likely will resume expanding when global growth returns to trend. China's continued high dependence on investment to generate growth contributes to upward pressure on global prices of oil and other commodities and could lead to continued outsized increases in China's energy consumption and carbon emissions.

Notes

1. *People's Daily*, "Central Economic Work Conference Convenes in Beijing December 3 to 5," December 6, 2004, www.people.com.cn (accessed July 21, 2006).

2. Wen Jiabao, "Report on the Work of the Government," *People's Daily*, March 14, 2006, http://english.people.com.cn (accessed March 14, 2006); New China News Agency, "We must concretely grasp eight work items to do well in next year's economic work," December 1, 2006, http://politics.people.com.cn (accessed December 12, 2006); Wen Jiabao, *Report on the Work of the Government* (Beijing, March 5, 2007); Wen Jiabao, *Report on Work of the Government* (Beijing, March 5, 2008), www.npc.gov.cn (accessed April 18, 2008).

3. Ben S. Bernanke, "The Chinese Economy: Progress and Challenges" (speech, Chinese Academy of Social Sciences, Beijing, December 15, 2006).

4. National Bureau of Statistics of China, *China Statistical Yearbook 2007* (Beijing: China Statistics Press, 2007), 60.

5. For details, see Nicholas R. Lardy, "China: Toward a Consumption-Driven Growth Path," Policy Briefs in International Economics 06-6 (Washington: Peterson Institute for International Economics, October 2006), www.petersoninstitute.org.

6. National Bureau of Statistics of China, *China Statistical Yearbook 2007*, 72. All of the analysis of the expenditure components of GDP—i.e., consumption, investment, and net exports—is based on the revised GDP expenditure data for the years 1978 through 2005 released by the National Bureau of Statistics of China, *China Statistical Yearbook 2006*, in late September 2006. Data for 2007 were released in May 2008 and are available from ISI Emerging Markets CEIC Database, available by subscription at www.securities.com (hereafter CEIC).

7. By definition, the national saving rate is equal to investment as a share of GDP plus the current account as a percent of GDP. In China, these were 42 and 9 percent of GDP, respectively, in 2006.

8. National Bureau of Statistics of China, *China Statistical Yearbook 2007*, 75.

9. The declining share of consumption in GDP is due to both a decline in household disposable income as a share of GDP and a decline in consumption as a share of disposable income. Some analysts believe that the National Bureau of Statistics of China undercounts household consumption, particularly of services, and thus

the share of household consumption in GDP is biased downwards. If GDP was undercounted by 8 or 12 percent, and the entire increment was private consumption of services, household consumption would have constituted 42 and 44 percent, respectively, of GDP in 2005; see Dragoneconomics Research & Advisory, "Consumption: A Chinese Puzzle," *China Insight*, no. 33 (February 13, 2007). Even on these alternative assumptions, however, private consumption as a share of GDP would be unusually low by international standards. These adjustments would also lower the investment share of GDP by three and four percentage points, respectively. The higher consumption and lower investment share of GDP would mean the degree of internal imbalance is less than that reflected in the official data. Note, however, that on these alternative assumptions, China's large and growing external imbalance would decline by only a few tenths of a percentage point of GDP.

10. US data are available at US Department of Commerce, Bureau of Economic Analysis, National Income and Product Accounts Tables, www.bea.gov (accessed May 15, 2008).

11. UK data are available at UK Statistics Authority, National Statistics, "First Release: UK Output, Income and Expenditure, 4th Quarter 2007," www.statistics. gov.uk; Indian data are available at Press Information Bureau, Government of India, "Press Note: Quick Estimates of National Income, Consumption Expenditure, Saving, and Capital Formation, 2006–07," January 31, 2008, http://mospi. nic.in (accessed May 15, 2008).

12. National Bureau of Statistics of China, *China Statistical Yearbook 2007*, 75; CEIC.

13. Ibid.

14. Louis Kuijs and Tao Wang, "China's Pattern of Growth: Moving to Sustainability and Reducing Inequality," World Bank Policy Research Working Paper 3767 (Washington: World Bank, November 2005), 2.

15. Martin Wolf, "Why Is China Growing So Slowly?" *Foreign Policy* (January–February 2005), www.foreignpolicy.com (accessed August 4, 2005).

16. Calculated on the basis of the Indian Ministry of Statistics and Program Implementation, *National Account Statistics*, http://mospi.nic.in; IMF, *International Financial Statistics*; National Bureau of Statistics of China, *China Statistical Yearbook 2006* (Beijing: China Statistics Press, 2006), 34, 36, 171.

17. From 1978 through 2000, China's trade turnover (imports plus exports) measured in value terms expanded at an average rate of 15 percent per year. From 2000 through 2006, the pace accelerated to 25 percent per year.

18. Kuijs and Wang, World Bank Policy Research Working Paper 3767.

19. National Bureau of Statistics of China, *China Statistical Yearbook 2005*, 208, and *China Statistical Yearbook 2007*, 214. For recent years China's statistical authorities have released data on total investment in manufacturing and investment in manufacturing in urban areas. For these years urban investment has consistently accounted for about 75 percent of all investment in manufacturing. Thus the rising share of urban investment going to manufacturing is likely a good proxy for the share of total investment going to manufacturing.

20. For a detailed analysis, see Daniel Rosen and Trevor Houser, "China Energy: A Guide for the Perplexed," (report, Washington: Peterson Institute for International Economics, May 2007), www.petersoninstitute.org.

21. National Bureau of Statistics of China, *China Statistical Abstract 2006* (Beijing: China Statistics Press, 2006), 147.

22. For example, in 2003 overall efficiency gains were the equivalent of about 30 percent of the adverse effects on energy efficiency stemming from the structural shift toward the most energy-intensive subsectors of the industrial sector. Jiang Jin, "Managing Energy Demand: The Bridge to Sustainability," *China Economic Quarterly* 10, no. 4: 31.

23. Shai Oster, "Pollution Takes Rising Toll in China," *Wall Street Journal*, August 4, 2006, http://online.wsj.com (accessed August 4, 2006).

24. Ma Guonan, "Who Foots China's Bank Restructuring Bill?" in *The Turning Point in China's Economic Development*, eds. Ross Garnaut and Ligang Song (Canberra: Asia Pacific Press at the Australian National University, 2006).

25. National Development and Reform Commission, *Report on the Implementation of the 2005 Plan for National Economic and Social Development and on the 2006 Draft Plan for National Economic and Social Development* (Beijing, March 5, 2006), www.npc.gov.cn.

26. This is hardly an argument against further appreciation of the renminbi, however. The longer China maintains an undervalued currency, the greater the distortion of investment in favor of tradables and the greater the size of the ultimate adjustment required when the currency does move toward a long-term equilibrium value.

27. People's Bank of China, Monetary Policy Analysis Small Group, *Report on the Implementation of Monetary Policy 2005Q2* (Beijing, August 4, 2005), www.pbc.gov.cn, 28.

28. ISI Emerging Markets CEIC Database, available by subscription at www.securities.com.

29. International Energy Agency, *World Energy Outlook—China and India Insights* (Paris, 2007).

30. For details, see chapter 7 of this book.

31. Marvin Goodfriend and Eswar Prasad, "A Framework for Independent Monetary Policy in China," IMF Working Paper 06/11 (Washington: International Monetary Fund, May 2006), www.imf.org (accessed October 6, 2006).

32. Organization for Economic Cooperation and Development, *China*, OECD Economic Surveys, 2005/13 (Paris, September 2005), 185.

33. National Bureau of Statistics of China, *China Statistical Abstract 2004* (Beijing: China Statistics Press, 2004), 41, 187.

34. This reallocation, of course, would reduce government savings, since the latter are defined as current revenues less current (i.e., noninvestment) outlays.

35. National Bureau of Statistics of China, *China Statistical Abstract 2006*, 52.

36. Louis Kuijs believes these funds are transferred to state-owned enterprises in electric power, water, transport, and other infrastructure sectors. See Kuijs, "How Will China's Savings-Investment Balance Evolve?" World Bank China Office Research Working Paper no. 5 (Beijing: World Bank China Office, May 2006), 7.

37. National Bureau of Statistics of China, *China Statistical Yearbook 2007*, 73, 92–93.

38. Kuijs, World Bank Research Working Paper no. 5.

39. IMF, *Regional Economic Outlook: Asia and Pacific* (Washington, May 2006), www. imf.org (accessed August 16, 2006); National Bureau of Statistics of China, *China Statistical Yearbook 2005*, 770; National Bureau of Statistics of China. *China Statistical Yearbook 2006*, 882.

40. China Economic Research and Advisory Programme, "China and the Global Economy: Medium-term Issues and Options," December 2005.

41. Consumption increased by 2.6 percent in households where one spouse was not in the labor force or unemployed and by 5.7 percent in households where both spouses worked. See Shin-Yi Chou, Jin-Tan Liu, and James K. Hammit, "National Health Insurance and Precautionary Saving: Evidence from Taiwan," *Journal of Public Economics* 87 (2002): 1873–94.

42. National Bureau of Statistics of China, *China Statistical Yearbook 2005*, 494; People's Bank of China, *Quarterly Statistical Bulletin,* no. 41 (Beijing, 2006), 33.

43. Before-tax profits of industrial firms with sales above RMB5 million were RMB1.95 trillion in 2006 (National Bureau of Statistics of China, *China Statistical Yearbook 2007*, 503–505). In 2004 the profits of all industrial firms exceeded those of firms with sales of more than RMB5 million by 15 percent. Assuming this ratio was unchanged in 2006, profits of all industrial firms in 2006 can be estimated at RMB2.2 trillion. China's three largest oil producers are subject to a windfall profits tax, which amounted to RMB45 billion in 2006. Profits also are subject to the corporate income tax. While the statutory rate is 33 percent, various tax waivers reduce the applied rate to 24 percent for most domestic enterprises (Zhu Zhe, "Unified 25% Corporate Tax Proposed," *China Daily*, December 25, 2006). Assuming the average corporate tax rate on domestic firms was 24 percent, after-tax profits can be estimated at RMB1.67 trillion or 8 percent of 2006 GDP.

44. Louis Kuijs, William Mako, and Chunlin Zhang, "SOE Dividends: How Much and to Whom?" World Bank Policy Note (Beijing: World Bank, October 17, 2005), www.worldbank.org (accessed August 9, 2006).

45. For example, effective August 19, 2006, the People's Bank of China raised the nominal interest rate on a one-year term corporate deposit to 2.52 percent. The corporate goods price index in August 2006 was up 2.9 percent compared with August 2005, making the real return –0.4 percent. Nominal returns on short-term deposits are less than 2.52 percent, as low as 0.72 percent for demand deposits, making the real return on deposits of less than one year as low as –2.2 percent. The next adjustment was effective May 19, 2007 when the one-year deposit rate was raised to 3.06 percent. But the corporate goods price index for May 2007 was up 5.1 percent compared with May 2006, making the real return –2 percent. The de-

mand deposit rate was left unchanged at 0.72 percent so by mid May the real return fell to –4.4. In short-deposit rates for corporates are becoming increasingly negative in real terms.

46. Kuijs, Mako, and Zhang, World Bank Policy Note.

47. Calculated from data in the flow of funds accounts reported in the annual *China Statistical Yearbook*. The flow of funds data for 2004, released in the fall of 2007, show a further 4.7 percentage point decline in household disposable income as a share of GDP in 2004 alone. However, because the 2004 flow of funds accounts are based on the revised GDP data released in late September 2006, the 2004 numbers on disposable income and GDP are not comparable with those previously published.

48. Nicholas R. Lardy, *China's Unfinished Economic Revolution* (Washington: Brookings Institution, 1998), 109.

49. Morris Goldstein and Nicholas Lardy, "China's Exchange Rate Policy: An Overview of Some Key Issues," in *Debating China's Exchange Rate Policy*, ed. Morris Goldstein and Nicholas Lardy (Washington: Peterson Institute for International Economics, 2008), 4–9.

50. The real interest rate is calculated as the one-year lending rate minus the inflation rate reflected in the corporate goods price index. The latter index is compiled and published by the People's Bank of China.

51. Jianwu He and Louis Kuijs, "Rebalancing China's Economy—Modeling A Policy Package," World Bank China Research Paper no. 7 (World Bank, September 2007), www.worldbank.org.cn.

52. World Bank, "Water Supply Pricing in China: Economic Efficiency, Environment, and Social Affordability," Policy Note (Washington, December 2007), 4.

53. Ministry of Finance, Ministry of Agriculture, and State Tax Bureau, "Notice Concerning Issues in Lowering the Agricultural Tax Rate and Carrying Out the Reform of Eliminating the Agricultural Tax in Trial Points" (Beijing, June 30, 2004), www.mof.gov.cn (accessed July 21, 2006).

54. Wen Jiabao, *Report on Work of the Government* (Beijing, April 18, 2008).

55. Based on the revised 2006 GDP figure of RMB21,192 billion the National Bureau of Statistics reported in April 2008. State Tax Bureau, "The Adjustment of the Individual Income Tax Will Bring RMB28 Billion in Benefit to Tax Payers" (Beijing, November 17, 2005), www.mof.gov.cn (accessed July 21, 2006); National Bureau of Statistics of China, "Report Concerning the Results of the Verified Final Data on 2006 GDP and the Verified Preliminary Data on 2007 GDP" (Beijing, April 10, 2008), www.stats.gov.cn (accessed June 12, 2008).

56. Ministry of Labor and Social Security, "Regulations on the Minimum Wage" (Beijing, December 30, 2003), www.trs.molss.gov.cn (accessed June 29, 2006).

57. Workers and staff is a category that includes a substantial portion of individuals employed in urban areas but excludes those working in private firms and the self employed, as well as foreigners and persons from Hong Kong, Macao, and Taiwan.

58. Beijing Municipal Labor and Social Insurance Bureau and Beijing Statistical Bureau, "Announcement on Developments in Beijing Municipal Wage and Social Insurance Affairs in 1999," www.bjld.gov.cn (accessed June 24, 2008); Beijing Municipal Labor and Social Insurance Bureau, "Notice Concerning the Adjustment of the Minimum Wage Standard in Beijing Municipality in 2007," www.bjld.gov.cn (accessed June 24, 2008); and ISI Emerging Markets, CEIC Database.

59. China Statistical Information Net, "Wages of Beijing Workers and Staff Increase Steadily; Differentials Across Industrial Branches Expand" (Beijing), www.hebei.gov.cn (accessed July 10, 2006).

60. This appears to have been partially offset by the actions of local officials in rural areas. In response to the abolition of the agricultural tax, which had accrued to local governments, they imposed increased levels of unauthorized fees on rural residents.

61. Data in the paragraphs that follow are taken from speeches presented at the National People's Congress in Beijing in early March 2008.

62. National Bureau of Statistics of China, *China Statistical Abstract 2007*, 209; National Bureau of Statistics of China, *Statistical Report on the Development of Labor and Social Insurance in 2007* (Beijing, May 21, 2008), www.stats.gov.cn (accessed May 21, 2008).

63. State Council, "Opinion on the Trial Implementation of the State Capital Management Budget" (Beijing, September 8, 2008), www.sasac.gov.cn (accessed September 25, 2007).

64. Profits of all industrial firms in 2006 are estimated to be RMB2.2 trillion (note 43). I assume that 41 percent accrued to state-owned and state-controlled firms, the share they accounted for in 2005; National Bureau of Statistics of China, *China Statistical Yearbook 2005*, 491, 497, and *China Statistical Yearbook 2006*, 509. Deducting the windfall profits tax of state-owned oil companies and the average corporate income tax of 24 percent (note 43) results in an estimate of after-tax profits of RMB650 billion.

65. Ministry of Finance, "Progress in the Work of Reforming Rural Taxes and Fees in 2004 and the Direction for Work in 2005" (Beijing, March 2, 2005), www.mof.gov.cn (accessed July 21, 2006).

66. Ministry of Finance, "The State Capital Management Budget Is Not the So-Called 'Taking from the Fat to Subsidize the Skinny'" (Beijing, September 14, 2007), http://news.xinhuanet.com (accessed October 3, 2007).

67. Zhe, *China Daily*, December 25, 2006.

68. The central bank did raise the demand deposit rate briefly by 9 basis points to 0.81 percent for five months in 2007, between July 21 and December 20.

69. National Bureau of Statistics of China, "Overall Stability in National Economic Circulation in the First Quarter" (Beijing, April 16, 2008), www.stats.gov.cn (accessed April 16, 2008).

70. Jonathan Anderson, *The Chinese Monetary Policy Handbook* (Hong Kong: UBS, November 2007).

71. An effective exchange rate is a weighted average of the bilateral exchange rates with each of a country's trading partners where the weights are the trade shares of each trading partner. A real exchange rate is one adjusted for relative price changes at home and abroad, typically based on consumer price data.

72. US Department of Labor, Bureau of Labor Statistics, "Import/Export Price Indexes," 2006, http://data.bls.gov (accessed April 17, 2008).

73. Nicholas R. Lardy, *Integrating China into the Global Economy* (Washington: Brookings Institution, 2002), 26.

74. National Bureau of Statistics of China, *China Statistical Yearbook 2007*, 72.

7

Energy Implications of China's Growth

It remains to be seen how flexibly the PRC will interpret self-reliance in this age of interdependence. The degree of flexibility may ultimately reflect, internally, the pace at which the PRC chooses to modernize its agriculture and industry and, externally, the direction in which PRC relations with the United States . . . develop.

— Choon-ho Park and Jerome Alan Cohen[1]

On one side of China's balance sheet stand shining economic achievements; on the other—inseparable from the nature of its industralization—lie disquieting energy and environmental liabilities. Between 1978 and 2000, the Chinese economy grew at 9 percent while energy demand grew at 4 percent. At the turn of the century, China accounted for 10 percent of global energy demand but met 96 percent of this demand with domestic energy supplies. After 2001, economic growth continued apace, but changes in the structure of the economy pushed energy demand up by 11 percent a year. Today China's share of global energy use has swelled to over 16 percent, forcing the country to rely on international markets for more of the oil, gas, and coal it consumes.[2] This fundamental shift in China's energy profile has created shortages at home and market volatility abroad and raised questions about whether China's growth trajectory is sustainable. China is now the world's second largest energy consumer and has likely become the leading source of greenhouse gas emissions.[3]

Understanding the changing relationship between macroeconomic trends and energy outcomes is critical in addressing energy security and environmental protection, both inside China and abroad. Conversely, how these issues are addressed will shape the macroeconomic trajectory and sustainability of China's development model. This chapter explores how China's energy footprint has evolved as a function of costs, the implications at home and abroad of China's energy use, and the policy agenda for dealing with those implications.[4]

Evolution of Energy Demand in China

Decades of state planning and ideological aspiration prior to reform in the late 1970s had distorted China's energy demand profile. Rather than embracing a development strategy compatible with its natural endowments (China is rich in labor, poor in capital, arable land, and technology) as Japan, Hong Kong, Taiwan, and others had done, leaders ignored comparative advantage and dragged China—kicking, screaming, and sometimes starving—toward Soviet-style industrialization. In fits and starts over 30 years, resources were shifted out of agriculture and into energy-intensive industries like steel and cement. Between 1949 and 1978, industry's share of economic output grew from 18 to 44 percent, and the amount of energy required to produce each unit of output tripled (figure 7.1).[5] This command-and-control fiasco resulted in severe inefficiency, which, ironically, created the potential for impressive catch-up growth later—what we think of as a Chinese miracle today.

In 1978 leaders began to unleash China's potential. Faced with continued worry about famine, Beijing let farmers "catch their breath" by reforming agricultural production targets and raising prices, with dramatic results. Farm output increased, and the early 1980s saw rural residents with more time on their hands, cash in their pockets, and freedom to use it as they chose. Much of this new wealth was invested into township and village enterprises (TVEs) set up to exploit what China was best suited for: labor-intensive light manufacturing. These TVEs became an engine of economic growth and the first step away from energy-intensive industry, a shift that would shape China's energy footprint for the next 20 years.[6]

Reform also brought changes within heavy industry, which reduced the energy intensity of Chinese growth. Economic incentives—the right to aspire to and keep profits—were introduced where only planned mandates existed. Awareness among enterprises of bottom-line profits made them focus more on top-line expenses, including on energy. And as enterprises were becoming more aware of the impact of energy costs on profitability, their energy bills were growing as a result of partial liberalization of oil, gas, and coal prices. The introduction of limited competition for both customers and capital, not just from other state-owned enterprises (SOEs) but also from a growing private sector, made energy cost management all the more important. Domestic competition was accompanied by gradual integration with world markets; lower trade barriers not only brought pressure on SOEs from energy-efficient foreign companies but also allowed them to acquire the more energy-efficient technology their competitors enjoyed. China's small existing base of modern plants and equipment enabled it to absorb new technology quickly, significantly improving the efficiency of the country's capital stock.[7]

By 2000, Chinese economic activity required two-thirds less energy per unit of output than in 1978 (figure 7.1). Energy intensity improvement on

Figure 7.1   Energy intensity of the Chinese economy, 1953–2007

Source: CEIC data from National Bureau of Statistics of China, *China Statistical Yearbook*, various years.

this scale was unprecedented for a large developing country and meant that in 2001, China accounted for 10 percent of global energy demand rather than the 25 percent based on 1978 energy performance.

Investment-Led Energy Surprise

At the start of the new millennium in 2001, China's leaders expected the energy intensity improvements that had been taking place since 1978 to continue. Economic reform was an accepted reality and was assumed to presage further energy efficiency. China had decided to join the World Trade Organization (WTO), locking in greater market competition at home and recognizing the importance of comparative advantage.[8] Most energy forecasters at home and abroad assumed that the structural shift away from energy-intensive heavy industry would persist; at least, no one expected the evolution to reverse quickly. Further, GDP growth was expected to expand by 7 to 8 percent for the coming decade, fast but not furious.[9] In 2001 both the Chinese government and the International Energy Agency (IEA) predicted 3 to 4 percent energy demand growth between 2000 and 2010 (figure 7.2).

Both wildly missed the mark. The economy grew much quicker than anticipated in 2001–06, but the real surprise was a change in the energy intensity of economic growth. Energy demand elasticity (ratio of energy demand

Figure 7.2 Energy demand, historic and recent forecasts, 1974–2030

billion tons of oil equivalent

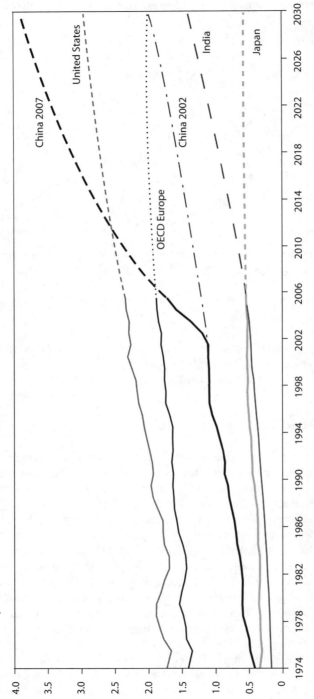

OECD = Organization for Economic Cooperation and Development

Note: The International Energy Agency, in its *2002 World Energy Outlook*, predicted Chinese energy demand would reach 2.1 billion tons of oil equivalent by 2030. Just five years later, in its *2007 World Energy Outlook* it raised its 2030 forecast for China's energy demand by 1.7 billion tons of oil equivalent (a 79 percent upward revision) to 3.8 billion tons of oil equivalent.

Sources: Historic data from International Energy Agency, *World Energy Statistics and Balances 2007*; projections from International Energy Agency, *2007 World Energy Outlook.*

growth to GDP growth) increased from 0.4 between 1978 and 2001 to 1.1 between 2001 and 2006.[10] Energy consumption grew four times faster than predicted to 16 percent of global demand in 2006. And yet on a per capita basis, China's energy demand remains one-sixth that of the United States, triggering anxiety about how much more growth is to come.[11]

This upside surprise not only shocked domestic and international energy markets but also prompted a fundamental reassessment of China's energy future—and hence the world's. In its *2007 World Energy Outlook*, the IEA raised its 2030 forecast for China's energy demand by 1.7 billion tons of oil equivalent (a 79 percent upward revision) to 3.8 billion tons of oil equivalent from the 2.1 billion tons of oil equivalent it had predicted in its 2002 outlook. The new forecast is more than India's total projected demand for that year.[12] Under this scenario, China will account for 22 percent of global energy demand, more than Europe, Russia, and Japan combined, easily surpassing the United States as the world's largest energy consumer.

What caused China's two-decade history of energy intensity improvements to change course? Many China watchers assume that the recent evolution of China's energy profile reflects growth in consumption and transportation—for instance, air conditioning and personal cars. This is not correct. Consumption-led energy demand will be the major driver in the future and is already significant in absolute terms, but the main source of today's growth is energy-intensive heavy industry. Industrial energy efficiency has continued to improve over the past six years: Every new steel mill is more efficient than the last one; but the structural shift away from heavy industry toward light industry has reversed, and a new steel plant—no matter how much more efficient than its predecessor—uses substantially more energy than a garment factory. Industry today accounts for two-thirds of final energy consumption in China, while the residential, commercial, and transportation sectors account for 12, 5, and 13 percent, respectively.[13] This is high by either developed- or developing-country standards (table 7.1).

When pundits express shock at how much more energy intensive China is than, say, Japan, they usually ignore the important factor of what the country makes. High energy intensity partly reflects the role of industry in the Chinese development model, as opposed to India, which has taken a more services-heavy approach, or Japan, which has lowered its energy intensity in part by migrating its energy-intensive sectors to China. As shown in table 7.2, industry accounts for 48 percent of all economic activity in China compared with India at 29 percent and Japan at 26 percent. So the fact that one unit of economic output requires five times as much energy in China as in Japan says more about the type of economic activity taking place in China than the efficiency with which it occurs (though energy efficiency in most industries in China lags OECD averages, discussed later). And economic activity in China is increasingly skewed toward investment.

Table 7.1   Energy demand by sector, 2005 (percent)

Sector	China	India	Russia	Brazil	Japan	EU-27	United States	World
Agriculture	4.6	7.2	2.3	4.9	0.9	2.2	1.1	2.4
Industry	63.8	52.1	38.4	41.1	38.3	32.4	26.8	37.8
Commercial	4.7	3.0	8.1	6.8	17.7	10.5	13.0	9.0
Residential	12.3	16.7	26.2	10.3	15.7	22.0	16.8	17.1
Transportation	12.8	18.5	22.7	36.9	26.9	29.8	41.4	31.5
Other	1.9	2.5	2.1	0.0	0.0	3.0	0.9	2.0
Total (million tons of oil equivalent)	890	199	417	128	348	1,249	1,546	6,893

Note: This table excludes biomass but includes nonenergy use of energy commodities.

Source: International Energy Agency, *World Energy Statistics and Balances 2007.*

Table 7.2   GDP by sector, 2005 (percent)

Sector	China	India	Russia	Brazil	Japan	OECD Europe	United States	World
Agriculture	12.5	18.8	5.5	5.7	1.5	2.3	1.0	n.a.
Industry[a]	47.5	28.8	39.5	29.3	26.2	27.3	20.7	28.2
Services	39.9	52.4	55.0	65.0	72.3	70.5	78.3	n.a.
Total (billions of US dollars)	2,303	809	765	882	4,554	13,671	12,434	44,730

n.a. = not available
OECD = Organization for Economic Cooperation and Development

a. Industry includes manufacturing and construction.

Source: Economist Intelligence Unit Country Data based on national sources.

Is it the case then that energy intensity booms whenever there is an investment boom in China? Investment as a share of China's GDP approached its current high of 43 percent two other times, in the late 1970s and the early 1990s, when it also created a surge in industrial activity.[14] From an energy standpoint, the current investment cycle is different. Based on a review of the literature, data analysis, and primary research, we postulate a number of things.

First, China is now producing domestically, rather than importing, more of the energy-intensive basic products (such as steel and aluminum) used to construct the roads and buildings investment pays for. China now accounts for 49 percent of global flat glass production, 48 percent of global cement production, 35 percent of global steel production, and 28 percent

Figure 7.3   China's share of global production, 2006

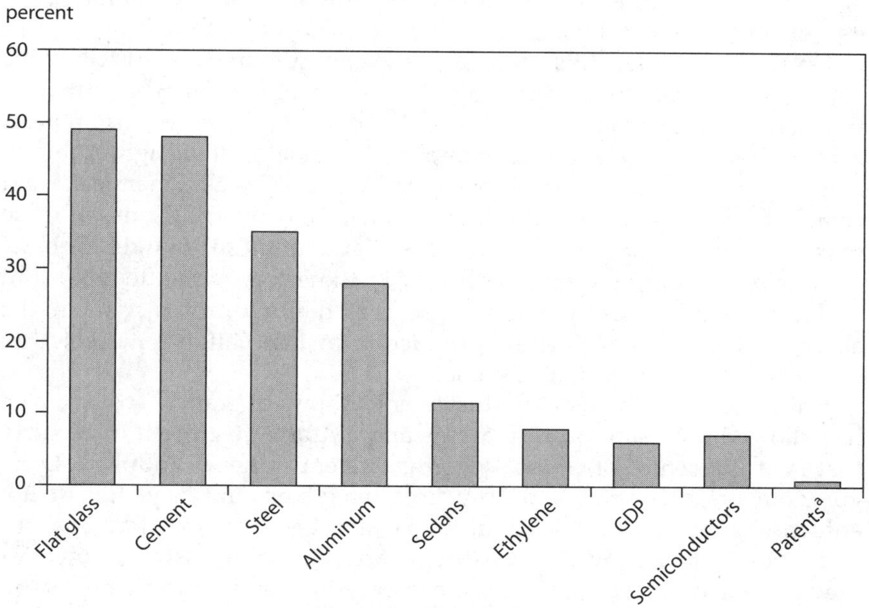

percent

a. Refers to share of US patents awarded to foreign countries.

Sources: CEIC data from ISI Emerging Markets; US Patent and Trademark Office; International Energy Agency; Pilkington, "Flat Glass Industry—Summary," www.pilkington.com; International Iron and Steel Institute, www.worldsteel.org; US Geological Survey; Comtex, www.comtex.com; and authors' estimates.

of global aluminum production (figure 7.3).[15] Some of this production reflects migration of industry from other parts of the world not only to serve Chinese demand but also for export. Where China used to be a net importer of many energy-intensive goods, it has now become a major global exporter of steel, aluminum, and cement.

Second, the energy impact of China's investment cycles is worsening: With each boom more finance is pumped in to build domestic energy-intensive industrial capacity. The implication is that energy policy alone cannot fix the energy problem, and it must be incorporated into the larger agenda for rebalancing China's growth; this agenda must include adjustments to the financial system, environmental protection regimes, trade policy incentives, and other variables discussed in this book.

Third, the changing composition of China's industrial structure is less the result of ideological aspiration (as it was for Mao Zedong) than competition among provinces and localities to grow GDP, tax revenue, and corporate profits.[16] Not just Beijing but also local interests, including industrial enterprises, set the rules of competition. And regardless of who sets the rules, implementation is a local matter. Within this context of competition, short-term economic incentives—low operating costs and profits—explain much of the increase in heavy industrial activity.

On the profit side, after-tax earnings in energy-hungry industries have been good, thanks to depreciation, dividend waivers for SOEs, transfer payments, and other factors. Heavy-industry profits have risen from near-zero in the late 1990s to a level comparable to that of their light-industry counterparts—ranging from 4 to 7 percent in steel, glass, chemicals, and cement in recent years.[17] With China modernizing over 170 cities of more than 1 million people, certainly there is a large domestic market for basic materials, and supply was squeezed by breakneck growth after 2001. But with overcapacity arising almost as soon as the first profits come in, the ability of firms to sell surplus production in international markets has been critical to remaining profitable.

China's energy-intensive industry enjoys low operating costs, which has allowed for rising profit margins and a dramatic growth in capacity that is at the center of China's overinvestment in heavy industry. Local governments often provide deeply discounted land, and they often do not enforce regulations to protect air and water. Construction time is short, and labor costs are low. These benefits apply to all industries; however, they are particularly valuable in the energy-intensive sector, where capital costs are large. The financial system also favors heavy industry: SOEs worry little about the threat of default, and borrowing rates are not even high enough to afford depositors a positive real rate of return. Not only are profit margins high (for borrowers, not depositors) but also SOEs do not have to distribute the profits to their shareholder (the state), leaving them with plenty to reinvest. The following subsections lay out these various operating cost advantages in detail.

Energy Prices and Environmental Costs

Energy prices in China, once highly subsidized, have gradually converged with world prices over the past 30 years. Yet, given local idiosyncrasies in pricing, dual supply channels for many legacy SOEs, arrears, and other factors, it can be difficult to accurately assess the price a specific firm pays for coal, gas, oil or electricity. Chinese prices for raw energy commodities including coal and natural gas, particularly in interior provinces close to resource deposits, can be significantly cheaper than those in the OECD. For coal, low prices result not from subsidization but rather from low extraction costs in areas isolated from international markets. As transportation bottlenecks ease, coal prices will continue to rise toward world prices. Coke, a coal-derived fuel used in steelmaking, was once significantly cheaper inside China than on international markets due to limitations on Chinese coke exports. In recent years, however, the gap between Chinese

Figure 7.4 Industrial electricity prices, 2006

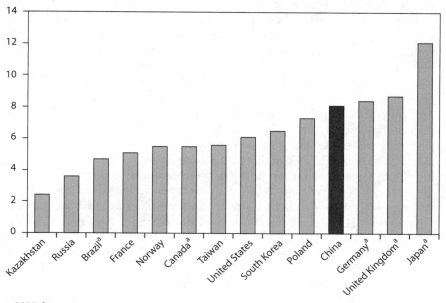

US dollars per kilowatt hour

a. 2005 data.

Sources: US Department of Energy, Energy Information Administration; International Energy Agency; CEIC data from National Development and Reform Commission Price Monitoring Center.

and global coke prices has significantly narrowed. Beijing directly controls natural gas prices, attempting to keep them competitive in the face of competition from the Middle East in gas-intensive industries like petrochemicals. But this approach has failed to encourage development and delivery of sufficient quantities of natural gas to meet demand, and authorities are allowing domestic prices to increase.

Reported prices of electricity—the form in which China's industry increasingly receives its energy—are high compared with those in developing and some developed countries (figure 7.4). However, based on our conversations with Chinese business leaders and industry analysts, it is likely that many industrial enterprises do not bear the full cost implied by national average figures from the Statistical Bureau. The National Development and Reform Commission (NDRC) sets electricity tariffs province-by-province based on the recommendations of local pricing bureaus, which answer to local officials. While the NDRC would like to see energy pricing rationalized to reduce overall energy consumption, it is sensitive to local social and economic development concerns. Energy-intensive firms in China typically consume more energy per unit of output than their peers in the OECD (on average, 20 to 40 percent more, according to some esti-mates[18]) and are thus sensitive to electricity price increases (as well as gas and coke prices, which may be low).

The recent surge in global commodity prices and inflation has chal-lenged Beijing's commitment to price reform. Gasoline and diesel prices, which are also directly controlled by the state, were increased by 10 and 7 percent, respectively, during 2007. In the six months following a price in-crease in October 2007, crude oil costs rose 33 percent, leaving Chinese gasoline and diesel prices 20 and 40 percent below US levels on average at the end April 2008.[19] Coal prices also increased significantly in 2007 and during the first quarter of 2008, yet Beijing has been reluctant to increase electricity prices. As with natural gas, price controls restrict supply rather than boost demand. Loss-making oil refineries cut back production, caus-ing filling stations to ration. In the first two months of 2008, some power generators were unwilling to buy coal at higher prices, leading to a draw-down in inventories, which contributed to the blackouts during the Chi-nese Spring Festival. By mid-June, these shortages had grown severe enough that the government had little choice but to raise prices, 18 percent for gasoline and diesel and 5 percent for electricity, improving the operat-ing economics of the country's refiners and power plants.[20]

Energy prices in China have not historically reflected environmental costs. Over 80 percent of the country's electricity is generated from coal. At the end of 2006, less than 15 percent of coal power plants had flue gas desulphurization (FGD) systems (used to remove SO_2 from emissions streams) installed and even fewer had them running.[21] Operating an FGD system reduces production efficiency by 4 to 8 percent and therefore con-tributes to higher electricity prices. If all the power plants in China in-stalled and operated FGD systems, average electricity tariffs could rise by 10 to 20 percent.[22] Industries that burn coal directly (such as steel and ce-ment) are subject to sulfur taxes, but these are generally too low to reduce pollution. Other air pollutants, such as nitrogen dioxide and mercury, are largely unregulated. Regulated or not, enforcement generally falls to the provincial and local governments, which must balance environmental concerns against economic growth priorities. In the absence of a strong environmental regulator, like the US Environmental Protection Agency, that balance is skewed toward near-term economic growth, as industry threatens to cut jobs and tax revenue if enforcement of environmental reg-ulations is ratcheted up.

Land and Construction

In China, land is not privately owned in perpetuity but owned and allo-cated by the government on the people's behalf. While private land own-ership does not exist, long-term (generally 50-year) leases do and are bought and sold between both individuals and enterprises. In more developed urban real estate markets like Beijing and Shanghai, there is little difference between these land leases and an ownership deed. They are priced at market terms and transferred between holders with little interference from the state. Outside the cities, however, the government largely handles land transfers. Local officials can take farmland to create industrial parks, compensating farmers only the agricultural value, not the industrial-use value. In other words, local officials can price land well below what a firm would pay elsewhere in the world, and since industrial users will pay taxes while farmers will not, there is a powerful incentive to put land to industrial use. While land use prices are rising in coastal areas, new swaths of heavily discounted farmland are being offered for industrial use in China's interior to lure investment.

In interviews with the authors, directors of energy-intensive firms in China emphasized the land cost advantage. The cost of transforming the land is low, and construction time short. Local governments often contribute generously to groundwork—grading, infrastructure buildout, and clustering related segments of the value chain. Relocating existing residents, carrying out environmental impact assessments, and other steps are accelerated in China to a degree not found elsewhere. Construction labor costs are dramatically lower in China than in the OECD countries. An aluminum smelter that would take three or more years to build in the United States at high labor and ground preparation costs can be constructed in China in under a year and at much lower daily cost.[23] (For political and social factors bringing about low land and construction costs in China, see chapters 4 and 5.)

Capital and Consolidation

Beijing does not intend for China's financial system to relentlessly favor heavy industry; nonetheless, the outcome has been just that: too much capital to build energy-guzzling industrial capacity. This outcome is rational from a short-term financial perspective because industrial operating costs are low, excess capacity can be exported without inducing normal exchange rate effects (thanks to the heavily managed exchange rate), and borrowers are mostly state-owned firms to which loan officers bear little career risk lending. Further, foreign firms are willing to join in many projects, contributing technology and creating backward linkages to developed-country markets.

While central authorities lean against approving investments in sectors where they see (national) overcapacity, local authorities encourage additional investments. Beijing has tried to curb lending to steel, aluminum, cement, and other industries in recent years. It has tried to prevent lending to new firms in the automobile sector; force consolidation in steel,

Table 7.3   Industrial profit margins, on an earnings-before-tax basis (percent)

Industry	1998	2002	2006
Heavy industry			
Iron and steel	0.80	4.60	5.20
Nonferrous metals	−0.80	3.20	6.80
Cement and glass	−0.40	3.70	5.30
Paper and pulp	1.80	5.00	5.20
Basic chemicals	1.00	4.00	5.60
Light industry			
Textiles and apparel	0.20	3.10	3.90
Furniture manufacturing	3.70	4.00	4.40
Computers and telecom	4.30	4.80	3.30
Electronic machinery	2.60	5.00	4.70

Note: Calculated as earnings before tax divided by total sales revenue.

Source: CEIC data from ISI Emerging Markets.

coal, and other sectors; and raise borrowing costs for energy-intensive industries in general. But in most cases, especially at the local level, financing of additional capacity continues, and little unauthorized capacity is ever shut down.

Since 1998, profit margins on an earnings-before-tax (EBT) basis[24] have recovered from less than 1 percent to between 4 and 7 percent for China's most energy-hungry industries (table 7.3). In 2007 profit margins in metals, glass, chemicals, and cement exceeded those in textiles, apparel, furniture, and electronics. The aluminum industry has seen a particularly dramatic increase in profitability, with EBT margins increasing from 5 to 14 percent in the past four years. Recent survey work calculating return on investment in 12,400 firms across the country supports sectorwide profit data trends.[25] Since 2002, iron and steel profits have surpassed those in most light industries.[26]

Some debate whether China's firms are truly profitable. Shan Weijian of TPG, an investment firm, argues that the value of debt-to-equity swaps and bank recapitalization has exceeded the entire pretax profits of the industrial sector since 1999—suggesting zero profitability but for lax bank financing on a gargantuan scale. This theory suggests that the direction China is headed is wrong but that from the borrowers' short-term perspective, does not contradict their instinct to pile into energy-intensive industries. Additionally, if banks are told not to lend or to charge higher rates, many SOEs can self-finance with retained earnings: Enterprise bank deposits—like household deposits—earn minimal interest, so there is little reason not to reinvest. If SOE shareholders—the government—were paid a reasonable share of profits as dividends, these firms' investment criteria

Table 7.4   Global steel industry: Production, market share, and industry concentration, 2006

Country/region	Production (million tons of crude)	Share (percent of global production)	Share of top three firms (percent of domestic production)[a]
China	422	34.60	14.10
EU-25	198	16.30	44.70
Japan	116	9.50	69.30
United States	99	8.10	59.70
Russia	71	5.80	55.10
South Korea	48	4.00	85.80
World	**1,219**	**100**	—

a. Share of domestic production from the three largest companies in 2005.

Sources: CEIC data from ISI Emerging Markets; International Iron and Steel Institute, www.world steel.org; company annual reports.

might be different, but the dividend policy reforms announced for 2008 are trivial in this regard.[27]

High profits impede rational resource allocation. The NDRC has promoted steel industry consolidation for years, not only to reduce energy consumption but also to nurture Chinese steel companies with scale to compete worldwide. Yet the number of steel enterprises doubled between 2002 and 2006, as firms saw profit opportunities and joined in. The three largest of China's 7,000 steel companies are now world class but accounted for only 14 percent of Chinese production in 2006. Compare this with Japan, South Korea, and the United States, where the top three companies each control well over half the market (table 7.4). China's steel industry is balkanized, with many provinces promoting their own champions. Local officials often resist attempts to consolidate firms. Conditions are similar in other energy-intensive industries. At the end of 2006, China had 381 aluminum companies, 3,388 paper and pulp companies, 2,982 glass companies, 5,210 cement companies, and 20,083 chemicals companies. Despite government attempts at consolidation, these industries have further fragmented, as rising profits and local encouragement attract more companies (table 7.5).

Were it not for the export safety valve, this pile-on would have created profit-eroding overcapacity. China's metals companies, in particular, have been able to utilize capacity and remain profitable by selling overseas, accounting for much of the growth in China's trade surplus since 2004. In 2002 China's steel imports exceeded exports by 450 percent. In 2006 exports exceeded imports by 230 percent, making China not only the world's largest steel producer but also the largest exporter. China's iron and steel industry was responsible for 18 percent of national energy consumption

Table 7.5   Industry concentration in China (number of firms)

Industry	2002[a]	2004	2006
Iron and steel	3,551	4,947	6,959
Nonferrous metals	1,332	1,766	2,798
Cement production	4,656	5,042	5,210
Glass and glass products	1,739	2,205	2,982
Paper and pulp	2,606	3,009	3,388
Chemical materials	12,481	15,172	20,083

a. 2002 figures are from a February 2003 survey.

Source: Beijing Kang Kai Information & Consulting data from ISI Emerging Markets.

that year, compared with only 10 percent for all the households in the country combined. Aluminum production, in which China now also runs a trade surplus, consumes nearly as much energy as the commercial sector, and production of chemicals, in which China still runs a trade deficit but a shrinking one, consumes as much as the transportation sector. Taken together, China's heavy industry is responsible today for 54 percent of the country's energy demand, up from 39 percent only five years ago.

The bottom line: Capital allocation is the palliative keeping China's energy-intensive market structure going when it should adjust. The consequences of making ill-considered investments in energy-intensive sectors must be permitted to bite at the firm level.

Local and Global Implications

The consequences of China's investment-led growth are significant both at home and abroad. In addition to the energy security and environmental challenges, the current investment-led, heavy industrial model of development leads to less-than-optimal economic growth and employment both for China and the rest of the world.

Energy Security

The impact of China's investment-led surge in heavy industry is felt first and foremost inside China. Between 2001 and 2006, electricity consumption doubled as new steel mills, aluminum smelters, and chemical industry parks were added to the grid. The power generation industry, still in transition from a government ministry to multiple state-owned enterprises, struggled to keep up with double-digit demand growth. During the late 1990s, Beijing restructured much of the state sector in advance of WTO accession, shutting down old inefficient industrial capacity. As a result, China found itself with an electricity surplus, and in 1999 policymakers issued a three-year moratorium on the construction of new power plants.[28] When demand started taking off in 2001, provincial officials struggled to win approval to build the generation capacity they would need to supply the new industrial activity taking place in their backyard. And when Beijing turned them down, many provinces went ahead and built the plants anyway, concerned that failure to do so would result in the loss of investment to competing provinces. In total, about 140 gigawatts of unauthorized capacity was built over a three-year period. Yet, this was not enough: Blackouts roiled the country during 2004 and 2005, raising energy security to the top of the political agenda.

China had long considered that its large reserves of coal—currently meeting 69 percent of the country's energy needs—would safeguard its energy security. Yet during 2002–05, China's coal-dominated energy supply system failed to deliver. Fatalities spiked at coal mines working overtime to meet surging demand. Clogged railways were unable to get enough coal to market to supply the newly constructed power plants, and a fragmented electrical grid was unable to get power where and when it was needed. And the surge in heavy industrial activity straining domestic coal and power supplies was forcing China to import more oil.

Between 1980 and 2002, China's oil demand grew by less than 6 percent per year on average. In 2003 and 2004, demand spiked to 9 and 17 percent, respectively.[29] While the growing number of passenger cars was responsible for some of this growth, expansion of heavy industry was the principal culprit: Newly constructed chemical industry parks required large amounts of naphtha, a petroleum-derived feedstock; firms increasingly turned to trucking to move products as the country's rail system was bogged down with coal shipments; and when the coal-fired power plants fell short in terms of electricity supply, industry scrambled to buy diesel and fuel oil to run back-up generators. As a result, China's dependence on imported oil grew from 30 percent in 2002 to just under 50 percent by 2006. China accounted for 36 percent of the growth in global oil demand during that period, compared with the United States at 14 percent.[30] This took oil markets by surprise and, along with political instability in the Middle East and hurricanes along the Gulf Coast of the United States, helped push oil prices toward historic highs. Most analysts had, in fact, anticipated a decline in Chinese oil demand growth from the rates seen in the 1980s and 1990s.[31] So when China's call on global oil markets doubled between 2002 and 2006, producers struggled to keep up.

Since the peak of the blackouts in 2004, China has increased its power generation capacity by 70 percent.[32] In 2006 and 2007, 200 gigawatts of new capacity was added to the grid, more than the entire installed base of Germany and Italy combined. While this rapid buildout temporarily alleviated electricity shortages and helped bring oil demand growth back in line, China's energy security problems are far from solved. To reduce coal mine fatalities and improve the efficiency of the coal sector, Beijing now factors coal mine fatalities into the criteria used to assess job performance of local government officials. In advance of the Communist Party Congress in October 2007, where Party members came up for job review, and the National People's Congress in March 2008, several small coal mines were closed, as local officials sought to prevent high-profile mine collapses in their jurisdictions during China's political season. This policy, which was successful from an environmental and workplace safety standpoint, meant that overall coal production growth slowed significantly in 2007. Coming into 2008, large coal companies, aware of reduced domestic supply and a tight international market, pushed for a 15 percent increase in annual contract coal prices. The power generators pushed back, concerned that with inflation headed toward 8 percent, the government would not allow them to pass higher coal costs through to electricity prices. Though the two sides ultimately settled on an 8 percent increase, neither party was eager to start fulfilling the new contracts.[33] Power companies started drawing down coal inventories rather than buying from miners at these prices, hoping that spot prices would fall. Then when severe snowstorms cut off coal delivery routes, inventories ran dry and blackouts ensued.

As long as coal and crude oil prices remain liberalized, and gasoline, diesel, and power prices remain controlled, China will have difficulty ensuring reliable energy supply to its citizens. This difficulty is compounded by the fact that demand growth continues to be industry-led, and thus volatile, oscillating with the boom and bust of investment cycles. In addition to making it difficult to plan domestic supply, volatile growth and controlled prices increase China's impact on international energy markets.[34]

Environmental Protection

Given limited supplies of natural gas and challenges in ramping up nuclear or renewable sources of energy, 80 percent of electricity in China comes from coal-fired power plants.[35] These power plants are the country's leading source of air pollutants including sulfur dioxide (SO_2) and particulate matter (PM). Annual SO_2 emissions have increased 30 percent since 2002 and are now nearly twice that of the United States.[36] While a steady increase in the average height of smokestacks at power plants and industrial facilities has reduced ambient air pollution levels from their historic highs in the 1980s, those improvements have slowed, and in many cases reversed, since 2003. China's State Environmental Protection Agency (SEPA) estimates that SO_2 pollution now costs the country $60 billion per year in economic impacts on public health and agricultural production.[37] Concentrations of particulate matter (PM10), which is tied to respiratory illness, are some of the highest in the world.[38] Only 1 percent of China's urban population lives in cities meeting SEPA's preferred PM10 standard.[39] In Beijing, PM10 levels are four times higher than in Los Angeles and six times higher than in New York. The World Bank estimates that all outdoor air pollutants combined account for between 350,000 and 400,000 premature deaths each year in China.[40]

China's investment-led industrial growth has also taken its toll on the country's water resources. Around urban areas, 90 percent of riverways are polluted, depriving millions of fresh, safe drinking water. Heavy metals and toxic organic chemicals from industrial wastewater are of greatest concern, increasing the risk of cancer, bone deformity, neurological disease, and complications during pregnancy. The World Bank estimates that air and water pollution, taken together, reduce overall Chinese economic output by 6 percent.

The environmental implications of China's booming heavy industry transcend borders. China's potential impact on international waterways was brought home when a CNPC petrochemical plant exploded in November 2005, sending a 100-ton benzene slick down the Songhua River through populated areas of China and into Russia. In the south, ambitious hydropower development plans, which have already resulted in the dislocation of 23 million people inside China, threaten to change the lives of millions more who live downstream on the Nu (Salween) and Lancong (Mekong) Rivers in Vietnam, Laos, Thailand, Cambodia, and Burma, not to mention further impact on the Yangtze in China.[41] And SO_2 emissions blowing eastward from China are a growing source of political tension with Korea and Japan.

The most global impact of China's energy use, and possibly the most significant in absolute terms, comes from carbon dioxide (CO_2). In 2007 China surpassed the United States to become the world's largest emitter of CO_2 on an annual basis (though still lagging considerably if measured in cumulative or per capita terms).[42] Industry in China is responsible for 68 percent of all emissions, compared with the United States, where energy used by consumers accounts for the majority of emissions.[43] If the current investment-led, heavy industrial model of economic development continues, the IEA estimates that China will account for 42 percent of the growth in CO_2 emissions worldwide between now and 2030.[44]

Employment, Income, and Growth

Overinvestment in heavy industry—which is generally capital not labor intensive—instead of light industry and services reduces job creation and the flow of salary income to consumers. Investment-led growth has also depressed the flow of interest income to households that would otherwise have increased their disposable income and thus promoted consumption (see chapter 6). As discussed earlier, low costs—one of which has been low-interest income to lenders relative to the profits enjoyed by borrowers—

have abetted the investment boom in heavy industry. Investment-led growth is also responsible for the environmental and pollution-related health costs of reckless industrial processes. The Chinese people increasingly have to bear these health costs on their own as medical care is underfunded in China. These costs are threatening household savings throughout the country, necessitating precautionary saving and hence depressing consumption.

The World Bank, working with Chinese government economists, has modeled the employment and household wealth effects associated with mollycoddling heavy industry. Balanced growth among sectors would increase employment growth by five times through 2025, increase incomes for those jobs thanks to 20 to 30 percent growth in productivity, aid more rapid urbanization and hence reduce rural-urban income inequality, and dramatically reduce negative environmental and health externalities due to reduced weight for dirty industries in the economy relative to less noxious services.[45]

Most importantly, these employment and rebalancing gains are *not* a trade-off between environmental protection and economic growth: Overall GDP growth is comparable in the business-as-usual and improved scenarios. The economic activity entailed in shifting from heavy industry to a less energy-intensive future makes just as great, if not greater, a contribution to GDP growth. A more benign energy future is not a luxury or otherwise incompatible with official pronouncements that China must deal with achieving "moderate prosperity" first before turning to sustainable development: More sustainable development is in fact the quicker route to moderate prosperity.

International Commercial Impacts

Just as China's post-2001 investment-led growth has had welfare consequences for households and other economic sectors at home, it has had commercial consequences abroad. If the 2002 pattern of industrial self-reliance versus reliance on heavy industrial imports had remained constant, by 2007 China's net imports would have grown by an additional 92 million tons of steel—the entire present steel output of the United States, employing 250,000 and creating $37 billion in economic activity.[46] Using this constant market share approach, China, on net, would have imported 2.2 million tons more of aluminum, 43 million tons more cement, and 8.7 million tons more paper. Taken together, domestic production substituted about $110 billion worth of heavy industrial imports (the four above plus some energy-intensive chemicals) in 2007.[47] The value added in this trade is, of course, a fraction of that total, and the corresponding export shares would be dispersed among many nations. If China had eschewed investment in these heavy industries, then it quite possibly would have invested in and amassed additional surplus in other light industries or even services. So it would be misleading to score 100 percent of forestalled trade as a welfare loss for the rest of the world. There may even be positive externalities for OECD nations where heavy-industry opportunities were impaired: Steel-consuming, higher value-added industries in these countries got cheaper intermediate inputs for their finished goods, while energy intensity was likely lowered and pollution reduced.

While it is a daunting and subjective challenge to compute the external impacts of China's penchant for heavy industry, it is important to recognize that they exist: China does not necessarily do the world a favor by overproducing. Moreover, there are other, dynamic welfare effects to be considered. A rebalanced China, better aligned with its natural endowment of labor, would be a bigger economy, grow faster, and be less prone to collapse and hence be a *better* engine of world growth. Also, heavy industry in China is less likely to attract innovation and hence technological change due to weaknesses in intellectual property protection and the difficulty of recovering R&D investments.[48] Similarly, institutional weaknesses in regulation and enforcement of pollution controls undermine the process of finding innovative ways to remedy environmental damage.

The Domestic Response

China's top leadership is becoming increasingly aware of the consequences of the current investment-led, heavy industry–dominated pattern of growth and expressing a desire to change course. In his address to the 17th Communist Party Congress in October 2007, President Hu Jintao pointed to the shortcomings of China's development model that "economic growth is realized at an excessively high cost of resources and the environment" and encouraged the formation of an "energy and resource-efficient and environment-friendly structure of industries."[49] Beijing has ambitions to reduce the energy intensity of growth in the years ahead. As part of the current 11th Five-Year Program the government has set a target of reducing energy intensity by 20 percent and air pollution by 10 percent by 2010. Each province has been asked to do its part to help the country meet this goal, and Beijing has warned that failure to do so will affect the career prospects of provincial officials, regardless of how they score on other metrics (like GDP growth and foreign investment).[50] To improve the odds of success, the NDRC, understanding that industrial energy use is at the core of the problem, compiled a list of the 1,008 top energy-consuming firms collectively accounting for one-third of total energy demand and instructed them to develop efficiency plans in cooperation with local officials.[51] Local governments have signed or are developing similar plans with an additional 100,000 smaller energy-intensive firms.[52] The NDRC also raised electricity prices for energy-intensive industry and stepped up efforts to ensure provincial enforcement.[53]

Power generation efficiency is also improving, thanks in part to a concerted effort by the NDRC to close small power plants. In 2007, 553 small inefficient plants, accounting for 14.4 gigawatts of capacity, were closed. Replacing this capacity with more efficient plants helped reduce the average amount of coal required for each kilowatt hour nationwide by 3 percent. This shaved overall coal consumption by 30 million tons and resulted in overall annual energy demand growth of 7.8 percent in 2007 rather than 8.6 percent.[54] Closing the remaining 100 gigawatts of small-scale power generation at this rate would reduce the energy intensity of economic growth by 0.75 percent each year through 2012.

SEPA, China's environmental watchdog, is gradually exerting more influence on the policymaking process. Most encouraging is the progress made in using economic incentives to reduce SO_2 emissions from power plants. The SO_2 pollution levy enacted in the late 1970s was too cheap, too narrow, and too weakly enforced to discourage power plants from polluting.[55] Recently, the sulfur levy was increased and, importantly, coupled with a market-based incentive: If plants install FGD systems, they can add the cost of installation and operation to the price they charge the grid companies for power. While absolute SO_2 emissions increased in 2006, the majority of new power plants had sulfur scrubbers installed.[56] As those sulfur scrubbers came online, SO_2 emissions declined by 4.7 percent in 2007.[57] In addition, SEPA is increasingly cracking down on polluting industries by denying permits: In 2006 110 projects were rejected on environmental grounds compared with only two during the entire preceding decade.[58]

These measures are yielding some positive results. Energy intensity declined by 1.8 percent in 2006 and 3.8 percent in 2007.[59] While this falls just short of the 4 percent per year needed to meet the 20 percent goal, policies put in place fairly recently are likely to show more progress in the years ahead. That said, improved energy efficiency and enforcement of environmental regulations alone will be insufficient to fundamentally change China's energy future. Even if Beijing is successful in meeting its 20 percent goal by 2010, overall energy demand will have increased by more than 40 percent since 2005, if economic growth continues at current rates. And much of the low-hanging fruit, in terms of efficiency improvements, has already been picked. To move China off its current trajectory, smarter energy and environmental policy will need to be coupled with a rebalancing of the economy as a whole.

Relationship to Overall Macro Rebalancing

In chapter 6 Nicholas Lardy centers the rebalancing imperative on raising consumption relative to investment and exports in national expenditures.

He highlights fiscal policies, financial system reforms, exchange rate system reforms, and increased energy prices as the four levers with which to propel consumption-led growth. For Jianwu He and Louis Kuijs, rebalancing also means raising consumption relative to investment and net exports.[60] They offer a longer laundry list of prescriptions for rebalancing, including the three components of Lardy's analysis plus more policy incentives (prices and taxes), labor and factor mobility reforms, center-local reforms, and more aggressive sector-specific industrial policies. Central authorities in China would disagree little with most of this; they do, as US Treasury Secretary Henry Paulson, Jr. often notes, have a difference of opinion on timing.

Unfortunately, there is little indication that Beijing has taken the steps necessary at the macro level to rebalance development. Money supply (M2) and bank lending have accelerated since 2005, despite administrative tightening on lending in late 2007 and a gradual rise in nominal interest rates since 2005. Dividend payment requirements for central SOEs were announced in 2007 for implementation in 2008 (on a trial basis in 2007) but at a very low rate. Fiscal reforms have not offset household anxieties that reduce consumption, and financial reforms are far from correcting the unfair division of investment income between borrowers and lenders. Appreciation of the renminbi against the US dollar remains modest in real terms, while the currency has moved even less against the real basket of currencies against which it trades. The simple bottom-line: As of end-2007, investment remains above 42 percent of GDP and growth in heavy industry continues to outpace that in light industry and services.

Attempts to change the economics of key energy-intensive industries may be having more success in reining in output growth. Policymakers have tried to restrict lending to the most energy-intensive sectors[61] and reduce incentives for these firms to export by cutting the value added tax rebate for many types of steel, aluminum, cement, and chemicals, effectively raising their price on international markets by 2 to 12 percent.[62] Energy and environmental compliance costs continue to rise for Chinese producers, and land use policies have made it more difficult for local officials to lure industry with land giveaways. In addition, changes in global steel, aluminum, and chemicals industries are putting competitive pressure on Chinese firms. In steel and aluminum, rising shipping costs have put China at a disadvantage vis-à-vis producers closer to ore reserves and Western markets. And with high crude prices and limited availability of natural gas, new capacity in the Middle East is challenging China's chemicals industry. In 2007, output from these industries continued to grow, but for steel, cement, and basic chemicals, the rate of growth declined from 2006, helping move China closer to its goal of reducing energy intensity by 20 percent by 2010.[63]

Rising resource costs, lending controls, and border adjustments alone, however, are unlikely to correct China's systemic bias toward heavy industry unless coupled with structural and institutional reforms. While physical output growth in energy-intensive industries slowed in 2007, higher prices and movement up the value chain meant their share of overall economic activity expanded. And while rising costs and stiff international competition are starting to put pressure on profit margins, investment in these industries has yet to slow relative to the economy as a whole. Improved efficiency and movement up the value chain have reduced the energy intensity of China's economic growth from its 2004–05 high, but for Beijing to quadruple economic growth by 2020 while only doubling energy demand, that growth will need to be rebalanced.

The Energy Footprint of a Rebalanced Chinese Economy

If Beijing pursued an inclusive rebalancing policy package, would the energy outcomes be positive? Yes, they would. A shift toward light manufacturing and services could unfold as quickly as the shift toward heavy industry eventuated in 2001–02. This is a critical point. As industry overwhelmingly drives China's energy demand, it is tied to investment cycles, which are volatile. In 2007, responding to the current investment-led heavy industry surge, the IEA raised its forecast for Chinese energy demand in 2030 by 79 percent from what it had forecast in 2002. Projections of China's energy future based on the current economic structure face similar risks, but in the other direction (i.e., less energy demand than expected).

One dollar of economic output from the apparel or electronics industry, as well as most service-sector activities, requires less than one-tenth the energy required to produce output of the same value from the steel or cement industries.[64] If services and light manufacturing were to significantly outgrow heavy industry in the years ahead, China's energy future would look much different than the alarming picture painted by today's forecasts. In the World Bank's rebalancing scenario mentioned earlier, not only does economic growth stay the same but also energy demand in 2030 declines by 25 percent from the business-as-usual projection, roughly equivalent to what the IEA sees China reaching in 2015—all this while increasing employment and returns to household savings.

That said, a Chinese economy rebalanced away from investment and net exports toward consumption will bring energy challenges of its own. Many Chinese households are today earning enough to afford energy-intensive consumer goods like air conditioners and automobiles. An emerging consumption-oriented middle class is more likely to work in an office than in a factory and can easily satisfy its food and shelter needs and have money left over to spend on consumer goods and services. If making the steel and glass to build office buildings and shopping malls drives China's energy demand today, lighting, heating, and cooling those malls and offices will drive China's energy demand in a consumption-led future. Likewise, the energy needed to make the cement and asphalt used to construct highways will be replaced by the energy needed to fuel the cars that will ply those highways.[65]

Dealing with the consequences of the energy demand of a rising middle class is, in many ways, easier than managing the consequences of today's investment-led energy demand. Consumption-led energy demand grows in a relatively steady, predictable manner compared with the volatile nature of investment-led demand. That means more reliable energy delivery inside China and less uncertainty in international energy markets. Also, as income (and thus purchasing power) grows, consumers are generally more willing and able to pay for cleaner energy supplies. While energy-intensive industry, in China as in most countries, fights environmental regulation out of fear of profit loss and decreased competitiveness, energy-intensive consumers also tend to be the same middle-class citizens pressuring government to clean up the air they breathe and the water they drink. Thus a consumption-led energy trajectory is more likely to unfold sustainable growth, from both energy security and environmental standpoints. Importantly, however, as we touch upon briefly in the following section, shrinking China's domestic energy footprint does not necessarily reduce the net global energy tab, since some other country will be making for export to China the same investment-heavy products that China rebalanced away from making for itself.

Conclusions and Policy Agenda

China's leaders are now aware that broad rebalancing must be part of dealing with energy and environmental challenges, but policies to do so have been slow to materialize. In addition, the macro rebalancing package, while necessary to address China's energy challenges at home, will not be sufficient when it comes to international energy security and global climate change. Outside China, unease over these issues is adding to already considerable anxiety about China's rise. In Washington, concern over these issues has centered on China's failed bid for Unocal; Chinese oil investment in Sudan, Iran, and Venezuela; and its contribution to climate change. Opinions and legislation on the US response to China's energy footprint are evolving rapidly.

The context should be kept in mind while contemplating ways to address this issue: China is an 800-pound gorilla on the world energy stage and cannot be ignored; but there is a 1,600-pound gorilla here too—the United States. Instead of defending that fact, US policymakers might see it as an opportunity. The scope of action needed from China seems impossibly ambitious as a unilateral matter, especially since China feels entitled to follow an industrial path that many OECD nations have taken. Acknowledging the need for it to improve the sustainability of its own energy profile may be by far the most powerful lever the United States has for impelling change elsewhere: There is an opportunity for a bargain in energy and the environment that gives policymakers in both China and the United States political cover for painful choices. And the world's two largest energy consumers and polluters will need to make numerous painful choices together in the decades ahead. Recognizing this, the two countries in June of 2008 launched a 10-year framework agreement for cooperation on energy and environmental issues.

Energy Security and the Role of Volatility

The energy security problem with China's investment-led energy demand is not so much the sheer volume of fuel the country needs—the world can deliver that supply if it has the time and confidence about demand—but the uncertainty and volatility it creates in international energy markets. Annual oil demand growth that jumps from 2 to 17 percent, accounting for anywhere between one-fifth and one-half of growth in global oil consumption in a given year, has contributed to the crude price premium as producers struggle to forecast future demand. China has also recently become a net importer of both coal and natural gas. Greater transparency and cooperation between China and other large energy-consuming countries on stockpile and inventory levels, ensuring sea lane safety, demand management, and development of alternative sources of energy would go a long way toward reducing price volatility and supply uncertainty, both for China and the rest of the world.

Yet as existing multilateral institutions work to facilitate such cooperation, China is missing from the table. The IEA counts only OECD countries as members, though some non-OECD countries, including China, hold "observer status." This collective of energy-consuming countries was established as a counterweight to the energy-producing collective, the Organization of Petroleum Exporting Countries (OPEC). While OPEC's share of global oil production is set to grow, the OECD's share of oil consumption is quickly declining, from 60 percent today to 47 percent by 2030. To stay relevant, the IEA must either adapt to the growing weight of the developing world, China in particular, or give way to a new institution that does not determine membership by income level. The United States has recently indicated it is interested in including China in the IEA, but it is unclear in what capacity and under what terms this participation would take place.[66]

Both the IEA and OPEC should also pay careful attention to the energy implications of China's macro rebalancing, if it were to occur. While moving from investment- and export-led growth to consumption-led growth would reduce China's domestic energy demand, it would likely increase energy demand elsewhere, as non-Chinese producers gain market share in industries like steel, cement, aluminum, and chemicals. To the extent that this readjustment rationalizes the energy footprint of global supply chains (i.e., moving energy-intensive industry closer to resource bases and to countries with more efficient production processes), global energy demand trend growth may be reduced. But the adjustment itself will likely create market volatility, and in some models a rebalanced China urbanizes faster, which raises questions about the net demand for energy-intensive goods in the medium term and beyond. Increased awareness and understanding of the linkage between macroeconomic trends and energy outcomes will help reduce market uncertainty.

Climate Change

The United States and China are both rich in coal and look to it to satisfy the majority of their electricity needs. China is building its power generation base from scratch and the United States is preparing to replace a generation of aging stock. In both countries, CO_2 is vented into the air from all the existing coal-fired plants and will be vented from all the plants currently on the drawing board.[67] Carbon capture and sequestration (CCS), which would mitigate CO_2 emissions from these plants, is a viable technology that still needs significant R&D before it can be widely commercialized. A recent MIT study on the future of coal pitches for several integrated projects to demonstrate the feasibility of CCS in a variety of countries and geological settings.[68] We believe this should be a priority area of cooperation between the United States and China. Industrial energy efficiency, biofuels, green buildings, and nuclear power are also important areas for collaboration.

While technical cooperation is important, particularly in the near term, it is no substitute for a multilateral framework to address climate change in which both the United States and China take part. The existing approach, as embodied in the Kyoto Protocol, is inadequate to address energy use in China and the rest of the developing world. While the vast majority of the CO_2 added to the atmosphere over the last century came from the West (and the United States in particular), most of the CO_2 emitted over the next century will come from the East (China in particular). Yet even in 2030, China will still be a relatively poor country, with per capita CO_2 emissions less than half those from the United States. As such China refuses to accept absolute limits on emissions, afraid that it will impede economic growth. That said, Beijing says it is willing to go beyond what was required under the Kyoto Protocol and commit to "nationally appropriate mitigation actions" under a post-Kyoto framework.[69] This willingness bodes well for global climate negotiations, not least because it removes the key obstacle to active US involvement. Washington has argued for over a decade that action by the developed world will be ineffective from a climate standpoint unless large developing countries like India and

China follow suit and harmful from an economic standpoint as energy-intensive industry in the developed world migrates to countries without similar costs on carbon emissions.

The nature of China's energy challenges informs the prognosis for a multilateral climate framework in which both China and the United States take part in three ways.

First, there is considerable scope for China to commit to emissions reductions, which would be positive for the country's economic growth. As 68 percent of the Chinese CO_2 comes from industry, rebalancing the economy away from heavy industry toward light manufacturing and services would maintain headline GDP growth at current levels while significantly reducing emissions.

Second, such rebalancing would allay industrial competitiveness concerns in the United States and other developed nations and increase the likelihood that they take action appropriate for their income level and historic emissions. While US climate leadership should not be conditioned on Chinese action, concerns that US national climate policy would result in an industrial exodus to China could translate into protectionist provisions or derail policy progress in Washington altogether. An agreement between the United States and China that both countries impose similar carbon costs on industry would enable bolder US domestic legislation and international negotiating positions.[70]

Finally, in considering the type of climate commitments China should be asked to make, it is important to remember that China's carbon future remains highly uncertain. A shift in the growth structure of the Chinese economy between 2002 and 2007 resulted in an upward revision of 70 percent in the IEA's 2030 forecast for China's CO_2 emissions, a change larger than *total* projected European emissions for that year. Successful rebalancing of economic growth, perhaps aided by new climate policy, could result in a similar large downward revision in expectations for future Chinese emissions. The difficulty in establishing a credible emissions baseline means that negotiating absolute caps on Chinese emissions, while politically challenging, is not advisable. It also means that any agreement on climate change needs to ensure that if China rebalances growth and its heavy industry migrates abroad, that shift in production reduces that industry's carbon footprint globally. Otherwise, from a climate standpoint, rebalancing the Chinese economy will just move China's emissions to other countries.

Notes

1. "The Politics of China's Oil Weapon," *Foreign Policy*, no. 20 (Autumn, 1975).

2. BP plc., *Statistical Review of World Energy 2007*; National Bureau of Statistics of China, *China Statistical Yearbook*; General Customs Administration, *China Customs Statistics*. The latter two, as well as all other Chinese statistics used in this chapter

(unless otherwise indicated) have been collected via CEIC, a commercial statistical database provided by ISI Emerging Markets. Henceforth, all figures accessed in this manner will be referenced as "CEIC" followed by the source publication or government agency.

3. International Energy Agency (IEA), *World Energy Outlook 2007* (Paris: Organization for Economic Cooperation and Development). This refers to annual emissions rather than cumulative emissions, in which the United States still leads.

4. This chapter draws heavily from Daniel Rosen and Trevor Houser, *China's Energy Evolution: The Consequences of Powering Growth at Home and Abroad* (Washington: Peterson Institute for International Economics, forthcoming).

5. CEIC data from National Bureau of Statistics of China, *China Statistical Yearbook*.

6. For more on energy dynamics in China's reform period, see Kenneth Lieberthal and Michel Oksenberg, *Policy Making in China: Leaders, Structures, and Processes* (Princeton, NJ: Princeton University Press, 1988). On the launch of reforms in general, see Barry Naughton, *Growing out of the Plan: Chinese Economic Reform, 1978–1993* (New York: Cambridge University Press, 1995); Susan L. Shirk, *The Political Logic of Economic Reform in China*, California Series on Social Choice and Political Economy, no. 24 (Berkeley: University of California Press, 1993); Barry Naughton, *The Chinese Economy: Transitions and Growth* (Cambridge, MA: MIT Press, 2007); Kenneth Lieberthal and David M. Lampton, *Bureaucracy, Politics, and Decision Making in Post-Mao China*, Studies on China (Berkeley: University of California Press, 1992); Nicholas R. Lardy, *Integrating China into the Global Economy* (Washington: Brookings Institution Press, 2002); Nicholas R. Lardy, *China's Unfinished Economic Revolution* (Washington: Brookings Institution, 1998); Kenneth Lieberthal, *Governing China: From Revolution through Reform*, 2d ed. (New York: W. W. Norton, 2004).

7. Analysis of what contributed to China's reduction in energy intensity can be found in Karen Fisher-Vanden et al., "Technology Development and Energy Productivity in China," *Energy Economics* 28, no. 5–6 (2006); Fuqiang Yang et al., "A Review of China's Energy Policy" (Lawrence Berkeley National Laboratory, 1995); Jin-Li Hu and Shih-Chuan Wang, "Total-Factor Energy Efficiency of Regions in China," *Energy Policy* 34, no. 17 (2006); Lynn Price et al., "Industrial Energy Efficiency Policy in China," in *ACEEE Summer Study on Energy Efficiency in Industry* (2001); Karen Fisher-Vanden et al., "What Is Driving China's Decline in Energy Intensity?" *Resource and Energy Economics* (2004); Richard F. Garbaccio, "Price Reform and Structural Change in the Chinese Economy: Policy Simulations Using a CGE Model," *China Economic Review* 6, no. 1 (1994). See in particular the forthcoming study by Lin Jiang of the Lawrence Berkeley National Laboratory on energy intensity in China, 1996–2003.

8. Daniel Rosen, "China and the World Trade Organization: An Economic Balance Sheet," Policy Briefs in International Economics 99-6 (Washington: Institute for International Economics, June 1999), www.petersoninstitute.org (accessed June 10, 2008).

9. Zhou Dadi and Mark D. Levine, "China's Sustainable Energy Future: Scenarios of Energy and Carbon Emissions" (Energy Research Institute and Lawrence Berkeley National Laboratory, 2003).

10. CEIC data from *China Statistical Yearbook.*

11. Between 1997 and 1998, energy demand in China fell in absolute terms while GDP grew at 7.8 percent, resulting in a particularly sharp decline in energy intensity. Thomas Rawski and others have argued that this is evidence that China overreported economic growth during those years; Thomas G. Rawski, "What is Happening to China's GDP Statistics?" *China Economic Review*, no. 12 (2001). Jonathan E. Sinton and David G. Fridley examine the sources of the decline in energy demand and isolate it to a fall in direct coal use in a handful of energy-intensive sectors, resulting from industry consolidation, increased efficiency, and a dramatic improvement in the quality of coal (Jonathan E. Sinton and David G. Fridley, "What Goes Up: Recent Trends in China's Energy Consumption," *Energy Policy*, March 2000). Even if the years 1997–2000 were an anomaly (either on the GDP or energy demand side of the equation), the underlying story remains the same. Energy demand grew at an average annual rate of 5 percent between 1978 and 1996 and 11 percent between 2001 and 2007 (a change in energy demand elasticity from 0.51 to 1.03).

12. IEA, *World Energy Outlook 2007* and *World Energy Outlook 2002* (Paris: Organization for Economic Cooperation and Development).

13. CEIC from *China Energy Statistical Yearbook.* This figure on residential use, as those used throughout this chapter, excludes consumption of biomass fuels like wood and crop waste. The use of such fuels is difficult to quantify and unlikely to increase much in absolute terms as China develops.

14. Nicholas R. Lardy, "China: Towards a Consumption Driven Growth Path," Policy Briefs in International Economics 06-6 (Washington: Peterson Institute for International Economics, 2006).

15. Michael Taylor, "Energy Efficiency and CO_2 Reduction Opportunities in the Global Cement Industry" (paper presented at the IEA-WBCSD Cement Industry Workshop, Paris, September 4, 2006); Pilkington, "Flat Glass Industry—Summary," www.pilkington.com; International Iron and Steel Institute (IISI), www.worldsteel.org; Abare Economics, www.abareconomics.com; CEIC from *China Statistical Yearbook.*

16. In his recent textbook, *The Chinese Economy*, Barry Naughton argues (p. 347): "The development of a market economy in China has shaped the economy in complex and sometimes apparently contradictory directions that are far different from what a central planner would ever have envisaged." Andrew Wedeman's *From Mao to Market* catalogues many of the intraprovincial trade wars that still go on but through industrial policy tactics rather than outright roadblocks (Andrew Wedeman, *From Mao to Market: Rent Seeking, Local Protectionism, and Marketization in China*, Cambridge, UK: Cambridge University Press, 2003). Scott Kennedy's recent work demonstrates the extent to which firms and their industry associations now drive industrial policy, rather than industrial policy disciplining them; Scott Kennedy, *The Business of Lobbying in China* (Cambridge, MA: Harvard University Press, 2005).

17. CEIC from *China Statistical Yearbook.* For opposing views on how good profits really are in recent years, see Louis Kuijs, William Mako, and Chunlin Zhang,

"SOE Dividends: How Much and to Whom?" World Bank Policy Note (Washington: World Bank, 2005); Weijian Shan, "The World Bank's China Delusions," *Far East Economic Review* 166, no. 29 (2006); Weijian Shan, "China's Low-Profit Growth Model," *Far Eastern Economic Review* 169, no. 9 (2006); Bert Hofman and Louis Kuijs, "Profits Drive China's Boom," *Far Eastern Economic Review* 169, no. 8 (2006); Jonathan Anderson, "The Furor over China's Companies," in *Asian Focus* (Hong Kong: UBS, 2006); David Dollar and Shang-Jin Wei, "Das (Wasted) Kapital: Firm Ownership and Investment Efficiency in China," IMF Working Paper 07/9 (Washington: International Monetary Fund, 2007).

18. Jiankun He, "Achieving the 2010 20-Percent Energy Intensity Target through Industrial Technology Advancement" (paper presented at the Senior Policy Advisory Council Meeting & Forum on Implementing China's 2010 20-Percent Energy Intensity Reduction Target, Hainan, China, November 2006); Yanjia Wan, "China's Energy Efficiency Policy in Industry" (paper presented at the "Working Together to Respond to Climate Change" Annex I Expert Group Seminar in Conjunction with the OECD Global Forum on Sustainable Development, Paris, March 27–28, 2006).

19. CEIC from NDRC Price Monitoring Center and US Department of Energy, Energy Information Administration.

20. Xinhua News Agency, "China to Raise Prices of Refined Oil, Electricity," June 19, 2008, http://news.xinhuanet.com.

21. Estimates for the amount of power generation capacity with FGD installed range from 60 to 90 gigawatts out of a total base of 622 gigawatts.

22. Calculated based on the share of total power generation coming from coal, the amount of FGD already installed and running, and the current tariff increase allowed for power plants that run FGD systems.

23. Based on conversations with both US and Chinese aluminum industry analysts, January and February 2007.

24. Calculated as earnings before tax divided by total sales revenue.

25. Dollar and Wei, "Das (Wasted) Kapital."

26. Ibid.

27. *People's Daily*, "Chinese Central SOEs Return 17 bln Yuan from 2006 Profits," September 20, 2007, http://english.people.com.cn (accessed December 19, 2007).

28. IEA, *China's Power Sector Reforms: Where to Next?* (Paris: Organization for Economic Cooperation and Development, 2006); C. P. Andrews-Speed, *Energy Policy and Regulation in the People's Republic of China*, International Energy and Resources Law and Policy Series, no. 19 (The Hague: Kluwer Law International, 2004).

29. CEIC from *China Statistical Yearbook*.

30. BP plc., *Statistical Review of World Energy 2007*.

31. See IEA, *World Energy Outlook 2002*. Also see IEA's *Oil Market Reports* (http://www.iea.org) as well as OPEC's *Monthly Oil Market Reports* (http://www.opec.org) from 2002 to 2005.

32. January 2005 through April 2008. CEIC from the China Electricity Council.

33. *China Coal Monthly,* "Annual Contracts Settled, Prices up RMB 35/t," January 30, 2008.

34. Daniel H. Rosen and Trevor Houser, "China Energy: A Guide for the Perplexed" (Washington: Peterson Institute for International Economics, 2007).

35. CEIC from *China Statistical Yearbook.*

36. World Bank and China's State Environmental Protection Administration, "Cost of Pollution in China: Economic Estimates of Physical Damages" (Beijing, 2007); Xiaohua Sun, "Pollution Control Targets Not Met," *China Daily,* February 13, 2007.

37. *South China Morning Post,* "500b-Yuan Loss from Sulfur Cloud," August 4, 2006.

38. Particulate matter are fine particles emitted from the combustion of fossil fuels (as well as volcanoes, forest fires, and dust storms) that are linked to heart disease and impaired lung function.

39. World Bank and China's State Environmental Protection Administration, "Cost of Pollution in China."

40. Joseph Kahn and Jim Yardley, "As China Roars, Pollution Reaches Deadly Extremes," *New York Times,* August 26, 2007.

41. Xinhua's China Economic Information Service, "Full Text: Report on the Work of the Government," March 17, 2007. See also Andrew C. Mertha, "Water Warriors: Political Pluralization in China's Hydropower Policy" (St. Louis: Washington University, 2007); Milton Osborne, *River at Risk: The Mekong and the Water Politics of China and Southeast Asia* (Lowy Institute for International Policy, 2004).

42. IEA, *World Energy Outlook 2007.*

43. IEA, "IEA CO2 Emissions from Fuel Combustion" (Paris: Organization for Economic Cooperation and Development, 2007). Here "industry" includes both direct and indirect emissions. "Consumers" refers to transportation, residential, and commercial energy demand.

44. IEA, *World Energy Outlook 2007.*

45. Jianwu He and Louis Kuijs, "Rebalancing China's Economy—Modeling a Policy Package" (Washington: World Bank, 2007).

46. IISI, *Steel Statistical Yearbook 2006;* US Department of Labor, Bureau of Economic Analysis, "Industry Economic Accounts" (Washington, 2007); US Department of Labor, Bureau of Labor Statistics, "Current Employment Statistics Survey" (Washington, 2007).

47. CEIC from General Customs Administration, *China Customs Statistics.*

48. See "OECD Reviews of Innovation Policy: China," Synthesis Report (Paris, 2007), which catalogues in detail the missing "framework conditions" that undermine the innovation in China, www.oecd.org (accessed December 17, 2007).

49. Xinhua News Agency, "Full Text of Hu Jintao's Report at 17th Party Congress," October 24, 2007.

50. Mure Dickie and Richard McGregor, "Jiangsu Sets the Pace on How to Assess Officials," *Financial Times*, March 15, 2007; Xinhua News Agency, "Chinese Officials Face Scrutiny over Failure to Meet Emission Targets," November 29, 2007.

51. Lynn Price and Wang Xuejun, "Constraining Energy Consumption of China's Largest Industrial Enterprises through the Top-1000 Energy-Consuming Enterprise Program" (Lawrence Berkeley National Laboratory, 2007).

52. Zhou Dadi, "Sustainable Energy Development in China" (background paper for the Westminster Consultations, March 21, 2007, on file with authors).

53. Reuters News, "China Tells Provinces to up Guzzlers' Power Tariffs," April 16, 2007.

54. *China Coal Monthly,* "China Closes 14.4GW of Small Units in 2007," February 25, 2008.

55. Tingsong Jiang and Warwick J. McKibbin, "Assessment of China's Pollution Levy System: An Equilibrium Pollution Approach," *Environment and Development Economics* 7, no. 1 (2002).

56. *Power in Asia*, "Beijing Urges Greater FGD Use," January 31, 2008.

57. Xinhua News Agency, "China's Economic, Social Development Plan," March 20, 2008. Full text of the government's report to the National People's Congress, March 5, 2008.

58. Andrew Batson, "China's Environmental Agency Gets Teeth," *Wall Street Journal*, December 18, 2007.

59. Reuters News, "China Jan-Sept Energy Intensity Falls 3 Pct," November 30, 2007.

60. Jianwu He and Louis Kuijs, "Rebalancing China's Economy—Modeling a Policy Package," World Bank China Research Paper, no. 7 (Washington: World Bank, September 2007).

61. Juan Chen, "China Regulators to Share Data to Curb Loans to Polluters," Dow Jones International News, July 19, 2007.

62. Jon Eichelberger, Brendan Kelly, and Eugene Lim, "China Adjusts Export Vat Refund Rates" (Shanghai: Baker & McKenzie, 2007).

63. CEIC from *China Statistical Yearbook.*

64. Ibid.

65. A more complete discussion of "consumption-led energy demand" can be found in Rosen and Houser, "China Energy: A Guide for the Perplexed."

66. Shai Oster, "U.S. Asks China to Join Global Energy Group," *Wall Street Journal*, May 21, 2008.

67. There are a couple of small exceptions in the United States, including the government-funded FutureGen project, which plans to capture and sequester its CO_2 stream.

68. Massachusetts Institute of Technology, *The Future of Coal* (Cambridge, MA, 2007).

69. UN Framework Convention on Climate Change, "Bali Action Plan" (2007).

70. Trevor Houser, Rob Bradley, Jacob Werksman, et al., *Leveling the Carbon Playing Field: International Competition and US Climate Policy Design* (Washington: Peterson Institute for International Economics, 2008).

8

Why Does the United States Care about Taiwan?

I sincerely hope that the two sides of the Taiwan Strait can seize this historic opportunity to achieve peace and co-prosperity. Under the principle of 'no unification, no independence and no use of force,' as Taiwan's mainstream public opinion holds it, and under the framework of the ROC [Republic of China] Constitution, we will maintain the status quo in the Taiwan Strait. . . . In resolving cross-strait issues, what matters is not sovereignty but core values and way of life.

—Ma Ying-jeou, presidential inaugural address,
Taipei, May 21, 2008

Taiwan has long been the most sensitive issue in US-China relations and likely will remain so for many years to come.[1] The impasse across the Taiwan Strait serves as one of the most dangerous flashpoints in the world, the one issue that could lead to military conflict at a moment's notice between the United States and China today.

China is fond of calling this matter a remnant of China's civil war and a relic of the Cold War. Indeed it is. However, the issue has evolved substantially from this historical context over the years, making the Taiwan impasse in some ways even more relevant and immediate today than ever. Many in the United States and elsewhere may reasonably ask why the United States cares so much about this island off China's coast and why Washington remains committed to it when this commitment could lead to war not only with a nuclear weapons state but also with the world's most important rising power. Likewise, it is reasonable to ask why China cares so deeply about the island that it is willing to jeopardize many other political and economic interests to concentrate on gaining control over the territory.

The answers, like US-China relations more broadly, are complex. They have as much to do with history as with present realities. This chapter provides that context and, in particular, explains the continuing strategic interest of the United States and China in Taiwan.

Why Does China Care about Taiwan?

To most Chinese, Taiwan represents something far more important than mere territory. It is the final piece in China's attempts to overcome the legacy of its "century of humiliation" spanning the 19th and early 20th centuries, when it was colonized and divided by outside powers. Japan had colonized Taiwan in 1895 as a spoil of the Sino-Japanese War and relinquished control only after its defeat in World War II.

The return of Taiwan is also wrapped up in China's traditional measure of national power and self-respect dating back to its imperial days: its "unity." Affirmed through consistent official—government, media, and educational—propaganda for decades, Taiwan's status as a part of historic China, and as a lingering symbol of China's historic victimhood, is an unquestionable article of faith and self-evident truth that resonates deeply with an overwhelming number of Chinese citizens, even among those the outside world might consider the most reformist or progressive on issues like human rights and democracy. For Chinese citizens to think otherwise, or even to raise questions about prevailing opinion toward Taiwan's status (and even official Chinese policy), threatens to call into question their love of the "motherland" and thus their patriotism. Few assume this posture in today's China.

This was not always so. Before the Ming dynasty (1368–1644 AD), the island had little association with mainland China. The Portuguese and the Dutch colonized Taiwan during the 16th and 17th centuries, respectively, and only under the Qing (1644–1911 AD) was the island retained forcefully as a protectorate.[2] During Qing rule, native uprisings were common, and central control inconsistent and tenuous. Taiwan thus has had a murky status historically and a legacy of local resistance to Chinese rule.

While both the Chinese communists under Mao Zedong and the Nationalists (Kuomintang) under Chiang Kai-shek eventually came to assert that Taiwan is part of China, neither side mentioned or focused on the issue until World War II when Taiwan became a potential spoil of war upon the defeat of Japan, which had colonized the island in 1895, and the waning days of the Chinese civil war in the late 1940s.[3] After Chiang's Nationalists were defeated in the Chinese civil war and fled to the island in 1949, they continued to assert their "Republic of China" regime remained the rightful government of all of China, just from offshore in the temporary capital of Taipei. The communists for their part viewed Taiwan as the final stage of the civil war and came to consider restoration of the country's unity—also to include Hong Kong and Macao—as essential for the regime's legitimacy.

Chinese leaders also have viewed Taiwan in terms of national security, specifically as being vulnerable to foreign powers' strategy of encirclement and containment. This perspective reflected China's traditional suspicions about the outside world and historically rooted consciousness about threats to the Chinese heartland from its periphery that periodically led to the nation's subjugation or division.[4] Beijing is particularly sensitive to talk of the island as an "unsinkable aircraft carrier," a term coined by the Japanese during their colonization of the island and continued during the Cold War when the United States maintained military bases on Taiwan and a formal alliance with the Nationalist (Republic of China) government in Taipei.

Chinese strategists have written about the importance for China's security of gaining control out to the "first island chain": They view Taiwan as part of a band of territory around China's eastern maritime periphery that includes US allies Japan, Korea, and the Philippines and thus is of strategic concern. Also of significance are the benefits to China's economy from increasing cross-strait trade and investment flows.[5]

One may argue that the People's Republic of China government itself, through the success of national education and propaganda, has created the conditions whereby the Taiwan issue has become a matter of regime survival and that it may be in China's own interest to consider how to get out of the corner in which it has placed itself. But it is essential to understand that the Chinese people today believe deeply that Taiwan is a historical part of China and that its separation is a legacy of foreign-instilled humiliation.

Whether the people on Taiwan have similar views today is of lesser importance to the Chinese. Likewise, China considers any questions from outsiders about Taiwan's rightful place as part of China as insulting and rude involvement in China's internal affairs that reflects ignorance, ulterior motives, or just fundamental ill will toward the rise of China. Until or unless the views of the Chinese people change, this deep emotional resonance with and popular connection to Taiwan cannot be ignored as a fundamental context for US and others' handling of the Taiwan situation.

Why Has the United States Cared about Taiwan?

The United States has its own historical perspective on Taiwan. The US connection in fact predates consideration of the island itself. Its roots stem from US historical engagement of China dating back to the 19th century and fascination in particular with the Republic of China under Chiang Kai-shek's Kuomintang Party. The rise of the Republic of China under Chiang and his US-educated Christian wife Soong Mei-ling (Madame Chiang) during the 1930s and 1940s represented the culmination of decades of US hopes and dreams to remake China in the Western image. Generations of American missionaries had traveled to China since the 19th century to save souls, do good works, and bring "enlightened" Western ways to a vast new frontier. News about China was transmitted back to the United States through US churches, which increased interest and awareness of Chinese affairs within US society. The rise of Chiang—a Christian convert—and his wife to power seemed to be a validation of their efforts and a measure of their success.

China under Chiang received a boost from US media and popular culture. *Time Magazine* editor Henry Luce, himself a missionary's son, used his magazine to tout the Chiangs as a bulwark for a modern, Westernized, and Christian China and against "warlordism" and atheistic communism. Pearl Buck's enormously successful novel and movie, *The Good Earth*, onto which Americans were able to project their Depression-era struggles to China's age-old hardscrabble conditions, further solidified America's connection to China and Chiang. The Japanese attack on Pearl Harbor made the United States and China both victims of, and immediate war-time allies against, international fascism, particularly Japan. When Madame Chiang made a triumphant visit to the United States in 1943, during which she addressed a joint session of Congress in flawless English, US ties to the Chiangs as China's hope only deepened in the American psyche.

The reality of Chiang's life and governance was obviously more complex. His personal commitment to Christianity, for instance, was inconsistent, and his rule was hardly as enlightened, clean, or democratic as many Americans had assumed (in fact, Chiang had flirted with fascistic models in the 1930s). Nonetheless, when Chiang's Kuomintang forces succumbed to Mao's communists and fled to Taiwan in 1949, many in the United States were stunned and angered. Some vilified the Harry S. Truman administration and US State Department's China specialists for allowing communism to expel an old ally and end the long-standing US project to change China. With concern over international communism growing as the Cold War dawned, the refrain of "Who Lost China?" became a heated cry in US policy and partisan circles. Others simply felt betrayed that the Chinese people, upon whom US citizens had bestowed so much time, toil, and emotion over many years, would turn their backs on "enlightenment" and choose communism.

For others, however, the Kuomintang's retreat simply tied the United States emotionally to the transplanted Chinese on Taiwan. Those who had felt betrayed by the mainland's turn to communism could now turn to the Republic of China based in Taiwan as the last best hope to transform China.

Nonetheless, in early 1950, the State Department had determined that, despite concern about communist victory on the mainland, the United States was in no position, militarily or otherwise, to prevent Mao's forces from finishing off the Kuomintang on Taiwan. This posture changed in June 1950, however, when North Korea invaded the South to begin the Korean War. The North's aggression provoked a new strategic calculation that the United States needed to demonstrate a firm commitment to defend against aggressive communist expansion anywhere and shore up the morale of its allies during the early stages of the Cold War.

The change in strategic mindset caused the United States to maintain its formal diplomatic ties with the Republic of China on Taiwan and led to the establishment of a treaty alliance in 1954 that incorporated the island into the US-led collective security system in East Asia. Taiwan became an essential component of the West's containment policy against international communism. The United States maintained military bases on the island as an "unsinkable aircraft carrier" from which to project power and fulfill its security commitments in East Asia.

In 1954 and 1958, Taiwan became a military flashpoint when China threatened two small Kuomintang-controlled islands—Quemoy (Jinmen) and Matsu—just off its coastline. The Dwight D. Eisenhower administration viewed Chinese pressure in each instance as a test of Western resolve against communist aggression worldwide, and threatened use of nuclear weapons in response, deepening a sense among many US and Kuomintang policymakers that the defense of Taiwan was not only of great symbolic value but also a vital Cold War interest. The crises also raised the first specter of the United States potentially becoming entrapped in a war— even nuclear war—with China over the island. This danger of miscalculation leading to conflict caused the United States and China to begin direct if quiet ambassadorial talks in the mid-1950s, first in Geneva and then Warsaw.

Over time, US relations with the people on Taiwan deepened in many other practical respects. The Taipei government provided economic and technical assistance in support of US operations in Vietnam (although offers of combat assistance were turned down for fear of provoking China). Taiwan's economy expanded rapidly beginning in the early 1960s, with an export-led growth strategy that moved the island from an agricultural to a flourishing industrial-based capitalist economy. By the 1980s, Taiwan had become one of Asia's economic "tigers."

At the same time, personal contacts between US and Taiwan government, academic, and business elite flourished. Americans who sought to study Chinese language or culture traveled to Taiwan, as the mainland remained closed to outsiders and marked by strange convulsions of revolutionary fervor and ideological zeal, epitomized by China's Great Proletarian Cultural Revolution.[6] By contrast, although remaining an authoritarian state, Taiwan seemed eminently friendly and open, and a capitalist ideal, deepening the connection many Americans had with the people on the island and creating expectations among the Taiwan people that the United States would remain its friend and benefactor.

Nonetheless, over time international realities made it more controversial and difficult to defend diplomatic recognition of a small government in exile on Taiwan and isolation of the Chinese communists in Beijing. John F. Kennedy pledged privately in 1963 that he intended to recognize the People's Republic but could only do so after he was reelected, given the fierce political opposition he would face from anticommunist conservatives. It thus ultimately fell to Richard Nixon, one of those anticommunist conservatives, to redefine US Cold War strategy by reaching out to Mao's China, marking the beginning of the end of the US focus on Taiwan as a critical strategic component in waging that war.

The United States recognized that it could not entirely abandon Taiwan to China without seriously damaging its international credibility and reputation, let alone as a matter of decency and fairness to an old friend. Indeed, in the bilateral communiqué that resulted from Nixon's breakthrough trip to China in 1972, the Taiwan issue was central. The two sides agreed to disagree on the issue, and finessed their differences in diplomatic language, setting down on paper the divergence in perspectives, which continues to this day: While China affirmed that Taiwan is "a province of China," the United States would only "acknowledge" that "all Chinese on either side of the Taiwan Strait maintain that there is but one China and that Taiwan is part of China." The United States also "reaffirm[ed] its interest in the peaceful settlement of the Taiwan question by the Chinese themselves." US agnosticism over the ultimate resolution of the Taiwan impasse but requirement that any resolution be peaceful and, by implication, achieved through dialogue laid out the fundamental outlines of the American position, which continues to this day.

In negotiating the communiqué, the Nixon administration recognized that regardless of the future development of relations with China, US commitment to Taiwan's security and peaceful resolution of its relationship with the mainland would remain important for US credibility with other allies and friends who relied on the United States for their security and for maintaining peace and stability in East Asia more broadly. In this view, failing to live up to its long-standing commitment to the people on Taiwan would leave doubts in others' minds about whether the United States was a reliable ally over the long run. With the Vietnam War coming to a close, and the United States retrenching in its military engagement of East Asia as a result, these questions about US reliability were immediate and relevant, with the potential, in the minds of US and regional strategists, to undermine the viability of the entire US alliance-based structure that underpinned US regional influence, and security in East Asia more broadly.

This perspective contributed to the delay in completing the task of normalization through the mid-1970s, as both Gerald Ford and Jimmy Carter resisted China's demands that the United States end arms sales to and break off all ties with the Taipei government as conditions for normalization. In the end, establishment of official diplomatic relations between the United States and the People's Republic of China on January 1, 1979, led to the end of formal US–Republic of China diplomatic ties, the eventual termination of the Mutual Defense Treaty,[7] and termination of US military presence on the island. But it did not lead to the end to military arms sales,[8] unofficial ties with Taipei, or to the fundamental and long-standing US requirement that the ultimate resolution of the Taiwan impasse be peaceful.

The US Congress, concerned that the United States remain true to its commitment to Taiwan's security and that China not be tempted to miscalculate US resolve against the use of force, passed the Taiwan Relations Act on April 10, 1979, establishing a quasi-formal defense commitment to Taiwan. The Act called all nonpeaceful means to determine the future of Taiwan, including boycotts and embargoes, "a threat to the peace and security of the Western Pacific area and of *grave concern* to the United States" (emphasis added), leaving ambiguous exactly how the United States would respond but making clear the seriousness with which Washington would view aggressive challenges to Taiwan's security.

Likewise, the Act stated that the United States will provide necessary "defense articles and defense services" to ensure that Taiwan can maintain "a sufficient self-defense capability." The United States itself would "maintain the capacity . . . to resist any resort to force or other forms of coercion that would jeopardize the security, or the social or economic system, of the people on Taiwan." To conduct subsequent unofficial relations with Taiwan, the bill established a private nonprofit corporation, the American Institute in Taiwan, that would be staffed with employees who were formally not employed by the US government (although in practice, they tended to be either retired officials or active-duty personnel who took a leave of absence from government to take the post).

The Taiwan Relations Act was a watershed for US relations with Taiwan, establishing as a matter of domestic law an explicit authorization and explanation of US interests and policy concerning Taiwan in the face of alliance severance and derecognition of the Republic of China government in Taipei. In particular, this included continuing arms sales to the island, albeit limiting them formally to those of a "defensive character." The Act also made a connection between the peaceful settlement of the Taiwan question and the US commitment to maintaining peace and stability in the region, which carried important implications for Taiwan's security given the severance of the US–Republic of China alliance.

For obvious reasons, the Chinese have considered the Taiwan Relations Act irrelevant to US commitments concerning Taiwan as reflected in the bilateral communiqués, and a violation of the spirit, if not the letter, of the normalization agreement. Nonetheless, none of the Act's precepts was inconsistent with prevailing US government positions on Taiwan as reflected in public statements and private conversations with the Chinese nor were any precepts criticized by the Carter administration or by any subsequent US administration.

In 1982, in the midst of a deteriorating climate in US-China relations over Taiwan arms sales, the Ronald Reagan administration produced three related statements that further defined and refined US-Taiwan policy in a new era. The first was a private statement of reassurance to Taiwan that its interests would not be sacrificed in the course of ongoing discussions between the United States and China over Taiwan arms sales and other matters.[9]

The second was another bilateral US-China communiqué,[10] which came under pressure from China. It committed the United States to reduce steadily, in "qualitative" and "quantitative" terms, arms sales to Taiwan.

The third was a clarification of this communiqué by the State Department's leading official responsible for Asian affairs, who told Congress that the decline of US arms sales would be a function of China's demonstrated commitment to peaceful resolution of the Taiwan issue and of Taiwan's defense needs.[11] In other words, the Reagan administration did not alter fundamental US policy concerning Taiwan, even regarding arms sales.[12]

The United States thus continued through the final years of the Cold War its commitment to peaceful, noncoercive resolution of the cross-strait impasse, and to Taiwan's security more broadly, despite an evolution in relations with China. By the 1980s, the issue became as much about commitment to an old friend as about containing communism or rising Chinese power in Asia. Nonetheless, as time passed, changes in Taiwan itself and in US perspectives toward China added to the mix of US interests in Taiwan's future and to the legacy of US support for the people on the island.

Why Does the United States Still Care about Taiwan?

The end of the Cold War and the rise of Chinese power in recent years have complicated US calculations concerning Taiwan. Given the changes in the international environment since the Cold War, the geopolitical value of Taiwan has arguably gone down even as the value of a constructive relationship with China—in economic, political, and other terms—has gone up. And of course the dangers of facing off against China militarily, over Taiwan or otherwise, have never been higher and will only increase. However, the United States continues to care about Taiwan for several important reasons.

First, at a coldly strategic level, the US government continues to assess that remaining true to its long-standing commitment to the people on Taiwan is critical for the continued credibility of US strategic commitments throughout East Asia. The United States remains the essential guarantor of East Asian security and balance of power through its military presence and alliances. Perhaps uniquely in the world, countries in the region continue to rely on and welcome this commitment from the United States to safeguard regional peace and stability and prevent the rise of a regional hegemon.

Although the region greatly fears US-China military conflict over Taiwan, should the United States abandon Taiwan to China, either explicitly or through compromise on its long-standing policy against coercive means of resolution, the region—particularly but not limited to allies such as Japan and South Korea—would question overall US resolve in the face of a rising China and have reason to fear abandonment of their interests and other regional commitments. It is not an exaggeration to suggest that the US position in Asia, and the psychology of security that it has produced, would be seriously undermined as a result, leading to regional instability as nations with long histories of mutual suspicion react to this perceived new security vacuum. For fear of alienating China, regional policymakers and strategists will not publicly state this concern about how Taiwan is handled but privately convey such sentiment.

At a more visceral level, Taiwan's evolution from a one-party authoritarian state to a multiparty democracy and open society over the past 20 years has also added a critical new component to US interest in the security and viability of Taiwan. In 1987, Chiang Kai-shek's son, Chiang Ching-kuo, lifted martial law, and in 1988, the Kuomintang allowed the formation of opposition parties. Competitive legislative elections were held, and direct election of the "President of the Republic of China" began in 1996. Taiwan's authoritarian past is a distant memory.

Indeed, from a systemic standpoint, Taiwan has undergone what many in the United States hope to see take place on the mainland: a transition to a more open, fair, and stable democratic society based on the rule of law. The political, social, and cultural freedoms enjoyed by the Taiwan people today are akin to the values instinctively attractive to and promoted by the United States.

Under such circumstances, enabling Taiwan society to continue to safeguard its way of life and to chart its own future, without coercion but short of formal independence, has seemed appropriate to US policymakers, particularly given Taiwan's status as an old friend and the achievements it has made with the help of its friendship with the United States. Indeed, it was the development of Taiwan's democracy that led the Bill Clinton administration to clarify US policy by requiring not only that any resolution be peaceful and noncoercive but also, more specifically, that it be "acceptable to the people of Taiwan." The George W. Bush administration seemed to accommodate Chinese concerns about the one-sided nature of this statement by modifying it to say that any resolution be acceptable to the people on "both sides of the Taiwan Strait."

Taiwan's economic achievements are another often-overlooked reason why the United States continues to care about the island. Taiwan is the United States' ninth-largest trade partner, with nearly $65 billion in bilateral trade in 2007. It has become the global leader in computer and telecommunication component technology, serving as a linchpin in the development of this critical sector. While unification with the mainland may not necessarily derail the entrepreneurial success of Taiwanese companies, maintaining the stability and viability of Taiwan's economy has become important to the health of the global and American economies.

Finally, and perhaps most importantly, many in the United States be-lieve that how China handles Taiwan will be an important measure of both how China deals with disputes as it rises and how the United States—and the world—will manage the challenges of a rising China. If the United States or others were to begin to compromise on their fundamental and long-standing commitments and interests because of concern about Chi-nese reaction, this would risk sending a signal of license to Beijing on other matters. As indicated earlier, it may also send a signal to other nations about a shift in the balance of regional and perhaps global power, leading those nations to make strategic choices accordingly that may not benefit the US position in Asia.

So while Taiwan may appeal naturally to American sensibilities for many reasons—as an old friend, a vibrant democracy, and an open soci-ety—it remains to some degree, as during the Cold War, a symbol of something larger: how America manages a broader international security challenge. To many US strategists, the Taiwan issue therefore is not about "containing" China, keeping China divided, or preventing China's rise, as many Chinese assert, but about ensuring that as it does rise, Beijing con-forms to its own stated goal of doing so peacefully, through dialogue rather than threats, through win-win solutions rather than coercive force.

Limits to US Support

The United States has stated publicly and repeatedly that it "does not support" Taiwan's independence. In 1998, President Clinton publicly af-firmed for the first time the so-called three no's policy of the United States toward Taiwan: no support for Taiwan's independence; no support for "two Chinas" or "One China, One Taiwan;" and no support for Taiwan membership in international organizations that require statehood. This policy has roots in statements former secretary of state and national secu-rity adviser Henry Kissinger made during his first visit to Beijing in 1971, but it was never affirmed publicly by a US president as US policy until Clinton's declaration.

A Taiwan declaration of independence, therefore, is a clear red line for the United States that would call into question US political and perhaps military support for Taiwan. Short of such a declaration, however, it has become more complicated and challenging for the United States to define exactly what is and is not acceptable behavior, particularly by Taiwan, given the natural evolution in the cross-strait situation.

Indeed, the natural evolution of Taiwan society has complicated cross-strait affairs. Taiwan's democracy has led to the political rise of "native Taiwanese," defined as those whose ancestors did not come to the island with the Kuomintang in 1949 but had lived there for many prior genera-tions. The Kuomintang had suppressed this group's culture, language, and history in favor of those of the mainland Chinese. The simmering resentment of these Taiwanese toward what they considered mainland Chinese political occupation was unleashed when democracy led to the election in 2000 of a president from a native Taiwanese-dominated party. Chen Shui-bian's Democratic Progressive Party favored independence and soon sought to reassert traditional Taiwanese customs and culture while distancing the island increasingly from any notion of a "Republic of China," or of China more broadly.

Generational change has also had measurable impact on cross-strait affairs. With the passage of time new generations of Taiwan citizens have emerged who have no recollection of or direct connection to mainland China and have gradually severed any loyalty that even the sons and daughters of Kuomintang exiles had toward the land of their parents and grandparents. Instead, they have come to consider themselves generally more "Taiwanese" than "Chinese"—or both[13]—with a distinct modern identity for which they demand respect and recognition, even if short of formal statehood.

The implications of this development have alarmed China. China fears that Taiwan may be drifting away inexorably over time and thus has been extremely sensitive to moves by Taiwan's leadership that China perceives as further severing any formal or symbolic linkages to China. These concerns were particularly acute during Chen Shui-bian's presidency, which rejected accepting the fundamental principle of "One China," Beijing's precondition for any official dialogue between the two sides. In response, China sought not only to punish Chen and his supporters directly but also to pressure the United States to help. Beijing often charges that US actions, such as arms sales or other support, demonstrate bad faith and embolden Taiwan "independence advocates."

This state of affairs has naturally complicated US policy toward both Taiwan and China. Short of supporting independence, the United States since the 1990s has had to determine to what degree changes in the aspirations of Taiwan's 23 million people are legitimate, accord with US values and interests, and thus deserve greater dignity, recognition, and support. This includes whether to support a larger role for Taiwan in international affairs, traditionally under the compromise moniker of "Chinese Taipei," or to accord Taiwan's leadership greater official respect in other ways.

At the same time, the United States in recent years has sought to establish constructive relations with China to deal with a wide array of critical issues, from counterterrorism to nonproliferation and from trade to climate change. Washington became particularly concerned during much of the Chen administration, then, about the seeming insensitivity of Taiwan at times to these and other US interests, both related and unrelated to China, particularly as the Chen government sought to affirm Taiwan's dignity and identity in ways that many saw as being on the border of acceptability and provocation.

For instance, Chen referred continually to Taiwan as a "sovereign country;" echoed the words of former president Lee Teng-hui that mainland China and Taiwan each make up a "country on each side of the Taiwan Strait" (*yi bian, yi guo*); announced the abolition of a Kuomintang-era council and guidelines dedicated to unification (although he subsequently amended this announcement by saying that they would be inoperable rather than abolished); and took the name of "China" off all state-operated companies, and that of Chiang Kai-shek off all official landmarks, including the island's international airport and central square. In 2003, Chen's government discussed promulgating a ballot referendum to be held concurrently with the 2004 presidential election that called for a new Taiwan constitution. This prospective move caused great consternation not only in Beijing but also in Washington, which feared that a new constitution could be viewed as a de facto declaration of Taiwan's permanent separation from China.

Likewise, the Chen government sponsored a ballot referendum during the March 2008 Taiwan presidential election that asked whether Taiwan ought to seek membership in the United Nations under the name "Taiwan." While seemingly innocuous—and pointless, since China would veto any effort by Taiwan to join the United Nations—the Bush administration considered the initiative a highly provocative step toward changing the formal name of the country that suggested independence from China. The referendum failed.

Indeed, the Bush administration responded over time with increasing annoyance and open opposition to such moves. It fumed at President Chen's consistent insensitivity to US desires to maintain cross-strait stability so Washington could focus on other more immediate and critical global challenges. President Chen defended his actions as the only responsible course for a president elected to serve the interests and protect the dignity of the 23 million people on Taiwan. The personal animus of President Bush for President Chen became an open secret.

In the face of changing goals, ambitions, and policies of a new generation of leadership in Taipei, the Bush administration eventually clarified US Taiwan policy to oppose "provocation" or "unilateral decisions by either side" to change the status quo. The United States has taken upon itself to define the meaning of these terms, including "status quo," and to react accordingly. In private, President Bush has also reportedly conveyed to the Chinese US "opposition" to Taiwan's independence, a substantial change from traditional US policy that avoided taking a position on the issue, and this formulation in particular. Overall, since the late 1990s the United States has found itself more actively involved in cross-strait affairs to prevent potential miscalculation or perceived provocations by either side from spilling over into confrontation.

To complicate matters further for US-Taiwan relations, questions have arisen over the past decade over Taiwan's commitment to its own defense in the face of a rapidly modernizing Chinese military. Legislative gridlock has prevented passage of arms procurement packages and defense budgets have declined. Both Chen and Taiwan's new president, Ma Ying-jeou, have vowed to increase Taiwan's defense budget to 3 percent of GDP; whether that will happen and is adequate for Taiwan to face the clear challenge remains to be seen. While Taiwan can never keep up with China's military development, its inability or unwillingness to expend the resources and signal a serious commitment to its own defense could undermine the commitment of US policymakers and members of Congress to support Taiwan's interests—including the potential to put US forces in harm's way on behalf of the island.

Given the stakes of US commitments to peace and stability in East Asia and to a peaceful resolution of the Taiwan issue specifically, successive US administrations have made it clear they do not appreciate surprises from Taipei and have urged Taiwan to be respectful of the sensibilities and interests of its "ally" when it decides to take action on issues that touch even remotely on Taiwan's sovereign status. The March 2008 election of Ma Ying-jeou, a Harvard Law School graduate with long experience in the United States, exemplary English-language ability, and an expressed discomfort with Chen's tactics, has raised hopes in Washington that the era of surprises and gratuitous provocation is over. Furthermore, as a Kuomintang "mainlander"—someone whose family fled to Taiwan from mainland China as a result of the Chinese civil war and thus relatively trusted by Beijing as more strongly connected to his "Chinese" roots—Ma has raised high expectations of a new stability and even progress in cross-strait relations in coming years. Whether these high expectations will be met remains to be seen.

Alternative Approaches to Dealing with the Taiwan Impasse

Despite the principles and strategy that underlie US policy toward Taiwan, the current situation of continued tension in US relations with China over Taiwan, and the hair-trigger nature of the cross-strait impasse—where an incident, accident, or miscalculation at any time by either China or Taiwan could lead to hostilities that draw in the United States for the sake of its credibility—are clearly not in the interest of the United States or the region. As a result, many specialists have grappled with ways to further refine US policy and engagement on the issue to deter provocation, prevent miscalculation, provide more predictability in the relationship, and generally reduce tensions to promote a more stable environment in which both sides can work out their differences over time.

Several innovative approaches have been broached. In 2005, China scholar and former White House official Kenneth Lieberthal suggested that China and Taiwan conclude an explicit modus vivendi lasting 20 to 30 years, in which China would vow not to use force to settle the impasse in return for Taiwan vowing not to declare independence.[14] The United States would offer its good offices to facilitate dialogue and to help line up international support to guarantee the arrangement. Lieberthal acknowledged that mutual mistrust, lack of adequate communication channels, and uncertainty over the compatibility of each side's positions might be unsurpassable obstacles to reaching such a deal. However, Taiwan's new president, Ma Ying-jeou, campaigned on a platform that included the idea of a Lieberthal-like modus vivendi, and the notion may be tested in some form in coming years.

Similarly, Joseph Nye in 1998 recommended a three-part package of unilateral steps by the United States, China, and Taiwan that would provide greater policy clarity and reassurance to all sides. Nye proposed that (1) the United States declare its opposition to both Taiwan's independence and use of force by China and that (2) China offer greater international space to Taiwan under a "one country, three systems" formula on the condition that (3) Taipei make a clear and public commitment not to declare or move toward independence but instead engage in cross-strait dialogue and promote greater cross-strait economic and personal interchange.

Some have suggested that the United States consider taking more direct responsibility for mediating the Taiwan dispute. They note that among the major challenges around the world in recent times, such as Northern Ireland, Israel-Palestine, even Kashmir, the Taiwan case is unique in that the United States has explicitly ruled out any mediating role to help resolve the impasse.[15] Given the clear and direct interest of the United States in a peaceful resolution, and its responsibility for the peace and stability of East Asia more broadly, these observers question the wisdom of maintaining this position.

Another view that has gained some momentum among conservative circles in particular is that the United States scrap adherence to a "One China" policy, which no longer reflects today's reality. In this view, the original formula in which the United States "recognizes" that people on both sides of the strait consider Taiwan to be part of China does not apply, since that condition arguably is no longer met in Taiwan. Furthermore, they note, continuation of a "One China" policy when combined with quiet reassurance that the United States "opposes" Taiwan's independence risks misunderstanding and miscalculation in Beijing that the United States might tacitly acquiesce to a limited military action against the island should Beijing and Washington agree that certain actions and trends in Taiwan are unacceptable.

Still others contend that Taiwan is simply not worth the damage US commitments are causing to healthy and constructive US-China relations. The notion that Taiwan remains the "turd in the punch bowl" (as one senior military official famously termed it in the 1990s) when it comes to US-China relations indeed exists among some US strategists and specialists in US-China relations. Nonetheless, few individuals have suggested publicly or even in formal private settings that the United States simply abandon its commitments to Taiwan. So far, these individuals may only go so far as to suggest that should Taiwan provoke conflict across the strait, the United States should not be obliged to come to its defense and that that message should be sent clearly to Taipei to constrain any "problematic" activity so it does not interfere with stable US-China relations.

Likewise, it should be noted that a few individuals in the United States take the radically alternative view that the United States should not allow China to regain control of Taiwan regardless of the circumstances—even if the Taiwan people were to acquiesce—because of the perceived strategic value of Taiwan to China and concurrent strategic vulnerability of the United States and its Northeast Asian allies that would result. Such a position, however, would run counter to decades of US stated policy, undermine US credibility as a force for peace and stability in East Asia, and simply be untenable to enforce against the will of the two sides to resolve their differences peacefully and determine their own future according to their common interest.

How Should the United States Think about Taiwan Today?

As noted, the Chinese consider Taiwan to be the most sensitive and important issue in US-China relations. The United States would prefer that this not be so, but it must take into account—though not necessarily always accommodate—Chinese sensibilities on the issue as a core element of a stable bilateral relationship.

US support for Taiwan in political and military terms is becoming increasingly complicated as time passes. China's rise makes the cost of US intervention higher and leads fewer nations around the world to dare speak out in support of the Taipei government, even as democracy and generational change in Taiwan are creating a new, less predictable decision-making dynamic on the island and leading to greater demands for international recognition of its de facto independent identity.

Indeed, for all intents and purposes, Taiwan is an independent entity that is governed from Taipei and not in the least from Beijing. Thus to some on Taiwan and elsewhere, it may not be fair that the United States and others do not accord official recognition to Taiwan's flag or anthem or offer Taiwan a place in the United Nations alongside other sovereign states. However, Taiwan's situation is unfortunately not a matter of fairness. The growing power of China and its commitment to prevent international recognition of Taiwan as a sovereign entity is the reality in which Taiwan finds itself. The island—and the United States—would be foolish to ignore this reality in its policies.

Nonetheless, the United States has every reason to maintain the fundamentals of its long-standing, if continually refined, Taiwan policy: peaceful (noncoercive) resolution through dialogue, agnosticism on ultimate outcome, no unilateral changes in the status quo, and no provocation by either side. The imperatives of strategy and values that underlie continued US commitment to Taiwan since the earliest days of the Cold War, as outlined earlier, may have evolved somewhat but remain as valid and important to US interests today as ever.

Few observers question that China will use force against Taiwan if it declared independence. This is a nightmare scenario for all sides. A December 2007 "Committee of 100" poll affirmed that only 32 percent of Americans favored US military intervention on Taiwan's behalf should a declaration of independence trigger hostilities across the strait.[16] However, Taiwan is unlikely to make such a clear declaration. The question is to what degree Americans should support military intervention if hostilities break out short of an independence declaration, for instance, if caused by a so-called provocative act that Beijing deems has crossed a red line. Just as complicated is the degree to which the United States should support other Taiwan moves that seek to promote its international profile, dignity, or other interests in ways that are not clearly provocative but that Beijing views as such.

The United States, in fact, should insist that any actions by Taiwan that come close to affecting the island's sovereign identity be at least communicated to, if not closely coordinated with, Washington. It would be unreasonable for Taiwan to expect the United States to automatically accept actions that are not worked out in advance with Washington given the stakes of miscalculation for US and regional interests, let alone Taiwan's own security. Even under a US policy that encourages China and Taiwan to work out their differences on their own, the United States does have an interest in understanding the direction of Taiwan policy in this regard and in communicating to Taiwan's leaders the implications of such policy for US interests and strategic calculations.

Taiwan's democracy also does not mean that the United States must or will support the island at every turn. The United States, for instance, should not support Taiwan actions that will complicate US relations with China unnecessarily or for reasons of Taiwan's domestic politics, rather than for essential issues related to Taiwan's national health, security, dignity, or development.

Indeed, given the changes on Taiwan, the US government should consider engaging in more types of direct contact with Taiwan officials in order to avoid miscalculation and miscommunication between the two sides.[17] Although China traditionally has not supported such official contact, it may in fact serve Beijing's interests that the United States be able to send its messages clearly to Taipei as necessary.

Likewise, the United States should withstand the temptations offered by China to work on the issue bilaterally, to "comanage" Taiwan, over the heads of the Taiwan people. In the interest of US credibility with allies and friends, the viability of any ultimate arrangement, and basic fairness to the Taiwan people, the United States should ensure at every turn that China understands that the road to resolution runs through Taipei and that it must engage directly with Taiwan's elected leadership if it desires any progress.

At the same time, while US policy is to not support Taiwan's membership in international organizations that require statehood, it does not make sense for the United States to oppose Taiwan's involvement, short of membership, in such international organizations or activities. It also seems reasonable that the United States adhere to the unstated corollary of its policy and support Taiwan's membership in appropriate international organizations that do not require statehood.

Putting the issue of sovereignty aside, Taiwan's advanced economy and society clearly can and should contribute to global efforts to address a range of international challenges. Given the dangers of infectious disease in East Asia, particularly in the aftermath of the severe acute respiratory syndrome (SARS) scare in Taiwan in 2003, for example, Taiwan's involvement in the World Health Organization would be particularly reasonable and important. The United States ought to support Taiwan's involvement not only as a matter of propriety but also in the interest of international safety and well-being, while continuing to affirm its firm opposition to any unilateral moves by Taiwan to change its undefined sovereign status.

On the issues of US arms sales and defense cooperation with Taiwan, the Chinese often charge that they promote separation and prevent unification. Indeed they do seek to prevent unification based on aggression or coercion, but that has been US policy for decades. Arms sales and defense cooperation should continue as a way to demonstrate adherence to long-standing US commitments, under the Taiwan Relations Act and otherwise; help the island maintain at least some of the "sufficient self-defense capability" that the Act calls for; and promote an environment where Taiwan would have the confidence it needs to enter into dialogue with its mainland counterparts on an equal basis to discuss reducing tensions and eventually resolving the impasse. The intent should be to promote deterrence and prevent Chinese miscalculation that resolving the situation through nonpeaceful means is a viable option.

At the same time, the US military needs to be prepared and able to intervene if called upon during a crisis. Obviously this is a worst-case scenario and one to be avoided. However, while the United States can be agnostic politically about Taiwan's ultimate sovereign status, it cannot afford to be agnostic about military planning, which should be done in coordination with Taiwan's military.

Indeed, nothing about Taiwan's ability to defend itself, US contingency planning, or overall US support for the island's dignity and security prevents China from winning over the hearts and minds of the Taiwan people to achieve the "peaceful reunification" and cross-strait stability Beijing says it seeks. The lack of trust between the two sides is the fundamental problem creating tensions and danger across the Taiwan Strait.

The United States, therefore, must continue to maintain a delicate balance in dealing with both Beijing and Taipei. The key is to give neither China nor Taiwan confidence that the United States would support unilateral moves toward a permanent solution of the impasse so as to avoid miscalculation by either side that might drag the United States into a crisis. In the end, it is the peace and stability of East Asia, and the maintenance of regional security more broadly, that the United States should consider its priority interest.

The good news is that Ma Ying-jeou's election in March 2008 and inauguration in May have led to a clear opportunity for a new start in cross-strait relations, one that both sides seem to have recognized and already seized. Chinese president Hu Jintao and Ma have echoed each other's words about how to move forward in relations at least in the near to mid-term,[18] with Hu apparently comfortable with the deliberate pace preferred by Taiwan's president to accentuate economic, societal, and cultural contacts first and defer to the indefinite future any conversation about harder political issues.[19] Formal dialogue between the two sides has already resumed, with the first meeting in a decade between Taiwan's Straits Exchange Foundation (SEF) and China's Association for Relations Across the Taiwan Strait (ARATS) held in June 2008.[20]

Taiwan's people expect the election of Ma to lead to increased cross-strait stability, economic development, respect from the mainland for the island's dignity and achievements, and reduction in the island's international isolation. Such high expectations will require even more flexibility and patience from the mainland in coming years, qualities that may be challenged over time as the Chinese people on the mainland harbor their own expectations of progress toward their national goals. Indeed, China is debating the fresh challenge of how to handle a Taiwan leader who is not provocative but committed to many of China's own stated aims for deeper and expanded cross-strait ties. Even as Ma has called for stability in cross-strait relations during his presidency under the "three no's" principle of "no unification, no independence, and no use of force," he has commented that reunification cannot happen until China is a democracy. Some are concerned that a gap may develop in expectations between the two sides over time, leading to renewed tensions or frictions.

Nonetheless, the more China and Taiwan take responsibility for managing cross-strait stability, the less the United States will be required to assume this task. The United States has been a critical component of the cross-strait dynamic but may be decreasingly so in coming years. This is

a good thing—although US engagement and vigilance will remain necessary for the foreseeable future to ensure continued progress and peace
and safeguard Taiwan from coercion.

China likes to say that were it not for the Korean War, Taiwan would be
part of China today. This is almost certainly true. However, regardless of
how we got to this point, the responsibility today ultimately lies with Beijing to build the mutual trust and confidence necessary to attract the people of Taiwan and peacefully resolve the long-standing impasse. At the
same time, Beijing will continue to claim that US support for Taiwan
demonstrates bad faith toward China. But to be pro-Taiwan should not be
construed as being anti-China. The Taiwan people have created a good
life for themselves, with an open, economically developed, democratic society that conforms to US values and interests. In fact, it is the type of society that China says it hopes for itself. How China resolves the Taiwan
issue will say much about how it will handle other disputes, internal and
international, as it grows in power.

Notes

1. For a brief primer on policy and perspectives surrounding the Taiwan dispute, see Derek Mitchell's chapter "China's Foreign and Security Policy: Partner
or Rival?" in *China: The Balance Sheet—What the World Needs to Know Now about
the World's Emerging Superpower* (New York: PublicAffairs, 2006). For a history of
the evolution of the Taiwan issue, see Alan D. Romberg, *Rein in at the Brink of the
Precipice: American Policy Toward Taiwan and US-PRC Relations* (Washington: Henry
L. Stimson Center, 2003). For a comprehensive analysis of cross-strait relations, see
Richard C. Bush III, *Untying the Knot: Making Peace in the Taiwan Strait* (Washington: Brookings Institution Press, 2005).

2. The name "Taiwan" didn't even appear in Chinese documents until the late
Ming period (1368–1644), when the island became an outpost for defeated Han
loyalists. Chinese maps during the early Qing dynasty (1644–1912) also failed to
include the island. Kangxi, the great Qing emperor (1654–1722), reportedly dis-
missed Taiwan as "no bigger than a ball of mud" and said his dominion would
"gain nothing by possessing it, and it would be no loss if we did not acquire it."
See Alan M. Wachman, *Why Taiwan: Geostrategic Rationales for China's Territorial Integrity* (Stanford, CA: Stanford University Press, 2007).

3. The Republic of China under the Kuomintang also considered Outer Mongolia
part of China, a claim renounced only by a Democratic Progressive Party government over the last decade but not yet reflected in changes in the official Republic
of China constitution still in force on Taiwan. Ironically, the People's Republic of
China, due to pressure from the Soviet Union and in the name of communist solidarity, formally relinquished any Chinese claims to Mongolia upon assuming
power, when it recognized the Mongolian People's Republic in 1949.

4. The first known recorded evidence of China's strategic concern about Taiwan
was in the late 1700s during the Qing period. Shi Lang, a strategist advising Qing

Emperor Kangxi, argued that Taiwan was important in several dimensions: as a buffer against pirates, criminals or others from afar who wished ill to China; to prevent the island from becoming a base for rebellious elements at home; or as a bridge to project power into vital sea lanes. See Wachman, *Why Taiwan*.

5. For more information and statistics on cross-strait economic flows, see the "one pager" on the China Balance Sheet website, www.chinabalancesheet.org/snap shots.html.

6. Historians mark the Cultural Revolution as running from 1966 to 1976, the year Mao died, although the movement reached its peak during the first five years. See endnote 16 in chapter 2.

7. Under the terms of the normalization agreement, the Chinese agreed to allow the United States to terminate the Mutual Defense Treaty according to the terms and timing of its own provisions, to take effect after one year, on January 1, 1980. In return, the United States agreed on a one-year moratorium on arms sales to Taiwan.

8. Indeed, Jimmy Carter revealed during a December 2007 conference in Beijing that Deng Xiaoping had acknowledged privately on the eve of the normalization announcement that China recognized the United States would continue to sell Taiwan defensive arms after normalization and after abrogation of the bilateral defense treaty. "Publicly they [the Chinese] are going to disapprove of this action, but privately they have acknowledged that it will be done," according to Carter, who reportedly read from a December 14, 1978, entry to his diary. Agence France Presse, "China Agreed US Could Sell Arms to Taiwan, Says Carter," December 6, 2007.

9. The so-called Six Assurances, made to Taiwan in 1982, included the following: The United States (1) has not set a date for ending arms sales to Taiwan; (2) has not agreed to consult with China on arms sales to Taiwan; (3) will not play any mediation role between Taipei and Beijing; (4) has not agreed to revise the Taiwan Relations Act; (5) has not altered its position regarding sovereignty over Taiwan; and (6) will not exert pressure on Taiwan to enter into negotiations with China.

10. This agreement, signed on August 12, 1982, is called the "Third Communiqué," with the first being the February 1972 Nixon-Mao statement released at the end of Nixon's landmark visit and the second being the January 1, 1979 normalization agreement.

11. This statement by Assistant Secretary John Holdridge echoed a private "codicil" to the communiqué written by President Reagan, which was revealed publicly for the first time in 2000 in James Mann's book *About Face* and officially published in April 2001.

12. Nonetheless, the United States did reduce arms sales to Taiwan for many years given the continued imbalance in Taiwan's favor during the 1980s, and continued to seek to demonstrate fealty to the communiqué's precepts through the 1990s, often through creative bookkeeping.

13. According to a survey conducted in December 2007, only 5.4 percent of those living on Taiwan identify themselves as "Chinese only"—the lowest level on record—while 43.7 percent identified themselves as "Taiwanese only" and 44.5 per-

cent as "both Taiwanese and Chinese"; Election Study Center, National Chengchi University, "Changes in the Taiwanese/Chinese Identity of Taiwanese as Tracked in Surveys by the Election Study Center, NCCU (1992–1997)," December 2007, http://esc.nccu.edu.tw.

14. Kenneth Lieberthal, "Preventing a War Over Taiwan," *Foreign Affairs* (March/April 2005). Lieberthal has also been associated with a similar 50-year plan.

15. See the "Six Assurances" in note 9.

16. Committee of 100, "Hope and Fear: American and Chinese Attitudes Toward Each Other," December 2007, www.survey.committee100.org (accessed December 17, 2007).

17. In 1994, the Clinton administration underwent a "Taiwan Policy Review" that resulted in promulgation of internal guidance for how, when, where, and on what US officials could engage with the Taiwanese government and its representatives. The outlines of this guidance have remained in force through the George W. Bush administration. Included are explicit restrictions against meeting Taiwanese government representatives in the White House, State Department, Defense Department, or Twin Oaks, the Washington estate that serves as the residence of Taiwan's "representative" (de facto ambassador). The level of US government officials who may travel to Taiwan remains unclear under the review but in practice has resulted in restrictions on officials at or above the deputy assistant secretary level, including military flag officers, except those granted "special permission." For their part, Taiwan's president, vice president, premier, foreign minister, and defense minister are not allowed to visit Washington. The executive secretary of the State Department reconfirms the official guidance annually at the start of each fiscal year (October).

18. In his inaugural address, Ma cited Hu Jintao's recent comments on cross-strait affairs several times as reflecting his own views on the way forward. Ma Ying-jeou, "Taiwan's Renaissance" (presidential inaugural address, May 20, 2008), www.chinapost.com.tw.

19. In his October 15, 2007 work report to the 17th Party Congress, Hu Jintao affirmed the "need to increase contacts [and] strengthen economic and cultural exchanges in more areas and at higher levels." To that end, reforms have already been instituted to allow direct cross-strait charter flights and visa liberalization to allow greater numbers of mainland tourists to travel to Taiwan. In his April 29, 2008 conversation with Kuomintang Party chairman Lian Chan, Hu also called for "building mutual trust, shelving controversies, finding commonalities despite differences, and creating together a win-win solution" across the Taiwan Strait.

20. Taiwan and China established the Straits Exchange Foundation and the Association for Relations Across the Taiwan Strait, respectively, to handle cross-strait dialogue on technical or business matters. They are semiofficial organizations and required as substitutes for "government" agencies given the unique political relationship between the two sides in which neither technically acknowledges the other's officialdom as legitimate entities.

9

China's Military Modernization

To strengthen national defense and the armed forces occupies an important place in the overall arrangements for the cause of socialism with Chinese characteristics. Bearing in mind the overall strategic interests of national security and development, we must take both economic and national defense development into consideration and make our country prosperous and our armed forces powerful while building a moderately prosperous society in all respects.

—Hu Jintao, October 15, 2007[1]

In November 2006 a Chinese submarine broached the surface in the vicinity of a US Navy aircraft carrier battle group steaming in the East China Sea, underscoring that the naval service of the People's Liberation Army (PLA) is operating farther from China's shores than it has at any time in modern history. In January 2007, a Chinese ground-based missile destroyed a Chinese satellite in space, not only creating a major debris field but also dramatically illustrating the potential vulnerabilities of militaries that rely on outer space for operational communications and battle space awareness. In April 2007, the PLA conducted a much publicized combined exercise with the armed forces of Russia, demonstrating a nascent ability to move men and matériel across China's land borders. In December 2007, a front page article in the *Washington Post* described the PLA's efforts to recruit the best and brightest students from China's most prestigious universities to join its ranks.[2]

These developments indicate that year after year the PLA is making substantial strides in enhancing its operational capabilities and increasing its institutional capacities. These examples are but a few of the fruits of over 15 years of sustained and focused military modernization in China.

The military's budget has continued to increase at double-digit rates every year but one (officially) since 1993 (see box 9.1). At the same time, the need for a more capable military is a recurrent theme in the official rhetoric of China's leaders, as Hu's quote above indicates. Unlike the 1970s and

---

Box 9.1   China's defense budget

The question of China's defense budget is something of a parlor game among observers of China's military. China's declared 2008 defense budget was $58.8 billion, an increase of 17.6 percent over 2007. However, China's actual defense-related expenditures are assumed to be much higher than this, with expenses related to research and development, strategic and paramilitary forces, and foreign arms procurement, among other items, all excluded from the formal budget. Organizations such as the Institute for International Strategic Studies (IISS), the RAND Corporation, the Stockholm International Peace Research Institute (SIPRI), and the US Department of Defense (DoD) have each offered estimates of China's actual annual defense expenditures based on various standards and models. DoD estimates are commonly the highest among them, although SIPRI and IISS also provide purchasing power parity (PPP)–based estimates that result in higher figures. Economists use PPP currency conversion rates to account for differences in price levels between countries, resulting in more meaningful international comparisons of consumption.

1980s, when military modernization was relegated to fourth place among Deng Xiaoping's "Four Modernizations," today's Chinese leaders talk of giving equal attention to economics, social issues, and national defense.[3]

It is not surprising that Beijing has refocused on modernizing its armed forces to keep pace with its overall development in recent years. Nonetheless a Chinese state increasingly capable of conducting military operations beyond its shores or over its land borders in the Asia-Pacific region is an unprecedented development.

Even assuming the most benign intentions on the part of Beijing, a more capable PLA that can sustain force in the Asia-Pacific region, coupled with China's economic traction, has the potential to significantly alter the geostrategic and geopolitical landscape in Asia for the first time since the end of the Second World War. The modernization of the PLA will clearly have as great an impact on other countries in the region as on the United States—India, Japan, South Korea, Southeast Asian nations, Russia (despite the public celebration of their strategic partnership), and, of course, Taiwan. While China so far has depended upon the political-diplomatic and economic elements of national power to pursue its national objectives in the region, Chinese strategists, civilian and military, see an enhanced PLA as an essential component of building its comprehensive national power.

China's Assessment of Its Military Needs

The operational capabilities the PLA is demonstrating today did not come about overnight. As is the case with any nation's armed forces, the weapons systems and technologies today's PLA is fielding, and the doctrines and training regimens being developed to employ them, are the result of yesterday's decisions, plans, and programs.

The PLA, in fact, is reaping the rewards of fundamental decisions that were made some 15 years ago, with subsequent adjustments as needed. On January 13, 1993, Jiang Zemin, then Chinese Communist Party (CCP) secretary general and chairman of the Central Military Commission (CMC), delivered a speech to an expanded meeting of the CMC in which he promulgated a new national military strategy for the PLA to guide its future modernization efforts.[4] The "Military Strategic Guidelines for the New Period" issued at that meeting launched the Chinese armed forces into a period of focused and sustained modernization that continues today.

At the time, Chinese leaders and military planners made two fundamental analytical judgments that led to the decision for a new period of military modernization: They (1) revised their assessment of China's security situation and (2) took account of the changing nature of modern warfare.

On the first account, Chinese analysts took stock of the collapse of the Soviet Union and the post-Cold War environment and concluded that, first, there were no prospects for a major war involving China and any other large power, and thus China's overall security situation was positive;[5] second, there nonetheless existed many uncertainties and pockets of instability in the world and conflicts involving challenges to Chinese interests along its periphery, including Taiwan; and third, instead of the "multipolar world order" that Chinese analysts predicted would unfold in the post–Cold War era, the reality was a "unipolar world order" with the United States remaining the sole superpower for the foreseeable future. For these reasons, the timing for developing a more capable military was deemed positive, and the need for a more capable military to supplement other elements of Chinese national power was deemed essential.

Whereas this first assessment provided a strategic rationale for the need for a more capable military, the second Chinese assessment provided the impetus for the *type* of modern military that would be required. In particular, US capabilities demonstrated during the first Gulf War in 1991 shocked the PLA leadership into confronting the stark reality that the armed forces of China were incapable of late 20th century state-of-the-art warfare, let alone able to cope with the high-tech information-dominated "revolution in military affairs" unfolding in the early 21st century. New developments in military affairs demonstrated by the United States and others since the first Gulf War—Kosovo, Afghanistan, the second Iraq War—have caused the PLA to further adjust its modernization goals. China needed a military that would be able to cope with future conflicts that exhibited the following characteristics:

- fought for limited political objectives and limited in geographic scope;
- short in duration but decisive in strategic outcome—i.e., a single campaign may decide the entire war;

- high-intensity operations, characterized by mobility, speed, and force projection;

- high-technology weapons causing high levels of destruction;

- logistics-intensive with high resource consumption rates, with success dependant as much on combat sustainability as on the ability to inflict damage upon the enemy;

- information-intensive and dependent upon superior C4ISR (command, control, communications, computers, intelligence, surveillance, and reconnaissance) capabilities and near-total battle space awareness;

- simultaneous fighting in all battle space dimensions, to include outer space and the electro-magnetic spectrum; and

- carefully coordinated multiservice (army, navy, and air force), "joint" operations.

The PLA's Taiwan contingency has served as a catalyst for its modernization program. However, even if there were no Taiwan issue to focus PLA attention, it is likely that the PLA would *still* be on the same reform and modernization path it is on today simply due to the basic requirements that this capabilities-based assessment demands.

Key Elements of China's Military Modernization

China's leadership has taken a holistic approach that cuts across every facet of activity within the armed forces.[6] Beijing correctly understands that military modernization is not just about modern weapons and technologies but also about institutions, people, corporate culture, and a host of other issues that require time and attention. The PLA's approach to modernization can be divided into three pillars of reform and modernization.

Pillar 1: Development, Procurement, Acquisition, and Fielding of New Weapons Systems, Technologies, and Combat Capabilities

The first pillar normally receives most of the attention in the media and in foreign-government assessments of the PLA. Chinese decisions on development, procurement, acquisition, and deployment of combat and combat-support capabilities provide the best window into the PLA's assessment of future warfare and the type of conflict it is preparing to face in the future. The capabilities include:

- end-item purchases from Russia such as SU-27 and SU-30 aircraft, Kilo class diesel-electric submarines, Sovremennyy class guided missile destroyers with advanced antiship cruise missiles (SS-N-22 Sunburn), air defense systems, air-to-air missiles, and precision guided munitions;

- domestically produced conventional weapons systems, such as Chinese-made submarines and surface vessels, modern J-10 aircraft, armor, and communications equipment;

- production of conventional missiles and upgrading the quality and survivability of China's nuclear arsenal from silo-based to road-mobile and from liquid-fueled to solid-fueled;

- basic research and development to indigenously produce state-of-the-art military technologies, especially in information technology, to enhance operational C4ISR[7];

- upgrading of its strategic nuclear forces to become more survivable and hence a more credible deterrent. China's December 2006 defense white paper highlighted the role of the PLA Navy—meaning its nuclear capable submarines—in conducting "nuclear counterattacks";

- advancement of its space capabilities, including communications, navigation, reconnaissance, satellites, and antisatellite (ASAT) weapons.[8] The 2006 white paper on China's space activities makes clear the strategic importance of space exploration and capabilities to China's national defense[9]; and

- research into cyber and information warfare as technological force multipliers.[10]

Pillar 2: Institutional and Systemic Reform

This pillar includes the vast array of organizational changes, procedural adjustments, and other critical changes to the PLA's corporate culture that are focused on raising the levels of professionalism of the officer corps and enlisted force. The objective is to make the force adept at employing and maintaining new battlefield technologies. Under this pillar, one could list:

- improvements to the quality of the PLA's officer professional military education system;

- more stringent requirements for officer commissioning, standardization of criteria for promotion, and stricter adherence to mandatory retirements;

- diversification of the sources of commissioned officers beyond the PLA's rather insular military academies to include some of the most prestigious universities in China such as Tsinghua University and Peking University;

- creation—for the first time—of a corps of professional noncommissioned officers who will serve full 30-year careers and be afforded career-long access to professional development;

- force structure adjustments that include a significant new emphasis on the navy, air force, and strategic missile forces, downsizing of staffs, consolidation of ground force units at the division and brigade levels, and new battlefield logistics paradigms; and

- outsourcing common-use goods to commercial suppliers in order to strip the PLA of unnecessary production units.

At the same time, China has not abandoned its traditional "people's war" concept that put a premium on mobilizing civilians at home for military purposes. China has reenergized its attention to its 800,000-strong reserve force and militia units and reanimated civilian-military exercises in recent years to coordinate rear area defense functions in case of a crisis. Medical, engineering, and logistical support in particular are starting to be "outsourced" to the civilian sector, enabling the PLA to focus more on its forward activities. The PLA has also established programs to pay for the schooling of the nation's best and brightest engineering students at prestigious universities such as Qinghua in return for several years of postgraduate service in developing the nation's weapons and information technology.

Pillar 3: Development of New War-Fighting Doctrines

To be able to fight future "high-technology" conflicts, the PLA is making significant changes to the doctrine used to guide commanders and their staffs in planning and operations.[11] China is making the following doctrinal adjustments:

- from wars of attrition to quick decisive campaigns;

- from single-service operations to joint multi-service operations;

- from concentration of units and personnel to concentration of capabilities;

- from emphasis on defense to the primacy of offense;

- from the need to absorb operational blows to the need to be able to execute operational-level preemption;

- from historic focus on land warfare to a holistic view of simultaneous operations in land, maritime, aerospace, electro-magnetic, and cyber battle space dimensions; and

- from focusing on the enemy's weakest geographic sectors to focusing on the enemy's most critical capabilities.

Overall, these concepts, among others, engender a major paradigm shift whereby the PLA is now fixed on being able to prosecute short campaigns to paralyze and deny access to opposing forces rather than long wars of attrition, and to level the technological playing field at the inception of hostilities by concentrating its best capabilities against the enemy's most important assets, particularly high-tech communications and information technologies (e.g., computers and satellites).

Remaining Questions about China's Military Modernization

Having been relegated to the lowest rung of Deng Xiaoping's "Four Modernizations" for many years, China's military started from a low base.

China says it has as many uncertainties about the future global security environment as any nation and that its "Taiwan problem" remains an important consideration. China finally has the technological base to improve the PLA's equipment with indigenous production in some key areas such as information technology and aerospace. And of course, the Chinese economy can now afford to underwrite a sustained modernization program that includes buying from Russia and other supplier nations the systems it cannot produce itself, as well as increasing pay and allowances for its personnel.

Beijing claims that suspicions and concerns about its military modernization are without foundation and that it is merely developing a responsible and proportional defensive capability. Nonetheless, China's military modernization is taking place at a time when China is increasingly confident about its growing power and role in the world and inclined to be proactive in shaping the international system, not just react to it as in the past. In addition, many unresolved regional disputes involving China remain, such as in the East China Sea (with Japan), South China Sea (with several Southeast Asian states), India, and, of course, Taiwan. A good deal of wariness abroad about PLA modernization stems from uncertainty about how Beijing intends to use this increasing capability to pursue its larger national interests.

A second source of uncertainty is the transformative nature of what the PLA leaders are trying to accomplish, and in fact they use the term "transformation" (*zhuangbian*) to impart just how ambitious their plans are. Overall, there is simply no roadmap or precedent in the PLA's past for what China's military leaders are seeking to achieve for its future.

The trajectory of the current modernization program seems to be one that will eventually result in a PLA that can project force in the Asia-Pacific region beyond China's borders, has incipient expeditionary capabilities, will get better at sustaining operations along exterior lines of communications, and will develop selective but effective pockets of tech-

---

Box 9.2   Aircraft carriers

In recent years, rumors have abounded about Chinese interest in developing or acquiring aircraft carriers. China today does not possess any operational carriers. However, there is reason to question how long this will remain the case. Reports have surfaced of "heated debates" on the issue within the Chinese system and there is no question that China is actively studying if not working toward a carrier option in the future.[1]

Analysts have surmised that China's leadership is hesitant to pursue an aircraft capability due to several concerns. Some note that deploying such an inherently offensive, power projection capability would undermine China's claims to a "purely defensive" military. Others contend that China does not have the "escort fleet" necessary for carrier support and protection and that limited resources may be applied better to other needed capabilities. Others assert that the People's Liberation Army (PLA) simply does not yet have the know-how to produce them.

Nonetheless, given China's growing global economic footprint, the increasing numbers of Chinese citizens abroad who may need emergency rescue, and China's increasing dependence on sea lanes for oil and trade more broadly, the debate continues in China over the necessity of developing and deploying carriers.

China has purchased four decommissioned carriers from Australia, Russia, and Ukraine for study and commercial entertainment (the carriers *Minsk* and the *Kiev* became centerpieces of military-themed amusement parks in Shenzhen and Tianjin, respectively).[2] Only one, the *Varyag*—originally reported to become a floating casino—seems a candidate for refurbishment to operational status after reports surfaced that it had been docked at the PLA Navy's Dalian Shipyard. Only time will tell whether, and if so when, aircraft carriers will enter China's operational future.

---

1. See Andrew S. Erickson and Andrew R. Wilson, "China's Aircraft Carrier Dilemma," *Naval War College Review* 59, no. 4 (Autumn 2006): 12–45.

2. Ibid., 18–19.

---

nological capacity. Assuming all goes well, this trajectory puts the PLA on a path to becoming for the first time one of the most operationally capable military forces in the Asia-Pacific region, yet one whose ultimate strategic goals remain uncertain or at best a work in progress (see box 9.2 on aircraft carriers).

A third source of concern is that, in their aggregate, the types of new combat capabilities and supporting technologies that the PLA has been fielding over the past few years have the potential to pose direct challenges to the US military's previously uncontested technological and operational advantages. While the PLA is not likely to become a "peer competitor" or overtake the US armed forces in operational capability—let alone in battle-tested war-fighting experience—any time soon, the PLA will become a regional force to be taken very seriously. China's military will develop key pockets of capacity that will be potentially problematic for the US armed forces, such as cyber warfare and counterspace operations. The PLA's modernization adds a new and complicating factor in the US strategic calculus, raising the stakes, for instance, in any potential Taiwan Strait crisis as the PLA develops more options for the use of military force.

Beyond Taiwan, the PLA and the US armed forces, whether entirely intended or not, appear to be pursuing competitive military strategies and approaches to force building and force posture in the region. While the United States remains committed to its traditional objective of maintaining access to the region, the PLA is building a force that is apparently geared toward impeding or denying that access.[12] And as the PLA seeks to increase China's strategic depth off its coast, with its aircraft flying further out at sea, and its surface and subsurface vessels operating increasingly in blue waters, the US military and the PLA are going to have more maritime and aerospace encounters in common areas, some planned and some—like the collision between a US EP-3 surveillance aircraft and a PLA fighter in April 2001—unplanned, raising new dangers of tension and potential conflict.

The modernization of the PLA adds a new and uncertain element to the overall strategic dynamic of the Asia-Pacific region as well. To the degree that the PLA is actually able to enhance and sustain its military development as an effective operational force, the geopolitical instincts and defense policies of other nations in the region may also shift as they detect and accommodate perceived new regional trends. Some nations might tilt toward China, while others might deepen their ties to the United States and/or strengthen their own military capabilities as a hedge against China. Either way, the result is a challenge to the traditional calculations of the regional balance of power in which the United States has a great stake and the maintenance of which the United States has been committed to on behalf of regional allies and friends for decades.

A fourth complicating factor revolves around transparency. Different views about and approaches to transparency in military affairs between the United States and China continue to be a source of mutual frustration and sometimes strain military relations even during the best periods of military-to-military interactions in past years.

Because the PLA considers itself the weaker party vis-à-vis the US military, the standard PLA approach is to show relatively little because, as the PLA often says, "the weak do not expose themselves to the strong." PLA officials are usually quick to point out that the PLA is the least open sector of the Chinese government. It is closed not only to foreigners but also to the average Chinese citizen and even to many within Chinese officialdom. Therefore, they would argue, the US concept of transparency in the military relationship cannot be transferred to the Chinese system. More-

Table 9.1   Competing statistics on China's military expenditure, 2006
(billions of US dollars)

Source	Expenditure
Official budget[a]	35.0
SIPRI estimate[b]	51.9
DoD low estimate[c]	80.0
DoD high estimate[c]	115.0
IISS estimate (PPP)[d]	122.0
SIPRI estimate (PPP)[e]	188.2

PPP = purchasing power parity

a. US Department of Defense (DoD), *Military Power of the People's Republic of China 2006,* Annual Report to Congress (Washington), www.defenselink.mil, 7.
b. Stockholm International Peace Research Institute, SIPRI Military Expenditure Database, http://milexdata.sipri.org.
c. M. D. Maples, "Current and Projected National Security Threats to the United States" (statement for the Record, US Senate Armed Services Committee, Washington, February 27, 2007).
d. International Institute for Strategic Studies (IISS), *The Military Balance 2007* (London), 346.
e. Stockholm International Peace Research Institute, *SIPRI Yearbook 2007* (Oxford University Press, 2007), 270.

over, PLA officials point to China's now-biennial publication of defense white papers explaining Chinese defense policies and wonder why US officials are still asking about the purpose and intentions behind Chinese military modernization if Beijing has already explained this in public.

Indeed, China has made some progress over the past decade in its military transparency, including its release of increasingly detailed white papers and greater engagement with foreign militaries.[13] Chinese defense officials and specialists are more available than ever to discuss Chinese defense affairs with foreign visitors, and Chinese media dedicated to defense issues reveal some of the ongoing internal PLA debates and developments. China has also been increasingly responsive to US requests for access to Chinese military sites and hardware.

Nonetheless, overall, the PLA remains an opaque institution. US officials (and others) question why some of the most fundamental issues about the PLA, such as the number of personnel in each service or the true aggregate of China's defense expenditures, are still not deemed fit by Beijing to be placed in the public domain (see table 9.1 for various estimates of China's defense expenditures). They reveal frustration at the never-ending negotiations with the PLA to visit Chinese military installations beyond show units, to see new equipment, and to receive the level of access to the Chinese armed forces that US officials assert the Chinese are afforded when they visit the United States in the course of military exchanges. US military officials also note that transparency is not simply a favor one does for another: The more transparent a nation is about itself, the less other nations' militaries have to assume the worst and respond accordingly, leading to potential misunderstanding, miscalculation, and an action-reaction cycle of military preparations to the detriment of all sides.

Finally, when addressing China's transparency, US observers often note uncertainty about the state and nature of China's civil-military dynamic. While few doubt that the Chinese Communist Party remains firmly in control of the PLA, recent Chinese actions—such as the January 2007 antisatellite test and the decision to refuse US Navy port calls to Hong Kong in November 2007—continue to raise fundamental questions about how national security issues are coordinated in Beijing and the degree of authority the PLA may or may not have to take unilateral action that affects larger Chinese national security or foreign relations.

Questions also persist about the nature and type of military advice senior PLA leaders offer its senior civilian leadership. There remains a near-total lack of public transparency on this issue even as, unlike in years past, the PLA now has near-total monopoly on military expertise upon which the civilian Party leaders must depend.

Future of PLA Modernization

The exact size, organization, and—most importantly—actual operational capabilities of the PLA in the next decade are impossible to detail at this point with precision. This is, after all, a military that has not engaged in significant observable combat for almost 30 years (since 1979 in Vietnam). Consequently, analysts and scholars studying the Chinese armed forces from publicly available data are forced to accept a certain dearth of empiricism.

Nevertheless, looking out over the next decade, one may detect six general observable trends in China's evolving defense establishment.

The PLA will continue to increase in professionalism, in the corporate and institutional sense, and enhance its operational capabilities. The PLA will be increasingly capable of sustainable *regional* force projection, although not yet capable of *global* conventional force projection.[14]

The PLA in the next decade will remain large in terms of numbers—today at 2.3 million—and in fact larger than China's leadership would prefer it to be.[15] While units will be of uneven quality in terms of equipment and trained personnel, the PLA is expected to maintain a core of highly trained and well equipped units that will make China's military one of the premier regional military forces in Asia.

The PLA is only in the early stage of becoming a "joint" organization that gives equal emphasis to the various branches of service. However, given another decade the PLA will likely become much more adept at orchestrating complex campaigns that involve land, sea, and air forces as well as cyber and outer space. Indeed, the PLA will almost certainly have enhanced space-based C4ISR capabilities that include architectures to enable new command-and-control relationships and for enhanced battle space awareness.

It is certainly not inevitable that the PLA will be successful in achieving all of its aspirations, however. A host of formidable systemic problems endemic to the PLA, challenges from within greater Chinese society, and wild card events in the international environment could preclude this massive defense establishment from achieving its objectives.[16] Systemic impediments include:

- low level of education of most of the PLA's enlisted members and training and readiness problems inherent in a conscript force in which draftees serve only two years;

- competition with the private sector to recruit the best and brightest to fill the ranks of the officer corps and then retain them;

- concerns in the PLA about the trainability of rural recruits, service evasion by educated urban youth, and issues with the military socialization of a generation of soldiers from one-child families;

- uncertainty whether the PLA has "adaptive capacity," i.e., the ability to adapt quickly to events on the ground when faced with rapidly evolving emergency or conflict situations;

- deeply entrenched bureaucratic interests in the PLA that resist systemic change;

- a professional culture, including a rigidly hierarchical system, that is uncomfortable with the decentralization of decision-making that high-tech war demands; and

- economic and political barriers at the local level that preclude the PLA from downsizing and economizing even further.

In the end, however, the PLA has proven that it is an organization that learns and evolves effectively—i.e, it understands what is broken and what must be fixed and changed. This in itself is impressive. Today there is no greater critic of the PLA than the leadership of the PLA.

US Response to China's Military Modernization

Given the modernization of the Chinese armed forces and the uncertainties of China's growing military capabilities, the United States needs to consider four issues.

First, the United States must continue to modernize and transform its own forces. The United States needs to do so, however, not only because of China but also because of the uncertain global security landscape that is unfolding on various fronts, including the Middle East as the Iraq War draws down and in South Asia. As defense planners make their case for building the "military after next," it will be tempting but shortsighted to use China and the PLA as the "poster child" for justifying what will certainly be a long-term and very expensive reconstitution and modernization effort of the US military in coming years. By considering its interests more broadly, the United States may still ensure that the gap between the military capabilities of the United States and the PLA remain wide and formidable, while providing a sense of balance and reassurance in Asia and beyond.

In particular, however, the United States will need to pay attention to safeguarding its critical C4ISR assets to ensure their survivability during hostilities. Given China's attention to antisatellite capabilities, computer network warfare, and ballistic missiles, redundancy and hardening of US high-tech capabilities will be essential to reduce US vulnerabilities and maintain military predominance during a crisis.

Second, the United States must continue to reach out to the PLA on as many levels as the two respective systems in Washington and Beijing can bear. The United States should do this for several reasons:

- *to ensure that the PLA understands the capabilities of the US armed forces.* Left isolated and insular, the PLA will slip into an alternative reality that could lead to miscalculation on its part.

- *to reduce risk and avoid miscalculation.* Any US military officer can likely do little to dissuade Chinese counterparts from their most deeply felt suspicions about US motives. The same is likely true for Chinese officers dealing with US counterparts. But winning "hearts and minds" should not be the objective of exposing each military to the other. A more realistic and necessary rationale is to ensure that when Chinese or US military officers have to make critical judgments or decisions—or advise their senior leadership—about how to deal with the other, they will decide based on knowledge, observations, and personal experiences, not ideological biases or politically correct shibboleths. They also should develop working relationships that allow development and implementation of bilateral confidence-building measures and crisis management regimes to prevent the possibility of accident and miscalculation from occurring and potentially escalating to something worse.

- *to find areas of cooperation when cooperation is in the national interest of both parties.* It is important to remember that while the United States and China are not allies, and complex issues divide the two, neither are they enemies nor predestined to become so. The two armed forces could

very well find themselves working *with* each other under certain circumstances even as they both hedge against each other in other areas.
Maritime security, humanitarian assistance/disaster relief, search and
rescue operations, peace operations, and environmental safety are some
of the areas where the United States and China have common interest,
and given time and commitment between the two sides, they may provide a roadmap for greater joint efforts toward common security, in coordination with other nations, in coming years.

At the same time, the United States should also be careful not to engage
with China's military to the point of assisting with the operational effectiveness of the PLA. The United States should remember that while it desires greater cooperation and wants to avoid an adversarial relationship,
the two countries remain suspicious of one another given different strategic visions, values, and interests. China remains uncomfortable with US
preeminence in East Asia, and both sides realize they may find themselves in a confrontation over Taiwan. US military engagement of China
in fact is constrained by US law.[17] The close connection between the private and military sectors in China also requires care among those in the
US private sector about the types of cooperation, including technology
transfer, offered to China; this too has been prescribed by law.[18]

Third, the United States must continue to maintain a credible forward
military presence in the Asia-Pacific region. Traditionally, US forces in the
Asia-Pacific region have labored under "the tyranny of distance," the natural constraint placed on the US military's operations in the region due to
the region's vast area. The ability to move forces through the region as
quickly as possible will not only enhance deterrence but also, more critically, facilitate real operations. The ability to base forces in Japan and South
Korea; increase US presence and capabilities in Guam; maintain high-
frequency deployments at sea to ensure freedom of navigation and maritime safety; and gain greater access to key regional locations for US forces
for training, exercises, and logistical support will remain keys to maintaining peace and stability in the region, related but not limited to China.

Fourth, US defense officials, and others, must continue to devote time,
effort, and resources to military diplomacy and operational cooperation in
the Asia-Pacific region more broadly. The United States should welcome
the opportunity to participate in multilateral venues and forums as a member of the Asia-Pacific community of nations. At the same time, the United
States must not remain stagnant in its regional alliances and bilateral relationships, but rather redefine and reorient them to fit the traditional and
nontraditional security requirements that are priorities for the region. Traditional requirements relate to hard deterrence, sea lane security, and balance of power considerations noted above. Nontraditional elements would
include training, equipping, and participating in joint efforts to provide

rapid humanitarian assistance and disaster relief to affected areas; ensuring adequate and secure supplies of energy; addressing climate change and other elements of environmental protection; combating drug and human trafficking; and staunching emerging health hazards, particularly infectious disease.

Both the PLA and the Pentagon are considering the other in their military planning. Some on both sides in fact argue that military conflict between the United States and China sometime in the future is inevitable. This, of course, is not true. However, both sides need to act with great care and develop vehicles for and habits of communication to prevent tensions or disputes from escalating unnecessarily, to the detriment of East Asia's peace and stability. This is especially critical as both militaries begin to operate more in common sea and air space. Given undeniable strides in PLA modernization, and remaining uncertainties in Chinese strategic intentions, however, the emergence of an increasingly capable and credible Chinese military ensures that the military factor will remain an important variable in the US-China relationship in years to come.

Notes

1. Xinhua News Agency, "Hu Jintao zai Zhongguo gongchandang di shiqi ci quanguo daibiao dahui shang de baogao" ["Hu Jintao's Report to the 17th Party Congress"], October 15, 2007, http://news.xinhuanet.com.

2. Maureen Fan, "China Scouts Colleges to Fill Ranks of Modern Army," *Washington Post*, December 17, 2007, A01.

3. Premier Zhou Enlai originally introduced the Four Modernizations in 1975. The Four Modernizations, in order of importance, are agriculture, industry, science and technology, and national defense.

4. Excerpts from the speech Jiang Zemin delivered, entitled "The International Situation and the Military Strategic Guidelines," can be found in *Selected Works of Jiang Zemin*, volume 1 (Beijing: People's Publishing House, August 2006), 278–94.

5. China originally reassessed its security situation in 1985, as the Soviet threat receded. In May that year, Deng Xiaoping, serving as chairman of the Central Military Commission, announced in a speech that China no longer faced a near-term military threat and that China ought to focus on development in a peaceful era. The 1993 review did not alter this fundamental assessment, although it took additional international trends into account to reach its conclusions.

6. For an official, unclassified US Department of Defense (DoD) assessment of China's military strategy, organization, and operational concepts, see *Military Power of the People's Republic of China 2008: A Report to Congress*, www.defenselink.mil. The Office of the Secretary of Defense is required by law—Section 1202 of the FY2000 National Defense Authorization Act—to submit a report annually "on the current and future military strategy of the People's Republic of China."

7. In 1998 the PLA created a fourth general department, the General Equipment Department, in yet another rectification of the PLA research and development system. The other PLA general departments are the General Staff Department, General Political Department, and General Logistics Department.

8. For instance, in January 2007, China tested its offensive antisatellite capability with the successful interception of a defunct Chinese weather satellite by a ground-based vehicle. In October 2007, China launched its first robotic lunar exploration mission, demonstrating an array of sensor, control, communications, and spaceflight technologies with broad military applications. The planned October 2008 launch of China's third manned space mission, Shenzhou VII, which will include China's first spacewalk, continues to highlight the Chinese human spaceflight program, with corresponding implications for systems integration and other critical technological capabilities.

9. Information Office of the State Council of the People's Republic of China, *China's Space Activities in 2006* (Beijing, October 2006), www.cnsa.gov.cn.

10. In the past few years some Western governments have alleged, and the Chinese have vociferously denied, that Beijing is actively probing, and attempting to hack into, government information systems, especially defense information technology systems. There is indeed increasing concern—and evidence—that the PLA is developing and testing cyber warfare capabilities.

11. For a detailed look at the PLA's new operational level doctrine, see David M. Finkelstein, "Thinking About the PLA's 'Revolution in Doctrinal Affairs'," in *China's Revolution in Doctrinal Affairs: Emerging Trends in the Operational Art of the Chinese People's Liberation Army*, eds. David M. Finkelstein and James Mulvenon (Alexandria, VA: The CNA Corporation, December 2005), 1–27.

12. See Michael A. McDevitt, Asian Military Modernization: Key Areas of Concern (unpublished paper prepared for the Institute of International Strategic Studies and the Japan Institute of International Affairs, June 5, 2008). McDevitt argues that, "Specifically, China is putting in place a credible way to deny access to US forces by knitting together broad area ocean surveillance systems, a large number of submarines, land based aircraft with cruise missiles, and ballistic missile systems that can target ships on the high seas. The operational objective is to keep US naval power as far away from China as possible in case of conflict."

13. According to China's 2006 defense white paper, "Since 2002, China has held 16 joint (sic) military exercises with 11 countries." An article in early January 2008 asserted that "China's armed forces conducted more joint (sic) exercises and joint (sic) training with foreign armed forces in 2007 than in any other recent year"; Xinhua News Agency, "Chinese Armed Forces Step Up Joint Exercises and Training with Foreign Armed Forces, Strengthen Mutual Trust and Cooperation," January 7, 2008. This increasing commitment to combined exercises with other nations, including most notably the August 2007 exercise with Russia and Central Asia—dubbed "Peace Mission 2007" and which involved the movement of 1,600 Chinese ground, air force, and logistics troops across the PRC border into central Russia—is indeed a major change from past Chinese policy, which explicitly rejected such activities. For numbers of Chinese troops deployed in Peace Mission 2007, see *Bei-*

jing Review, August 7–15, 2007, and Xinhua News Agency, "All Chinese Exercise Troops Return Home From Russia," August 26, 2007.

14. Some Chinese security analysts now talk about the need to develop capabilities to project conventional forces for what US military planners used to refer to as "Operations Other Than War" such as noncombatant evacuations. With over 670,000 Chinese citizens working and studying abroad in 2006 (see *People's Daily Online,* "Government to Protect Workers Abroad," May 16, 2007) and Chinese businesses operating in some of the world's worst neighborhoods, Chinese citizens are in harm's way as never before. See also David M. Finkelstein, "China's Quest for Energy and the 'Contradictions' of Beijing's 'Go Out Strategy'" (lecture, World Affairs Council, September 11, 2007). According to Finkelstein's data, between 2004 and 2007, nearly a thousand Chinese citizens had to be evacuated from war zones, disaster areas, and riots around the world, and Beijing still largely depends on other nations for assistance when its nationals must be evacuated from crisis zones. The expanding interests of a globalizing China are stressing security planners and gaining the attention of the PLA. As one Chinese Navy admiral wrote in 2006, "The present level of military force can hardly meet demand. China's military forces lag far behind . . . in its ability to tackle traditional security threats, fight terrorism, deliver humanitarian aid in case of natural disaster, undertake UN peace-keeping operations, and help overseas Chinese evacuate in an international crisis"; Yang Yi, "Peaceful Development Strategy and Strategic Opportunity," *Contemporary International Relations* 16 (September 2006).

15. The demobilization of massive numbers of soldiers is a regime stability issue for China that is handled with great care. Since 1985, the PLA has cut more than 1.5 million troops. Another 200,000-person reduction was recently completed. The economic burdens on local governments of integrating demobilized troops and their families back into the civilian sector is likely the greatest factor inhibiting the PLA from scaling down to a much leaner force—one that can be evenly trained and equipped for excellence across the board.

16. See David M. Finkelstein and Kristen Gunness, eds., *Civil-Military Trends in Today's China: Swimming in a New Sea* (Armonk, NY: M.E. Sharpe Publishers, 2007).

17. Section 1201 of the National Defense Authorization Act for FY2000 (Public Law 106-65) disallows "inappropriate exposure" of operational matters to the PLA and outlines specific areas of military-to-military engagement that are proscribed. A decade earlier, following the violent crackdown on Tiananmen Square protesters in 1989, the United States imposed legal prohibitions—first by presidential order in June 1989, then by Public Law 101-246 in 1990—on the government sale or commercial export to China of any military equipment or relevant technology, conduct in which the United States had been actively engaged during much of the 1980s. These sanctions remain in effect, albeit subject to presidential waiver.

18. An assortment of US Commerce Department regulations restricts sensitive commercial equipment and technology transfers to China, among other countries. In June 2007, the Commerce Department's Bureau of Industry and Security issued regulations that imposed new controls on the export of certain high-technology

items that could contribute to China's military build-up specifically, even while reducing barriers for prescreened customers in China. The US Congress established the China Economic and Security Review Commission to provide additional oversight in this regard. The commission's mandate is to "monitor, investigate, and submit to Congress an annual report on the national security implications of the bilateral trade and economic relationship between the United States and the People's Republic of China, and to provide recommendations, where appropriate, to Congress for legislative and administrative action."

10

China and the World

Today, China holds high the banner of peace, development and cooperation. It pursues an independent foreign policy of peace and commits itself firmly to peaceful development . . . . China firmly pursues a strategy of opening-up for mutual benefit and win-win outcomes. It is inclusive and is eager to . . . play its part in building a harmonious world of enduring peace and common prosperity.

—Hu Jintao, October 15, 2007[1]

Not long ago it was common to discuss China's emergence as one of the world's major powers as a future prospect but not an imminent one. It was expected that China's enormous challenges of poverty and underdevelopment would constrain its ability to project power or influence global events for the foreseeable future, while nations observed closely the growing giant largely for indications of aggressive intent toward Taiwan, internal turmoil, or hostility toward the dominance ("hegemony") of major powers, particularly the United States. China itself commonly demurred that it did not seek international or regional leadership and simply sought to focus on its own internal development over the next generation or more. In the early 1990s, Deng Xiaoping articulated the maxim for how China should approach international affairs: "Observe calmly; secure our position; cope with affairs calmly; hide our capacities and bide our time; be good at maintaining a low profile; and never claim leadership."

Although China's rise has not come close to the level of global power of the United States, or that of Great Britain during the 19th century, its rapidly growing economic, political, and cultural engagement and influence around the world today is as undeniable as it is remarkable. China has emerged as an engine of global economic growth, with $1.8 trillion in foreign currency reserves in May 2008 and plans to apply hundreds of billions of dollars of this to international investment in coming years through its sovereign wealth fund. Its driving need for all kinds of commodities, from oil and aluminum to cement and copper, has driven up world prices.[2] China is the world's third largest trader in terms of volume

Table 10.1   China's top trading partners, 2007

Country/region	Trade volume (billions of US dollars)	Share of China's total trade (percent)	Percentage increase in bilateral trade volume from 2006	Percentage change in share of China's total trade
European Union	356.1	16.4	27.0	0.5
United States	302.0	13.9	15.0	−1.0
Japan	236.0	10.9	13.9	−0.9
ASEAN	202.5	9.3	25.9	0.2
Hong Kong	197.2	9.1	18.8	−0.3
South Korea	159.9	7.4	19.1	−0.2
Taiwan	124.4	5.7	15.4	−0.4
Russia	48.1	2.2	44.3	0.3
Australia	43.8	2.0	33.1	0.1
India	38.6	1.8	55.5	0.4
Total	2,173.8	78.7	—	—

ASEAN = Association of Southeast Asian Nations

Note: Trade volumes in this table differ slightly from those in table 10.2 because the data in this table are from Chinese statistics, while those in table 10.2 are from China's trading partners' statistics.

Source: Ministry of Commerce of the People's Republic of China, "Top 10 Trading Partners" (Beijing, March 17, 2008; in Chinese).

(see table 10.1 for China's top trading partners), with GDP rising to $3.24 trillion in 2007 and GDP growth in 2007 reaching just under 12 percent.[3] It has risen rapidly to become the largest trading partner of many nations, particularly in Asia.

China has also become an important and active player in critical global security issues ranging from North Korea, Iran, and Sudan to global warming, HIV/AIDS, and energy security. Its officials and scholars have become more open to discussing China's evolving perspectives—and on-going internal debates—about a full range of international issues. In the process, Beijing has displayed increasing self-confidence and assertiveness in publicly promoting its interests and principles and in defying the United States, the European Union, and other major powers when challenged or embarrassed, for example, over currency valuation, domestic unrest, and human rights, acting less like a subordinate power and more like a defiant and coequal player in international affairs.

Perhaps most important, the world's perception of Chinese power and importance internationally today, and ever-growing influence year by year, has evolved measurably.[4] It is now commonly stated that no major international challenge can effectively be met without China's assistance. In short, China's "rise" has come sooner than expected.

China's embrace of globalization in all its forms has meant that its global interests, and thus its outreach, have increased commensurately. As a permanent, veto-wielding member of the United Nations Security Council, China has unique status and authority to act—or block action—on the critical international challenges facing the world, be it weapons proliferation, terrorism, climate change, energy security, or extreme human rights abuses perpetrated by national despots. China continues to demur that it is merely a developing country and does not seek to change the international system. But some of its rhetoric and actions suggest otherwise (chapter 1), and the weight inherent in the rise of a nation of 1.3 billion people (and counting) affirms a self-evident truth: It is not *whether* China will exert influence on the international system but *how*.

Indeed, the world is increasingly accommodating China's emergence. In Asia, few if any regional initiatives are undertaken or national foreign policies developed without first considering what China thinks and how China might react. Elsewhere in the developing world, China's growing influence is forcing international aid agencies to contend with a new competitor and forcing Western nations to look again at how they deal with pariah states.[5]

At the same time, Beijing looks at its growing power in complex ways. Chinese leaders consider what Chinese theoretician Zheng Bijian has termed the "multiplication and division" principle inherent in China's development: that all problems that arise in China are multiplied by 1.3 billion people, while all achievements are divided by the same amount. When China looks at itself, therefore, it sees something rather different than do those outside the country: It is focused as much on the per capita societal challenges it faces as on the collective measure of its economic or political power.

Nonetheless, Chinese officials and scholars are talking more openly about China's growing influence in international affairs and their plans for developing that influence further over time. Beijing has identified what it has termed a "strategic opportunity" in coming years, in which "peace and development" remain the predominant global trends even as the United States remains concentrated on the Middle East and South Asia and on a "war on terrorism" that has been focused largely outside East Asia. International revulsion over US foreign policy in recent years has also presented itself as an opportunity for China to focus inward, enhance its global attractiveness, present alternative models of international conduct, and shape the international system in ways that meet its national interests.

Evolution of Goals and Principles Underlying China's Foreign Policy

Many of the basic goals, principles, and rhetoric of China's foreign policy have remained consistent since at least Deng Xiaoping's time. China's foremost goal is safeguarding its sovereign independence, territorial integrity, and national development.

No longer concerned about challenges to its political existence, and having long ago abjured support for or export of radical Maoist ideology, China's external policies in recent years have largely been defensive: They have sought to create international conditions that will enable Beijing to focus the majority of its energies inward—on the nation's substantial domestic challenges and steady development of what it calls "comprehensive national power."[6] Specifically, China's foreign policy has sought to prevent the creation of anti-China blocs, particularly in its neighborhood, which could constrain its freedom of action and economic growth; ensure access to overseas markets for its products and to critical natural resources necessary for its internal development, including but not limited to energy; secure its periphery to prevent cross-border challenges to its domestic stability, particularly in Tibet and Xinjiang; and promote a multipolar world that will constrain the power and influence of great powers, particularly the United States.

The exception to China's defensive orientation arguably concerns Taiwan (chapter 8). China asserts that its policy is defensive—to prevent Taiwan's drift toward de jure independence. China has demonstrated willingness to apply a full array of economic and diplomatic leverage to reward countries that avow a "One China" policy and deny Taiwan an international profile and to punish those that do not. China has also directed its military modernization primarily to address a Taiwan contingency (see chapter 9), which Beijing calls a deterrent and Taipei (and many in the United States) views as threatening and provocative. Beijing has met with increasing success in isolating Taiwan internationally as more states make the calculation that they should not antagonize the world's leading emerging power on its most sensitive national interest.

At the same time, China continues to seek to reassure the international community about the overall positive, peaceful, and constructive implications of its rise. China's outreach and public rhetoric continue to be couched in terms of high moral principle: "win-win" solutions, democracy in international affairs, noninterference in others' internal affairs, and commitment to dialogue and development to solve the world's ills.[7] During the 17th Party Congress in October 2007, the phrase "peaceful development" was added to the lexicon and enshrined as a matter of China's national strategy (as was the broader goal of "foster[ing] a security environment conducive to peaceful development").[8]

The phrase "harmonious world" also recently entered China's rhetorical lexicon under Hu Jintao (see chapter 2). Meant to contrast with previous Maoist ideals of "struggle" and "revolution," "harmony" (*hexie*) is a principle that harkens back to historical Chinese cultural traditions of Confucianism and Taoism and is meant to accentuate China's modern commitment to international stability. China's kinder, gentler approach has sought to make China's rise in power more acceptable and perhaps legitimate in the eyes of the world, particularly along its periphery, which otherwise might view China's emergence with alarm and coalesce to contain or balance against it.

Attention to principle, morality, and virtue as legitimating elements of one's policies has a long history in China, also reaching back to its Confucian philosophical roots. Adhering to virtue and principle in one's conduct, according to this Chinese tradition, affirms one's right to lead. In a contemporary context, China has also come to recognize the value of such ideals in developing Chinese soft power abroad, specifically as potential cultural and intellectual contributions to international society that may promote China's influence and status as a major world leader (see next section). It is indeed no coincidence that China has named after Confucius the institutes it continues to establish around the world to promote the study of Chinese language and culture.

In practice, however, China's idealistic tenets have often fused seamlessly with its very practical national interests. Promoting the noninterference principle has enabled China to demonstrate solidarity with many developing-world nations against the West and prevent any precedents from being set to allow the international community to intervene in its own internal affairs. China's continued refrain of "dialogue" as virtually a panacea for all international problems is certainly constructive and unassailable as a matter of principle and one that many Chinese truly consider more viable than more coercive approaches to problems. Nonetheless, it has enabled China (among other nations) to avoid taking actions that might negatively affect its economic or strategic interests in places such as Burma, Sudan, and Iran. Ironically, this posture has often served China's political interests well by gaining it leverage with both the international community and nations facing international criticism as each vies for China's support and assistance in seeking an advantage over the other.

As a result, some in the West have charged China with being a "free rider" in international security affairs, leading to calls for China, in Robert Zoellick's words, to become a "responsible stakeholder" in global affairs to uphold established norms and principles of the international system.[9] Others will question whether Chinese international conduct is in fact moral and virtuous given that its noninterference policies have had the perceived effect of protecting brutal governments in Burma, Sudan, and Zimbabwe from international pressure.

The Chinese will argue in return that their concepts of virtue and morality simply differ from those of the West: China's "relativist" morality, they say, is one that respects different cultures, social systems, and traditions to decide for themselves how to conduct their affairs, while the West's "universalist" notion of morality, where certain norms and values transcend cultures, social systems, and borders, is intrusive, disrespectful, and destabilizing. This difference in conception and implementation of virtue and morality in international affairs will likely continue to play out in the international arena in coming years, with both the West and China (and others) certain to come under pressure to compromise on their own terms as a greater consensus forms.

Role of Soft Power in Chinese Foreign Policy

China is voracious in its interest to listen, learn, and evolve according to proven best practices around the world and to assess what the Chinese call the "trends of the times." Officials and scholars have closely studied how other nations have succeeded—and failed—throughout history and sought consciously to avoid their mistakes and learn the lessons of their success to apply at home. China is rigorous in assessing the global and regional environment that it faces and accommodates its policy accordingly—an accommodation that alters China's chosen means to achieve its objectives even if its ends remain constant.

Joseph Nye's concept of "soft power"[10] is an area of particular strategic interest and tactical focus for today's China. Consistent with its desire to enhance its international image, reassure nations of its benign nature as it rises, and prevent the formation of counterbalancing coalitions, China has paid attention to the concept since the early 1990s and in recent years has explicitly stated in public and private the priority it places on developing and cultivating soft power through its actions and policies.[11]

China in fact sees traditional concepts of power as an essential complement to soft power: Without economic and military strength, Beijing has assessed, the appeal of one's cultural and intellectual contributions will suffer in turn.[12] China has recognized the importance of moving out on both legs of hard (military) and soft (economic[13] and cultural) power in its development of "comprehensive national power."[14]

China at one level seeks to counter "China threat" theories by "deepening [the] world's understanding of China."[15] More fundamentally, however, China has been seeking to identify something universal that separates it favorably from the West, a unique and positive contribution to international society and world culture that will be distinctively associated with China. In Beijing's view, China's current promotion of concepts such as "peaceful development," "harmony" (including a "harmonious world" abroad and "harmonious society" at home), "win-win solutions," and "strategic partnerships" fit this mold. However, traditional Chinese cultural values, codes, and maxims, particularly those associated with Confucianism, are considered more fundamental and universal cultural contributions that China can promote in years to come.

To back up its high-minded rhetoric, China has not only provided substantial overseas financial and infrastructural assistance but also sent its doctors and teachers abroad; funded education opportunities in China for foreign nationals; encouraged the spread of traditional Chinese medicine; and promoted the study of the Chinese language abroad (specifically simplified Chinese characters, which not coincidentally are used by the mainland but not by Taiwan) by building more than 200 Confucius Institutes around the world.[16] The combination of idealistic rhetoric and constructive action indeed has reassured and sometimes enticed nations in Southeast Asia, Africa, and elsewhere, enhancing the foundation of China's soft power development over time. This is particularly true in the developing world, where China is focusing much of its attention on cultivating its soft power.[17] Public opinion polls demonstrate that China's popularity in fact remains high in most developing areas, whether in Southeast Asia, Africa, or Latin America, largely because of perceived economic benefits from engagement with China.[18]

However, many challenges are appearing in China's bid for soft power there and elsewhere. Attitudes toward China within the developed world, for instance, have grown more negative in recent years—in Europe, the United States, Japan, and even South Korea.[19] Of more concern to China, popular attitudes toward it in critical developing neighbors India and Russia have also declined. The economic challenge from China is a major factor, but concerns about China's growing military power are also evident in all these countries—including Russia.

Even in those areas of the developing world with more positive attitudes toward China, problems have surfaced. Many stories have emerged in the media about a backlash within African populations against low-grade Chinese goods supplanting African goods in local markets, Chinese labor being used instead of local labor for infrastructure projects, Chinese investors' disinterest in local environmental standards, and charges of Chinese neocolonialism due to extraction of resources rather than investment in industry. Some in Africa contend that these stories are overblown and do not reflect the reality of China's overall positive contributions to local economies and infrastructure. Indeed, African nations have often stated that they prefer China's attitude of respect, equality, and partnership in its economic outreach to the perceived condescension of the West's "charity" and "help."[20]

Nonetheless, the Chinese government is clearly concerned about trends in the region and the impact they are having on its soft power strategy around the world. In continuing its "go out" (*zou chuqu*) policy of actively encouraging, and indeed facilitating, Chinese corporate activity overseas, the Chinese government in August 2006 promulgated new regulations demanding companies pay attention to issues of corporate responsibility and what it termed "localization"—respect for local customs, safety standards, and labor.[21] Enforcement among Chinese corporations, and even provinces, that are doing business internationally has proved difficult, increasingly complicating the Chinese government's ability to control completely the conduct and success of its soft power strategy.[22] Given its potential impact on China's image overseas, how Chinese companies should engage with the world will reportedly be a subject of priority attention and debate within the government in coming years.

Meanwhile, international condemnation of China's domestic record on human rights, rule of law, political freedom, corruption, and export product safety has infuriated Beijing. This is true not only because of traditional Asian notions of "losing face" or contentions that it "hurts the feelings of 1.3 billion Chinese people," as the Chinese are wont to say, but also because these public criticisms affect China's international reputation and thus its soft power. China has responded to international public criticism more forcefully in recent years, viewing it as a Western method to embarrass and thus keep China down.

On the other hand, on occasion, Chinese authorities have welcomed international attention to some of China's internal problems as a way to gain leverage within their system to address these issues. China's environmental problems, including water and air pollution and desertification, have been one notable arena where China's leaders have used the international media in this regard.

Joseph Nye has stated that in a global information age, "success depends not only on whose army wins but also on whose story wins."[23] In the end, soft power is not just a function of popularity; it is the ability to get others to do things in one's interest through one's attractiveness. There are in fact few examples yet of China demonstrating this ability. China remains at a nascent stage in its soft power development. But Beijing is clearly making a serious, concerted, and conscious effort to this end, with enough patience to continue working toward its goal for years to come.

China's International Relationships

> For developed countries, we will continue to strengthen strategic dialogue, enhance mutual trust, deepen cooperation and properly manage differences to promote long-term, stable and sound development of bilateral relations. For our neighboring countries, we will continue to follow the foreign policy of friendship and partnership, strengthen good-neighborly relations and practical cooperation with them, and energetically engage in regional cooperation in order to jointly create a peaceful, stable regional environment featuring equality, mutual trust and win-win cooperation. For other developing countries, we will continue to increase solidarity and cooperation with them, cement traditional friendship, expand practical cooperation, provide assistance to them within our ability, and uphold the legitimate demands and common interests of developing countries. We will continue to take an active part in multilateral affairs, assume our due international obligations, play a constructive role, and work to make the international order fairer and more equitable.

— Hu Jintao, October 15, 2007[24]

In the explicit hierarchy of importance that China places on its international relationships, "major power" relations, particularly with the United States, remain at the top, followed by relations with neighboring states, and then developing nations elsewhere.[25] Interaction with the developing world has risen in relative importance in recent years, beginning during the later years of Jiang Zemin but accelerating under Hu Jintao. China recently added multilateralism to its list of priority relationships, particularly as it recognized the ability of multilateralism to safeguard its interests, specifically within the United Nations, reassure nations of its commitment to the international system, and appeal to its developing-world brethren more broadly.

China typically divides its bilateral relationships into two categories: "strategic partner" and "cooperative partner" in order of importance. When China concludes a strategic partnership agreement with another country or region, however, it is not meant by either party to be taken literally. China seeks such agreements in order to highlight the relative importance of a particular bilateral and multilateral relationship to its global interests.[26] Strategic partnerships are also meant to serve as an explicit Chinese alternative to the concept of alliances, which Beijing has denounced as exclusionary, provocative, and harmful to China's interests, since the US alliance system dominates East Asian security and surrounds China. Beijing has also pursued free trade agreements and other preferential trade arrangements, often less for economic reasons (these agreements generally have enormous loopholes and exceptions) than as political vehicles to highlight its commitment to particular relationships.[27]

Major Powers

United States

Given its priority attention to economic development and potential threats to its national sovereignty and territorial integrity, China continues to consider the United States its most important bilateral relationship. China recognizes that US economic, political, and military power remains predominant in the world, and specifically in Asia, making hostile relations a costly distraction that would complicate, if not obstruct, China's economic development and achievement of overall strategic goals. US investment and technology and its domestic market continue to be critical for China's development needs, albeit to a decreasing degree as China diversifies its economic ties.

China feels relatively confident about the trajectory of its relationship with the United States, despite controversies over trade, Tibet, Taiwan, and other matters. Growing economic interdependence between the two countries, absence of recent public crises between the two sides akin to the

1999 bombing of China's embassy in Belgrade or the April 2001 spy plane incident, and general US official distraction from China after September 11, 2001 have created a degree of comfort about relations with the United States in recent years. Chinese officials and scholars worry, however, that the United States may rediscover China in coming years as its attention to the Middle East and Islamic extremism recedes. China hopes in the interim to deepen economic interdependence and establish new vehicles for cooperation with the United States. China will continue to develop a web of alternative relationships with other powers in East Asia and beyond to promote a more multipolar world. China continues to mistrust US intentions toward it and suspects that the United States does not welcome—and indeed may seek to prevent—the rise of China as a potential peer competitor over time.

Russia, India, Japan, and Europe

China's relations with other major powers such as Russia, India, Japan, and Europe have moved in varying directions in recent years. Official relations with Russia appear as warm as ever. The two nations have put their border dispute far behind them and continue to find common cause in seeking to constrain US power, prevent intervention in their internal affairs, and take advantage of complementary interests of supply (Russia) and demand (China) in their bilateral trade, particularly in the energy and arms sales sectors. Russia continues to serve as China's leading source of advanced military equipment and technology. Each permanent members of the United Nations Security Council, they have coordinated their approaches on several key international security issues, blocking sanctions against Iran, Burma, and Zimbabwe, and actively opposing US deployment of missile defense as destabilizing and contemptuous of their respective national interests.

The China-Russia partnership[28] has also included joint development (with Central Asia) of the Shanghai Cooperation Organization (SCO) and organization of SCO-sponsored multilateral military exercises. China's considerable political and operational investment in this initiative reflects that Central Asia has become a priority area for China's strategic planning.

Nonetheless, China's relations with Russia will not lead to a formal, operational alliance to oppose the United States, nor will the SCO become a military bloc seeking to balance the North Atlantic Treaty Organization (NATO), despite some of the more breathless interpretations of these relationships. Indeed, many Russian strategists remain quite wary about the implications of China's rapid growth for Russian political and economic security, particularly its growing influence in Russia's depopulated but energy-rich northeast regions. Popular attitudes toward China within Russia remain quite poor.

China has stabilized its relationship with India,[29] seeking to put aside their troubled recent history to focus on common interests of economic development and trade. Beijing is nervous about increasing closeness in US-India relations and as a result has more evenly balanced its engagement in South Asia between India and long-time ally Pakistan. Nonetheless, China's military development, and India's long memory of Chinese military and political support for Pakistan and of the traumatic 1962 border war, has led India to remain quite mistrustful of its huge eastern neighbor. China's desire to set aside their continuing border dispute in order to stabilize relations has met with reluctant acceptance in New Delhi, which itself seeks to promote a peaceful international environment in which to focus on its profound internal development challenges.

Since early 2007, Beijing has even begun to change its approach toward Japan, about which the Chinese hold a deep-seated antipathy rooted in modern history. Chinese leaders realized that China's public propaganda was creating mistrust in Japan and fueling sustained animosity from the Chinese people, which threatened to solidify hostile relations between the two over the long run. With bilateral economic relations increasingly critical for China's (and Japan's) growth, China has moderated its negative media propaganda, and used Premier Wen Jiabao's visit in April 2007 and President Hu Jintao's April 2008 visit, the first Chinese presidential trip in a decade, to focus on developing relations for the future rather than focusing on the troubled past. With the relative thaw in China-Japan relations, China has moved to patch up the one gap in its strategy to maintain positive relations with all its neighbors (the thaw in relations with Taiwan after Ma Ying-jeou's inauguration as the island's leader in May 2008 has been the other major development in this regard).

China's relationship with Europe, however, has soured noticeably in recent years. In 2005, the European Union was prepared to lift its arms embargo on China in keeping with its desire to promote economic relations and its newly minted strategic partnership. Since then, the economic opportunity of China, while still viable, has revealed its dark side. Like the United States, Europe's concerns are intensifying around endemic intellectual property rights violations, product safety concerns, China's undervalued currency, a ballooning bilateral trade deficit, and loss of the region's low-tech manufacturing industry. China's refusal at times to acknowledge that lopsided trade relations are a problem has further inflamed European sentiment.

As the voice of new EU members from former communist Eastern Europe grows louder, China's political system and human rights record are also becoming more relevant in bilateral relations. China's unconditional aid policy in Africa has infuriated European nations that consider Chinese intervention unhelpful to their efforts to promote human rights, good governance, and environmental health on the continent. China's assistance to the Burmese junta has led to popular revulsion, as have reports of Chinese cyber attacks on British military facilities, raising a new awareness of security challenges posed by China. Even France and Germany, whose former leaders had once been China's best friends in Europe, have become more skeptical of China. German Chancellor Angela Merkel withstood the fury of China when she hosted the Dalai Lama and was even quoted as favoring a "united front" to address the rise of authoritarian powers such as China.[30] Nonetheless, China is the European Union's second largest trade partner, behind the United States, providing ballast for the relationship even as Europe's honeymoon with China, apparent earlier this decade, appears to be over.

Neighbors

China's high priority focus on neighboring countries is consistent with imperial China's many centuries of concern about threats emanating from its periphery. Overall, China has been very successful in implementing this strategy, as it has established positive relationships with virtually all its neighbors in recent years. Wariness in the region remains, however.

China has generally emphasized nonmilitary aspects of its comprehensive national power in reaching out to its neighbors, adopting a three-pronged approach of setting aside areas of disagreement, focusing on confidence-building measures, and engaging in economic integration and multilateral cooperation to address shared concerns and promote regional stability to allow China to focus inward. China has settled virtually all its border disputes[31] and is now focusing on developing infrastructure ties (roads, railways, and pipelines) with nations throughout Northeast, Southeast, Central, and South Asia to bind itself more closely to them and promote a sense of regional identity and solidarity. China has been active in assisting the development of a host of new regional dialogue vehicles, including the Shanghai Cooperation Organization (involving Central Asia and Russia), mentioned earlier; "ASEAN Plus Three" (members of the Association of Southeast Asian Nations plus China, Japan, and South Korea); and ASEAN Plus Six (the three plus India, Australia, and New Zealand).

China is also increasingly important economically to the region as intraregional trade flourishes. China is willing to tolerate trade deficits with many East Asian countries, and interdependence grows annually. Trade between China and ASEAN has grown by more than 20 percent each year since 2002,[32] and another round of tariff reductions between China and ASEAN due to take effect in 2010 will cause trade between them to soar anew. In 2007, the volume of China-Japan trade surpassed US-Japan trade; the same occurred between China and South Korea in 2004 and with Australia in 2006. (Table 10.2 shows how China has grown in importance to selected countries' economies.)

Nonetheless, regional nations remain quite wary, if quietly so, of the ultimate implications of the emergence of the new regional powerhouse.

Table 10.2 China's rank among countries' top trading partners

Country	2000	2006	2007	Total trade with China, 2007 (billions of US dollars)	Balance of trade with China, 2007 (billions of US dollars)
Australia	5	2	1	46.4	−4.8
South Korea	3	1	1	140.5	18.1
Japan	2	2	1	236.6	18.6
India	10	2	1	38.6	−9.6
United States	4	2	2	386.7	−256.3
European Union	4	2	2	482.7	−252.4
Indonesia	5	3	2	25.0	−0.2
Russia	6	4	3	48.2	−8.8

Sources: 2000 rankings calculated from data in United Nations, *International Trade Statistics Yearbook*, 2004; 2006 rankings calculated from data in International Monetary Fund, *Direction of Trade Statistics Quarterly*, September 2007; **Australia data:** Australia Department of Foreign Affairs and Trade, "Trade Topics: A Quarterly Review of Australia's International Trade" (Autumn 2008), www.dfat.gov.au (converted to US dollars by author at December 2007 exchange rates); **South Korea data:** XTVWorld.com, "China Is Korea's Largest Trading Partner," January 17, 2007, http://press.xtvworld.com; **Japan data:** Japan External Trade Organization, "China Overtakes the U.S. as Japan's Largest Trading Partner," February 28, 2008, www.jetro.go.jp; **India data:** *Times of India*, "China Is India's Largest Trade Ally," January 17, 2008, http://timesofindia.indiatimes.com; **US trade volume and trade balance data:** US-China Business Council, "U.S.-China Trade Statistics and China's World Trade Statistics," www.uschina.org; **US 2007 ranking:** US Census Bureau, "Top Ten Countries with which the U.S. Trades for the Month of December 2007," www.census.gov; **EU trade volume and trade balance data:** *International Herald Tribune*, "Facts on the EU-China Trade Relationship," April 23, 2008, www.iht.com; **EU 2007 ranking:** Xinhua News Agency, "China, EU Start Up High-Level Economic, Trade Dialogue," April 25, 2008, http://news.xinhuanet.com; **Indonesian trade volume and trade balance data:** Hong Kong Trade Development Council, "Sino-Indonesia Trade Volume Surges 30% in 2007," February 13, 2008, http://emerging.hktdc.com; **Indonesia 2007 ranking:** *Jakarta Post*, "China Sticks to Open Market Despite Side Effects," January 26, 2008, www.thejakartapost.com; **Russian trade volume and trade balance data:** *RIA Novosti*, "Russia-China Trade up 44% to Record $48 Bln in 2007," June 15, 2008, http://en.rian.ru; **Russia 2007 ranking:** Ministry of Commerce of the People's Republic of China, "Potential for Chinese Exports to Russia to Increase," March 4, 2008, http://win.mofcom.gov.cn.

Territorial disputes in the East and South China Sea, and lingering border issues with India and Korea, have led to concerns about how China will choose to resolve these matters over time. While Chinese rhetoric and posture to date have accentuated high-minded win-win values, Asia understands the cold realities of power balances. As China emerges, it need not throw its weight around for its growing diplomatic, economic, and military posture to have a quietly coercive effect on the policy decisions of neighboring states in the future.

Developing World

China continues to use its self-proclaimed status as the "world's largest developing nation" to appeal to developing-world sensibilities and pro-

Table 10.3   China's top five sources of crude oil imports, 2003–07 (percent)

Country	2003	2004	2005	2006	2007
Saudi Arabia	16.6	14.0	17.4	16.4	16.1
Angola	11.0	13.2	13.7	16.2	15.3
Iran	13.6	10.7	11.2	11.6	12.6
Russia	5.7	8.7	10.0	11.0	8.9
Oman	10.1	13.3	8.5	9.1	8.4

Sources: 2003–05 data are from *Statistical Yearbooks* published by the General Customs Administration of the People's Republic of China (PRC); 2006 data calculated from PRC customs statistics cited in Landun Group (Tianjin) Limited, "Africa Becomes One of China's Increasingly Diversified Sources of Oil Imports" (in Chinese), June 9, 2007, www.tjlandun.com; 2007 data are from General Customs Administration of the PRC, "2007 Witnessed Steady Increase in the Nation's Crude Oil Imports and Dramatic Decrease in Exports" (in Chinese), February 28, 2008.

mote solidarity with developing nations.[33] Many developing states, particularly in Africa, view China as "one of them" due to their common colonial legacy, long-standing ties starting from their postcolonial beginnings during the Cold War, and desire to resist pressures from the West.

China's voracious appetite for energy and other raw materials, and need for markets for its low-grade goods, has made its relationship with the developing world nowadays far more than "fraternal." The Middle East alone provides about half of China's oil imports, with Africa accounting for another one-third (see table 10.3 for China's key sources of crude oil). China is also turning increasingly to Latin America to help satisfy its need for oil, minerals, soy, and other primary commodities, and trade between the two exceeded $100 billion in 2007, according to Chinese officials, three years ahead of Hu Jintao's seemingly ambitious goal to reach this level by 2010.[34]

China's trade with Persian Gulf states alone has doubled since 2000 to $240 billion and is slated to grow several more times over the next decade, leading some observers to dub growing ties a "new Silk Road."[35] With its large pool of surplus cash, and finding the US market increasingly hostile to its outreach, Gulf investors have also begun to look closely at China as a preferred investment destination. One Beijing-based consulting firm estimates Gulf investors will move a third of their portfolios, or about $250 billion, to China over the next five years.[36]

Chinese foreign assistance to the developing world has been diverse and active, including debt relief; grants and loans; and construction of schools, roads, bridges, hospitals, rail lines, power generation, communication links, and other critical infrastructure, earning the appreciation of many countries (and some approbation from local populations; see above). China has also provided substantial sums of military assistance; China's cheaper, if less capable, equipment better fits the budgets of developing nations. At the same time, China has used its diplomatic weight in the United Nations, large-scale participation in peacekeeping efforts, and participation in a variety of multilateral forums to demonstrate its good faith commitment to addressing developing-world interests. In return, China has put pressure on states to adhere to a "One China" policy that isolates Taiwan, as virtually all of the remaining nations that officially recognize the Republic of China government in Taipei over the People's Republic of China in Beijing are in the developing world.[37]

China's Impact on the International System

As of June 2008, 1,955 Chinese personnel were deployed to 12 UN peacekeeping missions; of the five permanent members of the UN Security Council, China is among the largest contributors of peacekeeping personnel to UN missions.[38] According to its own accounting, China has joined more than 130 (intergovernmental) international organizations and committed to 267 multilateral treaties.[39] Far from its posture just a generation ago, China today has also become an increasingly constructive member of the international nonproliferation regime[40] and international peace operations.

As China has begun to think and act globally, it has had to adapt to an international system traditionally dominated and developed by the major Western powers. China is generally comfortable with the world's major international institutions such as the United Nations and the World Trade Organization (WTO). With a professed commitment to international law, equality of states, and democratization of international affairs, and eager to reassure the world of its responsible conduct and peaceful rise, China views these institutions as helpful in promoting its strategic goals and principles. Beijing is also confident that its privileged role as a veto-wielding permanent member of the UN Security Council and advantage of numbers in concert with developing-world allies will provide the necessary reassurance that the work of these institutions will not violate its sovereignty and national interests and that its voice in developing and implementing international rules within them is heeded.

China is less comfortable with other aspects of the current international system. US global predominance is clearly uncomfortable for Beijing, as is the current US-dominated, alliance-based security structure in both Asia and Europe. Nonetheless, China has become less vocal in opposition in recent years so as not to alarm the United States or others in East Asia that support the maintenance of this structure.

Instead, China has supported the development of new alternative forums in Asia and elsewhere to promote confidence-building, cooperation, and regional security. Beijing has also entered into dialogue arrangements with established regional organizations elsewhere to increase its international voice, gain economic advantage, and pursue its vision of international confidence-building and security cooperation.[41] China's relative, if nascent, success has been assisted in part by US disregard for, and often absence from, many multilateral forums around the world in recent years.

Some observers suspect that China is playing a longer-term game in East Asia of diluting the importance of US alliances for international security and demonstrating the viability of alternative vehicles. China's involvement in the development of the Shanghai Cooperation Organization in Central Asia and ASEAN Plus Three in East Asia are offered as examples of this intent. Likewise, China's substantial political and financial commitment to help stabilize the region's financial system through the development of a regional lender of last resort, under the so-called Chiang Mai Initiative, is considered a challenge to the predominance of the United States in international financial matters through the International Monetary Fund (IMF). China in fact has called for a "new international economic order," although its exact outlines are unclear beyond putting more of a burden on the developed world to make sacrifices and concessions to create more equitable global development (see chapter 1).

China is quietly uncomfortable with the very notion trumpeted by the West of its "integration" into the current international system. While not opposed necessarily to the principles that underlie institutions such as the Group of Eight (G-8) and the International Energy Agency, Beijing's increasing pride and self-confidence lead it to hesitate joining groups that it had little role in developing or whose rules it did not help to establish. Chinese officials and scholars have debated in private the viability and implications of developing alternative structures to organizations such as the G-8 in which China may be present at the creation and thus serve as a coequal partner in establishing international rules.

To date, however, China's interest in keeping a relatively low profile, focusing inward, and reassuring the world about the implications of its rise has led to a reluctance to take the lead in developing new global institutions or challenging old ones for fear of attracting unwanted attention and taking on new responsibilities that will create unnecessary distractions for itself. At the same time, the international community has tried to reassure China of the benefits and flexibility of the current international system and taken steps to encourage its continued integration into it: In 2006, the IMF increased China's voting share by 15 percent, and in 2008 the World Bank named a senior Chinese economist as its chief economist, the first to hold the post from a developing country.

Nonetheless, China's policy of providing foreign aid without conditions, and sometimes in direct competition with alternative offers from the IMF or other established international institutions,[42] has raised questions about China's potential impact on an international system that in recent years has sought to promote sustainable development and political and social justice by conditioning aid on adherence to standards of good governance, labor and environmental protection, and human rights. Chinese officials have occasionally offered China's development model as an option for developing nations, most notably African states[43] and North Korea. They have refrained from claiming that China's specific experience is the only alternative blueprint for developmental success, however. In essence, the principle of development China promotes, as noted earlier, is that no single model for national development fits all and that each nation must decide for itself its preferred developmental path and outsiders should not interfere.[44]

Regardless, China's growing influence on accepted international norms and principles need not be explicit to have an impact. To date, the Chinese development model has gained currency simply because of China's apparent success, and the attractiveness of China's hands-off standards-free policy to authoritarian leaders and even some populations tired of perceived heavy-handedness and condescension from Western aid donors.

Finally, China has demonstrated in recent years some disinclination to accept particular international standards for reasons of pride or otherwise, which has raised questions about China's consistent commitment or adherence to spoken and unspoken rules of the current system. China has viewed the first formal US filings of WTO complaints against China, for instance, in highly political/strategic terms rather than as a legal matter or normal matter of economic intercourse, suggesting a potential lack of understanding about the rules-based process.

A pattern in military affairs is particularly noticeable and alarming. China ignored international law in holding a US flight crew for 12 days on Hainan Island in April 2001 after a US spy plane was forced to make an emergency landing after colliding with a Chinese fighter. To the Chinese, the US surveillance plane, despite being in international waters, offended the Chinese sense of propriety. A stand-off ensued and ultimately was resolved by China in a manner that took little account of international law. Subsequent efforts to implement a 1997 agreement to regulate future interaction of US and Chinese air and naval forces operating in proximity in international space, as was developed between the United States and the Soviet Union during the Cold War, have led nowhere, threatening that a Hainan-like incident (or worse) could be repeated.

Likewise, when China launched its test of an antisatellite weapon in January 2007, it failed to provide public notice consistent with accepted international practice, putting at risk other nations' space assets. In November 2007, China denied two US minesweepers permission to make port in Hong Kong to refuel as a storm approached, violating an unwritten law among the world's navies. Instead of taking responsibility for the mistake, Beijing suggested that the move was in response to, alternatively, US arms sales to Taiwan or a recent visit to the United States of the Dalai Lama. Such selective adherence to international law and accepted international standards, which China may ignore when piqued or its national pride offended, is a potentially dangerous development, particularly in the military realm where accidents, miscommunication, or misunderstanding can have dire consequences.

Implications for the United States of China's Rise in Global Influence

China's expanding engagement with the world is not an alarming development but an expected, natural, and overall welcome one. Another constructive actor in addressing common concerns, particularly one as important as China, will be invaluable in dealing with everything from underdevelopment to nonproliferation to environmental degradation and in building confidence and reducing historical tensions throughout Asia and elsewhere.

However, China's rise does pose a series of potential challenges to US interests. China's appeal within the developing world offers an alternative model and source of support for these nations, to the benefit of many for sure but to the potential detriment of international governance and other standards. New dialogue vehicles in which China plays a central role seem intended to counterbalance US alliances in East Asia. China's growing political and military power is complicating US predominance in the region, including its ability to fulfill its commitments to allies and others, including Taiwan, and thus an overall balance of power that favors stability.

China's growing economic, political, and military power is also leading many nations, including US allies, to soft-pedal concerns about Chinese behavior, offering an increasingly self-confident Chinese leadership more license to assert itself in international affairs. China's increasing willingness to affirm its noninterference principle by wielding, or threatening to wield, a veto in the United Nations Security Council on various sanctions resolutions will complicate the West's ability to apply this tool to pressure regimes to adhere to international norms and obligations. Growing Chinese international stature and self-confidence also means fewer releases of human rights activists, less reticence about openly pursuing its military development, and increasing defiance when confronted with criticism.

The United States and China do not like to acknowledge publicly that they are engaged in a kind of competition, but they are, if latent and relatively benign at this point (except the issue of Taiwan). As in economic affairs, however, competition need not be zero-sum but can be quite healthy for sharpening and focusing one's own activities more effectively. China's rise in influence can be viewed as a prism through which the United States might look afresh at its own international policies and principles, reaffirming many and reassessing others.

For instance, following China's pragmatic and effective approach of listening closely to the perspectives of others and accommodating their sensibilities without sacrificing its own interests would be an effective and constructive method of "competing" with a rising China. Chinese competition might awaken the United States to the developing world's desire for partnership rather than charity and renew its attention to developing-world challenges and perspectives. China's recognition of the importance and complementarity of hard and soft power for the development of a nation's comprehensive national power may also serve as a model for US policy. Indeed, the new US concept of "smart power" reflects this effective integration of hard and soft power.[45]

At the same time, in this new environment the United States will need to be careful to avoid being reticent about defending principles and perspectives in its interest because of concerns about antagonizing the world's largest rising nation. The United States should not be shy about enunciating without hyperbole its differences with China.

Likewise, virtually all of East Asia continues to support the US alliance system and military presence as a stabilizing factor in regional security; the United States need not be defensive about maintaining both even in the face of Chinese concern. Indeed, how the United States handles its security relationships in East Asia in relation to China's rise will have a profound effect on Washington's ability to manage both in the future. Today, the United States' East Asian allies—Japan, South Korea, Australia, Thailand, and the Philippines—may continue to rely on the United States for their security, but their economic security is increasingly tied to China. This situation will increasingly complicate alliance partnerships on issues related to China. The United States will need to recognize this fact, while working with allies to reach out to China to cooperate on a range of regional security issues in which China's engagement will be critical, such as energy, infectious disease, environmental protection, and climate change. The United States likewise should accept invitations by China, if and when they come, to contribute to forums and initiatives of which Beijing is a central part.

The United States should not be shy about continuing to challenge China's assertion of a noninterference principle. Washington should take the lead in working with China to find a responsible balance between sovereignty and responsible intervention. Indeed, China and others in the developing world well recognize that in a tightly interconnected world, what happens inside another's borders can have a profound impact on one's own affairs and interests and thus make pure notions of national sovereignty a luxury.

In fact, open public frustration with, and pressure on, China when Beijing invokes noninterference to defend its policies have shown results. Beijing openly condemned Burma's violent suppression of peaceful demonstrators in the fall of 2007, even supporting a UN Security Council resolution on the matter. Beijing also supported UN Security Council resolutions sanctioning Iran and North Korea and pressed Sudan's leader to accept a UN/African Union force in Darfur. China will continue to be concerned about its international reputation. Careful and quiet international encouragement, combined with its own increasing recognition of the impact of the internal affairs of other states on its own security and economic equities, may help continue the evolution of Chinese perspectives, although China is unlikely to change its public adherence to the noninterference principle due to the many political, economic, and strategic benefits it receives overall from the policy.

To exaggerate the threat from China will be counterproductive for American interests, since the world is not looking for a new Cold War in which it will have to choose between these two major powers in years to come. The United States would build up international goodwill and respect for its leadership through an honest, candid, and sober assessment of, and response to, China's rising influence on world affairs and national interests. Recent poll numbers suggest that the challenges that naturally attend the rise of a major power like China have become more apparent in recent years and have served as a wake-up call for many nations. The United States should not revel in this development, but it does serve to remind observers that the rise of Chinese influence will not be a simple or uncomplicated process and will be shaped by many factors in years to come.

Indeed, taking an unreasonably hostile or confrontational approach to China will feed Chinese suspicions about US disrespect and intention to curb its rise as a major power. The danger here is particularly acute with the Chinese population, which has become more sensitive about slights to China's dignity, as witnessed by its reaction to the international protests related to Tibet and the Olympic torch relay around the world in early 2008. The Chinese government will have to manage this growing Chinese populism in coming years, but one should not ignore its impact on China's future international orientation.

The United States must remain vigilant about the effects of China's rise on its domestic and international interests, but Washington should not look instinctively to blame or denounce China as a scapegoat for problems. In fact, by taking responsibility for the impact of its own policies that are contributing, for instance, to product safety concerns, trade deficits, and global environmental problems, the United States will not only do its part to resolve these matters but also send a reassuring message to the world about its humility and thus gain in world opinion and soft power influence. China's best advantage is international skepticism toward the United States. The United States can best maintain its stature and influence, then, by addressing this skepticism; indeed, the best antidote to concerns about rising Chinese influence remains in the control of the United States itself.

At the moment China wants to gain more influence and more respect but not necessarily more responsibility in the world. China apparently feels trends are in its favor, despite internal challenges, and that time is on its side. It is willing to be patient as it focuses its attention, both domestic and international, on safeguarding its urgent internal needs. China currently accepts that the United States will take lead responsibility for maintaining security in East Asia and elsewhere. It will continue to accept this situation in the near to medium term, if grudgingly, as long as its interests are protected—particularly but not limited to Taiwan—its counsel sought, and more vehicles for bilateral and multilateral consultation are available to dilute exclusive reliance on US alliances and unilateralism.

The year 2008 will serve as a watershed for China's relations with the world. The Olympics serve as a proud announcement of its arrival and desire for acceptance as an important and constructive player on the world stage. International sympathy and material assistance in response to the tragic earthquake in Sichuan in May 2008 created an opportunity for China to demonstrate its openness to and interconnection with the world and to reassure international society of its peaceful and "harmonious" intent. Coinciding with the conclusion of the Olympic Games and the imminent 30th anniversary celebration of China's establishment of its "reform and opening up" policy, Beijing is reportedly set to discuss its strategy and goals for the next 30 years, reviewing lessons learned from the successes and mistakes of the past to chart its future course.

In the process, China will continue to consider international conditions and perspectives of the international community as it develops its policies. The United States and its allies will need to consider how to involve themselves constructively in those discussions both directly and indirectly through policies that demonstrate how Chinese interests are better served through continued integration into the normative and rules-based system rather than promotion of unreliable or destabilizing alternatives. Indeed, international influence—and potential US-China collaboration or competition—in coming years will likely be determined in the realm of international norms and rules rather than force of arms.

The world will remain skeptical and wary of all major powers, including both China and the United States, in years to come. The United States, however, arguably still has a greater reservoir of global respect and appreciation than does China, which is a nascent player on the world stage with an uncertain future. The United States should neither be distracted from nor overreact to the challenges of a rising China but instead focus on its own strengths and advantages of hard and soft power to maximize the effective coordination of both in its conduct of foreign policy. By doing so, the United States can become more credible and effective in promoting its principles, protecting its national interests, and managing—in concert with allies and friends—an international situation in which the ultimate impact of China's emergence remains uncertain. Pursued with humility and resolve but without malice, the result can truly be a "win-win" situation for all, including for an increasingly influential, proud, and assertive China.

Notes

1. Xinhua News Agency, "Hu Jintao zai Zhongguo gongchandang di shiqi ci quanguo daibiao dahui shang de baogao," ["Hu Jintao's Report to the 17th Party Congress"], October 15, 2007, http://news.xinhuanet.com.

2. For instance, China consumes over a quarter of global production of oil, coal, and copper (China Geo-Tech Secretariat, www.chinageotech.org, 2007) and nearly half the world's cement (*Financial Times*, "Lefarge Aims to Double Investment in China," December 2, 2007). As of 2005, China was the world's top consumer of steel, coal, grain, and meat (BBC News, "China Emerges as a Global Consumer," February 27, 2005).

3. Economist Intelligence Unit, Country Report for China, June 4, 2008.

4. In a public opinion poll conducted in late 2007 by the Bertelsmann Foundation of Germany, www.bertelsmann-stiftung.org, among residents in Brazil, Britain, China, France, Germany, India, Japan, Russia, and the United States, 50 percent of those polled viewed China as a world power today, and 57 percent said it would be a superpower by 2020. By contrast, only 67 percent said the United States would remain a superpower in 2020.

5. In December 2007, for example, the European Union relented from past practice by inviting Zimbabwe's dictator Robert Mugabe to attend an EU-Africa summit meeting.

6. China developed the concept of "comprehensive national power" as an index by which to measure its power against other countries. According to one definition, it refers to the sum total of the powers or strengths of a country in terms of its economy, military, science and technology, education, resources, and influence. China Institutes of Contemporary International Relations, *Global Strategic Patterns: The International Environment of China in the New Century* (Shishi Press, 2000).

7. In fact, the principles of "peace, development, and cooperation" hold the highest place in Chinese rhetoric: During the 17th Party Congress, Hu Jintao affirmed that China will "hold high the banner of peace, development and cooperation, pursue an independent foreign policy of peace, safeguard China's interests in terms of sovereignty, security and development, and uphold its foreign policy purposes of maintaining world peace and promoting common development."

8. Before formal adoption at the 17th Party Congress, Chinese Premier Wen Jiabao elaborated on the concept of "peaceful development" in a major speech, in which he asserted that "To take a path of peaceful development is a strategy and foreign policy to which China is committed. It is definitely not an expediency. In following this guiding principle, we should seize opportunities, remain unswayed by provocations and concentrate on our development, and we will not seek a leadership role in the international arena. It is thanks to following this policy that we have been able to gain more room for the conduct of China's diplomacy." Premier Wen Jiabao, "Our Historical Tasks at the Primary Stage of Socialism and Several Issues Concerning China's Foreign Policy," *People's Daily*, February 27, 2007.

9. Robert B. Zoellick, "Whither China: From Membership to Responsibility?" (remarks, as prepared for delivery, to National Committee on US-China Relations, New York City, September 21, 2005), www.state.gov.

10. Nye defines soft power as the "ability to get what one wants through attraction rather than coercion or payments," through "the attractiveness of a country's culture, political ideals, and policies"; Joseph S. Nye, Jr., *Soft Power: The Means to Success in World Politics* (New York: PublicAffairs, 2004).

11. See, for instance, Li Jie, "Soft Power Building and China's Peaceful Development," *China International Studies* (Winter 2006): 164–79. At the time of writing this author served as deputy director of the Department of Policy Planning in China's Ministry of Foreign Affairs. The piece has been widely read in Chinese academic circles and is one of many in English- and Chinese-language journals in China that reflect heightened official interest in building up China's soft power.

12. "Hard power is the basis of the growth of soft power . . . when hard power is weakening, the appeal of soft power will also decline, and when the growth of soft power lags behind, the expansion of hard power will be hindered" (Ibid., 167).

13. Nye was somewhat ambiguous about whether economic power should be categorized as hard or soft power, with most political scientists ultimately placing it in the latter. Walter Russell Mead, however, developed an alternative category, calling it "sticky power," attractive in origin but ultimately trapping others in one's orbit. Walter Russell Mead, "America's Sticky Power," *Foreign Policy* (March/April 2004).

14. An explicit example of how deeply the concept of soft power is reaching into the mindset of the Chinese elite is a quote from the director of China's new National Center for Performing Arts, who commented that the new center represents "a concrete example of China's rising soft power and comprehensive national strength." Joseph Kahn, "Chinese Unveil Mammoth Arts Center," *New York Times*, December 24, 2007. See also Yan Xuetong, "The Rise of China and its Power Status," *Chinese Journal of International Politics* 1 (2006), 16. (Originally published in *Science of International Politics*, Institute of International Studies, Tsinghua University.)

15. Li Jie, *China International Studies* (Winter 2006), 171.

16. However, one Confucius Institute director has suggested that only half or fewer of the 210 Confucius Institutes may be actually operational.

17. Pang Zhongying, director of the Institute for Global Studies at Nankai University, identified the developing world as the "main battlefield" in which China should acquire and expend soft power. Pang Zhongying, "China's Soft Power" (talk delivered at the Brookings Institute, October 24, 2007).

18. Pew Global Attitudes Project, "Global Unease with Major World Powers," June 27, 2007.

19. Ironically, in France, where Li Jie had touted the "Year of Chinese Culture" in 2006 and a supposed "China Craze" as emblematic of the progress its soft power is having around the world, 51 percent of the people had an unfavorable view of China, with 84 percent considering China's growing military power a "bad thing"—the highest percentage of any European nation polled—and 64 percent viewing China's growing economy the same way (Pew Global Attitudes Project, "Global Unease with Major World Powers"). A recent survey also indicated that China's soft power still trails that of the United States and Japan in the region

(Chicago Council on Global Affairs and East Asia Institute, "Soft Power in Asia: Results of a 2008 Multinational Survey of Public Opinion," June 17, 2008).

20. While China is perceived to treat developing countries with "respect" in its economic engagements, the World Bank has reported that one-third of Chinese enterprises have lost money on their foreign investments and 65 percent of their joint ventures had failed. Bates Gill and James Reilly, "The Tenuous Hold of China Inc. in Africa," *Washington Quarterly* (Summer 2007), 49.

21. Ibid., 47.

22. Mitchell, "China and the Developing World," 125.

23. Joseph S. Nye, Jr., "The Rise of China's Soft Power," *Wall Street Journal Asia*, December 29, 2005.

24. Xinhua News Agency, October 15, 2007.

25. Many observers, including some in China, argue today that China places its relations with neighbors at least equal to relations with the United States and other major powers. In its own parlance, China consistently applies unique terms to qualify its various international relationships: Relations with developed nations are termed "key" (*guanjian*); neighboring countries are a "priority" (*shouyao*); and developing nations are called the "basis" (*jichu*) of China's foreign policy, each rather ambiguous in distinctiveness from the other.

26. For an updated chart listing China's strategic partnership and cooperative partnership agreements, see the "Issue Overviews" section of the China Balance Sheet website, www.chinabalancesheet.org.

27. China has signed free trade agreements with six countries and areas: Chile, Pakistan, ASEAN, New Zealand, Hong Kong, and Macau. The agreements with Macau and Hong Kong are known as closer economic partnership arrangements.

28. For an overview of Sino-Russian relations and implications for the United States, see Derek J. Mitchell, "China and Russia," in *The China Balance Sheet in 2007 and Beyond* (Washington, May 2007).

29. For a comprehensive examination of China's relations with India, see Derek J. Mitchell and Chietigj Bajpaee, "China and India," in *The China Balance Sheet in 2007 and Beyond* (Washington, May 2007).

30. *Economist*, "The Company She Keeps," November 29, 2007.

31. Notable exceptions are Aksai Chin and Arunachal Pradesh with India; demarcation of the East China Sea and sovereignty over the Diaoyutai/Senkaku islands with Japan; and the Paracel and Spratly Islands in the South China Sea with Southeast Asian nations, including Vietnam, the Philippines, Indonesia, and Malaysia.

32. Rate for 2002–05 calculated from data in the *ASEAN Statistical Yearbook 2006*; information for 2006 from *Taipei Times*, "China-ASEAN Trade Reached US$160.8 Billion Last Year," January 15, 2007; information for 2007 from Xinhua News Agency, "China, ASEAN become 4th-largest trade partners in 2007," February 29, 2008.

33. For a comprehensive examination of China's relations with the developing world, see Derek J. Mitchell, "China and the Developing World," in *The China Balance Sheet in 2007 and Beyond* (Washington, May 2007).

34. Ambassador Zhou Wenzhong, "China's Relationship with Latin America" (speech at Inter-American Dialogue, May 13, 2008).

35. See Stephen Glain, "The New Silk Road," *Forbes Asia*, June 2, 2008, 62–63; and Stephen Glain, "The Modern Silk Road," *Newsweek*, May 26/June 2, 2008, 32–33.

36. JL McGregor & Company, "A Note on Middle East Investment in China," 2008, 3.

37. As of June 2008, 23 countries recognized the Republic of China: Palau, Tuvalu, Marshall Islands, Solomon Islands, Kiribati, Nauru, Guatemala, Paraguay, St. Vincent and the Grenadines, Belize, El Salvador, Haiti, Nicaragua, Dominican Republic, Honduras, Panama, St. Kitts and Nevis, Saint Lucia, Burkina Faso, São Tomé and Principe, Swaziland, Gambia, and the Holy See (Vatican).

38. United Nations Department of Peacekeeping Operations, Monthly Summary of Contributors of Military and Civilian Police Personnel, June 2008, www. un.org.

39. "China's Peaceful Development Road," State Council Information Office White Paper, December 22, 2005, http://english.people.com.cn. Note that the Chinese version of this white paper reveals that China did not complete the steps of signing and ratifying many of the 267 treaties.

40. Evan Medeiros, *Reluctant Restraint: The Evolution of China's Nonproliferation Policies and Practices, 1980-2004* (Stanford, CA: Stanford University Press, 2007).

41. For a list of international organizations in which China participates, see Mitchell, "China and the Developing World," 128.

42. For example, in 2007, a conditional World Bank loan to revamp Nigeria's crippled railway system was thrown out at the last minute when the Chinese government offered a larger, no-strings-attached contract through the China Civil Engineering Construction Company with Chinese financing. In early 2006, China offered a low-interest $2 billion loan to the Angolan government, allowing Angola to shelve a prospective IMF package conditional on increased accountability and transparency in the oil sector.

43. During an African leaders summit in late 2006, Chinese leaders reportedly promoted the notion of special economic zones to promote development, as China had done during its developmental stage beginning in the early 1980s.

44. "We respect the right of the people of all countries to independently choose their own development path." Hu Jintao's report delivered at the 17th National Congress of the Communist Party of China, October 15, 2007.

45. Center for Strategic and International Studies, *A Smarter, More Secure America*, Report of the CSIS Commission on Smart Power (Washington, November 26, 2007).

11

Conclusion

> *No one can look at Asia and take [all the] Chinese out of it and say you can have any policy in the Pacific that will succeed in preventing war without having the Chinese a part of it. It's just as cold-blooded as that.*
>
> *No one in this world knows how great the gulf is between their philosophy and ours, their interests and ours. But also no one in this world, I think, knows better than I do, how imperative it is to see that great nations that have enormous differences . . . have got to find ways to, you know, talk, get along.*
>
> — President Richard M. Nixon, January 26, 1972

China has changed a lot in the last 36 years since President Nixon made this observation. But the essential tenet of US policy toward China over that period has not. While the two countries have quarreled and been confrontational on many occasions, "engagement" has been the unquestioned principle that has guided the administrations of seven US presidents in relations with China. In its most primitive form, that policy seeks to draw the United States and China together through dialogue to avoid costly miscalculation. More broadly, the engagement strategy has sought to develop equities for China in the US-led global order to (1) deter China from disrupting that order and (2) encourage China to adopt a form of government most compatible with maximizing benefits through participation in that order.

As the preceding chapters make clear, that strategy has been marvelously successful in many respects. Despite the gulf in philosophy between the two countries, the United States and China have not fought on either sides of a war. Through its participation in the global order, China has brought hundreds of millions of Chinese out of poverty and firmly tied its economic fate to that of the rest of the world. China's government has had to adjust to a new reality in which its authority is more limited than before, and the manner in which it adopts new policies has had to become more transparent, pluralistic, and less capricious than before.

But engagement is hardly an unqualified success. China's participation in the global order and development of stakes in that order has not prevented China from challenging that order as described in chapter 1; indeed, developing states increasingly cite China as an alternative model to that order. China's economic explosion through trade and opening up has come at a dramatic cost to domestic Chinese social equities and the global environment. The wonder of integrating one-quarter of the world's working population into the global economy has not always been perceived as such by political and economic interests in other parts of the world, including the United States. And ultimately, engagement has not brought about a sea change in Chinese governmental protection of human rights, religious freedom, or other US values of political import. At times, the political cost-benefit analysis of "engagement" seems to tilt rather pointedly toward the "cost" side of the spectrum.

Perhaps the problem is that the engagement policy has been too successful. Drawing China into the world's economy as a diplomatic concept was a fine idea, but the original architects of the engagement policy may not have envisioned the scenario in which China would become the world's second or third largest economy (depending on the methodology one uses) in just 30 years. The pace of change in China and the impact of that change on the global community have been enormous. This book has reviewed many of the issues confronting China and the world as a result of China's (and "engagement's") successes. The question now confronting the United States is: Is engagement still the appropriate policy to manage a risen China?

This book has attempted to provide specific guidance for policymakers confronting that question. The preceding chapters have covered the waterfront of policy challenges and opportunities in China.

China's domestic political situation is far from static. As detailed in chapters 2 to 5 China faces significant domestic challenges, whether resulting from corruption or from the relationship between Beijing and China's local and provincial power centers. Efforts to manage domestic dislocations caused by rapid economic growth have helped foster greater policymaking plurality and fueled Beijing's interest in "democratic" reform. But China's political evolution is not clearly leading to a result modeled on Western forms of participatory government. Indeed, for all the talk of democracy by Hu Jintao and the employment of local political laboratories to field test forms of participatory government, China is shaping up to be a distinct alternative to Western democracies as a model for developing states. That has clear implications for the United States in its role as a leader in institutions of global governance like the United Nations, but also in looking at overseas development assistance as a tool of US "soft power."

China's unbalanced economic development also poses unique new challenges, as noted in chapters 6 and 7. Its current economic development model, especially its energy-intensive heavy industry and investment-led growth, has aggravated income inequality, undermined employment gains, heightened trade tensions, and contributed to serious energy and environmental problems for both China and the rest of the world. The government has taken some steps to shift the source of economic growth from investment and export-led development to domestic consumption, but these steps have been slow in coming and are not enough. More vigorous government policy action is needed in the fiscal, financial, exchange rate, and pricing domains. Failure of the government to promptly make the necessary policy changes may lead to a slowdown in China's impressive growth, put continued upward pressure on global oil and commodity prices, and further increase China's energy use and carbon emissions.

As the final three chapters make clear, China is also presenting new and clear challenges to America's role as guarantor of security in Asia. Its military modernization is proceeding at a pace something akin to its economic development but on terms significantly less visible to outside observers. The new activity on China's part means that opportunities for friction and miscalculation along the lines of the 2001 collision between a US EP-3 surveillance aircraft and a People's Liberation Army fighter will be more common. Although it is far from certain that China has specific goals for its new military might, increasing instances in which it is flexing its muscle—from the 2007 antisatellite test to new submarine facilities—suggest that China will continue to bump against the United States in US conduct of its now 60-year role in the Pacific. Making room at the table for China and allowing China to grow equities as a "responsible stakeholder" in this field present particularly problematic challenges to American policymakers. Even apart from China's growing coercive power, China's increasing attractiveness as an alternative development model is a source of normative power for China, although its extent should not be exaggerated.

Perhaps the greatest challenge to American policymakers from China's rise is on the United States' own domestic political front. The specter of Chinese military power clearly has the potential to alarm the American public. Fears of job losses to China, rightly or wrongly, have stimulated protectionist impulses. Philosophical and ideological differences are a wedge that can easily separate the United States and China further. Some American policymakers and politicians will be tempted to exploit or fan these political differences. Using China as a foil would be in keeping with some tried and tested political practices in the United States. Overcoming some of these instincts will not be easy for elected officials. Indeed, China bashing as a political sport is unlikely to disappear anytime soon.

Even though China presents challenges to US supremacy, the two sides are not bound for conflict. China and the United States share a wide variety of broad common interests that yield opportunities for global partnership. The United States can play a much bigger role in helping China improve its domestic institutional capacity to deal with its internal challenges. On economic issues, the two could do much to provide world leadership on climate change, energy, and international trade as outlined in chapter 1. Militarily the two sides have some obvious fault lines but share basic desires for international stability that provide a basis for cooperation. There may be a role for cooperation in international development as well.

The authors of this book have concluded that there is no meaningful alternative to a policy that seeks to enfranchise 1.3 billion people. It is no longer possible, even if desirable, to isolate or contain China. China's economic, military, and normative "soft" power demands a US response that cannot be primarily based on confrontation or estrangement. At a basic level, therefore, there is no reasonable alternative to "engagement."

However, the presumption that there is room for China in the US-defined and US-led global world order has proven to be flawed. China's economic, political, and security rise has been so meteoric that it no longer comfortably fits into the global architecture in which the United States has at least fitfully tried to make a place for it. China has definite equities in global economic, security, and political matters. But the architecture through which to engage China, and to demand China's responsibility as a stakeholder, does not now exist.

The Bretton Woods and other post-World War II architectures are inadequate given China's transformative role regarding the norms of international trade and finance, climate change, intellectual property protection and innovation, energy consumption, and regional military alignments. Relying solely on the existing institutions without significant overhaul to accommodate China's rise may be an exercise in futility. At a minimum, they are inadequate to manage the domestic political fallout in the United States (as well as in Western Europe and elsewhere) from China's economic rise.

The authors have variously offered potential architectural solutions for the United States to better engage China as it continues to rise, including in chapter 1 on the international economic oder. The critical step for the United States is to recognize that the time for blithe acceptance of simple engagement as a root policy for China is at an end. The next US administration confronts a radically different world order than that Richard Nixon faced when he recognized the importance of engaging one-quarter of the world's population.

There may be no alternative to engagement with China. There is an urgent need, however, to develop alternative vehicles through which to engage China. Recognizing this imperative is the first step toward addressing the opportunities and challenges of China's rise.

The United States is still the primary actor in international affairs. China does not now look to challenge it in that role, but China clearly challenges current US assumptions about that role.

In 1957 the launching by the Soviet Union of the satellite *Sputnik* sent the American people into a mild panic. The perception that the Soviet Union had surpassed the United States in technological prowess caused its share of handwringing, but rather than despair, the United States scrambled to reform its educational and scientific capacity to cope with the new challenge. Americans met the perceived threat, in other words, with positive action to reform their own capacity. In the early part of the 21st century, albeit on a much grander scale, the rise of China presents *Sputnik*-like challenges to Americans' perceptions of themselves and their leadership role in the world. As this book goes to print, many American hands are wringing about China's rise. Whether the United States rises to China's challenge and uses it as an opportunity to build its capacity for future leadership will say much about whether it will continue to lead. On balance, China's rise could turn out to be a good thing for the United States.

Bibliography

Bergsten, C. Fred, Bates Gill, Nicholas Lardy, and Derek Mitchell. 2006. *China: The Balance Sheet: What the World Needs to Know Now about the Emerging Superpower.* New York: PublicAffairs Books.

Bergsten, C. Fred, and the Institute for International Economics. 2005. *The United States and the World Economy: Foreign Economic Policy for the Next Decade.* Washington: Institute for International Economics.

Bush III, Richard C. 2005. *Untying the Knot: Making Peace in the Taiwan Strait.* Washington: Brookings Institution Press.

Cooper Ramo, Joshua. 2004. *The Beijing Consensus.* London: Foreign Policy Centre.

Dickson, Bruce. 2003. *Red Capitalists in China.* Cambridge: Cambridge University Press.

Dittmer, Lowell, and Guoli Liu, eds. 2006. *China's Deep Reform: Domestic Politics in Transition.* Lanham, MD: Rowan & Littlefield.

Emmott, Bill. 2008. *Rivals: How the Power Struggle between China, India, and Japan Will Shape Our Next Decade.* Orlando: Harcourt, Inc.

Esty, Daniel C. 1994. *Greening the GATT: Trade, Environment, and the Future.* Washington: Institute for International Economics.

Fewsmith, Joseph. 2001. *China Since Tiananmen: The Politics of Transition.* New York: Cambridge University Press.

Finkelstein, David M., and Kristen Gunness, eds. 2007. *Civil-Military Trends in Today's China: Swimming in a New Sea.* Armonk, NY: M.E. Sharpe Publishers.

Gilley, Bruce. 2004. *China's Democratic Future.* New York: Columbia University Press.

Goldstein, Morris, and Nicholas R. Lardy, eds. 2008. *Debating China's Exchange Rate Policy.* Washington: Peterson Institute for International Economics.

Houser, Trevor, Rob Bradley, Jacob Werksman, Britt Childs, and Robert Heilmayr. 2008. *Leveling the Carbon Playing Field: International Competition and US Climate Policy Design.* Washington: Peterson Institute for International Economics.

Kennedy, Scott. 2005. *The Business of Lobbying in China.* Cambridge, MA: Harvard University Press.

Lampton, David M. 2008. *The Three Faces of Chinese Power: Might, Money, and Minds.* University of California Press.

Lardy, Nicholas R. 1998. *China's Unfinished Economic Revolution.* Washington: Brookings Institution Press.

Lardy, Nicholas R. 2002. *Integrating China into the Global Economy.* Washington: Brookings Institution Press.

Leonard, Mark. 2008. *What Does China Think?* New York: PublicAffairs Books.

Lieberthal, Kenneth, and David M. Lampton. 1992. *Bureaucracy, Politics, and Decision Making in Post-Mao China.* Berkeley: University of California Press.

Lieberthal, Kenneth, and Michel Oksenberg. 1988. *Policy Making in China: Leaders, Structures, and Processes.* Princeton, NJ: Princeton University Press.

Lieberthal, Kenneth. 2004. *Governing China: From Revolution through Reform,* 2d ed. New York: W. W. Norton.

Manion, Melanie. 2004. *Corruption by Design: Building Clean Government in Mainland China and Hong Kong.* Cambridge, MA: Harvard University Press.

Mann, James. 2007. *The China Fantasy: Why Capitalism Will Not Bring Democracy to China.* New York: Penguin.

Medeiros, Evan. 2007. *Reluctant Restraint: The Evolution of China's Nonproliferation Policies and Practices, 1980–2004.* Stanford, CA: Stanford University Press.

Minxin Pei. 2006. *China's Trapped Transition: The Limits of Developmental Autocracy.* Cambridge: Cambridge University Press.

Mulvenon, James, and David M. Finkelstein. 2005. *China's Revolution in Doctrinal Affairs: Emerging Trends in the Operational Art of the Chinese People's Liberation Army.* Alexandria, VA: The CNA Corporation.

Murphy, Melissa. 2008. *Decoding Chinese Politics: Intellectual Debates and Why They Matter.* Washington: Center for Strategic and International Studies.

Naughton, Barry. 1995. *Growing Out of the Plan: Chinese Economic Reform, 1978–1993.* New York: Cambridge University Press.

Naughton, Barry. 2007. *The Chinese Economy: Transitions and Growth.* Cambridge, MA: MIT Press.

Nye Jr., Joseph S. 2004. *Soft Power: The Means to Success in World Politics.* New York: PublicAffairs Books.

Osborne, Milton. 2004. *River at Risk: The Mekong and the Water Politics of China and Southeast Asia.* Sydney, Australia: Lowy Institute for International Policy.

Peerenboom, Randall. 2007. *China Modernizes: Threat to the West or Model for the Rest?* Oxford: Oxford University Press.

Romberg, Alan D. 2003. *Rein in at the Brink of the Precipice: American Policy Toward Taiwan and US-PRC Relations.* Washington: Henry L. Stimson Center.

Shambaugh, David. 2008. *China's Communist Party: Atrophy and Adaptation.* Washington: Woodrow Wilson Center Press.

Tang Wenfang. 2005. *Public Opinion and Political Change in China.* Stanford, CA: Stanford University Press.

Wachman, Alan M. 2007. *Why Taiwan: Geostrategic Rationales for China's Territorial Integrity.* Stanford, CA: Stanford University Press.

Wang Shan. 1994. *Luo Yi Ning Ge'er, Disanzhi Yanjing Kan Zhongguo* [*Looking at China Through a Third Eye*]. Taiyuan: Shanxi People's Publishing House.

Wedeman, Andrew. 2005. *From Mao to Market: Rent Seeking, Local Protectionism, and Marketization in China.* Cambridge, UK: Cambridge University Press.

Zheng Yongnian. 2007. *De Facto Federalism in China: Reforms and Dynamics of Central-Local Relations.* Singapore: World Scientific Publishing Co.

About the Authors

C. Fred Bergsten has been director of the Peterson Institute for International Economics since its creation in 1981. He has been the most widely quoted think tank economist in the world over the eight-year period 1997–2005. He was ranked in the top 50 "Who Really Moves the Markets?" by *Fidelity Investment's Worth*, and as "one of the ten people who can change your life" in *USA Today*.

Dr. Bergsten was assistant secretary for international affairs of the US Treasury (1977–81); assistant for international economic affairs to Dr. Henry Kissinger at the National Security Council (1969–71); and a senior fellow at the Brookings Institution (1972–76), the Carnegie Endowment for International Peace (1981), and the Council on Foreign Relations (1967–68). He is co-chairman of the Private Sector Advisory Group to the United States–India Trade Policy Forum. He was chairman of the Competitiveness Policy Council, which was created by Congress, throughout its existence from 1991 to 1995; and chairman of the APEC Eminent Persons Group throughout its existence from 1993 to 1995. He chaired the "shadow G-8" that advised the member governments on their annual summit meetings during 2000–2005.

Dr. Bergsten has authored, coauthored, or edited 38 books on international economic issues including *China: The Balance Sheet—What the World Needs to Know Now about the Emerging Superpower* (2006), *The United States and the World Economy: Foreign Economic Policy for the Next Decade* (2005), *Dollar Adjustment: How Far? Against What?* (2004), *Dollar Overvaluation and the World Economy* (2003), *No More Bashing: Building a New Japan-United States Economic Relationship* (2001), and *The Dilemmas of the Dollar* (2d ed., 1996). He has received the Meritorious Honor Award of the Department of State (1965), the Exceptional Service Award of the Treasury Department (1981), and the Legion d'Honneur from the Government of France (1985). He has been named an honorary fellow of the Chinese Academy of Social Sciences (1997). He received MA, MALD, and PhD degrees from the

Fletcher School of Law and Diplomacy and a BA magna cum laude and honorary Doctor of Humane Letters from Central Methodist University.

Charles Freeman holds the Freeman Chair in China Studies at the Center for Strategic and International Studies (CSIS) in Washington, DC. The Freeman Chair was established by the Freeman Foundation, to which Charles Freeman has no relation, to advance the study of China and to promote understanding between the United States and the countries of the Asia-Pacific region. He concentrates on economic, political, and social changes in greater China and on US-China relations, with particular attention to economic and trade matters. He joined CSIS after two years as managing director of the China Alliance, a collaboration among four US and Canadian law firms to counsel clients on trade, investment, and government relations strategies in China.

Between early 2002 and late 2005, Freeman was assistant US trade representative (USTR) for China affairs, the United States' chief China trade negotiator, and played a primary role in shaping overall trade policy with respect to China, Taiwan, Hong Kong, Macao, and Mongolia. During his tenure as assistant USTR, he oversaw US efforts to integrate China into the global trading architecture of the World Trade Organization and negotiated with China to resolve a wide range of market access issues and other trade interests on behalf of the United States.

His career-long experience with China and other parts of Asia spans tours of duty in government, business, and the nonprofit sectors. Prior to joining the Office of the USTR, Freeman served as international affairs counsel to Senator Frank Murkowski (R-Alaska), where he advised on trade, foreign relations, and international energy matters. His private-sector experience also includes stints as a Hong Kong–based executive with the *International Herald Tribune* and as a Boston-based securities lawyer and venture capitalist concentrating on developing markets in Asia and Eastern Europe. He also previously worked in Hong Kong as director of economic reform programs in China and Taiwan for the Asia Foundation.

Freeman received his JD from Boston University School of Law, where he was an editor of the *Law Review* and graduated with honors. He earned a BA degree from Tufts University in Asian studies, concentrating in economics, also with honors. He also studied at Fudan University in Shanghai and at the Taipei Language Institute.

A second-generation "China hand," he grew up between Asia and the United States and speaks Mandarin Chinese. His civic activities include service on the board of directors of the National Committee for US-China Relations.

Nicholas R. Lardy, called "everybody's guru on China" by the *National Journal*, has been a senior fellow at the Peterson Institute since 2003. He was a senior fellow in the Foreign Policy Studies Program at the Brookings Institution from 1995 to 2003. He was the director of the Henry M. Jackson School of International Studies at the University of Washington from 1991 to 1995. From 1997 through the spring of 2000, he was the Frederick Frank Adjunct Professor of International Trade and Finance at the Yale University School of Management.

His most recent publication (coedited with Morris Goldstein) is *Debating China's Exchange Rate Policy* (2008). Other publications include *China: The Balance Sheet—What the World Needs to Know Now about the Emerging Superpower* (2006), *Prospects for a US-Taiwan Free Trade Agreement* (2004), *Integrating China into the Global Economy* (2002), *China's Unfinished Economic Revolution* (1998), *China in the World Economy* (1994), *Foreign Trade and Economic Reform in China, 1978–1990* (1992), and *Agriculture in China's Modern Economic Development* (1983). He is a member of the Council on Foreign Relations and is a member of the editorial boards of the *China Quarterly, Journal of Asian Business, China Review*, and *China Economic Review*.

He received his BA from the University of Wisconsin in 1968 and his PhD from the University of Michigan in 1975, both in economics.

Derek J. Mitchell is senior fellow and director for Asia in the CSIS International Security Program (ISP), having joined the Center in January 2001. He concurrently serves as director of CSIS's new Southeast Asia Initiative, which was inaugurated in January 2008 and is the Center's first initiative dedicated to the study of Southeast Asian affairs. He is responsible for managing all Asia-related studies conducted at ISP, which currently include projects involving the security of the Taiwan Strait, the future of the US-Japan and US–South Korea alliance, China's foreign and security policy and US-China relations, and the integration of India into the strategic mix of East Asia. He was special assistant for Asian and Pacific affairs in the Office of the Secretary of Defense (1997–2001), when he served alternately as senior country director for China, Taiwan, Mongolia, and Hong Kong (2000–2001), director for regional security affairs (1998–2000), senior country director for the Philippines, Indonesia, Malaysia, Brunei, and Singapore (1998–99), and country director for Japan (1997–98). He was the principal author of the Department of Defense (DoD) 1998 East Asia Strategy Report, and he received the Office of the Secretary of Defense Award for Exceptional Public Service in January 2001.

Prior to joining DoD, Mitchell served as senior program officer for Asia and the former Soviet Union at the National Democratic Institute for International Affairs in Washington, DC. From 1993 to 1997, he developed the institute's long-term approach to Asia and worked on democratic development programs in Armenia, Burma, Cambodia, Georgia, Pakistan, and Thailand. In 1989, he worked as an editor and reporter at the *China Post* on Taiwan. From 1986 to 1988, he served as assistant to the senior foreign policy adviser to Senator Edward M. Kennedy.

He received a master of arts in law and diplomacy degree from the Fletcher School of Law and Diplomacy in 1991 and a bachelor's degree from the University of Virginia in 1986. He studied Chinese language at Nanjing University in China and speaks Mandarin Chinese proficiently. He is the coauthor of *China: The Balance Sheet—What the World Needs to Know Now about the Emerging Superpower* (2006) and coeditor of *China and the Developing World: Beijing's Strategy for the 21st Century* (2007).

About the Organizations

Center for Strategic and International Studies

At a time of new global opportunities and challenges, the Center for Strategic and International Studies (CSIS) provides strategic insights and policy solutions to decision makers in government, international institutions, the private sector, and civil society.

CSIS was launched at the height of the Cold War, dedicated to the simple but urgent goal of finding ways for America to survive as a nation and prosper as a people. During the following four decades, CSIS has grown to become one of the nation's and the world's preeminent public policy institutions on US and international security.

Founded in 1962 by David M. Abshire and Admiral Arleigh Burke, CSIS is a bipartisan, nonprofit organization headquartered in Washington, DC with more than 220 full-time staff and a large network of affiliated experts. Former US senator Sam Nunn became chairman of the CSIS Board of Trustees in 1999, and John J. Hamre has led CSIS as its president and chief executive officer since April 2000.

CSIS experts conduct research and analysis and develop policy initiatives that are organized around more than 25 programs grouped under three themes: defense and security, global challenges, and regional transformation.

With one of the most comprehensive programs on US defense policy and international security, CSIS proposes reforms to US defense organization, security policy, and the defense industrial and technology base. Other CSIS programs offer solutions to the challenges of proliferation, transnational terrorism, homeland security, and postconflict reconstruction.

With programs on demographics and population, energy security, global health, technology, and the international financial and economic system, CSIS addresses the new drivers of risk and opportunity on the world stage.

CSIS is the only institution of its kind with resident experts studying the transformation of all of the world's major geographic regions. CSIS specialists seek to anticipate changes in key countries and regions—from Africa to Asia, from Europe to Latin America, and from the Middle East to North America.

From its beginning, CSIS has been committed to bipartisan problem solving. While partisan competition advances ideas, America prospers when policy leaders develop a consensus across the political spectrum. CSIS actively unites leaders from both parties to join in shared problem solving.

Peter G. Peterson Institute for International Economics

The Peter G. Peterson Institute for International Economics is a private, nonprofit, nonpartisan research institution devoted to the study of international economic policy. Since 1981 the Institute has provided timely and objective analysis of, and concrete solutions to, a wide range of international economic problems. It is one of the very few economics think tanks that are widely regarded as "nonpartisan" by the press and "neutral" by the US Congress, and it is cited by the quality media more than any other such institution.

The Institute, which has been directed by C. Fred Bergsten throughout its existence, attempts to anticipate emerging issues and to be ready with practical ideas, presented in user-friendly formats, to inform and shape public debate. Its audience includes government officials and legislators, business and labor leaders, management and staff at international organizations, university-based scholars and their students, other research institutions and nongovernmental organizations, the media, and the public at large. It addresses these groups both in the United States and around the world.

The Institute's staff of about 50 includes more than two dozen experts, who are conducting about 30 studies at any given time and are widely viewed as one of the top group of economists at any research center. Its agenda emphasizes global macroeconomic topics, international money and finance, trade and related social issues, energy and the environment, investment, and domestic adjustment measures. Current priority is attached to globalization (including its financial aspects) and the backlash against it, global trade imbalances and currency relationships, the creation of an international regime to address global warming and especially its international trade dimension, the competitiveness of the United States and other major countries, reform of the international economic and financial architecture and particularly sovereign wealth funds, and trade negotiations at the multilateral, regional, and bilateral levels. Institute staff and research cover all key regions—especially Asia, Europe, Latin America, and the Middle East, as well as the United States itself and with special reference to China, India, and Russia.

Institute studies have helped provide the intellectual foundation for many of the major international financial initiatives of the past two decades: reform of the International Monetary Fund (IMF), adoption of international banking standards, exchange rate systems in the G-7 and emerging-market economies, policies toward the dollar, the euro, and other important currencies, and responses to debt and currency crises. The Institute has made important contributions to key trade policy decisions including the Doha Round, the restoration and then the extension of trade promotion authority in the United States, the Uruguay Round and the development of the World Trade Organization, the North American Free Trade Agreement (NAFTA) and other US free trade agreements (notably including Korea), Asia Pacific Economic Cooperation (APEC) forum and East Asian regionalism, initiation of the Strategic Economic Dialogue between the United States and China, a series of United States–Japan negotiations, reform of sanctions policy, liberalization of US export controls and export credits, and specific measures such as permanent normal trade relations (PNTR) for China in 2000 and import protection for steel.

Other influential analyses have addressed economic reform in Europe, Japan, the former communist countries, and Latin America (including the Washington Consensus), the economic and social impact of globalization and policy responses to it, outsourcing, electronic commerce, corruption, foreign direct investment both into and out of the United States, global warming and international environmental policy, and key sectors such as agriculture, financial services, steel, telecommunications, and textiles.

The Institute celebrated its 25th anniversary in 2006 and adopted its new name at that time, having previously been the Institute for International Economics. It moved into its award-winning new building in 2001.

Acknowledgments

The authors express their great appreciation to the following people for their support of the China Balance Sheet Project.

Project co-chairs: C. Fred Bergsten and John J. Hamre
Advisory committee: See list on page 255
Senior advisers: Bates Gill and Ben W. Heineman, Jr.
Project adviser: Adam S. Posen
Contributing authors: David Finkelstein, Trevor Houser, Melissa Murphy, Daniel H. Rosen, and Andrew Wedeman
Editorial adviser: Carla Freeman
Project coordinators: Eve Cary and Carl Rubenstein
Research associates: Giwon Jeong and Alyson Slack
Research interns: Shiuan-ju Chen, Orlando Crosby, Fergus Green, Xuan Gui, Liana Lim Hinch, Arthur Kaneko, Roy Levy, Stephen Meyers, Prashanth Parameswaran, Alexis Rado, Shelley Su, Pak To Wong, and Xiao Zhang
Copyeditor and editorial coordinator: Madona Devasahayam
Publication team: Marla Banov, Jim Dunton, Susann Luetjen, David Roth, and Edward A. Tureen

The China Balance Sheet Project Advisory Committee

We have been fortunate to be able to draw on the extensive knowledge of a remarkable group of experts on China and US-China relations, representing a range of perspectives. Many of these advisers participated in brainstorming meetings or provided comments on draft versions of this volume, and we are deeply grateful for their guidance and support. However, the findings and opinions expressed in this book solely reflect those of the authors. They do not necessarily represent the views of our advisers or other supporters.

Among those from whom we solicited views are:

William Alford, Harvard University Law School
Jonathan Anderson, UBS Investment Bank
Jeffrey Bader, Brookings Institution
Charlene Barshefsky, WilmerHale
Doug Bereuter, The Asia Foundation
Samuel Berger, Stonebridge International, LLC
Dennis Blair, National Bureau of Asian Research
Pieter Bottelier, School of Advanced International Studies
Richard Bush, Brookings Institution
Kurt Campbell, Center for a New American Security
Richard Cooper, Harvard University
Bruce Dickson, George Washington University
Thomas Donilon, O'Melveny & Myers, LLP
Michael Dooley, University of California
Robert Ebel, Center for Strategic and International Studies
Elizabeth Economy, Council on Foreign Relations
James Feinerman, Georgetown University
William Ferguson, Citigroup

Joseph Fewsmith, Boston University
David Finkelstein, CNA
Charles Freeman, Center for Strategic and International Studies
Michael Gadbaw, General Electric Company, retd.
Paul Gewirtz, Yale University
Bonnie Glaser, Center for Strategic and International Studies
Morris Goldstein, Peterson Institute for International Economics
Michael Goltzman, The Coca-Cola Company
Thomas Gottschalk, Kirkland & Ellis, LLP
Maurice Greenberg, C.V. Starr & Company, Inc.
Scott Hallford, Federal Express
Carol Lee Hamrin, Global China Center
Harry Harding, George Washington University
Benjamin Heineman, Harvard Law School
David Henson, Caterpillar Inc.
Carla Hills, Hills & Company
Richard Holbrooke, Perseus, LLC
Jamie Horsley, Yale University
Janet Howard, The Coca-Cola Company
Richard Jackson, Center for Strategic and International Studies
L. Oakley Johnson, American International Group Inc.
James Kelly, Center for Strategic and International Studies
Henry Kissinger, Center for Strategic and International Studies
William Lane, Caterpillar Inc.
Lawrence Lau, Chinese University of Hong Kong
Malcolm Lee, Microsoft China
Cheng Li, Hamilton College
Kenneth Lieberthal, University of Michigan
James Lilley, former US Ambassador to China
Xiaobo Lu, Columbia University
Keith Maskus, University of Colorado at Boulder
Michael McDevitt, CNA
William McDonough, Merrill Lynch & Co., Inc.
Carola McGiffert, Center for Strategic and International Studies
Eric McVadon, Institute for Foreign Policy Analysis
Evan Medeiros, RAND Corporation
R. Scott Miller, Procter & Gamble
T. James Min, DHL Express
G. Mustafa Mohatarem, General Motors Corporation
Peter Morici, University of Maryland
James Mulvenon, Center for Intelligence Research and Analysis
Kevin Nealer, Scowcroft Group
Paul Neureiter, ACE USA
Matt Niemeyer, ACE USA
Marcus Noland, Peterson Institute for International Economics

Minxin Pei, Carnegie Endowment for International Peace
Dwight Perkins, Harvard University
Ernest Preeg, Manufacturers Alliance
Clyde Prestowitz, Economic Strategy Institute
Jean Pritchard, The Boeing Company
Thomas Rawski, University of Pittsburgh
William Reinsch, National Foreign Trade Council, Inc.
Stephen Roach, Morgan Stanley
Alan Romberg, Henry L. Stimson Center
Daniel Rosen, Rhodium Group
J. Stapleton Roy, Kissinger Associates, Inc.
Scott Rozelle, Stanford University
James Sasser, Former Ambassador to China
Phillip Saunders, National Defense University
Randy Schriver, Armitage International
Elizabeth Nash Schwartz, The Boeing Company
Jeffrey Shafer, Citigroup
David Shambaugh, George Washington University
Anne Solomon, Center for Strategic and International Studies
Michael Swaine, Carnegie Endowment for International Peace
Murray Scot Tanner, Consultant
Frederick Telling, Pfizer, Inc.
Anne Thurston, School of Advanced International Studies
Jennifer Turner, Woodrow Wilson International Center for Scholars
Arthur Waldron, University of Pennsylvania
Stephen Yates, DC Asia Advisory, LLC
Shirley Zebroski, General Motors Corporation

Index

administrative reform, 66
Administrative Supervision Law, 61
Afghanistan, 193
Africa, China's relations with, 215, 219, 222
agricultural production, reform of, 138
agricultural tax, 121
aircraft carriers, 198*b*
air pollution, 152–53, 156
anti-China blocs, prevention of, 212
antigovernment demonstrations, 91, 96–97, 100, 103*n*
Anti-Monopoly Law, 13, 39, 42, 61
APEC (Asia Pacific Economic Cooperation), 16
ARATS (Association for Relations Across the Taiwan Strait), 186, 189*n*
armed forces, modernization of. *See* military modernization
arms sales
   from Russia, 197
   to Taiwan, 175–76, 188*n*
   from US, 207*n*
ASEAN (Association of Southeast Asian Nations), 15–16, 220, 224
Asian financial crisis (1997–98), 19*b*
Asian Monetary Fund, 17
Asian trading bloc, creation of, 15–16, 22
Asia Pacific Economic Cooperation (APEC), 16
Asia-Pacific region
   military power in, 199, 204–205
   security of, 223–24, 227, 229, 237
Association for Relations Across the Taiwan Strait (ARATS), 186, 189*n*
Association of Southeast Asian Nations (ASEAN), 15–16, 220, 224
Australia, trade agreement with, 15–16

bank deposits, 114, 117, 118, 119*f*, 121
   interest rates on, 116, 118–19, 119*f*, 125–26, 133*n*–135*n*
banking system
   development of, 112
   reform of, 125–26
bank lending, 157
beggar-thy-neighbor policies, 24
Beijing Consensus, 38, 60
   versus Washington Consensus, 46, 53*n*, 70*n*
"Beijing model" of development, 70
Beijing Olympics, 46, 80, 92, 228, 229
Beijing Spring, 36, 52*n*
Belgrade, Chinese embassy in, bombing of, 46, 47, 218
Bernanke, Ben, 106
border disputes, 220, 221
Brazil, 27
bribery, 92, 94–95, 102*n*. *See also* corruption
brick kiln scandal, 82
Burma, 11, 219, 227
Bush, George W., 26, 177, 180, 189*n*

cadre(s), 41, 54*n*, 61
   corruption and, 95–96, 100
cadre responsibility system, 61, 100
capital intensity, 110–11, 111*f*
   energy implications of, 147–50
capital transfers, consumption-driven growth and, 116–17
carbon capture and sequestration (CCS), 161
carbon dioxide (CO_2), 153
CCDI (Central Commission for Discipline Inspection), 99
CCP. *See* Chinese Communist Party

CCS (carbon capture and sequestration), 161
center-local relations, 5, 75–89
  Communist Party control and, 82–84
  corruption and, 77, 79, 91, 97–98
  current factors causing friction in, 78–79
  key policies and, 80–82
  policy recommendations, 84–85
  US perception of, 75–76
Central Commission for Discipline Inspection (CCDI), 99
Central Economic Work Conference, 105, 120
Central Military Commission (CMC), 61, 193
Central Party School (CPS), 41, 54*n*, 61, 73*n*
Chiang Ching-kuo, 177
Chiang Kai-shek, 171, 177, 180
Chiang Mai Initiative, 17, 224
China Investment Corporation (CIC), 24, 51*n*
China National Offshore Oil Corporation (CNOOC), 20, 25
China Society for Economic Reform, 40
Chinese Academy of Social Sciences, 97
Chinese Communist Party (CCP), 33
  anticorruption campaigns, 98–100
  center-local relations and, 82–84
  17th Congress work report to, 33–34, 41–42, 50, 61
  on consumption-driven growth, 105
  control of military by, 201
  corruption and, 5, 61, 94–100
  domestic protests against, 13
  "emancipation of the mind" campaigns, 42, 43*b*, 60, 66
  future of, 4–5, 57–74, 96–97
  intellectual activism and, 35–36
  leadership system, 63
  ongoing support for, 66–68
  political reform and, 44, 45, 63–64, 73*n*
  public opinion of, 68
  ruling capacity of, 61–62, 66, 94
Chinese People's Political Consultative Conference (CPPCC), 63
Christian missionaries, from US, 171–72
CIC (China Investment Corporation), 24, 51*n*
C4ISR capabilities, 202, 203
civilian population, mobilization for military purposes, 196
climate change. *See* environmental issues
Clinton, Bill, 177, 178, 189*n*

CMC (Central Military Commission), 61, 193
CNOOC (China National Offshore Oil Corporation), 20, 25
CNPC petrochemical plant, explosion of, 153
coal consumption, 111–12
coal mine fatalities, 151–52
coal prices, 116, 128, 144–46, 152
coal reserves, 151, 161
coke prices, 144–46
Cold War
  lessons from, 238–39
  Taiwan and, 172–73, 174, 175–76
colonization, 170
combat capabilities, 194–95
Communist Party. *See* Chinese Communist Party
"comprehensive national power," concept of, 230n
conditionality, of foreign aid, 20–21, 219, 224–25, 233*n*
Confucianism, 213, 214
Confucius Institutes, 215, 231*n*
conservatives. *See* "Old Left"
construction, 147
consumer price index, 125
consumer safety policies, 78–79, 81, 83, 85
consumption
  as share of GDP, 106–109, 107*f*–108*f*, 117–18, 129, 130*n*, 133*n*
  shift toward, 5–6
consumption-driven growth, 105, 120–28
  adverse effects of, 128–30
  environmental issues and, 111–12, 129–30, 158–59
  exchange rate policy and, 119–20, 126–27, 129–30
  financial reform and, 118–19, 125–26
  fiscal policy and, 116–18, 120–25, 128, 157
  price reforms and, 120, 127–28
  promotion of, 115–20
cooperative partnerships, 217
Corporate Income Tax Law, 41
corporate tax policy, 117–18, 123–25, 133*n*
corruption, 5, 91–104
  antigovernment demonstrations and, 91, 96–97, 100, 103*n*
  causes of, debates on, 97–98
  combating, 98–100
  cost of, 95–96
  land use policy and, 82
  levels of, 92–94, 93*f*, 101*n*
  at local level, 77, 79, 91, 94–97

Party governance and, 5, 61
  policy recommendations, 100–101
Corruption Perceptions Index
  (Transparency International), 92–93,
  93f
CPPCC (Chinese People's Political
  Consultative Conference), 63
CPS (Central Party School), 41, 54n,
  61, 73n
criminalization of the state, 5, 95. *See also*
  corruption
cultural promotion, 214–15
Cultural Revolution, 53n, 173, 188n
  corruption and, 93
  development debate and, 41
  political reform and, 59, 63
currency markets
  consumption-driven growth and,
    119–20, 126–27, 129–30
  intervention in, 14, 17–19, 24
current account surplus, 114, 115f
  exchange rate policy and, 17, 18b–19b

Dalai Lama, 220
dangnei minzhu (inner-party democracy),
  promotion of, 62–63, 73n
Darfur, 228
decentralization, 76–77, 97–98
defense budget, 191, 192b, 200, 200t
deliberative democracy (*xieshang
  minzhu*), 57
democracy, 11
  Chinese-style, 4–5, 11, 44, 57–74
  corruption and, 92
  future of, 66–68
  at grass-roots level, 64–65, 69
  implementation of, 60–65
  inner-party, promotion of, 62–63, 73n
  intellectual debate on, 37, 43–45
  policy recommendations, 68–70
  rhetoric versus reality, 65–66
  in Taiwan, 177, 178–79, 184
democratic consultation process (*minzhu
  kentan*), 64–65
democratic deficit, 44, 59, 69
democratic parties, multiparty
  cooperation and, 63–64
Democratic Progressive Party (Taiwan),
  179, 187n
"demythification" of the West, 47
Deng Xiaoping
  on China as superpower, 1, 21
  development initiatives, 3, 9, 43b, 60, 106
    debate over, 34, 35–41

on foreign policy, 49, 209, 211
  "Four Modernizations," 192, 197,
    205n
  on military, 205
  "New Left" position and, 41
  on political reform, 41, 45, 57, 58
developing country/countries. *See also*
  specific country or region
  attitude toward China in, 215, 226
  China's relations with, 221–23, 232n
  China's status as, 16, 221
  in climate change response, 161–62
  global systemic modifications and, 22
development
  "Beijing model" of, 70
  China as model of, 225, 236
  debates over, 38–40
  energy demand and, 138–39
  "Washington model" of, 70
diesel prices, 146
dividend tax rates, 123–25, 157
Doha Round, 15–16, 21, 22
dollar dumping, 18b–19b
domestic consumption. *See* consumption

East Asia Free Trade Area, 16, 24
economic growth
  capital intensity of, 110–11, 111f
  center-local relations and, 78, 79, 85
  consumption-led (*See* consumption-
    driven growth)
  corruption and, 96
  energy implications of (*See* energy
    demand)
  imbalanced regional pattern of, 110
  investment-led (*See* investment-driven
    growth)
  pace of, 9, 28, 106, 137
  sources of, 106–109, 107f
  strategy for, 109–15
  sustainability of, 5–6, 105–36, 236–37
    global implications of, 114–15,
      129–30
economic nationalism, 13, 38–39
education, 122–23
Eisenhower, Dwight D., 173
elections, village committee, 64
electricity prices, 145f, 145–46, 152, 156
electric power, 128, 150–52, 156, 161
"emancipation of the mind" campaigns,
  42, 43b, 60, 66
employment, effect of development on,
  110–11, 153–54
employment laws, 81–82, 84, 88n

energy demand, 6, 19–20, 137–68
  of consumption-driven growth, 111–12,
    129–30, 158–59
  evolution of, 138–39
  global, China's share of, 137, 141
  of investment-driven growth, 139–50
  local and global implications of,
    150–55
  macro rebalancing and, 156–59
  policy agenda, 159–62
  predictions of, 139f, 139–41
  by sector, 141, 142t
energy demand elasticity, 139–41
energy efficiency, improvements in, 156
energy intensity, of Chinese economy,
    138–44, 139f, 155
energy markets, investment in, 20,
    24–25, 159
energy prices, 116, 127–28, 144–46, 152.
    See also oil prices
  environmental costs and, 146
  volatility in, 160–61
energy security, 150–52, 159–61
engagement, principle of, 235–36
environmental issues, 6
  center-local relations and, 80, 83
  development debate and, 38
  global economic system and, 24–26, 29
  growth at any cost and, 78, 85
  multilateral framework to address,
    161–62
  policy agenda, 161–62
environmental protection, 152–53
environmental protection bureaus (EPBs),
    79, 83
environmental regulations, enforcement
    of, 156–57
European Union
  adherence to international rules, 12
  China's relations with, 219–20, 231n
  Doha Round and, 15
  as global superpower, 9, 32n
  "G-2" relationship and, 26, 28–29
  protectionism in, 14, 105–106
  response to Asian trading bloc, 16
exchange rate, effective, 136n
exchange rate policy, 14, 17–19, 24
  consumption-driven growth and,
    119–20, 126–27, 129–30
exports
  reliance on, 114
  as source of economic growth, 108–109,
    109f, 126

fang/shou (loosening, then tightening), 59
fen zao chi fan policy (fiscal contracting
    system), 76
"fifth generation" leadership, 58, 68
financial reform, consumption-driven
    growth and, 118–19, 125–26
fiscal contracting system (fen zao chi fan
    policy), 76
fiscal policy
  consumption-driven growth and,
    116–18, 120–25, 128, 157
  decentralization and, 76–77
Five-Year Programs, 39, 155
flue gas desulphurization (FGD) systems,
    146, 156
food and drug safety, 81, 83, 85
Ford, Gerald, 174
foreign aid, 20–21, 222–23
  conditionality of, 20–21, 219, 224–25,
    233n
foreign direct investment, corruption
    and, 96
foreigners, living in China, 1
foreign exchange markets. *See* exchange
    rate policy
foreign exchange reserves, 18b–19b, 24–25
foreign firms, rules concerning, 13, 39, 42, 61
foreign policy, 7, 21, 209–33
  Communist Party line on, 34
  goals and principles underlying, 211–14
  "G-2" relationship and, 28–29
  intellectual debate on, 46
  regional trade agreements and, 16, 22,
    24, 220–21
  soft power in, 214–16
Four Cardinal Principles, 34, 45, 64
"Four Modernizations," 192, 197, 205n
"fourth generation" leadership, 58, 63
freedom of information regulations, 61
free trade agreements (FTAs), 15–17, 22,
    24, 217, 220, 232n
Free Trade Area of the Americas, 24
Free Trade Area of the Asia Pacific, 16–17

gasoline prices, 146
GDP
  consumption as share of, 106–109,
    107f–108f, 117–18, 129, 130n, 133n
  industry profits as share of, 112, 113f,
    135n
  investment as share of, 106, 107f,
    109–10, 129, 142
  by sector, 141, 142t

General Agreement on Tariffs and Trade
(GATT), 27
global economic leadership
partnerships in, 27, 237–38 (*See also*
"G-2" relationship)
responsibility for, 28
global economic order, 9–32
China's criticism of, 21–22, 224
effect of Chinese economic growth on,
114–15, 129–30, 154–55
intellectual debate on, 28, 48–50
reform of, 22–30, 224–25
systemic issues in, 11–21
global economic output, China's share of,
3, 31*n*
global economic superpower(s), 9, 10*b*
China as, 1–2, 4, 7, 9, 10*b*, 209–10
global energy use
China's share of, 137, 141
multilateral framework to address,
161–62
Global Environmental Organization, 25
globalization
backlash against, 13, 37–38
China's attitude toward, 211
intellectual debate over, 46
military modernization and, 207*n*
global production, China's share of,
142–43, 143*f*
global security environment
China's role in, 210, 227
military modernization and, 197, 203
global warming. *See* environmental issues
"go out" (*zou chuqu*) policy, 215–16
government consumption. *See*
consumption
government transparency, improvement
in, 61, 62–63, 66, 100
grass-roots level, democracy at, 64–65, 69
"green credit" policy, 83
green GDP Program, 83
"green trade" policy, 83
"G-2" relationship, 4, 23–31
climate change issues and, 29
shifts in US mindset required for, 27–28
"G-3" relationship, 29
"G-5" relationship, 29
Group of Eight (G-8), 29, 32*n*, 224
Group of Seven (G-7), 21, 29, 32*n*
Guangdong Province
corruption in, 96
Shenzhen special economic zone in,
65, 100

Guangzhou, corruption in, 95
guanxi (social connections), 97

"harmonious society" concept, 49, 54*n*,
82, 110, 214
"harmonious world" concept, 49–50,
212–14
harmony (*hexie*), principle of, 212–14
health services, 116, 117, 122, 122*t*, 154
heavy industry
energy security and, 150–52
environmental implications of, 152–53
overinvestment in, wealth effects of,
153–54
shift away from, 138, 139, 141
Heilongjiang scandal, 94–95
Hong Kong, 99, 100
household consumption. *See* consumption
Hu Jintao
17th CCP Congress work report, 33–34,
41–42, 43*b*, 50, 61
center-local relations and, 82–83
on corruption, 91
economic development vision, 39–40,
110, 155
on foreign policy, 49, 209, 212, 216, 230*n*
on military modernization, 191
"New Left" position and, 40
on political reform, 44, 45, 58, 60, 65
study sessions, 52*n*
on Taiwan, 186, 189*n*
transfer of power to, 63
visit to Japan, 219
human rights, 216, 219
hydropower development, 153

IEA. *See* International Energy Agency
IMF (International Monetary Fund), 13,
14, 17, 21, 126, 224
import safety issues, 81, 83, 85
income gains
center-local relations and, 79
consumption-driven growth and, 121,
130*n*–131*n*, 134*n*
effect of development on, 153–54
income inequality, 110
India
China's relations with, 219
consumption share of GDP, 110
Doha Round and, 15, 22
economic power of, versus China, 10*b*
energy demand in, 141
trading bloc with, 16

industrialization, energy demands of, 138
industrial pollution, 153
industrial reform, energy demand and,
    138, 139, 141, 143–44, 147–52
industry concentration, 149–50, 150*t*
industry profits
    energy demand and, 148, 148*t*
    as share of GDP, 112, 113*f*, 135*n*
inflation, 125
information warfare, 195, 206*n*
inner-party democracy (*dangnei minzhu*),
    promotion of, 62–63, 73*n*
institutional weaknesses, center-local
    relations and, 78–79
intellectual debate, 4, 33–56
    on causes of corruption, 97–98
    current dynamics in, 36–37
    on development, 38–40
    on foreign policy, 46
    future of, 50–51
    on global economic system, 28, 48–50
    on nationalism, 44, 46–48, 56*n*
    policy response to, 40–43
    on political reform, 37, 43–45
    reevaluation of reform, 37–38
    role of, 35–36, 52*n*
intellectual property rights (IPR)
    protection, 78–79, 80–81, 84, 87*n*
interest coalition building, 85
interest rates
    on bank deposits, 116, 118–19, 119*f*, 121,
    125–26, 133*n*–135*n*
    on loans, 120
    real, 134*n*
International Energy Agency (IEA), 20, 24
    Chinese status in, 160, 224
    energy demand predictions, 139, 139*f*,
    158, 162, 163*n*
International Monetary Fund (IMF), 13,
    14, 17, 21, 126, 224
international monetary system, 17–19
international relationships, 216–23, 232*n*.
    See also foreign policy; *specific country*
    with developing world, 221–23
    with major powers, 217–20
    with neighbors, 220–21
international rules
    adherence to, 11, 12, 15–17, 23–24, 223,
    225–26
    China's influence on, 225
    climate change and, 24–26
international system. *See also* global
    economic order
    China's impact on, 223–26

internet postings, 96–97
investment
    consumption-driven growth and,
    120, 129
    in energy markets, 20, 24–25, 159
    by local government, 82
    in manufacturing, 112, 131*n*
    manufacturing and services share of,
    110–11, 111*t*
investment-driven growth, 106, 107*f*,
    109–10, 129
    domestic response to, 155–58
    energy implications of, 139–50
    international commercial impacts of,
    154–55
    wealth effects of, 153–54
IPR (intellectual property rights)
    protection, 78–79, 80–81, 84, 87*n*
Iran, 19*b*, 20
Iraq War, 193, 203

Japan
    China's relations with, 219
    colonization of China by, 170
    economic power of, 10*b*
    energy intensity in, 141
    "G-2" relationship and, 26, 29
    Liberal Democratic Party (LDP), 67, 72*n*
    postwar global order and, 22
    trading bloc with, 16
Jiang Zemin, 38
    as Central Military Commission
    chairman, 61, 193
    on foreign policy, 217
    "New Left" position and, 40–41
    "Three Represents" theory, 61, 71*n*
job creation, effect of development on,
    110–11, 153–54

Kennedy, John F., 173–74
Kissinger, Henry, 30, 178
kleptocracies, local, 94–96
Korea, trading bloc with, 16
Korean War, 172, 187
Kosovo, 193
Kuomintang (KMT), 170, 171, 187*n*
    political reform and, 67, 177
Kuwait, 19*b*
Kyoto Protocol, 161

labor costs, construction, 147
labor laws, 81–82, 84, 88*n*
land policy, 79, 82, 84, 146–47
land use violation charges, 96

Latin America, China's relations with, 222
Lee Teng-hui, 47, 180
legal system
    anticorruption campaigns and, 99–100
    reform of, 61–62, 66
loans
    interest rates on, 120
    nonperforming, 112, 114
local government
    central policy implementation by (See center-local relations)
    corruption in, 77, 79, 91, 94–97
    democracy in, 64–65
    energy policies, 155
    investment by, 82
    minimum wage rates, 121
    public opinion of, 66, 91
    social welfare responsibility, 77, 79, 85

mafia states, local, 91, 95
manufacturing, investment in, 112, 131n
Maoflag.net, 45
Mao Zedong, 143, 170, 172
Marxism-Leninism, 44, 51n, 59
May Fourth Movement, 44, 55n
Ma Ying-jeou, 169, 181, 182, 186, 189n, 219
media, watchdog role of, 99–100
mergers and acquisitions, laws concerning, 13, 39, 42, 61
Merkel, Angela, 220
metals companies, 149–50
Middle East, China's relations with, 222
migrant workers, rights of, 38
military assistance, to developing world, 222–23
military budget, 191, 192b, 200, 200t
military conflict, over Taiwan, fear of, 169, 176–77, 184, 204
military education system, 195–96, 202
military exercises, joint, 191, 206n
military modernization, 6–7, 191–208
    future of, 201–202
    international security issues and, 11
    key elements of, 194–97
    questions about, 197–201
    regional force and, 197–99, 201, 204–205
    Taiwan and, 181, 212
    transparency and, 199–201
    US response to, 199, 202–205, 237
military needs, assessment of, 192–94
military technology, 194–95, 197, 203, 206n
minimum wage policy, 121
Ministry of Environmental Protection, 83

Ministry of Labor and Social Security, Regulations on the Minimum Wage, 121
minzhu kentan (democratic consultation process), 64–65
mispricing, 6
missiles, 195, 203
missionaries, from US, 171–72
modernization
    military (See military modernization)
    socialist, 58
modus vivendi, China-Taiwan, 182
money supply (M2), 157
Mongolia, 187n
morality, differing notions of, 213–14
multifactor productivity growth, 109–10
multilateralism, 217
multiparty cooperation, 63–64
multipolar world order, 193
Mutual Defense Treaty (Taiwan), 174, 188n

NAFTA (North American Free Trade Agreement), 16
National Bureau of Corruption Prevention (NBCP), 99, 100
National Defense Authorization Act, 207n
National Development and Reform Commission (NDRC), 112, 128, 145, 149, 155
National Endowment for Democracy, 64
nationalism
    economic, 13, 38–39
    intellectual debate over, 44, 46–48, 56n
Nationalists. See Kuomintang
National Land Superintendency, 84, 100
National People's Congress (NPC), 39–40, 43b, 61, 66, 83
national security
    military needs and, 193, 197
    Taiwan and, 170–71
native Taiwanese, 178–79
NATO (North Atlantic Treaty Organization), 218
natural gas prices, 145–46
NBCP (National Bureau of Corruption Prevention), 99, 100
NDRC (National Development and Reform Commission), 112, 128, 145, 149, 155
net exports of good and services
    reliance on, 114
    as source of economic growth, 108–109, 109f, 126

"New Left," 34, 52n–53n
  Communist Party work report and, 34
  in corruption debate, 98
  criticism of globalization, 13
  democratization debate and, 44, 60
  development debate and, 38–40, 54n
  nationalism and, 47–48
new weapons systems, 194–95
New Zealand, trade agreement with,
    16, 31n
Nixon, Richard M., 174, 188n, 235, 238
nongovernmental organizations (NGOs),
    global systemic modifications and, 22
noninterference principle, 212–13, 227–28
nonmarket economy, 10
nonperforming loans, 112, 114
North American Free Trade Agreement
    (NAFTA), 16
North Atlantic Treaty Organization
    (NATO), 218
North-South conflict, 22
NPC (National People's Congress), 39–40,
    43b, 61, 66, 83
nuclear forces, 11, 195

OECD (Organization for Economic
    Cooperation and Development),
    20, 160
oil demand, 151, 160–61
oil imports, sources of, 222, 222t
oil prices, 20, 24, 115, 116, 127–28, 146, 152
oil shocks, 22
"Old Left," 53n
  Communist Party work report and, 34
  democratization debate and, 45
  development debate and, 38
Olympics (Beijing), 46, 80, 92, 228, 229
"One China" policy, 182, 212, 223
"one country, three systems" formula, 182
Organization for Economic Cooperation
    and Development (OECD), 20, 160
Organization of Petroleum Exporting
    Countries (OPEC), 20, 22, 160
Outer Mongolia, 187n

Pakistan, 219
particulate matter (PM), 152–53, 166n
patriotism, Taiwan and, 170
Paulson, Henry, Jr., 26, 105, 157
"peaceful democracy" theory, 69
peaceful development, concept of, 48–50,
    212, 214, 230n
peacekeeping operations, 223
Peace Mission 2007, 206n

pension schemes, 116
People's Bank of China, 114, 126, 133n
People's Liberation Army (PLA)
  adaptive capacity of, 202
  Communist Party control of, 201
  democratization and, 67
  modernization of (See military
    modernization)
  as regional force, 197–99, 201
  size of, 201, 207n
  systemic reform of, 195–96, 201–2, 206n
  Taiwan contingency, 194, 197
People's Republic of China, opening of, 1,
    13, 209
"people's war" concept, 196
per capita income, 10, 110
Persian Gulf states, China's relations
    with, 222
Persian Gulf Wars, 193
PLA. See People's Liberation Army
policy intellectuals. See also intellectual
    debate
  role of, 35–36, 52n
Political Bureau
  Standing Committee, 35
  study sessions, 42, 52n
political reform, 4–5, 236. See also
    democracy
  Communist Party leadership on, 34
  corruption and, 98, 100–101
  evolution of, 58–60
  incremental, 59, 62, 68
  intellectual debate on, 37, 43–45
  shock therapy of, 57, 68
  in Taiwan, 67, 68, 177, 178–79, 184
political system, 11, 32n
pollution, 112. See also environmental
    issues
  center-local relations and, 80
  regulation of, 146, 156–57
  sources of, 152–53
power, concepts of, 214–16, 227, 231n,
    236, 238
power generation industry, 128, 150–52,
    156, 161
price(s), energy, 116, 127–28, 144–46, 152,
    160–61. See also oil prices
price inflation, 125
price reforms, 116, 120, 127–28
production, global, China's share of,
    142–43, 143f
production capacity, surplus, adverse
    effects of, 112
product safety policies, 78–79, 81, 83, 85

profitability, in tradable goods sector, 113*f*, 114, 135*n*
  energy demand and, 148, 148*t*
profit margins on earning-before-tax (EBT) basis, 148, 148*t*
Property Law, 41, 54*n*, 61
protectionism, 14, 105–106
public opinion
  of China, 215, 226, 230*n*, 237
  of Communist Party, 68, 96–97
  of local government, 66, 91
  of United States, 47, 228

quality monitoring systems, 83

Reagan, Ronald, 175–76
recentralization, 77, 98
regional security, 223–24, 227, 229, 237
  military modernization and, 197–99, 201, 204–205
regional trade agreements, 15–17, 22, 24, 217, 220–21
renminbi
  appreciation of, 14, 18*b*–19*b*, 116, 120, 127, 129–30, 132*n*, 157
  revaluation of, 126–27
Republic of China. *See* Taiwan
"Right"
  Communist Party work report and, 34
  in corruption debate, 97–98
rule of law
  anticorruption campaigns and, 99–100
  Party governance and, 61–62, 66
rural welfare programs, 122–23
Russia
  arms sales from, 197
  China's relations with, 218
  corruption in, 98
  in G-7 summit meetings, 32*n*
  joint military exercise with, 191

san nong ("three rural" issues), 38
SARS (severe acute respiratory syndrome), 185
SASAC (State-Owned Asset Supervision and Administration Commission), 124
Saudi Arabia, 29
saving rate, national, 114, 117, 118, 119*f*
Scientific Development Concept, 34, 39, 43*b*, 54*n*
  center-local relations and, 82–83
  debate over, 66
SCO (Shanghai Cooperation Organization), 218, 220, 224

seafood imports, 81
SED (Strategic Economic Dialogue), 26–27, 29
SEF (Straits Exchange Foundation), 186, 189*n*
selective partnership, 32*n*
SEPA (State Environmental Protection Agency), 80, 83, 112, 152, 156
Shanghai clique, 40
Shanghai Cooperation Organization (SCO), 218, 220, 224
Shenzhen special economic zone, 65, 100
Sichuan Province
  earthquake in, 96, 229
  township elections in, 65
Singapore
  People's Action Party (PAP), 67
  rule of law in, 99
Six Assurances, 188*n*
smart power, 227
social connections (*guanxi*), 97
socialism, primary stage of, 41, 45, 60
socialist market economic system, 35
socialist modernization, 58
social unrest, increase in, 37, 52*n*, 91, 96–97, 100, 103*n*
social welfare
  consumption-driven growth and, 116–17, 122, 128
  government expenditure on, 122*t*, 122–23
  local responsibility for, 77, 79, 85
SOE (state-owned enterprise)
  energy demand and, 138, 144, 157
  reform of, 38–39, 123–25
"soft authoritarianism," 61, 67
soft power, 214–16, 227, 231*n*, 236, 238
Soong Mei-ling (Madame Chiang), 171–72
sovereign wealth funds, 24–25
Soviet Union
  collapse of, 58, 193
  Sputnik launch by, 238–39
space capabilities, 191, 202, 203, 206*n*, 225
special and differential treatment, 16
special economic zone, 65, 100
State Auditing Administration, 99
State Environmental Protection Agency (SEPA), 80, 83, 112, 152, 156
State-Owned Asset Supervision and Administration Commission (SASAC), 124
state-owned enterprise (SOE)
  energy demand and, 138, 144, 157
  reform of, 38–39, 123–25

steel industry, 149t, 149–50
Straits Exchange Foundation (SEF), 186, 189n
Strategic Economic Dialogue (SED), 26–27, 29
strategic opportunity, 211
strategic partnerships, 214, 217
Subsidy Code (GATT), 27
Sudan, 20
sulfur dioxide (SO$_2$), 152–53, 156
sulfur scrubbers, 156
summit meetings
   G-7, 32n
   US-China, 4, 27
   US-EU, 32n
super ministries, establishment of, 73n
Supreme People's Procuratorate, 100
surplus production capacity, adverse effects of, 112

Taiwan, 6, 169–89
   alternative approaches to, 181–83
   Chinese attitude toward, 170–71, 186, 212
   declaration of independence, 178–80, 182, 184–85
   economic success of, 173, 177
   historical perspective on, 170–76, 187n–188n
   international recognition of, 183–84
   Japan-China relations and, 219
   military conflict over, fear of, 169, 176–77, 204
   military modernization and, 181, 194, 197, 212
   National Health Insurance in, 117
   political reform in, 67, 68, 177, 178–79, 184
   self-defense capability, 180–81, 185
   UN membership and, 180, 183
   US attitude toward (See US-Taiwan relations)
Taiwan Relations Act, 175, 185
tax(es), consumption-driven growth and, 116–17, 121, 123–25, 128, 133n, 135n, 157
tax collection, center-local relations and, 76, 77, 79
tax division system, creation of, 77
territorial disputes, 220–21, 232n
think tanks, 35, 36
Third Communiqué, 188n
three no's policy, 178, 186
"Three Represents" theory, 61, 71n
"three rural" issues (san nong), 38

Tiananmen Square crackdown (1989), 35, 37, 44, 47, 58, 67
Tibet, 67, 212, 228
Tokyo Round, 27
township and village enterprises (TVEs), 138
"track two" dialogue, 5, 69–70
tradable goods sector, profitability in, 113f, 114, 135n
   energy demand and, 148, 148t
trade, share of Chinese economy, 9
trade agreements, regional, 15–17, 22, 24, 217, 220–21
trade laws, 81–82
trade policy, 14–17
trade surplus, 14, 31n
   exchange rate policy and, 17
   growth sustainability and, 106, 109, 129, 154–55
trading partners, 209–10, 210t, 220, 221t
transformation (zhuangbian), 197
transparency
   government, improvement in, 61, 62–63, 100
   in military affairs, 199–201
Transparency International, Corruption Perceptions Index, 92–93, 93f
transportation, 159
Truman, Harry S., 172
TVEs (township and village enterprises), 138

unemployment insurance, 116, 117, 122, 122t
unipolar world order, 193
United Nations
   Security Council, 211, 218, 223, 226, 227
   Taiwanese effort to join, 180, 183
United States
   adherence to international rules, 12
   arms sales, 207n
   carbon emissions, 153
   Chinese dollar holdings and, 18b–19b
   climate change policy, 161–62
   consumption share of GDP, 108
   current account deficit, 14, 17
   Doha Round and, 15
   domestic politics in, 237
   economic crisis in, 17, 18b–19b
   energy demand in, 141, 151
   foreign opinion of, 47, 228
   foreign policy of, 211, 227, 228
   as global superpower, 9, 32n
   historical perspective on Taiwan, 171–76

implications of China's rise for, 226–29
interest coalition building by, 85
missionaries from, 171–72
perception of Chinese central authority, 75–76
protectionism in, 14, 105–106
response to Asian trading bloc, 16
response to Chinese military modernization, 199, 202–205, 237
role in East Asia, 227–29, 237
trade deficit, 17
US-China relations, 217–18. *See also* "G-2" relationship
center-local relations and, 80–82, 84–85
consistency in, 3, 235–36
corruption and, 101
current challenges in, 2
democratization and, 68–70
energy demand and, 159–60
global economic strategy and, 22–30
history of, 1
intellectual debate and, 50–51
military modernization and, 199, 202–205
policy recommendations, 235–39
Taiwan and, 182–83 (*See also* Taiwan)
US Food and Drug Administration (FDA), 81
US-Taiwan relations
alternative approaches to, 181–83
current, 176–78
historical, 171–76
limits of support, 178–81
policy recommendations, 183–87
Unocal, 20, 159

value added tax rebate, 157
Vietnam War, 173, 174, 201
village committee elections, 64

wages
effect of development on, 153–54
minimum, 121
war-fighting doctrines, development of, 196
Washington Consensus, 3, 21, 38
versus Beijing Consensus, 46, 53*n*, 70*n*
definition of, 53*n*
shock therapy of radical reform, 57
"Washington model" of development, 70
water pollution, 153
wealth effects model, 154
weapons systems, 195

Wen Jiabao
center-local relations and, 82–83
economic development vision, 39–40
on foreign policy, 230*n*
on government transparency, 100
"New Left" position and, 40–41
"new socialist countryside" program, 122
on political reform, 41, 45, 57, 58, 60
report to National People's Congress, 43*b*
transfer of power to, 63
on unsustainable economic growth, 105
visit to Japan, 219
Wenling (Zhejiang Province), democratic consultation process in, 64–65
West
"demythification" of, 47
"universalist" morality in, 213–14
white papers
defense, 200, 206*n*
democracy, 58, 59
political party system, 63
rule of law, 61–62
"win-win" solutions, 214, 229
workers' compensation, 116
World Bank, 13
corruption indices, 92–93, 93*f*
energy demand predictions, 158
wealth effects model, 154
World Health Organization, 185
World Trade Organization (WTO)
China's entry into, 9, 13, 37, 46, 48, 139, 223
Doha Round, 15–16, 21, 22
rules of, compliance with, 12, 15–16, 23–24
World War II, 170, 172

Xiamen City
campaign against petrochemical plant in, 87*n*
corruption scandal in, 95
xieshang minzhu (deliberative democracy), 57

Yasukuni Shrine, 46

Zhou Enlai, 205*n*
zhuangbian (transformation), 197
Zhu Rongji, 39, 51*n*
Zoellick, Robert, 26, 213
zou chuqu ("go out") policy, 215–16

BOSTON PUBLIC LIBRARY

3 9999 06257 952 7

Egleston Square Library Branch
2044 Columbus Avenue
Roxbury, MA 02119

WITHDRAWN

No longer the property of the
Boston Public Library.
Sale of this material benefits the Library